WHY PRISON?

Prison studies has experienced a period of great creativity in recent years, and this collection draws together some of the field's most exciting and innovative contemporary critical writers in order to engage directly with one of the most profound questions in penology – *why prison?* In addressing this question, the authors connect contemporary penological thought with an enquiry that has received the attention of some of the greatest thinkers on punishment in the past. Through critical exploration of the theories, policies and practices of imprisonment, the authors analyse why prison persists and why prisoner populations are rapidly rising in many countries. Collectively, the chapters not only provide a sophisticated diagnosis and critique of global hyper-incarceration but also suggest principles and strategies that could be adopted to radically reduce our reliance upon imprisonment.

DAVID SCOTT is a senior lecturer in criminology at Liverpool John Moores University.

CAMBRIDGE STUDIES IN LAW AND SOCIETY

Cambridge Studies in Law and Society aims to publish the best scholarly work on legal discourse and practice in its social and institutional contexts, combining theoretical insights and empirical research.

The fields that it covers are: studies of law in action; the sociology of law; the anthropology of law; cultural studies of law, including the role of legal discourses in social formations; law and economics; law and politics; and studies of governance. The books consider all forms of legal discourse across societies, rather than being limited to lawyers' discourses alone.

The series editors come from a range of disciplines: academic law; socio-legal studies; sociology; and anthropology. All have been actively involved in teaching and writing about law in context.

Series editors

Chris Arup
Monash University, Victoria
Martin Chanock
La Trobe University, Melbourne
Sally Engle Merry
New York University
Susan Silbey
Massachusetts Institute of Technology

A list of books in the series can be found at the back of this book.

WHY PRISON?

Edited by

David Scott

CAMBRIDGE
UNIVERSITY PRESS

University Printing House, Cambridge CB2 8BS, United Kingdom

Cambridge University Press is part of the University of Cambridge.

It furthers the University's mission by disseminating knowledge in the pursuit of
education, learning and research at the highest international levels of excellence.

www.cambridge.org
Information on this title: www.cambridge.org/9781107030749

© Cambridge University Press 2013

First published 2013

A catalogue record for this publication is available from the British Library

Library of Congress Cataloguing in Publication data
Why prison? / edited by David Scott.
    pages   cm. – (Cambridge studies in law and society)
ISBN 978-1-107-03074-9
1. Prisons.   2. Punishment.   3. Crime.   4. Criminal justice, Administration of.
I. Scott, David Gordon, editor of compilation.
HV8665.W43   2013
365–dc23
                                                    2013005147

ISBN 978-1-107-03074-9 Hardback

CONTENTS

FIGURES AND TABLES

CONTRIBUTORS

Vanessa Barker is Associate Professor of Sociology at Stockholm University. She is the author of *The Politics of Imprisonment: How the Democratic Process Shapes the Way America Punishes Offenders* (2009) and is currently working on a comparative analysis of global mobility and penal order.

Emma Bell is senior lecturer at the University of Savoie in Chambéry, where she teaches British history and contemporary British politics. Her research aims to situate British penal policy in its wider social, political and historical context. She is the author of *Criminal Justice and Neoliberalism* (2011), in which she attempts to understand the so-called 'punitive turn' in British criminal justice policy under the New Labour administration and examine its links to neoliberal political economy. In September 2012 Emma was elected as the new coordinator of the European Group for the Study of Deviance and Social Control.

Mary Bosworth is Reader in Criminology, University of Oxford and, concurrently, Professor of Criminology, Monash University Australia. She is co-editor of the journal *Theoretical Criminology* and recent book titles include *Explaining U.S. Imprisonment* (2010a) and *What is Criminology?* (2011).

Mark Brown teaches criminology at the University of Melbourne. He has written on a number of aspects of punishment, penal history and theory. He is currently engaged in research projects on the process of desistance from offending, on the modern history of the prison in Australia and on the jurisprudence of offender risk. He is also writing a book on penal power and colonial rule in India.

Michelle Brown is Assistant Professor of Sociology and faculty fellow at the Centre for the Study of Social Justice at the University of

Tennessee. She is the author of *The Culture of Punishment: Prison, Society, and Spectacle* (2009), co-editor of *Media Representations of September 11* (Chermack et al., 2003) and co-author of *Criminology Goes to the Movies: Crime Theory and Popular Culture* (2011).

Vickie Cooper is a lecturer in criminology at Liverpool John Moores University. She has published literature on housing and homelessness and is currently involved in a research project on homelessness and imprisonment in Liverpool with the Howard League for Penal Reform.

Alessandro De Giorgi is Associate Professor of Justice Studies at San José State University, California. He has a PhD in criminology from Keele University, UK. His research interests include theories of punishment and social control, global migrations, political economy and urban ethnography. Currently, he is conducting an ethnographic research on ex-prisoners released into a poor and segregated neighbourhood of Oakland, California. He is the author of *Re-Thinking the Political Economy of Punishment: Perspectives on Post-Fordism and Penal Politics* (2006).

Marie Gottschalk is Professor of Political Science at the University of Pennsylvania. She is the author of, among other works, *The Shadow Welfare State: Labor, Business, and the Politics of Health Care in the United States* (2000) and *The Prison and the Gallows: The Politics of Mass Incarceration in America* (2006). She is completing a new book, *Caught: The Future of the Carceral State and American Politics*.

Magnus Hörnqvist is an associate professor at the Department of Criminology, Stockholm University. He works in a tradition from Foucault and Marx, critically analysing power in prisons, the labour market and other social settings. His publications include *Risk, Power and the State: After Foucault* (2010).

Emma Kaufman received her BA from Columbia and her MPhil and DPhil from Oxford, where she was a Marshall and Clarendon Scholar. She was a guest scholar at the University of California,

San Diego's Centre for Comparative Immigration Studies from 2011 to 2012 and now attends Yale Law School. Emma's doctoral research examined the treatment of foreign national prisoners in the British penal estate. She has published on American immigration imprisonment, gender and punishment and British prison policy.

Thomas Mathiesen is a professor of sociology of law at the University of Oslo. He co-founded the Norwegian prisoners' association KROM in 1968 and is the author of a number of highly influential books, book chapters and journal articles, including *The Politics of Abolition* (1974), *Prison on Trial* (1990, 3rd edn 2006) and *Silently Silenced: Essays on the Creation of Acquiescence in Modern Society* (2004). His most recent book is entitled *Towards a Surveillant State: The Rise of Surveillance Systems in Europe* (in press).

Keally McBride is Associate Professor of Politics and International Studies at the University of San Francisco. She has published on a variety of themes in contemporary life and power, including *Collective Dreams: Political Imagination and Community* (2005), *Punishment and Political Order* (2007) and most recently with Margaret Kohn, *Political Theories of Decolonization: Postcolonialism and the Problem of Foundations* (Kohn and McBride, 2011). She is currently researching criminal law and the legacy of colonialism.

Erica Meiners teaches, writes and organises in Chicago. She has written about her ongoing labour and learning in anti-militarisation campaigns, educational justice struggles, prison abolition and reform movements and queer- and immigrant-rights organising in *Flaunt It! Queers Organizing for Public Education and Justice* (Quinn and Meiners, 2009), *Right to be Hostile: Schools, Prisons and the Making of Public Enemies* (2007) and articles in *Radical Teacher, Meridians, AREA Chicago* and *Social Justice*. She is a professor of education and gender and women's studies at Northeastern Illinois University, where she is a member of UPI/ Local 4100, and she also teaches at other free and community-based popular education sites in Chicago.

Julia C. Oparah (formerly Sudbury) is an educator, writer and activist
scholar with roots in Nigeria and the UK, who lives in Oakland,
California. She is Professor and Chair of Ethnic Studies at Mills
College, where she teaches classes on the African diaspora, 'women
of color' organising and the criminal justice system. Julia is author
of *Other Kinds of Dreams: Black Women's Organisations and the
Politics of Transformation* (1998), editor of *Global Lockdown: Race,
Gender and the Prison-Industrial Complex* (Sudbury, 2005c) and
co-editor of *Activist Scholarship: Antiracism, Feminism and Social
Change* (2009), *Outsiders Within: Writing on Transracial Adoption*
(2006) and *Colour of Violence: The Incite! Anthology* (2006). Julia is
co-founder of Critical Resistance, a national anti-prison
organisation, and has worked with Arizona Prison Moratorium
Coalition, Prison Activist Resource Centre, Justice Now!, Toronto
Prisoner Justice Action Committee and INCITE! Women of
Color Against Violence.

David Scott is a senior lecturer in criminology at Liverpool John
Moores University and, until recently, coordinator of the European
Group for the Study of Deviance and Social Control. He is an
associate editor of the *Howard Journal of Criminal Justice* and a
member of the steering group of the Reclaim Justice Network.
Recent book titles include *Controversial Issues in Prisons* (2010),
Critique and Dissent (Gilmore et al., 2013) and *The Caretakers of
Punishment* (in press (a)).

Joe Sim is Professor of Criminology at Liverpool John Moores University.
He is the author and co-author of a number of texts on prisons,
including *British Prisons* (Fitzgerald and Sim, 1982), *Medical Power
in Prison* (1990) and *Prisons under Protest* (Scraton et al., 1991). His
latest book is *Punishment and Prisons: Power and the Carceral State*
(2009).

Loïc Wacquant is Professor of Sociology at the University of California,
Berkeley, and researcher at the Centre européen de sociologie et de
science politique, Paris. A MacArthur Foundation Fellow and
recipient of the Lewis Coser Award of the American Sociological
Association, his research spans urban relegation, ethnoracial
domination, the penal state, incarnation, and social theory and the

politics of reason. His books have been translated in some twenty languages and include the trilogy *Urban Outcasts: A Comparative Sociology of Advanced Marginality* (2008a), *Punishing the Poor: The Neoliberal Government of Social Insecurity* (2009a) and *Deadly Symbiosis: Race and the Rise of the Penal State* (2013), as well as *The Two Faces of the Ghetto* (2013).

TABLE OF CASES

FOREWORD

On stemming the tide

Thomas Mathiesen

This is an important book.

Why prison? At the outset it seems obvious. We have prisons because we have crime. We have prisons also because we want to stop or at least reduce crime. But as David Scott shows in the opening chapter of this book, it is not so simple. There is an unclear relationship between prison and crime. Prisons have something to do with crime, but it is not clear how the two interact.

The question of 'why prison?' becomes all the more thorny when we go into detail. From a large number of empirical studies, we know that recidivism from standard prisons (and most prisons are 'standard' or less) is very great, despite attempts at rehabilitation. This holds for old as well as new attempts – from the 'Nothing works' period of the 1970s to the 'What works?' period of our own time (Mathiesen, 2011). Prisons are generally a fiasco. Why, then, do we keep on? *Why prison?*

FUNCTIONS OF PRISONS

Of course, prisons may have a variety of other presumed official functions. If they generally do not rehabilitate, prisons may, presumably at least, incapacitate the offender, through collective or individual incapacitation. Prisons may also deter others from committing crime. And prisons may provide retributive justice. But in terms of these official functions, prisons are also fiascos. When you look at it more closely (which I have spent large parts of my life doing), prisons in fact largely do not incapacitate and in very many cases do not deter others. In terms of retributive justice, there are far too many differences between individuals, groups, cultures and nations to make the construction of a common 'system of justice' possible (Mathiesen, 1990/2006). Why, then, do we continue this? *Why prison?*

We have to differentiate between the causes why prisons came to be and the causes why prisons persist today, despite their fiasco. The causes why prisons came to be, why they were 'invented', are historical and are to do with deep-seated changes in social structure in the 1600s and specifically in the 1800s. But from sociology, and perhaps particularly from Max Weber in his famous essay *The Protestant Ethic and the Spirit of Capitalism* (Weber 1930, original German edition 1904–5), we have learned that why something persists today may differ from why it came to be. Weber argued that the protestant ethic in its Calvinist variety was a necessary (though hardly a sufficient) condition for the rise of capitalism. Few would argue that the same conditions, and especially the Calvinist ethic, not only allow capitalism to exist but also allow it to thrive as a major economic system across the world today. So with prisons. The various historical conditions for their 'invention' are at least partly different from their stubborn persistence and, indeed, grave expansion in our own time.

Below I concentrate on the latter question. Through the years, I have ventured several attempts at explaining 'why prisons?' in this sense. One attempt came in my *Prison on Trial* (Mathiesen, 1990/2006). There I said that 'we have prisons despite their fiasco because there exists a pervasive and persistent *ideology of prison* in our society... An ideology of prison... renders the prison as an institution and a sanction meaningful and legitimate' (ibid.: 141–5, emphasis in original). The ideology has a supportive and a negating component.

Very briefly: assuming an advanced capitalist society, prisons serve, I said, four or five important ideological functions: (i) an *expurgatory* function (getting rid of a sizeable – and, I might have added, an increasing – proportion of the unproductive population); (ii) a *power-draining* function (getting rid of them in a controlled way, draining off whatever power they used to have); (iii) a *diverting* function (diverting our attention away from the deviance of those who have power in our class society); and (iv) a *symbolic* function (closely related to the diverting function). Because prisons are the most observable of all sanctions, I added a fifth function which I called an overt *action* function, important to those who administrate the sanctioning system and want to show that they do something about crime. I add here that the five functions are probably largely intended but considered as more or less illegitimate or as asides from the official functions by high-ranking decision-making personnel or politicians.

These five functions, I said, imbue prisons with something 'positive'; the prison performs something. Some of them are also visible.

That certainly goes for the first of the five – the expurgatory function of getting rid of a sizeable part of the unproductive population. Prisons in the Western world are filled with sick, vagrant, unemployed people.

But the ideology of prison also contains a negating function – that is, the fiasco of the prison is negated throughout the various public spheres of society.

Functions such as these are in my mind important. They may also contribute to an explanation of variations in the use of prisons. A state with a low unemployment rate, a high standard of living and a low degree of class division may be expected to have relatively few prisoners per capita, whereas the opposite situation may be expected to provide many prisoners. There are indeed such variations in the Western world.

AN ALTERNATIVE HYPOTHESIS: CONFIDENCE

However, though coming from a society which at present has the former features, and a low number of prisoners per capita, I venture an alternative hypothesis. The great differences in terms of prisoners per capita between various states in the Western world may partly be explained by differences in *confidence* in our various societies.

'Confidence' is a wide term, subject to interpretation. It may be seen as a synonym to 'trust'. I have confidence, or trust, in a person selling me groceries in a normal grocery store. I trust that the woman behind the counter will give me the correct change back. I have less confidence in a vagrant who wants to sell me a cell phone at a street corner. Roughly, confidence or trust may be seen in terms of two aspects: (i) abstract or general confidence; and (ii) concrete confidence in institutions, politicians or individuals. Law is presumably a system of confidence across time and space, though we may have our doubts. Much more could be said about confidence, but this is enough for the purposes here. Let us then explore this concept.

A study of confidence

On 22 July 2011, a bomb went off at the main government building in Oslo, causing serious destruction to the building and killing seven people. A little later on the same evening, sixty-nine young people were shot to death in a political summer camp on an island near Oslo. The blast and the later killings were committed by the same ultra-radical white extremist man.

A study of the confidence that people have in central social institutions and in foreigners was conducted (Wollebæk et al., 2011). Two representative population samples (1,000 people, internet users aged 16–79) were compared, one sample from a little before the terrorist attack in Oslo, in March/April 2011, and the other a short time after the terrorist attack, in August 2011. In addition, a panel study was carried out on persons who used so-called social media twice a week or more (a sample of people were asked questions in March/April, and again in August 2011).

In their study comparing the degree of confidence in Norway before and after 22 July 2011, Wollebæk et al. (2012:11) found a much higher degree of 'generalised confidence' ('most people are to be trusted') after the terrorist event than before. The increase had been clearest among grown-ups and middle-aged people, weaker among the oldest (ibid.: 12). The researchers found the greatest confidence in people close to those who were asked – family and so on (not an unexpected finding); the more abstract forms of confidence, where the respondents knew a lower proportion of the people in question, were somewhat weaker (ibid.: 13). But Wollebæk et al. (2012) summarise as follows:

> [T]here is a clear increase in confidence in groups where you most of the time do not know everyone personally. People convey increased confidence in people who live in the same community. Aside from increased confidence in other Norwegians, we find the strongest increase in the most demanding types of confidence, that is, confidence in people who are unlike ourselves even as far as central criteria goes, meaning nationality and religion... In Norway, confidence in other people is closely related to confidence in institutions.
>
> (Wollebæk et al., 2012: 15–16, my translation)

This was a time when criticism and antagonisms began to surface in Norway. So far, however, 'the findings unambiguously indicate increasing trust' (ibid.: 16). This is clearest regarding parliament and the government, but also regarding the courts, municipal authorities and the administration (ibid.), while the change was more moderate for the police, which, together with the government, was severely criticised during the months to come.

Oslo and Oklahoma
It may be instructive briefly to compare the Oslo case of 2011 with the Oklahoma case of 1995, where there are comparable data. The

Oklahoma City bombing in 1995 claimed 168 lives and injured more than 680 people, destroying or damaging 324 buildings within a 16-block radius. Right after the Oklahoma bombing, 38 per cent of a national sample said they were very worried about terrorism and 40 per cent were a little worried. Of the representative study, 2.5 per cent and 16.6 per cent respectively said the same in Norway right after the Norwegian events (Wollebæk et al., 2012: 18). The difference is very large. Wollebæk et al. (2011: 19–21) also report other comparative data from Oklahoma which point in the same direction.

A number of studies have shown that the level of confidence between people is higher in Norway and the other Nordic countries than elsewhere in Europe. During the last fifteen to twenty years, the development has been more varied in Western Europe, somewhat negative in Southern and Eastern Europe and quite negative in the USA (ibid.: 9). In other words, international data seems to corroborate the first set of findings, the 2011 findings, from Norway.

A second report

Wollebæk and associates wrote a second report. In their report *One Year after 22 July* (Wollebæk et al., 2012), they followed up their initial findings on opinions right before and right after 22 July 2011. Opinions a year afterward were somewhat different. Opinion surveys and panel studies were carried out during four different periods, entitled April 2011, August 2011, May 2012 and August 2012 (right after the publication of a critical '22 July Commission's Report'). The data showed that a development back to the time before 22 July 2011 had occurred. But the terror event had neither become a societal collapse nor something like a permanent rose-gathering.[1] In August 2012, the social

---

[1] Right after the attack, on 25 July 2011, an estimated 200,000 people carrying roses gathered at the Oslo City Hall to listen to speeches by, among others, the Prime Minister, the Crown Prince and the Mayor of Oslo. For a city of less than 620,000 inhabitants (1 July 2012; close to 925,000 when 10 nearby municipalities are included), 200,000 is a very large crowd. It was televised nationwide. Similar gatherings occurred in many other cities. The speakers emphasised more democracy and more openness – presumably basic Norwegian values – as Norway's reply to the terrorist. During the trial which followed in April 2012, an assembly of 40,000 people gathered at the City Square and outside the Court House, again carrying roses and singing a well-known children's song – in the rain. Members of Parliament also sang in the Parliament building that day. The full story of 22 July 2011 and its aftermath should one day be told in English. A good part of the story is told in my forthcoming book *Towards a Surveillant State: The Rise of Surveillance Systems in Europe* (Matheisen, in press).

engagement, confidence in people and confidence in institutions had returned to just about normal.

Fear and insecurity, as well as a belief in surveillance measures, were greater, but this may be due to the critical publication and widespread public debate on the '22 July Commission's Report', which also occurred in August 2012. With regard to surveillance on the internet, there is a clear tendency of opinion towards more surveillance of communication during the past year. The terrorist's communications and his ideologically supportive websites were most likely behind this. But there is an important difference between grown-ups and young people. Grown-ups, to a larger extent, accept surveillance of individuals and groups on the internet. Young people, to a larger extent, have attitudes which do not exclusively demand more control and surveillance (Wollebæk et al., 2012: 70).

The crucial question is, therefore, why is a culture of fear not more clearly established among the young? Victims of the terror were predominantly young people, shot at the island. The explanation may be tied to the fact that they live in a 'high trust society' (ibid.: 72).

In short, public opinion one year after the terrorist event in Norway was back to normal. It was not as high in terms of confidence as right after the attack, but it was certainly not lower.

It should also be added that terrorist attacks have previously shown a significant short-term effect on trust and political engagement. During the months following the 9/11 attack, trust between people as well as in the government, the police and in ethnic minorities increased in the USA. Trust in the government increased to a level not seen since the 1960s. But trust fell back to pre-2001 levels after a few months or bifurcated the population in terms of class (Sander and Putnam, 2010; Wollebæk et al., 2012: 5).

However, comparisons indicate that the proportion of the population which thinks that 'you can trust most people' is double the size in Norway compared with the USA (Wollebæk et al., 2012: 5). The difference is certainly significant.

Can we make use of this?

The crucial question is this: 'Can we make use of information such as this, and lower or at least significantly slow down the increase in the number of prisoners per capita in a society?' As David Scott has pointed out, Norway's number of prisoners per capita has increased, but is still relatively low, while the USA, on the other hand, has the highest figure of all twelve countries which he compares (748 per 100,000 – see Table 1.1). It should be added that the rate rises if you look at men only (who predominantly populate US prisons), and further to 1,261 per 100,000 Hispanics and Latino men and to a staggering 3,042 per 100,000 black men.

How, then, are we to 'stem the tide'?

- *There are material aspects that foster confidence in others*: urban structures should be fundamentally changed – low buildings instead of tall; tight-knit towns or sections of towns where people see and speak to each other instead of barren city sections; street lights should be lit.
- *There are aspects of formal control that should be changed*: the police should largely be unarmed instead of armed, police officers should be visible and polite rather than driving around in closed cars, and ethics and police politeness should be taught in police academies; it is wrong to assume that our own increase in sanctioning potential fosters security – it fosters increased fear. A measure of security arrangements should be organised, but very soon you reach an upper limit. The ideology of a precise relationship between effective means to reach goals should be tapered down, the 'round' police officer who also helps people and is a servant should be fostered.
- *There are aspects of togetherness that should be fostered*: transport should be collective, parks should be made into cultural centres and speakers' corners, poverty should be lifted, television should be tamed, public colonisation of civil life in the form of a culture of advertisements should be challenged, civil society should once again be made into a part of city life – and so on and so forth.
- *This involves a limitation on controlled city life, and an expansion of a social city life*: think tanks to create human contexts, rather than create more efficient control, should be established.

I have outlined briefly a line of reasoning. It needs much further thinking. If followed, it would imply a 'softer' or 'warmer' society; it would involve a sum of norms, trust and networks, what several researchers have referred to as increased 'social capital' (Sander and Putnam, 2010: 5; see also Barker, Chapter 7 of this volume). It would probably not abolish the main functions of prison mentioned earlier. For example, as long as we have a predominantly capitalist economy, confidence would not abolish the expurgatory function of getting rid of the unproductive poor (see Wacquant, Chapter 4).

But it would make the process less pronounced, possibly much less pronounced.

We are better at analysing the reasons why unwanted conditions flourish than how they are to be tamed. We should begin thinking about how to tame them.

In doing so, *Why Prison?* will be a very important and useful book.

1

WHY PRISON? POSING THE QUESTION

David Scott

The question 'why prison?' has never been more pertinent or compelling than it is today. Rates of penal incarceration in many countries around the world have reached record levels, and the combined world prison population recently surpassed 10 million.[1] When such enormous figures are presented to us it can be difficult to conceptualise what the data actually mean, but if all the people imprisoned in just three nations – the USA, China and Russia – were to stand next to each other, the resulting line would stretch across the surface of the planet. Notwithstanding a few notable exceptions, the global data are clear and decisive: penal incarceration has risen and continues to rise at an alarmingly fast pace (Walmsley, 2012). For Dario Melossi (2011: 50), global penal excess at the beginning of the twenty-first century is tantamount to a 'great internment'. Such phraseology immediately brings to mind a possible connection between the current penal incarceration binge and the emergence of the Great Confinement in the late sixteenth and early seventeenth centuries (Rusche and Kirchheimer, 1939/2003; Foucault, 1967). It also begs parallels with the emergence in the eighteenth century of a centralised bureaucratic state with the mandate to manage rising economic inequality and manifestations of class struggle. The mission of the new sites of state detention was unequivocal: to survey, classify, regulate and control unwanted and unwelcome populations

---

[1] Due to categorisation and recording problems, even this figure is likely to be an underestimate. For example, it is estimated that there are more than 650,000 people in detention centres in China. If these data are included, the overall total for China is 2.3 million and the world total 10.75 million (Walmsley, 2012: 1).

(Rothman, 1971; Foucault, 1977; Ignatieff, 1978; Melossi and Pavarini, 1981; S. Cohen, 1985; Scull, 1993). As Thomas Mathiesen (1990: 14) maintained some twenty or more years ago, the rapid and spectacular growth of penal incarceration since the early 1970s may indicate a new *third stage* in the development of imprisonment, this time in response to a perceived '*need for discipline in given segments and groups of the population*' (emphasis in original). Perhaps, then, we should not be surprised that prisons everywhere are bursting at the seams with the poor, marginalised and socially deprived.

Asking the question 'why prison?' connects contemporary critical analysis of penal incarceration with an enquiry that has been the attention of some of the greatest thinkers on the 'confinement project' in the past and provides the central premise of this edited collection. This introductory chapter is divided into three parts. The section directly below explores data from twelve countries to update and evidence Thomas Mathiesen's (1990) argument regarding the emergence of a third stage of penal incarceration. The discussion then moves on to critically evaluate five of the main 'common sense' justifications proposed in defence of the prison. Finding such justifications unconvincing, it is maintained that the global explosion in the use of imprisonment in the last four decades has more to do with its role in the control of certain identifiable groups of people rather than as a rational response to 'crime'. The introduction closes with a brief summary of the following fourteen chapters by some of the leading contemporary writers on imprisonment.

GLOBAL HYPER-INCARCERATION

Even the most cursory glance at Table 1.1, which details penal incarceration rates in twelve countries since 1970, can leave no doubt about current trends in the Western world. In ten of the twelve nations, which are either predominantly English speaking or located in Europe, the prisoner rate has increased in the last forty years. In one country, Germany, the prisoner rate rose in the late twentieth century but by 2010 had returned to virtually the same level as 1970. Only in Finland can we find evidence of a clear downward trend. This deviant case has attracted considerable academic attention (Lappi-Seppala, 2012), and it is worth noting that whilst in 1970 Finland had a prisoner rate second only to the USA, by 2010 it had by far the lowest recorded rate of the twelve selected countries. Let us take this analysis of prisoner rates further by first considering in some depth the USA, and then moving

TABLE 1.1 Selected prisoner rates (per 100,000) in twelve countries (1970–2010)

Country	1970	1980	1990	2000	2005	2010
USA	166	221	461	684	738	748
New Zealand	83	88	114	151	186	199
England and Wales	71	85	90	125	144	153
Australia	48	59	84	113	125	133
Canada	88	98	113	101	107	117
Spain	38	85	113	145	160	159
France	55	66	77	88	96	96
Netherlands	21	23	43	84	127	94
Germany	86	92	82	97	97	85
Sweden	65	55	58	60	78	78
Norway	44	44	56	57	68	73
Finland	113	106	69	55	74	59

(Source: Lappi-Seppala, 2012; Walmsley, 2012)

on to reflect upon the situation in four other Anglophone countries before concluding this overview with an account of the seven other selected countries in Europe, paying particular attention to the recently debated notion of 'Nordic exceptionalism'.

The USA today stands at the top of the world penal incarceration rate. It was not always so. For most of the twentieth century until the mid 1970s, the USA had a relatively stable rate of penal incarceration, remaining well below 200 per 100,000 of the national population.[2] In 1970 the average daily population (ADP) of those confined in prison or jail was 250,000,[3] yet the rise since this time has been quite staggering. By the early 1980s the USA prisoner ADP had doubled to more than 500,000 prisoners, and by February 2000 this number had surpassed 2 million (Lacey, 2011). In 2010 the USA imprisoned 2.3 million people at a rate of 748 per 100,000 and 7.3 million people – or 1 in 33 adults – were either in prison, on parole or on probation. Prisoner rates in the USA are now five times greater than those of Western-European and English-speaking countries.[4]

[2] I will subsequently just refer to the figure 100,000.
[3] There is some debate over the accuracy of this number, with one commentator pointing to the figure of 380,000 prisoners in the USA at this time (Wacquant, 2009).
[4] It should be noted that these USA data do *not* include juveniles and persons in police lockups, a figure which Loïc Wacquant (2009) estimates at around 140,000 people.

Whilst politicians in the USA have recently raised concerns about the financial cost of imprisonment (the USA spent $47 billion on prisons in 2008), penologists have primarily focused on the social dimensions of penal incarceration. The phenomenal rise in the US prison population has been described as 'mass imprisonment' for much of the last decade (Garland, 2001d). Recently, however, Loïc Wacquant (2010a) has argued that this term is inappropriate because penal excess has not been experienced by the 'mass' of the populace, but almost exclusively by poor black, Latino and Hispanic Americans. US prison data support his assertion. Whilst more than 1 in 100 American adults are in prison, the figure is 1 in 50 for Hispanic men and 1 in 20 for black men. The overall penal incarceration rate for men in the USA is 943 per 100,000. When analysed via categorisations of 'race', the rate falls to 487 for white men but rises to 1,261 for Hispanic and Latino men and 3,042 for black men (Lacey, 2011). African Americans make up 13 per cent of the general population but 60 per cent of the US prison population, and are eight times more likely to be incarcerated than the white population (Downes, 2012). The centrality of class should not be forgotten here. Undoubtedly middle-class black populations have benefited from social mobility. By some estimates the probability of middle-class African Americans going to prison dropped by 50 per cent in the last twenty years (Wacquant, 2001; 2010a). This being said, more African Americans are today under correctional supervision than were enslaved during the antebellum period (Alexander, 2011). Loïc Wacquant (2010a) refers to this phenomenon as 'hyper-incarceration', indicating the existence of 'penal excess' (J. Pratt, 2008b) without obfuscating its real target: poor and black or minority ethnic (BME) populations. The contention of this chapter is that such 'hyper-incarceration' also has a global dimension (A. Y. Davis, 2012).

In other Anglophone countries we can also find evidence of escalating prisoner populations and an intensification in the discipline and control of BME populations from the poorest segments of the working class. In New Zealand in the 1960s, the prisoner ADP was around 1,700, and although it remained relatively stable until the mid 1980s, from this point the prisoner rate rose from 80 per 100,000 to 126 per 100,000 in 1996 (Cavadino and Dignan, 2006). It increased still further to 199 per 100,000 in 2010 and in March 2011 the prisoner ADP peaked at 8,844. Like the USA, when prisoner rates are examined through the lens of 'race', disturbing patterns emerge. Maori men constitute 15 per cent of the national population but account for 51 per cent of the male prisoner population. They are eight times more likely to be imprisoned than non-Maori men by New Zealand criminal processes. In Australia there has been a steady rise in prisoner population since the 1970s, and by March 2012 it had a prisoner rate of 133 per 100,000 and a prisoner ADP of 29,226. Two of the most striking aspects of Australian prison populations are the divergences between different territories and the over-penalisation of Aboriginal and Torres Strait Islanders. In March 2012 the Northern Territory had a prisoner rate of 821 per 100,000, which, if it was nation in its own right, would be the number one penal incarcerator in the world. Aboriginal and Torres Strait Islander people represent just 2 per cent of the national population but 27 per cent of the prisoner population, and have an imprisonment rate of 2,247 per 100,000 (Australian Bureau of Statistics, 2012).

England and Wales has been on a clear expansionist penal trajectory since at least the 1970s.[5] Although there was a small reversal in this trend from 1989 to 1992 when the prison population fell from 50,000 to 41,000, since 1993 the prisoner ADP has increased year-on-year by an average of 3.7 per cent for nearly twenty years (Berman, 2012). The result is a more than doubling of the ADP of prisoners, which surpassed 80,000 for the first time in December 2006 and reached a record high of 88,179 prisoners on 2 December 2011. People categorised as either 'black' or 'black British' make up 2.7 per cent of the national population but 13.4 per cent of the prisoner population. 'African Caribbean' women make up 1 per cent of the national population but 24 per cent of women in prison, whilst 'African Caribbean' men are eight times more likely to face the sanction of penal incarceration than white men (Sudbury, 2005b; Berman, 2012). Canada, the final Anglophone country considered here, has experienced what may be described as a 'slow creep' towards hyper-incarceration. The prisoner rate in the 1970s and 1980s remained fractionally under 100 per 100,000, although in the last two decades it has consistently exceeded this rate and in 2011 stood at 117 per 100,000. It is important to note, however, that when data on those admitted to custody is analysed, Canada appears not less but more punitive than England and Wales. For example, in 2006 over 232,800 adults were admitted to some form of penal custody, a much higher number than in England and Wales, which is approximately 120,000 (Webster and Doob, 2007). Whatever the difficulties in comparing prisoner rates, Canadian prisons undoubtedly share the same mission

---

[5] This is also broadly the case for other countries in the UK.

to control impoverished BME populations and other members of the 'subproletariat' (Hall et al., 1978). Aboriginal adults make up 4 per cent of the national population but 21 per cent of male prisoners and 30 per cent of female prisoners. In some places such as in Manitoba or Saskatchewan, Aboriginals account for more than for 70 per cent of men and 80 per cent of women sentenced to imprisonment, despite being only 15 per cent of the population. Prisons have always drawn their clientele from the poorest segments of the proletariat but, as the above data indicate, the racist legacy of English colonialism is also clearly evident in prisoner populations across Anglophone nations.

Penal excess and the disproportionate imprisonment of impoverished BME populations are widespread in Western Europe. Spain, France and the Netherlands have all seen record-number prisoner populations in the last decade, although Germany has resisted this trend somewhat. Spanish prison populations have sharply increased since the early 1970s: the 2011 prisoner ADP of 73,459 is four times higher than the equivalent figure in 1970, and the enlargement of the prisoner population has been particularly marked since the new millennium (Institute of Penitentiaries, 2012). With a prisoner rate of 159 per 100,000, Spain is the highest penal incarcerator in Western Europe, and like many other countries in this region, Spain also has a large number of foreign nationals serving long sentences (De Giorgi, 2011; Walmsley, 2012; see also De Giorgi, Chapter 2 of this volume). The prisoner rate in France has fluctuated considerably (Cavadino and Dignan, 2006). In 1985, for example, the prisoner rate was 72 prisoners per 100,000. Within three years the prisoner population increased by over 12,000 to leave a rate of 92 prisoners per 100,000 in 1988, yet by 1990 it had fallen back to 81 prisoners per 100,000. Despite regular amnesties and pardons, there is evidence of a 'slow creep' in France.[6] In July 2012 the French prisoner ADP reached a record high of 67,373 prisoners – a prisoner rate of 101 per 100,000. Although foreign nationals comprised only 6 per cent of the population, they accounted for 21 per cent of the prison population.

The Netherlands, once eulogised as a leading example of penal tolerance, has witnessed one of the most dramatic increases in prisoner rates on the planet. In 1973 the Netherlands had a prisoner rate of just

---

[6] The last amnesty law in France was in 2007. The tradition of granting presidential pardons to mark the 14 July celebrations was also ended by President Sarkozy. The recently elected socialist President François Hollande has, so far, refused to sanction any further prisoner amnesties.

18 per 100,000. By 2005 the prisoner rate had ballooned to 127 per 100,000.[7] Indeed, of the twelve selected countries, only the USA has experienced a similar escalation in the use of penal incarceration. During this time the proportion of foreign national prisoners grew rapidly, rising from 12 per cent in 1981 to 26 per cent in 1992. Whilst there is some evidence that the Netherlands has turned a corner in terms of penal expansionism, with the prisoner rate declining to 94 by 2010, in the same year the share of foreign national prisoners rose to 32 per cent. The case of Germany is a little different, at least in terms of rising prisoner populations. Whilst the prisoner population did increase in the latter part of the twentieth century, in recent times it has declined. The 2010 figure of 85 per 100,000 had returned to the exact same figure as 1970. Notwithstanding, Germany does not deviate in terms of the over-representation of foreign nationals, with 34 per cent of its prisoners designated as 'immigrants' (De Giorgi, 2011). Undoubtedly it is those foreign nationals who face precarious working and living conditions that fill such prisons (Wacquant, 2006, 2010b; De Giorgi, 2011; see also De Giorgi, Chapter 2 of this volume).

Whereas Anglophone and many Western-European countries have indulged in penal excess, for some commentators Nordic countries are places of penal moderation with humane prison conditions (J. Pratt, 2008a, 2008b, 2011; Pratt and Erickson, 2012). Particular focus in recent years has been on Finland, as it is the one country in Europe which has seen a concerted long-term decline in prisoner populations. In the early 1950s the imprisonment rate in Finland stood at 200 per 100,000, and even in the 1970s the Finnish incarceration rate remained one of the highest in Europe. It was not until the 1990s that Finland reached a comparative rate with other Nordic countries, and in 2010 Finland had a prisoner rate of 59 per 100,000 (Lappi-Seppala, 2012). In contrast to many other European countries, Finland also has a low proportion of foreign national prisoners, constituting a relatively modest 13 per cent in 2011.[8] By comparison, Sweden and Norway have experienced a 'slow creep' in prisoner rates and have high numbers of (lower working-class) foreign nationals behind bars. In the 1950s Sweden had a prisoner rate of 35 per 100,000. This figure had doubled by the 1960s,

---

[7] The Netherlands include juveniles and other detainees in its official prison rates. The problem of how different detained populations included in the prisoner rates of different countries can make international comparisons difficult is discussed below.

[8] This is approximately the same number of foreign national prisoners as England and Wales in 2012.

and since the 1970s there has been a gradual increase in prisoner rates. In 2010 Sweden had a prisoner rate of 78 per 100,000, and foreign nationals constituted 28 per cent of the prisoner population (Dullum and Ugelvik, 2012; Walmsley, 2012). A 'slow creep' in Norwegian prisons has also been evident since the mid 1980s. Whilst there have been only modest increases, from for example 56 per 100,000 in 1990 to 73 per 100,000 in 2011, what is most notable is the drastic increase in the number of foreign national prisoner, rising from 19 per cent of the prison population in 2007 to 33 per cent by June 2012 (International Centre for Prison Studies, 2012). Though both Norway and Sweden continue to have low populations compared to most other countries in Europe, prisoner rates are not as low as they once were.

Before reaching any firm conclusions, some of the problems associated with analysing comparative prison data should be highlighted. Let us first consider the disquiet regarding 'Nordic exceptionalism' (Dullum and Ugelvik, 2012). Concerns have been raised about accepting official data without sufficient consideration of the 'subaltern' voices of prisoners, prisoner collective struggles or alternative 'non-official' sources of information (A. M. Jefferson, 2012). Critics note that rates of prisoners per 100,000 of the population may obscure as much as they reveal because: Nordic countries have, in the main, short sentences but reasonably large numbers of people processed through penal systems (Mathiesen, 2012); low prisoner rates do not indicate a humane penal system, and rates of self-inflicted deaths, which are relatively high in Nordic prisons, may prove more reliable in terms of indicating how prisoners experience penal incarceration (Mathiesen, 2012); it is impossible to grade pain (Christie, 1981), understand prison conditions outside the wider material conditions pertaining in a society (Neumann, 2012) or remove the inherent harms and pains of penal incarceration (Scott and Codd, 2010); and pre-trail detention and solitary confinement in Nordic nations provide a significant example of inhumane penal practices that are obscured by a focus on official quantitative data (Sharff-Smith, 2012). It is important to recognise that the intensification of penal discipline and control that Thomas Mathiesen (1990) highlights is not only about rising prisoner ADP rates.

The above problems regarding data on 'Nordic exceptionalism' are characteristic of general difficulties measuring international prisoner rates (Brodeur, 2007; Scott, 2008; Snacken and Dumortier, 2012). Official 'prisoner rates' are not standardised tools comparing 'like with like'. For a start, not all nations define 'prison' and their populations in the same way: some countries include juvenile offenders and/or those in psychiatric 'care' in penal custody statistics, whilst others provide data on adult prisoners only. Finland and Sweden include 15–17-year-olds in their prisoner rates, whilst the Netherlands include juveniles confined under both the civil and criminal law, resulting in competing estimations depending on which category is included or excluded (Tonry, 2007). In other words, widely different data are available on prisoner rates of the same country for a given year. This makes genuinely accurate measurement impossible. As in the Nordic case, the meanings of official prisoner rates are also contested. Measuring the prisoner ADP or prisoner rates may be less accurate at predicting sentencing trends than, for example, measures examining the average days served by prisoners or the relationship between arrests, prosecution and conviction in a given country (Pease, 1994). Though existing official quantitative data on prison populations should not be dismissed out of hand, it should be interpreted with the greatest of care and its limitations duly recognised.

There are also considerable differences in the way comparative data have been analysed. Three broad approaches can be identified: convergence, diversity and context. Theorists of convergence have aimed to highlight globalised socioeconomic and political developments in the last four decades that can explain the global penal incarceration binge (Garland, 2001c; Simon, 2007; Wacquant, 2009b) or identified particular clusters of nations that represent specific political economic or cultural commonalities (Cavadino and Dignan, 2006; Lacey, 2008; J. Pratt, 2011). Theorists of diversity have focused on the specific 'risk and protective factors' pertaining in a given nation shaping penal policy and incarceration rates (Tonry, 2007; Green, 2008; Snacken and Dumortier, 2012) or emphasised the manner in which the penal practices of each nation are so deeply embedded within their own history and culture that questions of their 'travels' must be considered very carefully (Melossi, 2011). A third approach recognises distinct national and historical penal practices but contextualises them within a recognition of the intensification of global economic and social inequalities underscoring liberal market and transnational capitalist economies, patriarchies, heteronormativity and neocolonial, racialised ideologies. This allows for an understanding of diversity between nations alongside recognition of a broader authoritarian drift towards a third historical stage of penal incarceration to control the global poor (Mathiesen, 1990; Sudbury, 2005a; A. Y. Davis, 2012; see also Scott, Chapter 15 of this volume).

Though it would be disingenuous to claim that the official prison data cited above, based as they are on quantitative snap shots of only twelve countries with no reference to rates in Africa, Asia or South America, alone provide incontrovertible evidence of global hyper-incarceration, it does strongly indicate a globalised trend towards an intensification of penal discipline. Prison populations, at different speeds in different countries, are in the main growing, and they not only contain poor people but disproportionately poor men and women classified as BME, migrants, refugees, asylum seekers or foreign nationals (see also De Giorgi, Chapter 2 of this volume). The question is: why?

QUESTIONING INCARCERATION

The global growth of penal incarceration could be taken to imply that prison has been successful in terms of meeting its stated aims. To some people it may even seem peculiar to ask the question 'why prison?' – surely the answer is self-evident: prisons have existed for centuries as places of punishment, so there must be a clear, uncontested rationale which explains their introduction, historical development and current expansion. And yet, like exposing an emperor with no clothes, when the apparently obvious reasons for imprisonment are closely examined, they are laid bare as a naked sham. Let us briefly, but critically, review five well-rehearsed arguments in defence of the prison.

1. Prisons are a natural and inevitable response to 'crime'

No straightforward relationship exists between 'crime' and imprisonment. Prisoners (in most cases) have breached and been prosecuted under the criminal law. This, however, must be understood within the context of the meaning, definition and differential application of the criminal label. 'Crime' is an unstable concept, and the diverse sets of behaviours it brings together are united only by the criminal process itself (Hulsman, 1986). Rather than being fixed and constant, the meanings and content of 'crime' change depending upon time, place, perpetrator and audience, with the criminal label more likely to be applied if the perpetrator is successfully distanced (Christie, 2004). Selective police surveillance in societies shaped by the determining contexts of capitalism, patriarchies and neocolonialism has resulted in the unequal application of criminal law against socially disadvantaged groups (Sim et al., 1987; Barton et al., 2006; Sim, 2009). For as long as we continue to classify and control certain behaviour by certain people using the criminal label, 'crime' will continue to have a relationship to rates of penal incarceration. How they interconnect, however, is extremely complex. 'Crime' and punishment have great symbolic resonance detached from actual or perceived rates of illegalities, and single criminalised acts can, and do, disproportionately impact on penal policies. A spate of high-profile killings or the horrific death of a child is likely in many countries to monopolise media agendas more than mundane but widespread troublesome incidents (Hall et al., 1978; Simon, 2007; Green, 2008; see also Scott, Chapter 15 of this volume). Because its definition and application is likely to remain unchallenged, 'crime' can be manipulated to justify authoritarian state intervention without an actual increase in prevalence (Hall et al., 1978; Sim et al., 1987). This indicates that it would be wrong to assume that the main cause of global hyper-incarceration is directly linked to rises in recorded 'crime'. Indeed, at times they do not even correlate. Let us consider recorded 'crime' rates in five of the countries highlighted earlier. In the 1990s there were increases in violent 'crime' in the USA, Canada, Germany and Finland. Only in the USA did this result in rapidly escalating rates of penal incarceration. In Germany and Canada, the prisoner rate showed only evidence of a 'slow creep' or remained reasonably stable, whereas numbers actually declined in Finland (Tonry, 2001; Lappi-Seppala, 2012). In England and Wales, after a number of decades in which 'official crime rates' had risen dramatically, 'crime' figures stabilised and then began to decline from 1993. Yet, in the twenty-year period since, the prison population has continued to rise without abatement. To dismiss 'crime' entirely from the equation would be a mistake, but there are clearly other reasons why prisons persist and continue to expand.

2. Prison prevents 'crime' by deterring offenders

Popularised by politicians and academics alike under the slogan 'prison works' (Murray, 1997), the idea that prisons have a deterrent effect appears almost self-evident. The logic behind deterrence is firmly rooted in the utilitarian calculus that to deter the rational offender requires the pain of imprisonment to outweigh the pleasure derived from 'crime'. Yet the role of prison as a means of deterring 'crime' is vulnerable to critique on a number of grounds, most damningly because most people who refrain from problematic conducts do so for reasons unconnected to the penal law. On the one hand, moral conscience or family reputation seem to act as the main barriers to wrongdoing for many. On the other hand, people already stigmatised, impoverished and excluded are less likely to fear further stigmatisation through criminal prosecution (Golash, 2005). The very logic of deterrence has also been questioned. Most people do not rationalise and calculate costs and benefits about 'crimes'. Further, not only is it actually impossible to determine if deterrence has a positive effect (we cannot measure what does not happen) but what evidence we do have – recidivism rates – overwhelmingly indicates that prison does not prevent 'crime'. In England and Wales, for example, recidivism is high for both young (75 per cent) and adult (50 per cent) ex-prisoners, and even here these data only measure those ex-prisoners who both offend and are caught (Scott and Codd, 2010). Indeed, prisons not only fail to deter 'crime' but also have criminogenic effects, which have surely only escalated in our time of global hyper-incarceration. Thus, rather than controlling 'crime', deterrence may more plausibly be considered as a means of controlling populations (Mathiesen, 1990). For Rusche and Kirchheimer (1939/2003) the value of human life is intimately tied to the current value of human labour, and in times of economic instability and financial crisis, prisons perform a key role in deterring the poor and marginalised through the principles of *lesser eligibility*. Unhygienic living conditions and penal servitude send a clear message to the labouring classes that if they do not conform to the rigours of the labour market, an even worse fate could yet befall them. This suggestion, however, indicates a more symbolic role for imprisonment, shifting attention away from any obvious 'crime'-prison link and towards a consideration of political economy (see also De Giorgi, Chapter 2 of this volume).

3. Prison turns bad criminals into good citizens

It is often argued that effectively managed prisons can provide an opportunity to reduce the likelihood of reoffending and to 'bring home' prisoner responsibilities. Rehabilitation in recent times has been associated with a treatment model where wrongdoing is conceived as an individual or social disease and, if the problems can be correctly diagnosed, offenders can be cured (Scott and Codd, 2010). Yet 'crime' is neither an 'illness' nor a 'disease' but a social construct, and by focusing upon perceived pathologies rooted in individual or social defects, rehabilitation as treatment is profoundly deterministic and denies human agency and moral choices (Scott, 2008, 2009). Treatment programmes individualise 'other' lawbreakers as cognitively different whilst at the same time ignoring wider problematic social circumstances and structural divisions such as poverty, sexism and racism (Kendal, 2002). The pains of incarceration are always more likely to dehabilitate rather than act as a conduit for reflection and growth (Mathiesen, 1990). Historically, rehabilitation has also been closely associated with work, penal servitude and discipline (ibid.). Although today some countries, such as the USA, pay mere lip service to the idea of rehabilitation; in others, as evidenced in penal policy documents such as *Breaking the Cycle* (Ministry of Justice (MoJ), 2010) in England and Wales, a focus on rehabilitation through work has once again come to prominence. Under this rationale, work is considered an essential part of a person's 'normal' activity and an effective means to cure laziness, instil discipline or simply use up time and energy that may otherwise be channelled into lawbreaking (Foucault, 1977). Although prisons are much more likely to create unemployability rather than a skilled reserve army of labour, the political appeal of prisons being perceived as a place of discipline and hard work grinding bad men and women good should not be dismissed out of hand. Indeed, this 'need for discipline' can help explain the authoritarian drift towards hyper-incarceration in many countries around the world.

4. Prisons protect the public from 'dangerous offenders'

Global hyper-incarceration cannot be explained due to rising recorded violent 'crime'. Though in popular mythology prisons contain 'dangerous offenders' who would present a serious future risk to public safety if not imprisoned, all the data indicate that the vast majority of prisoners are not 'dangerous', at least not when first imprisoned. Prisoners around the globe are generally people with impoverished social backgrounds who suffer from significant health problems and have perpetrated relatively minor property offences (Ruggiero et al., 1996; Weiss and South, 1998; Scott, 2008). In the USA, which has seen the greatest rise in penal incarceration in the last few decades, more than 1 million of the prison population have been incarcerated for non-violent offences. This rapid rise in penal incarceration cannot be separated from the increased criminalisation of drug usage in African American communities (Bosworth, 2010a; Alexander, 2011). 'Categorical suspicion' (Hudson, 2003) and the control of 'suspect communities' (Hillyard, 1995) is well documented in critical criminological analysis, and for some, contemporary penality is underscored by the logic of *actuarialism* (Simon, 1987; De Giorgi, 2011). Actuarialism entails the systematic analysis of the statistical distribution of criminal behaviours in a given population where criminalisation is closely linked to the group to which the offender belongs rather than the actual offence committed. Its effectiveness is dependent upon the aggregation of criminal character-istics and the subsequent use of techniques to identify those who most closely fit criminal risk profiles. This entirely removes individuals from the 'crime' control equation (Simon, 1987). Such a rationale sees the end of the acknowledgement of 'false positives' (people wrongly pre-dicted to offend in the future) as now the criteria of accuracy is judged solely on the correspondence between risk profiles and individual char-acteristics. Grounded in positivism and risk assessments, this approach is philosophically untenable because quite frankly we do not have the ability to accurately predict who will commit (serious) offences in the future (Mathiesen, 1990). Braithwaite and Pettit (1990) claim that even the best prediction techniques are wrong at least twice as often as they are right, whilst Deidre Golash (2005) estimates that predictions are generally wrong eight times out of nine. Prisons are not filled to the brim with dangerous offenders, but rather with lower working-class, BME, migrant and foreign national lawbreakers. What does remain plausible after such revelations is an analysis of advanced capitalist, neocolonial, patriarchal and heteronormative societies which identifies the prison as performing an important role in maintaining economic and social inequalities through the selective incapacitation of the 'detritus and the damned' (Mathiesen, 1990; A. Y. Davis, 2012; see also Cooper and Sim, Chapter 10 and Meiners, Chapter 13 of this volume).

5. Prison reflects our need to punish 'crime'

Penal incarceration appears so deeply entrenched in our cultural sensi-bilities that prison and punishment have become almost synonymous (Melossi and Pavarini, 1981). It has long been recognised that punish-ment may be intended as a moral message to denounce 'crime', with its severity reflecting collective indignation and revulsion (Durkheim, 1893/1984). The effect and intent of the expressive and symbolic role of incarceration are open to debate, but there are concerns that the penal obesity of the last four decades has so far failed to satisfy appetites for penal destruction. For some commentators, populist punitiveness drives contemporary penal excess, with its power being directly con-nected to the weakening of state bureaucracies and the rise in political influence of an unredeemable mob demanding longer and harsher sen-tences (J. Pratt, 2007). Evidence to support this assertion is a little thin on the ground; those studies that have investigated public opinions on punishment indicate that when people are well informed, they are considerably less punitive than public opinion polls suggest (Green, 2008). More sophisticated accounts have laid the problem of penal excess and the penalisation of sites of state detention at the door of increasing economic and social inequalities and weakening social solidarities (de Haan, 1990; Christie, 2000; Bosworth, 2010a) or explored the ways in which fears and anxieties concerning 'crime' have been deliberately orchestrated from above to shift attention away from the real problems in society (Hall et al., 1978; Beckett, 1997b; Simon, 2007; Sim, 2009; see also Bell, Chapter 3 of this volume). It is also questionable whether the demand for the infliction of pain and suffering is healthy, as the venom of punishment is poisonous for all it encounters. It is unlikely that suffering can expiate guilt or provide a good way of restoring relationships, and punishment is not a very effective means of moral communication (Mathiesen, 1990). Few would doubt that some kind of response is required for many of those behaviours currently defined as 'crimes', but there is no obvious reason why this should be imprisonment. Two wrongs can never make a right. We do not need to punish – alternative and rational means of redress and conflict resolution are feasible within the immanent possibilities of our times (de Haan, 1990; see also Scott, Chapter 15 of this volume). The more brutal we are to those who do wrong or exhibit unpleasant, unattractive and disturbing behaviours, the greater the acceptance of cruelty, the weaker the sensitivity to pain. Punitive societies are callous and morally indifferent to the suffering of others. Consequently the current global expansion of incarceration must be problematised and its targeting of the poor and BME populations exposed.

STRUCTURE OF THE BOOK

When 'common sense' assumptions and justifications of imprisonment are subjected to serious critical scrutiny, the prison appears to have no straightforward or obvious defence (Mathiesen, 1990; Golash, 2005; Scott, 2009). Despite the 'fiasco of its aims' (Mathiesen, 1990), abolitionist analysis of penal incarceration remains relatively marginalised in the academy, and is often politically de-legitimated. Indeed, rather than being in terminal decline, prison populations in countries all around the world have risen to unprecedented levels. This phenomenon demands serious academic attention, and in recent years the study of imprisonment has undergone a period of great creativity, which is reflected in the chapters brought together in this book. Though for Armstrong and McAra (2006: 22) contemporary critical analysis should aim to 'decentre the prison without dismissing it', arguably it seems more pertinent to ask why prison continues to perform such a central role in both the public imagination and social control of deviant populations. It is important therefore that the 'why prison?' question is posed in an intellectually honest and rigorous manner. As Keally McBride (in Chapter 11 of this volume) points out, questions concerning imprisonment today merely concern 'how can we justify incarceration?', 'what does prison do to those confined?' or 'who should be imprisoned?' rather than going back to the most fundamental question of all: 'why should prisons exist?' Although the 'why prison?' question can be approached in a number of different ways, for the purpose of this book, contributors have focused upon one or more of its following interconnected meanings:

1. Why does the prison continue to persist when there is so much evidence that it fails?
2. Why is the prison so deeply ingrained in popular culture and so widely considered as the most appropriate response to lawbreaking?
3. Why are we witnessing the penal colonisation of other sites of state detention and the rise of global prison populations at such an alarming rate?

The first three contributors – Alessandro De Giorgi, Emma Bell and Loïc Wacquant – scrutinise the prison's role in disciplining and controlling certain segments of the working class. In Chapter 2, Alessandro De Giorgi argues that in our late-capitalist 'wastelands of insecurity' we are witnessing the unleashing of the penal arm of capitalist states to govern the new global proletariat of working poor. Underscored by the principle of *less eligibility*, the prison is designed to deter 'the most marginal factors of the proletarian class from turning to "crimes of survival" as a form of resistance to waged labour'. Throughout the chapter he points to the need for an analytical framework that can recognise how and why the logic of penalisation stretches beyond the prison to encapsulate immigration controls, welfare regulation and broader 'processes of excommunication' of poor and migrant populations. After evidencing the hyper-criminalisation of immigrants in Europe, Alessandro De Giorgi lays down the foundations of a new 'cultural political economy of punishment' that can transcend the tradition's narrow focus on unemployment to conceptualise and problematise the economic and social structures of late-capitalist societies and their implications for the regulation of the global working poor. In a similar vein, Emma Bell examines the rise of 'egotistic individualism' (Reiner, 2007) and recent developments in penal policy in Britain in Chapter 3. Identifying the current Conservative-Liberal Democrat coalition government as a contemporary manifestation of 'authoritarian populism' (Hall, 1988), she revisits Thomas Mathiesen's (1990) 'unofficial aims of imprisonment' to explore their contemporary role in constructing symbolical boundaries and diverting attention away from increasingly stark social divisions. The penalisation of poverty is understood within the 'paradoxical' nature of public opinion and the rise of the 'security-industrial complex'. After discussing the so-called rehabilitation revolution and the interconnections between penal privatisation, penal labour and immigration controls, Emma Bell concludes her chapter by emphasising the continued symbolic potency of penal incarceration.

Reflecting upon his recent book *Punishing the Poor* (Wacquant, 2009b), Loïc Wacquant argues in Chapter 4 that hyper-incarceration must be understood as a political response to the social insecurities arising due to changes in labour markets and a backlash against greater racial equality. Inspired by the work of Pierre Bourdieu, and especially his notion of the 'bureaucratic field', the chapter identifies the restrictive turn from social welfare to workfare. Loïc Wacquant argues that the expansive cast of penal policies are two sides of a broader revamping of state policy towards 'problem categories and territories' which are united under the same 'behaviourist philosophy'. The prison consequently partakes in the re-engineering of the state and serves two key functions: the containment of an emergent regime of 'advanced marginality' and a signalling of the authority of rules at a time when state sovereignty is being eroded from above by capital mobility and from below by the diffusion of social insecurity. In so doing, he carefully weaves together the symbolic-materialist and instrumental-expressive divide that has characterised the sociology of punishment since the early interventions of Emile Durkheim and Marxist penologists such as George Rusche. As such, Loïc Wacquant not only explores why prisons are central to the overall workings of the contemporary capitalist state but also provides a clear warning that the containment of unwanted and impoverished populations by the 'penal state' represents a significant danger to the workings of democracy itself.

Magnus Hörnqvist, Michelle Brown and Vanessa Barker explore the cultural embeddedness of penal incarceration through analysis of participation in penal practices and penal policy formation. Chapter 5 provides an innovative analysis of why middle-class professionals work in penal bureaucracies. Posing this question within the context of both the 'invisibility' of the professional middle classes in the sociology of punishment and the apparent little obvious benefit gained by participating in the internal workings of the penal machine, Magnus Hörnqvist carefully considers 'how the professional middle class constitutes itself as a class in and through the desires, fears and fantasies played out within the institutional domain of the prison'. Drawing upon the insights of Pierre Bourdieu and Jacques Lacan, and utilising a number of examples from Swedish prisons, Magnus Hörnqvist reveals that not only are prisons places of 'pacification' facilitating social order and suppressing fear but that they also represent/create a unique environment facilitating engagement in both the pleasures and fantasies of violence and mundane humanitarian interventions – all done, of course, for the higher interests of the state.

Michelle Brown shines the spotlight on the negative consequences of public distance from penal processes in Chapter 6. Whereas the punished live through the brutal reality of penal incarceration, the penal spectator is shielded from the pains of confinement by 'experiential distance'. Despite widespread prison talk, the reality of penal incarceration remains largely inaccessible to white middle-class bystanders. Consequently, the cultural imaginary of the prison via media representations in TV dramas, documentaries and iconic films, alongside more direct physical engagement in prison tourism, become crucial in shaping public knowledge. Yet a little knowledge can sometimes be a bad thing, as the penal spectator is not required to give more than a 'distant look or fleeting glance' at the tragic quality of penal incarceration – the deliberate infliction of pain and suffering. It is not just the failure to break down emotional distance that is of concern, but also the fact that the penal spectator assumes he/she is now fully informed. Of central importance then are strategies that can find 'a way out' by publically exposing prisons for what they really are.

In Chapter 7, Vanessa Barker starts by locating penal excess and welfare retrenchment within a breakdown of American democracy, specifically the decline of public participation within the public sphere. For Vanessa Barker, imprisonment is inherently political – engendering state authority, the power to punish and the moral legitimacy of the infliction of pain – alongside possessing a powerful symbolic function. She argues that de-democratisation can lead directly to penal excess because weakened social bonds result in greater political rigidity and entrenched political positions. In contrast, however, more democracy can reduce penal excess because civic engagement is a form of collective agency and can be expressed through 'deliberative forms' of participation. Greater public participation, she maintains, results in enhanced engagement with pressing social issues and consequently more empathy, solidarity, trust and calls for welfare interventions to social problems.

The next three chapters by Mark Brown, Emma Kauffman, Mary Bosworth, Vickie Cooper and Joe Sim examine in-depth the relationship between imprisonment and other sites of state detention. In Chapter 8, Mark Brown argues that a singular focus on imprisonment has been detrimental to the broader understanding of confinement, and what is urgently required is a new way of thinking that can escape, once and for all, the 'iron cage of prison studies'. To free ourselves from such an intellectual straightjacket, we should investigate the prison as merely one form of 'involuntary detention'. Mark Brown outlines a theoretical rationale for such an analytical break and then asks the crucial question 'Why does it seem so much more suitable that a detention centre should look and feel like a prison, rather than, for example, a hospital or aged-care village?'. His arguments are illustrated by a consideration of a number of different contemporary sites of state detention: non-penal preventive detention derived from civil laws; 'slave like' immigration detention; and the control of terror suspects, migrants and refugees through the creation of 'international zones'. He then proceeds to construct a new way of conceptualising 'prison-like forms' through a re-articulation of existing criminological thought.

Chapter 9, by Emma Kaufman and Mary Bosworth, examines the hypothesis that prison and immigration detention perform a central role in the (re)production of the nation state. Identifying a major escalation in the control of 'non-citizens' in Britain since the mid 1990s, they explore the emergence of a symbiotic relationship between these two forms of state detention. Whilst still recognising that prison and immigration detention are distinct entities, they point to their similar mission to classify and contain those 'non-citizens' who should be excluded in the interests of national sovereignty. Acknowledging the historical connections between the two forms of confinement, Emma Kaufman and Mary Bosworth utilise ethnographic research to evidence how detainees experience immigration removal centres as equivalent to or even worse than prison. Vickie Cooper and Joe Sim explore the convergence of penal and welfare institutions in the governance of the homeless in Liverpool in Chapter 10. 'Locked out, locked up and quarantined', the homeless in Liverpool are regulated by 'processes of punishment' where disciplinary penal and welfare logics are deployed to reconstruct, rebuild and re-programme 'deviant subjectivities'. Exploring findings from an ethnographic study of homeless women in Liverpool, Vickie Cooper and Joe Sim highlight how the boundaries between penal and semi-penal institutions have become increasingly blurred. Emphasising how violence underpins state practices, they explore why attempts to normalise the homeless and other petty offenders have merely proved to be 'debilitating and disempowering'. Vickie Cooper and Joe Sim conclude by calling for the need for more 'utopian, socialist and abolitionist' strategies that can transcend the punitive ideologies and practices of the capitalist state.

The following two chapters by Keally McBride and Marie Gottschalk both reflect upon whether progressive penal reform can result from current pressures to reduce penal expenditure in the USA. Keally McBride argues in Chapter 11 that, since the 1970s, the assumption has been that people cannot be changed through imprisonment; therefore they should remain in prison for as long as possible. After exploring the deeply entrenched political desire to incapacitate those who fail to live their lives as 'economically driven creatures', she argues that because of the 'great recession', crime talk is increasingly becoming about 'balancing budgets' and being 'tough on crime and tough on criminal justice spending'. Indeed such are the consequences of the fiscal crisis, such as in the state of California, that today the logic of economic rationality may have become useful for those calling for radical reductions in prisoner populations. In Chapter 12, Marie Gottschalk highlights how the political agendas of four social movements in the USA have been exploited or manipulated by government organisations and law enforcement groups to ratchet up penalisation. The retributive victims' rights movement has been grounded in a 'zero-sum game predicated on tougher penalties for offenders'; the women's movement has made problematic alliances with the punitive lobby, fostering a reductive analysis of gendered violence as individual pathology; the prisoners' rights movement created a 'racially charged political atmosphere' leading to a backlash from conservatives and a lockdown on political activism behind bars; and the campaign to abolish capital punishment has brought 'popular sentiments and passions' to the forefront of the formation of penal policy and undermined more rational and objective debate. Throughout, Marie Gottschalk emphasises the complex interrelationship between social, economic and political dimensions and argues that 'ghosts of the past' cannot be exercised alone by the economic impact of the great recession – what we require in our troubled economic times is the mobilisation of progressive social movements that can generate and exploit political momentum in the direction of (radical) penal reduction.

Penal abolitionism as a social movement and analytical framework is explored in the final three chapters by Erica Meiners, Julia Oparah and David Scott. In Chapter 13, Erica Meiners critically examines the relationship between the school and the prison in the USA, emphasising the role public education performs in the surveillance, discipline and control of children of color and non-heterosexual youth. She emphasises how the 'logic of punishment' increasingly shapes the policy, ideology and practice of public schools which have begun to 'look and act a lot like detention centres'. For Erica Meiners, to escape from the 'prison-industrial complex' and its collateral consequences we need to abandon existing categorisations of childhood and develop a new way of thinking that can allow for the recognition of a (young) person's shared humanity. She argues that penal reform may simply extend the carceral mesh, and so what is required is the adoption of an abolitionist vision which can decolonise the punitive rationale lying at the heart of contemporary schooling practices in the USA. In Chapter 14, Julia Oparah asks the essential question: 'why no prisons?' Her chapter is organised around five key themes: (i) prison is a descendant of slavery; (ii) prison increases fear rather than provides safety; (iii) prison spending channels funds away from education, health and social welfare; (iv) prisons damage democracy; and (v) prisons reproduce violence and provide no protection from violence perpetrated in the community. She argues that, in sum, these five strategies reinforce the claim that the only rational response to the prison-industrial complex is abolition and concludes by identifying a number of progressive social policies that could be promoted immediately to challenge penal incarceration and provide genuine safety for all.

Bringing the book to a close, David Scott argues that prisons are 'unequalled in pain' in Chapter 15. This final chapter begins by highlighting the *raison d'être* of penal incarceration: the deliberate infliction of pain and the allocation of blame. The discussion then places global hyper-incarceration within the contexts of mounting economic inequalities and the social inequalities of class, 'race', gender and sexuality. Focusing on England and Wales as an illustrative example, the chapter identifies a number of factors driving the intensification of penal logic in advanced capitalist, patriarchal, neocolonial and heteronormative societies. The chapter then attempts to answer the question 'what can we do right now to reverse global hyper-incarceration?' from an 'abolitionist real utopia' perspective. In so doing, David Scott highlights a number of historically immanent alternatives to penalisation, emphasises the strategic importance of the 'attrition model' in reducing prison populations' and calls for more collective resistance against global hyper-incarceration though abolitionist-inspired social movements.

PART I

PENAL DISCIPLINE

2

PRISONS AND SOCIAL STRUCTURES IN LATE-CAPITALIST SOCIETIES*

Alessandro De Giorgi

POLITICAL ECONOMY OF PUNISHMENT

The main hypothesis of the neo-Marxist criminological current known as 'political economy of punishment' is that the historical emergence, persistence or decline of specific penal practices are connected to dominant relations of production in a given society. Although Marx himself never dealt systematically with the penal question, the epistemological background of the political economy of punishment can be traced back to the materialist approach outlined in his preface to A *Contribution to the Critique of Political Economy* (1859/1961).

> In the social production men perform, they enter into definite relations that are indispensable and independent of their will; these relations of production correspond to a definite stage of development of their material powers of production. The totality of these relations of production constitutes the economic structure of society – the real foundation on which legal and political superstructures arise and to which definite forms of consciousness correspond. The mode of production of material life determines the general character of the social, political and spiritual processes of life. (Marx, 1859/1961: 67)

The penal system is part of those superstructural state apparatuses (Althusser, 1971: 85–126) in charge of reproducing hegemonic class relations and perpetuating given geographies of power. Therefore, the

---

* This chapter provides a synthesis of my recent work in the field of the political economy of punishment. For more in-depth analyses of the issues covered in each of the following sections, see De Giorgi (2010; 2012).

historical and contemporary transformations of the penal field can only be understood by linking the dominant ideologies of law and order to the power structures that shape the field of capitalist production. Reinforcing existing taxonomies of social worthiness through the legal principle of retribution and its exclusive emphasis on individual responsibility and free choice, the penal field provides an ideological legitimation to the existing social order while obscuring the marks of class power borne by criminal law in a capitalist society. As Soviet legal scholar Evgeny Pashukanis (1924/ 1978: 174) argued in his *General Theory of Law and Marxism*, '[e]very historically given system of penal policy bears the imprint of the class interests of that class which instigated it'. Georg Rusche and Otto Kirchheimer would draw on this materialistic framework to develop a social history of Western penal systems, and in their classic text *Punishment and Social Structure* they laid the foundations of the political economy of punishment.

> Every system of production tends to discover punishments which corre-spond to its productive relationships. It is thus necessary to investigate the origin and fate of penal systems, the use or avoidance of specific punishments, and the intensity of penal practices as they are determined by social forces, above all by economic and then fiscal forces.
> (Rusche and Kirchheimer, 1939/2003: 5)

The task of a structural critique of punishment is to deconstruct the role played by the penal field in the reproduction of specific capitalist forma-tions: in this sense, the 'origin and fate' of penal systems has less to do with reformist ideas and humanitarian values than with the function of penal strategies in the perpetuation of existing structures of class power within a given system of production. In capitalist societies, such structures of class power are ultimately shaped by the labour market, which plays a crucial role in establishing the economic value of human labour and therefore the average living conditions of the proletarian classes. In turn, these classes represent the main targets of penal control in a class society, as their members are the ones who must be continually forced to fill the ranks of waged labour and accept existing conditions of exploitation. The central mission of the penal system is therefore to deter the most marginal fractions of the proletarian class from turning to 'crimes of survival' as a form of resistance to waged labour.

In a seminal article entitled 'Prison revolts or social policy: lessons from America', Georg Rusche (1930/1980) summarised this entire process with reference to the principle of *less eligibility*: in order to function as a deterrent for the poor, the penal system must impose on those it punishes standards of living that are in any case worse than those available to the most marginal among law-abiding proletarians.[1] As Rusche explained:

> One thing is certain: no society designs its penal system with a view to inciting crime... Therefore, if it is not to contradict its goals, the penal system must be such that the most criminally predisposed groups will prefer a minimal existence in freedom, even under the most miserable conditions, to a life under the pressure of the penal system... The above considerations can, in a general way, be formulated to mean that all efforts to reform treatment of criminals are limited by the conditions of the lowest socially significant proletarian stratum which the society is attempting to deter from crime. All reforms which go beyond this, no matter how humanitarian in their design, are inevitably condemned to Utopia.
>
> (Rusche, 1930/1980: 42)

Therefore, in a capitalist society the direction and intensity of criminal sanctions will be ultimately determined by the average living conditions of the most marginal fractions of the proletarian class – those most likely to engage in crimes of survival as a form of self-subtraction from waged labour. This means that whenever the supply of labour exceeds the needs of capitalist production, creating a surplus that operates as an industrial reserve army within the lower rungs of the class structure (Marx, 1867/1976: 781–94), penal practices will tend to become harsher, and draconian punishments will likely re-emerge from the shadows of penal history:

> Unemployed masses, who tend to commit crimes of desperation because of hunger and deprivation, will only be stopped from doing so through cruel penalties. The most effective penal policy seems to be severe corporal punishment, if not ruthless extermination... In a society in which workers are scarce, penal sanctions have a completely different function. They do not have to stop hungry people from satisfying elementary needs. If everybody who wants to work can find work, if the lowest social class consists of unskilled workers and not of wretched unemployed workers, then punishment is required to make the unwilling work, and to teach other criminals that they have to content themselves with the income of a honest worker.
>
> (Rusche, 1933/1978: 4)

---

[1] The principle of less eligibility was originally formulated in the early-nineteenth century in England, where it inspired the Poor Laws of 1834; since then, this principle has become a logical pillar of any welfare system, by establishing that no welfare provision can be so generous as to render public assistance preferable to waged labour (for a good historical reconstruction, see Sieh, 1989).

The materialist paradigm outlined by Rusche and Kirchheimer has inspired both historical and contemporary analyses of the penal system. On the one hand, the 'revisionist' histories of punishment that appeared between the 1970s and 1980s addressed the question 'why prison?' by connecting the birth of the penitentiary institution with the rise of the factory as the main site of production during the nineteenth century (Foucault, 1977; Ignatieff, 1978; Melossi and Pavarini, 1981). On the other hand, criminologists like Ivan Jankovic (1977), Dario Melossi (1993), David Greenberg (1977, 1980), Steven Box and Chris Hale (1985) and others developed neo-Marxist analyses of penal change in contemporary late-capitalist societies – in particular, of the unfolding of a punitive shift characterised by rising imprisonment rates in many Western societies during the last quarter of the twentieth century.

Most recent politico-economic critiques of punishment have tested Rusche and Kirchheimer's hypothesis by analysing the connections between rates of unemployment, adopted as indicators of the 'situation of the lowest socially significant proletarian class', and rates of penal incarceration, used as indicators of penal severity. In general, this literature has found that such relationship is observable and that trends in imprisonment seem to be correlated to unemployment levels in significant ways (see De Giorgi, 2006, ch. 1). However, I would argue that such a mechanical translation of the materialist framework raises some important questions, particularly from the point of view of the structural analysis of late-capitalist societies. The narrow quantitative focus on unemployment as the main indicator of current labour conditions reveals that the traditional political economy of punishment is rooted in a specific structure of capitalist production: the Fordist/Keynesian regime of accumulation.[2] This model of capitalist development was based on mass industrial production, highly regulated labour markets and a potentially expansive system of social welfare based on a clear distinction between employment and 'unemployment'. During the last three decades, however, this industrial-welfarist paradigm has been deeply transformed by the

[2] The concept of 'capitalist regime of accumulation' has been introduced by political economists belonging to the so-called 'regulation school' (see Aglietta, 1979; Jessop, 1990a). According to this perspective, each regime of accumulation includes four main elements: (i) a distinctive type of *labour process*, which identifies the dominant form of production and the corresponding technical composition of the workforce; (ii) a specific strategy of *macroeconomic growth*, which identifies the leading sectors of an economic formation; (iii) a particular system of *economic regulation*, which describes the prevailing regulatory framework; and (iv) a coherent mode of *societalisation*, which identifies the hegemonic forms of cultural, institutional and social organisation (see Jessop, 2002: 56–8).

emergence of what has been defined as a post-Fordist regime of accumulation and a neoliberal model of economic governance. This new regime of accumulation is defined by fundamental changes in the form of capitalist production of value and in the regulation of labour, such as the shift from industrial production to a service economy, the growing flexibility of work, the fragmentation of labour markets, the globalisation of capitalist networks of production, the growing transnational mobility of labour and the increased centrality of immigrant workers (see Amin, 1995; Hardt and Negri, 2000; Koch, 2006; Marazzi, 2011). What I would like to suggest here is that this reconfiguration of capitalist production has shaken the foundations on which the traditional political economy of punishment had built its analyses.

In the emerging post-Fordist scenario, purely quantitative economic indicators like official unemployment rates seem no longer able to provide a solid ground for a materialist critique of punishment in late-capitalist societies. In the USA, as well as in Europe, whole economic sectors – from domestic work to constructions, agriculture and low-skill service jobs – rely on a disposable army of insecure and vulnerable workers whose hyper-exploitation takes place precisely at the intersection of employment and unemployment, low-wage work and bare survival, precarious inclusion and social marginality. As economist Paul Streeten wrote in 1981:

> Employment and unemployment make sense only in an industrialized society where there are employment exchanges, organized and informed labour markets, and social security benefits for the unemployed who are trained workers, willing and able to work, but temporarily without a job... 'Employment' as interpreted in industrial countries is not the appropriate concept... To afford to be unemployed, a worker has to be fairly well off. To survive, an unemployed person must have an income from another source... Indeed, the very poor are not unemployed but work very hard and long hours in unremunerative, unproductive forms of activity. This discovery drew attention to the informal sector... The problem then was redefined as that of the working poor.
>
> (Streeten, 1981: 12–13)

The dismantling of the welfare state incited by the neoliberal ideology of deregulation and 'less government' has turned this economic borderland into a broadening wasteland of social insecurity populated by the new global proletariat that inhabits the urban peripheries of Europe and the inner cities of America: dispossessed urban minorities; marginalised youth; vulnerable immigrant labourers; the working poor. These are

the contemporary members of Rusche's 'lowest socially significant proletarian class' (Rusche, 1933/1978: 4). These are the ones who must
again be persuaded that accepting waged labour – even without contract
and social protections, for poverty wages and often under threat of
detention and deportation – is still preferable to being ensnared in the
expanding net of punitive regulation.

In these pages I would like to suggest that a contemporary materialist
critique of punishment should be able to investigate these structural
transformations from a broader perspective than the one afforded by a
reductionist analysis of unemployment and imprisonment. A neo-
Marxist critique of punishment in late-capitalist societies should be
based on a complex politico-economic analysis of the structural transformations faced by Western societies in the last thirty years. In addition,
such new political economy of punishment should attempt to overcome
the deterministic tendencies of orthodox Marxist criminology by inte-
grating the economic, institutional and cultural dimensions of the
transition of Western capitalist societies toward a post-Fordist regime
of accumulation. Finally, it should extend its critique beyond the narrow
focus on imprisonment to include the broad range of extra-penal punitive practices deployed by the emerging neoliberal state in order to
discipline the post-Fordist proletariat, particularly in fields like immigration control and welfare regulation. In the next two sections I focus
specifically on the consolidation of confinement as a strategy for the
control of the 'social surplus' generated by the converging forces of
capitalist globalisation, the crisis of the Fordist-Keynesian regime of
accumulation and the neoliberal assault on the welfare state.

The most dramatic instance of these punitive trends is clearly provided
by the US penal experiment of the last forty years; however, a significant
increase in penal incarceration and related practices of confinement, such
as the administrative detention of 'illegal immigrants', can also be
observed in several European countries whose variously confined populations are growing at a fast pace. Finally, in the last section I suggest some
possible new directions for materialist criminology, and I outline the
hypothesis of a 'cultural political economy of punishment'.

NEOLIBERAL PENAL DISCIPLINE IN THE USA

Recent literature in the sociology of punishment has focused on the
punitive turn that has affected several Western societies, particularly the
USA, during the last quarter of the twentieth century, resulting in

harsher penal policies, rising imprisonment rates and a widespread emphasis on incapacitation over rehabilitation (see Garland, 2001c; Tonry, 2004; Sudbury, 2005c; Simon, 2007). Loïc Wacquant has famously described the transition of late-capitalist societies from a Fordist/industrial model toward a post-Fordist/post-industrial model of capitalist accumulation as the shift from a 'social state' charged with mitigating the effects of economic inequality among marginalised populations to a 'penal state' in charge of enforcing the emerging neoliberal economic order through a punitive regulation of the poor:

> Thus the 'invisible hand' of the unskilled labour market, strengthened by the shift from welfare to workfare, finds its ideological extension and institutional complement in the 'iron fist' of the penal state... The regulation of the working classes through what Pierre Bourdieu calls the 'Left hand' of the state, that which protects and expands life chances, represented by labour law, education, health, social assistance, and public housing, is supplanted (in the United States) or supplemented (in the European Union) by regulation through its 'Right hand', that of the police, justice, and correctional administrations, increasingly active and intrusive in the subaltern zones of social and urban space.
>
> (Wacquant, 2009b: 6)

Emerging in the 1970s, and soaring in the following three decades, the 'Right hand' of the state has indeed become hegemonic in the USA and has increasingly gained strength in Europe: if in the USA the penal system has become a central tool for regulating the racialised poor, in Europe it appears to be specialising in the governing of 'third-world' immigrants (Melossi, 2003; Angel-Ajani, 2005; Palidda, 2011).

The graph reported below (see Figure 2.1) offers a disturbing picture of the rise of hyper-incarceration in the USA. Despite modest decreases in the last two years, the country's prison population has reached the historically unprecedented (and geographically unmatched) number of 2.3 million individuals confined within a penal network of almost 5,000 correctional institutions. With an imprisonment rate of 730 per 100,000, the 'productivity' of the American penal system is unequalled by any other country in the world.

Not all Americans, however, have shared the burden of hyper-incarceration. Overall, 66 per cent of the convicted population belongs to the vast group of 'non-white population'. In particular, African American men are dramatically over-represented in the prison population, with rates of conviction eight times higher than their white

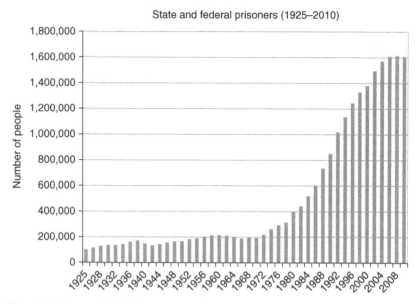

Figure 2.1 State and federal prisoners in the US (1925–2010)

counterparts. Among the black population, one of every three males aged 20 to 29 is today under some form of correctional supervision; an astonishing 3.1 per cent of black males in the nation is in state or federal prison (compared to 0.5 per cent for white males and 1.3 per cent for Latinos), while 7.3 per cent of black men aged 30 to 34 are currently incarcerated with a sentence of more than one year (Bureau of Justice Statistics, 2011). At current rates, a black male born in 2001 would have 32 per cent chance of ending up in prison during his lifetime – a probability that goes down to 17 per cent for Hispanic males of the same age group and to 6 per cent for white males (Mauer, 2006: 137). As Bruce Western has argued in his recent work on punishment and inequality in the USA, penal incarceration has been so intensely concentrated among poor/urban black males that it has become a 'modal life event' for marginalised African American men:

> The criminal justice system has become so pervasive that we should count prisons and jails among the key institutions that shape the life course of recent birth cohorts of African American men. By the end of the 1990s, black men with little schooling were more likely to be in prison or jail than to be in a labour union or enrolled in a government welfare or training program. Black men born in the late 1960s were more likely, by 1999, to

have served time in state or federal prison than to have obtained a four-year degree or served in the military. For non-college black men, a prison record had become twice as common as military service.

(Western, 2006: 31)

It is also worth remembering here that the prison system represents only one side of the US penal machinery. In fact, outside the walls of the prison, a true and proper 'nation within the nation' has formed as a consequence of the vertical increase in the semi-custodial or non-custodial punishments collateral to penal incarceration. Thus the total population living under some form of correctional supervision has reached the astonishing number of 7.1 million: a population comparable to that of Austria or Switzerland. This means that in the 'land of the free', 3 per cent of adults in the resident population live under conditions of institutionally diminished freedom (Glaze, 2011). The construction of what Nils Christie (1993) described as an emerging 'Western-style gulag' is the result of the post-civil-rights backlash invoked by Barry Goldwater in the 1964 presidential campaign, launched by Richard Nixon in the early 1970s and then carried on through the last quarter of the twentieth century by the following administrations under a bipartisan commitment to free market on the economic side and to punitive segregation on the penal side (see Wacquant, Chapter 4).

The foundations for the punitive overturn of the welfarist model of social regulation that had been consolidated in capitalist democracies in the aftermath of World War II were laid down during the early 1970s. Emerging as a new governmental rationality in an age of deep economic transformations, the US punitive turn has unfolded in the shape of an expanding penal net in charge of neutralising the racialised 'underclass' generated by the crumbling of the industrial economy and the neoliberal assault on welfare. This shift toward an exclusionary model of regulation of the poor put an abrupt end to the reformist era defined by David Garland (1995) as 'penal modernism', during which the USA exhibited prison populations comparable to (and in some states even smaller than) those of most other Western democracies. Thirty years later, US imprisonment rates are between five and eleven times higher than those of European nations.

These 'regressive' tendencies in penal policy should come as no surprise, if one keeps in mind that the principle of less eligibility sets the ultimate limit to any reform of penal practices. Indeed, Rusche himself warned in his 1933 article against any progressive view of the penal system as steadily evolving toward civilisation and humanity:

> Often, legal historians are guided not by an unprejudiced analysis of social laws, but by an evolutionary conception of the development of legal institutions: from barbaric cruelty to the humanitarianism of the relatively perfect legal system which we supposedly enjoy today. They overlook that we are dealing with a very long, now halting, now regressive movement.
>
> (Rusche, 1933/1978: 12)

Indeed, the rise of a penal populism demonising criminals as dangerous and irredeemable outsiders lent new legitimacy to a whole array of symbolic and draconian penal practices: life imprisonment for juveniles routinely tried as adults in cases of serious crime; 'Three Strikes and You're Out' laws mandating life in prison for recidivists; sex offender registration laws banning individuals convicted of any sex crimes from entire cities. This punitive shift has also prompted the resurgence of extreme, semi-corporal penalties like chain gangs, solitary confinement, 'supermax' prisons, chemical castration and other 'de-civilised' punishments, which the progressive ethos of the 1960s seemed to have consigned to the arsenal of history (J. Pratt, 1998).

At the same time, in different regions of the US penal field, a vast range of invisible punishments (Mauer and Chesney-Lynd, 2002) has proliferated at the intersection of penal and social policy, creating a 'carceral-assistantial' continuum (Wacquant, 2009b; see also Wacquant, Chapter 4 of this volume), the foundations of which were laid by President Clinton's welfare reform. Among a vast array of stigmatising measures aimed at forcing the loathed underclass into low-wage employment, the 1996 Personal Responsibility and Work Opportunity Reconciliation Act prescribed a lifetime ban on food stamps, educational grants and unemployment benefits for broad categories of drug offenders – whose numbers in prisons have risen from 50,000 in 1980 to more than 500,000 in 2010. Another example of the increasing use of welfare policies for crime-control purposes is provided by the draconian 'One Strike and You're Out' provisions implemented in many urban areas during the 1990s by the US Department of Housing and Urban Development, which allow public housing authorities to evict entire families and ban them for three years from federally subsidised housing for a single drug offence – even if just one member of the household is involved, the tenant is unaware of the illicit activity or the incident happened off-site (Stinson, 2004).

The process of social excommunication of the 'truly disadvantaged' (Wilson, 1987) prompted by the US punitive turn has not been limited to civil and social rights but has extended to political rights as well. Fourteen states currently impose a temporary voting ban on individuals convicted of a felony (even after the sentence has been fully served), while eight states impose a lifetime ban. Forty years after the civil rights revolution (and less than sixty years after the beginning of desegregation), 13 per cent of African American males are disenfranchised as a consequence of voting bans (Mauer, 2002: 50–8). During the 2000 presidential elections, almost 4.7 million US citizens could not vote as a consequence of previous criminal convictions (Manza and Uggen, 2006).

What is most important from the point of view of the political economy of punishment is that the punitive hysteria outlined so far does not reflect actual changes in criminal activity. Trends in crime and punishment have grown increasingly disconnected during the last three decades: even as crime rates declined steadily, the number of people arrested, convicted and incarcerated has continued to grow. The rhetoric of penal severity took root even in the absence of any connection to the crime problem, and public discourses on social problems traditionally framed in the language of social policy and welfare were now translated in the language of crime and punishment. Although in different forms and with varying degrees of intensity, both in the USA and in Europe, this paradigmatic shift emerged not in response to changes in criminal activity but rather as the new hegemonic approach to the government of the global poor in a post-industrial society.

ILLEGALISATION AND CRIMINALISATION IN EUROPE

At first sight it would be difficult to argue that contemporary European penal systems are experiencing anything comparable to the penal experiment that has taken place in the USA since the mid 1970s: today the USA has the largest prison population in the world and an imprisonment rate that is seven times higher than the European average (see Table 2.1). In this respect, statistical data would seem to support the arguments of scholars working from the perspective of comparative penality, who insist that the punitive turn in the USA is exceptional and that this exceptionality reflects the country's peculiar structures of race and class inequality, its legal traditions and its political system (Whitman, 2003; Tonry, 2004; Lacey, 2008).

TABLE 2.1 Imprisonment rates in selected
European countries and in the USA

Country	Imprisonment rate
Austria	102.6
Belgium	105
Denmark	71.3
Finland	62
France	103.5
Germany	87.6
Greece	105.6
Ireland	97.4
Italy	113.3
Luxembourg	137.4
Netherlands	70.8
Portugal	109.2
Spain	164.8
Sweden	74.1
United Kingdom	153.9
Average EU (15):	**103.9**
USA:	**730**

(Sources: Council of Europe, 2012; Glaze, 2011)

However, we may ask whether the *selectivity* of penal practices, and not only their scale, should be considered as an indicator of penal severity for the purpose of a structural critique of punishment. In other words, it could be the case that although the overall *extension* of the penal arm of the state remains comparatively limited in Europe, pointing to a general climate of penal moderation, the same penal arm is unleashed with unusual intensity when it comes to the criminalisation of some subpopulations, specifically the urban poor and third-world immigrants. In Europe, particularly since the early 1990s, xenophobic arguments against immigration have been framed around the myth of immigrants as a dangerous class (McDonald, 2009; De Giorgi, 2010; Palidda, 2011). Often articulated in a racialised language that postulates a link between ethnic origins and specific types of criminal activity, fear of immigrant crime has been amplified by political parties and ruling elites eager to capitalise on public insecurity in the construction of populist consent. In turn, these public discourses have become powerful catalysts for a punitive governance of immigration, as illustrated by the

TABLE 2.2   Hyper-criminalisation of foreigners in selected
European countries (2010)

Country	Imprisonment rate (nationals)	Imprisonment rate (foreigners)	Hyper-incarceration factor
Austria	61	438	7.1
Belgium	69	398.5	5.7
Denmark	59.3	247.2	4.1
Finland	55.6	254.8	4.5
France	90.2	312	3.4
Germany	70.3	265.4	3.7
Greece	49.4	713.3	14.4
Ireland	93.5	163.7	1.7
Italy	77.7	546.6	7.0
Luxembourg	74	217	2.9
Netherlands	58.2	374	6.4
Portugal	90.5	533.4	5.8
Spain	106	395	3.7
Sweden	61	244.3	4.0
UK	128.1	248.2	1.9
Average EU (15)	**76.2**	**356.7**	**4.6**

(Source: my elaboration on Council of Europe, 2012)

dramatic concentration of foreigners in the prisons of Europe (see Table 2.2).

The average immigrant incarceration rate of 356 per 100,000 across Europe means that immigrants are imprisoned on average 4.6 times more often than EU citizens, with some countries (e.g. Italy, Austria, the Netherlands, Greece) incarcerating them seven to fourteen times more than nationals – a rate of over-representation higher than that of the black population in the US prison system.[3] Here the image of European societies as strongholds of penal tolerance becomes increasingly blurred, leaving room for a reality of growing punitiveness and selective criminalisation. This conclusion is confirmed even by a cursory glance at recent imprisonment trends in Europe: in the last ten years, prison populations have been rising in several EU countries, with increases as

[3] It should also be noted that these data do not include the form of extra-penal incarceration to which only immigrants can be subjected: administrative detention. There are currently more than 200 immigration detention centres across Europe, in which more than 100,000 immigrants are detained each year.

high as 34 per cent in France, 23 per cent in Belgium, 20 per cent in the UK and 17 per cent in Italy, while the only major European country to have significantly reduced its prison population is Germany, with an 8.5 per cent reduction over the last ten years (Council of Europe, 2012) – all this, it should be noted, in a period of stable or declining crime rates across most European countries.

But why are immigrants hyper-incarcerated in Europe? Do they commit more, or more serious, crimes than nationals? Although historically the link between foreigners and crime has been a recurring element in cyclical moral panics about immigration and its control, the criminological literature on the argument has mostly disconfirmed this connection (see, e.g., National Commission on Law Observance and Enforcement, 1931; Sellin, 1938; Marshall, 1997; Tonry, 1997; Martinez and Valenzuela, 2006; Sampson, 2008).

Of course, any generalisation about the criminal involvement of migrants across Europe would be problematic, given that European countries are characterised by different economies, legal and illegal work opportunities and historical patterns of immigration; nor is it my intention here to propose a comparative analysis of immigrant crime (but see Lynch and Simon, 2003: 227–39). Instead, I will point to some structural conditions that seem to render immigrants particularly vulnerable to the selective criminalisation described here, in the field of both penal policy and immigration control (Angel-Ajani, 2005).

A first observation concerns the marginal position occupied by immigrants in the highly segmented illegal economies of the societies of destination: the immigrant labour force tends to concentrate in the lower tiers of criminal enterprises, where it specialises in low-skill services such as street-level drug dealing and prostitution. One could argue that the illegal economy mirrors what happens in the legal economy: immigrants take the jobs nationals are no longer willing to do (see Ruggiero, 2000). These activities tend to be not only less profitable but also particularly risky because of their high visibility, which results in more frequent arrests and in a growing hostility by local residents. As 'quality of life' approaches to urban safety take hold (equating the simple presence of immigrants on the streets to urban decay and criminal danger), the public's propensity to call the police for any minor sign of disorder increases, thus contributing to the exposure of undesirable immigrants to the exclusionary strategies of ethnic profiling and zero-tolerance policing (Angel-Ajani, 2003; Palidda, 2009).

Another significant factor in the hyper-criminalisation of migrants, particularly if undocumented, is provided by criminal activities collateral to illegal immigration: infractions committed almost exclusively by foreigners as a consequence of their insecure legal status. Besides the unauthorised entry or sojourn in the country, these 'crimes' include violations of criminal or immigration laws such as re-entering a country from which the migrant had been banned; forging visas, driving licenses and other documents; giving assistance or shelter to undocumented relatives or friends and so on. In a prohibitionist immigration regime such as the one currently in place throughout Europe, these criminalised behaviours constitute for many immigrants the only path toward some form of subordinate inclusion within the society of destination, usually at the intersection between legal and illegal economies and formal and informal labour markets. In other words, to the extent that immigrants are involved in criminal activities across Europe, this involvement appears to be substantially oriented toward those 'crimes of desperation' evoked by Georg Rusche in 1933: patterns of criminal behaviour prompted by the precarious legal status of migrants in the societies of destination and reinforced by their subordinate position in the post-industrial economy. In her recent work on the governing of labour migrations in Southern Europe, Kitty Calavita effectively summarises the circularity between the legislative 'production' of immigrant illegality and the economic exploitation of immigrant labour as follows:

> Immigrants are useful as 'Others' who are willing to work, or are compelled to work, under conditions and for wages that locals now largely shun. The advantage of immigrants for these economies resides precisely in their Otherness. At the same time, that Otherness is the pivot on which backlashes against immigrants turn. For, if marginalized immigrant workers are useful in part *because* they are marked by illegality, poverty, and exclusion, this very marking, this highlighting of their difference, contributes to their distinction as a suspect population.
>
> (Calavita, 2005: 11–12)

In this respect, restrictive immigration laws (with their arsenal of administrative and semi-penal sanctions) should be considered ancillary to traditional penal instruments in reproducing disadvantaged immigrants as a vulnerable and exploitable labour force. They concur to define a punitive regulation of migrations which, according to the less eligibility principle, is charged with deterring immigrants from finding alternatives to the precarious, unskilled and underpaid labour needed by the societies of destination.

TOWARD A POST-REDUCTIONIST POLITICAL ECONOMY OF PUNISHMENT

Based on the main premises of the political economy of punishment, so far I have tried to demonstrate how a paradigmatic shift in the capitalist regime of accumulation has prompted significant changes in punitive practices across late-capitalist societies. In societies such as the USA, which have traditionally leaned toward a *laissez-faire* model of capitalist development based on deregulated markets and minimal public interventions in the economy, the dismantling of the Fordist-Keynesian model has unfolded in a neoliberal variant characterised by extreme labour market flexibility, a vertical decline in labour unionisation, a drastic curtailment of welfare provisions and soaring levels of socioeconomic inequality (Sennett, 1998; Shipler, 2004; Katz and Stern, 2006). In European societies, stronger welfare states and a more established tradition of unionisation have somewhat shielded the national labour force from the crudest repercussions of the capitalist restructuring of the 1970s, which have instead concentrated on the much less protected immigrant workforce. In both cases, the crisis of the Fordist-Keynesian paradigm and the concurring process of capitalist restructuring have involved much more than the expulsion of industrial labour force from the system of production – the only aspect captured by the old political economy of punishment's narrow focus on unemployment and imprisonment.

The transition to a new regime of accumulation has taken the form of a broad capitalist offensive against the global (i.e. local and immigrant) labour force in a successful attempt to re-establish suitable conditions for capitalist valorisation in a globalised economy: stricter work discipline; higher levels of labour flexibility; more insecure working conditions; lower social protections; and an increased competition for low-wage work among the global poor. This process of capitalist restructuring has been successful in producing a dramatic shift in the balance of power from labour to capital.

It is in the context of this broader realignment of social power in late-capitalist societies that a materialistic analysis of contemporary penal change must situate its critique. And such critique must be able to take into account not only the measurable dynamics of the labour market, but also the political, institutional and cultural transformations that have contributed to redefine existing structures of socioeconomic inequality and to solidify a new regime of accumulation.

In order to illustrate some of the theoretical implications of this 'qualitative shift', I return once again to Rusche's original formulation of the concept of less eligibility as the logic governing the relation between punishment and social structure. As we have seen, Rusche argued that 'all efforts to reform the punishment of criminals are inevitably limited by the *situation of the lowest socially significant proletarian class* which society wants to deter from criminal acts' (Rusche, 1933/1978: 4, my emphasis). What I would suggest is that Rusche's concept of 'situation' lends itself to a much broader conceptualisation than the narrowly economistic reduction to unemployment rates privileged by the quantitative political economy of punishment. If the relative power of the workforce in a capitalist economy is ultimately determined by the price of its labour, the overall situation of that workforce – its position within existing hierarchies of social power – is not simply the outcome of labour market dynamics. Rather, it is shaped by a variety of non-economic factors that contribute to define the overall 'social value' of a capitalist labour force and of the social groups who fill its ranks. In this respect, the social value of labour results from the interaction between *economic* structures (modes of production, patterns of economic growth, labour market dynamics, wealth concentration or distribution), *governmental* strategies of social regulation (welfare/workfare systems, strategies of public intervention in the economy, penal politics and immigration control regimes), and *discursive/symbolic* processes of cultural reproduction (hegemonic scales of social worth, public discourses on deservingness and undeservingness, dominant representations of crime and punishment and social constructions of ethnic difference). In other words, the overall situation of marginalised social classes is determined by their place in the economic structure as much as by their position in the moral economy of capitalist social formations (see also Sayer, 2001).

Following this perspective, a post-reductionist political economy of the punitive turn in the USA and Europe should analyse the changing 'situation' of marginal classes in both contexts against the background of the economic and extra-economic processes that have contributed to reposition the post-Fordist proletariat within the social structure of late-capitalist societies. Over the last three decades, structural processes of capitalist transformation – deindustrialisation, downsizing, outsourcing, etc. – have significantly reduced the economic value of wage labour and consolidated a tendency toward rising work insecurity, declining wages, longer working hours and an overall increase in the socially acceptable levels of 'exploitability' of the labour force (Schor, 1992; Harris, 1997; Ehrenreich, 2001; Ehrenreich and Hochschild, 2002). At the same time, a broad reconfiguration of governmental strategies of social regulation – such as the transition from welfare to workfare, the adoption of restrictive immigration laws, the increasing commitment to privatisation and market deregulation and the emergence of neoliberal governance in fields like health care, housing, education, etc. – has eroded the Fordist-Keynesian compromise, deepening social fractures along lines of class, race, ethnicity and national origin. Finally, in the field of cultural signification the conservative hold on public debates about socioeconomic inequality, reinforced by periodic moral panics about street crime, immigration, drugs, welfare, etc. has consolidated hegemonic representations of the post-industrial poor – personified in particular by urban minorities in the USA and by third-world immigrants in Europe – as undeserving and potentially dangerous (Handler and Hasenfeld, 1991; L. Morris, 1994; Gans, 1995; Quadagno, 1995; Standing, 2011).

A non-reductionist materialist framework like the one sketched above would allow the political economy of punishment to overcome its traditional emphasis on the instrumental side of penality and to analyse the post-Keynesian state's increasing reliance on punitive regulation from the point of view of the broad reconfiguration of late-capitalist social structures in the last forty years. In this direction, a post-reductionist critique of the punitive turn should of course emphasise the structural dimension of recent penal practices, illustrating their instrumental role in 'imposing the discipline of desocialised wage work... by rising the cost of strategies of escape or resistance that drive young men from the lower class into the illegal sectors of the street economy' (Wacquant, 2009b: xvii). But it should also analyse the widespread governmental effects of penal technologies – particularly in conjunction with other tools of social regulation, such as immigration control and welfare policies – and elaborate a culturally sensitive materialist analysis of the symbolic dimensions of contemporary penal forms, emphasising how the hegemonic representations of deserving/undeserving and laborious/dangerous classes resonate with – and provide cultural legitimacy to – a regime of accumulation grounded in the material and discursive devaluation of the poor and their labour. From this perspective, penal politics would no longer be approached by the political

economy of punishment as an outgrowth of capitalist relations of production – a 'superstructure' of the capitalist economy, in the language of
orthodox Marxism – but rather as a set of material and symbolic practices that contribute in various forms to the reproduction of capitalist
social formations.

3

THE PRISON PARADOX IN NEOLIBERAL BRITAIN

Emma Bell

> I am sure that prison is the necessary punishment for many serious offenders. But does ever more prison for ever more offenders always produce better results for the public? Can we carry this argument on ad infinitum? I doubt it. . . Too often prison has proved a costly and ineffectual approach that fails to turn criminals into law-abiding citizens.
>
> (Clarke, 2010)

These words, spoken by the former UK Justice Secretary, shortly after assuming office under the Conservative-Liberal Democrat coalition government in 2010, were widely heralded as a u-turn on the previous Conservative government's hardline approach to criminal justice as epitomised by a former Home Secretary's much-quoted catchphrase, 'Prison Works' (Howard, 1993). Yet, although Kenneth Clarke appeared to manifest a desire to prevent the British prison population from spiralling out of control, he failed to fundamentally challenge the prison as an institution, criticising it mainly for its lack of cost-effectiveness and its failure to rehabilitate. In no way did he question the widely held notion that prison is an appropriate response to criminal behaviour, despite the fact that he was accused by the tabloid press as being 'a man who doesn't believe in prison' (Pandya, 2012). On the contrary, Kenneth Clarke considers prison to be a useful place in which offenders can be put to work so that they may more effectively integrate into society on their release – prisons are literally meant to 'work'.

Even Kenneth Clarke's modest proposals to bring about a small reduction in the prison population by, for example, reducing sentence lengths by 50 per cent for early guilty pleas (MoJ, 2010) was abandoned in the subsequent Legal Aid, Sentencing and Punishment of Offenders Act after the Prime Minister himself expressed concern that this would lead to over-lenient sentencing, thus sending out the wrong message to the criminal and eroding public confidence in the system. The prison population of England and Wales, already at record levels (85,000) in

2010 when the new government came to power, has continued to grow and now stands at over 87,000, the largest total prison population in the European Union (International Centre for Prison Studies, 2012). The prison population rate of England and Wales is 156 per 100,000 of the total population, similar to that of Scotland at 157 prisoners per 100,000, close to half that of Latvia but more than twice that of Switzerland (ibid.). It has risen by 90 per cent over the past twenty years and is expected to increase to almost 90,000 by 2017 (MoJ, 2012a). This is a conservative estimate, which fails to take into account the likely impact of the reforms included in the Legal Aid, Sentencing and Punishment of Offenders Act, notably the limitation of parole and other early release schemes and the return to 'two strikes' sentencing. In addition to these changes, it is likely that prison will continue to be used to sanction breaches of community sentences[1] and civil orders such as Antisocial Behaviour Orders (ASBOs).[2] Furthermore, prisons – euphemistically called 'immigration removal centres' or 'short-term housing facilities' – are to continue to be used to incarcerate newly arrived immigrants, immigrants awaiting removal, visa over-stayers, asylum seekers and other undocumented persons. It is estimated that between 2,000 and 3,000 immigrants are detained at any one time in the UK,[3] making the UK immigration detention estate one of the largest in Europe (Silverman and Hajela, 2012; see also Kaufman and Bosworth, Chapter 9 of this volume).

The aim of this chapter is to attempt to explain this 'prison paradox', namely why prison survives as an institution when it manifestly fails to fulfil its declared aims (see Scott, Chapter 1). To do so, it seeks to uncover the unofficial aims of imprisonment, placing these in their

[1] In 2009, it was estimated that the number of people imprisoned for breach of a non-custodial penalty had grown by 470 per cent since 1995 (MoJ, 2009: 7). Whilst the new Legal Aid, Sentencing and Punishment of Offenders Act allows the court to take no action or to impose a fine for breach of a community sentence, the court may re-sentence someone to custody even if the original offence was not serious enough to justify a custodial sentence. In addition, the Act allows offenders serving community sentences to be placed under curfew for 16 hours a day and permits their return to court if they break it.

[2] The ASBO, originally introduced in 1998 in order to sanction those responsible for behaviour thought to be 'likely to cause harassment, alarm or distress to one or more persons not of the same household as [themselves]', is to be rebranded and replaced by a Crime Prevention Injunction, which will be much easier to obtain than its predecessor since it is proposed that only the civil standard of proof will be necessary to impose such an order. Failure to respect the conditions of an ASBO or its new replacement may lead to a sentence of imprisonment.

[3] These statistics do not include undocumented persons who are detained in police cells or prison service establishments.

political, ideological and cultural context. It is argued that the context of neoliberalism has created the conditions that make the adoption of punitive responses to crime, notably over-use of imprisonment, more likely, even if such responses are not necessarily intrinsic to neoliberalism itself. Indeed, some key neoliberal thinkers such as Gary Becker (1968) believed that harsh punishment should not be disproportionate to the crime committed, yet prison is manifestly a wholly disproportionate response to many offences, especially when used to back up penalties such as ASBOs, which target non-criminal behaviour. To understand exactly how neoliberalism in practice, if not necessarily in theory, has impacted upon rising prison numbers, it is first necessary to provide a brief definition of neoliberalism in its contemporary British context. It is important to recognise that neoliberalism is a polysemantic and wide-ranging concept, which cannot simply be reduced to the economic dimension. Its significant impact on the legal, social, cultural and political fields brought about a profound reconfiguration of the role of government itself, leading the state to reassert its authoritarian regalian functions. Next, it is shown how the context of neoliberalism has led to a re-emphasis on what Thomas Mathiesen has described as the symbolic and diversionary functions of imprisonment (Mathiesen, 2000). Indeed, the prison may be regarded as a site of exclusion *par excellence*, serving to erect physical and symbolic boundaries between those who play by the rules of market society and those who do not. It is here that the diversionary function of imprisonment becomes evident, as popular attention is focused on the moral failings of those disadvantaged individuals who find themselves behind bars rather than on the government and the economic elites whose neoliberal policies have exacerbated the very social problems that are identified as criminogenic. In diverting public attention in this way, it is suggested that the government is engaging in 'authoritarian populism' (Hall, 1988) whereby it exploits an apparently widespread fear of crime to serve its own electoral ends. Yet, it is also serving the interests of the economic elites whose crimes remain shielded from public view and prosecution. This leads us on to a discussion of the symbiotic links which exist between government and the private sector. The final section explores the UK's *security-industrial complex*, looking at how the same economic elites, which have benefited most from the neoliberal project, are now significantly implicated in the delivery of punishment and rehabilitation for offenders and in the detention of immigrants.

NEOLIBERALISM IN CONTEMPORARY BRITAIN

'Neoliberalism' is a term that is much-used but rarely defined. It should not be reduced to its economic dimension alone. Whilst this is an essential component of neoliberalism (as exemplified by market and workplace deregulation; the breaking down of international barriers to the free movement of capital; the lowering of levels of corporate and income tax, particularly for the wealthy; and the privatisation of national assets under successive British governments from Margaret Thatcher through to David Cameron), the concept ought to be understood as a complex *system* which does not simply have an economic dimension but also social, political, legal and cultural dimensions (Dardot and Laval, 2009; G. Christoph, 2010).

In the legal field, neoliberalism has entailed the simultaneous deregulation of the financial and labour markets and the increased regulation of trade union activities. In addition, the law has been altered in such a way as to encourage the appropriation of natural resources, such as water (G. Christoph, 2010: 105–6), by private companies. In the social sphere, individualism became the *maître mot* as an anecdote to the 'dependency culture' that was so detested by Margaret Thatcher. Consequently, individuals who found it impossible to survive in the free market were left to flounder as the value of welfare benefits was drastically reduced and workers' means of defence were weakened through the restructuring of the labour market and the limitation of trade union rights. Individuals were to be understood primarily as rational economic actors who would be spurred on by the threat of poverty to succeed economically. Hence, a deliberate 'strategy of inequality' was pursued throughout the 1980s (Novak, 1984; Johnson, 1990; A. Walker, 1997; Jones and Novak, 1999; Hudson and Williams, 2000), marking a significant departure from the post-war Keynesian project which essentially sought to attenuate social divisions. Tony Blair's New Labour and Cameron's Conservatives adopted a slightly different rhetorical approach in an attempt to legitimise their respective political projects and offer an alternative to Thatcher's starkly individualistic approach as exemplified by her infamous assertion that 'there is no society' (Thatcher, 1987). Both leaders promoted the idea of a strong society (the 'big society' in Cameron's case – see below) in which individual citizens are to be held mutually responsible for one another, linked to each other and to government via a new social contract, which requires them to accept duties and responsibilities in return for certain rights. Yet, in practice, this has entailed significant continuity with the Thatcher years as individual over state responsibility for social problems has been promoted at all costs (Bell, 2011). This obsession has exacerbated inequalities and encouraged the development of what may be described as a neoliberal culture that promotes 'egotistic individualism' over 'reciprocal individualism' (Reiner, 2007: 18), creating a selfish, uncaring and 'exclusive society' (Young, 1999).

These changes in the social and cultural spheres have, in turn, created significant political changes, notably in terms of governance. Indeed, as politics have increasingly become primarily 'market-driven' (Leys, 2003) rather than motivated by social concerns, governments have been obliged to seek new platforms from which to appeal to their electorates. As will be explained below, authoritarian approaches to crime, which aim to provide physical security to the population at large, are but one manifestation of the neoliberal state's attempt to compensate for its failure to provide social and economic security. So, paradoxically, the frontiers of the capitalist state have not just been rolled back in the economic field but there has also been a simultaneous 'rolling forward' of the state as it seeks to attempt to manage the social fall-out of neoliberalism, of which crime may be regarded as just one manifestation. Despite the neoliberal rhetoric of freedom, the state has actually become increasingly powerful and authoritarian, especially under New Labour and now the Conservative-Liberal Democrat coalition, as it has extended its punitive reach into the social sphere, backing up attempts to tackle problem behaviour by penal solutions, namely imprisonment.

There is one final dimension of neoliberal governance, which ought to be highlighted before addressing the key question of why prison is such an attractive option in a neoliberal state such as Britain. There is the fact that although the authoritarian side of government has been reasserted, following the paradox of the free economy and the strong state (Gamble, 1988), it might also be argued that the power of the state has been weakened in favour of the large corporation, which has obtained an unprecedented degree of power and influence. Indeed, 'since it is impossible to envisage an economy that is not dominated by giant firms and in which they are unable to translate economic power into political influence, governments cannot be trusted not to be exceptionally responsive to these firms' interests' (Crouch, 2011: 171-2).

In the final section of this chapter, dedicated to the existence of a security-industrial complex in the UK, it is argued that penal policy is no exception to this assertion, even if the British government still continues to play a principal role in the delivery of pain.

THE SYMBOLIC FUNCTION OF IMPRISONMENT: THE PRISON AS A SITE OF EXCLUSION

The prison serves an important symbolic function, placing the offender outside the boundaries of 'normal' society, marking him out as 'other' and facilitating his control. The prison, as a site of exclusion, is particularly resonant in contemporary society, as increased freedom of movement has come to characterise the lives of the privileged classes in a globalised world. Those who are placed behind bars are already characterised by their essential otherness, despite the fact that the notion of a 'law-abiding majority' has been exposed as a myth, since criminal behaviour is actually widespread throughout society as a whole (Karstedt and Farrall, 2007). For Tony Blair, offenders were the 'selfish minority', to be distinguished from the 'law-abiding majority' (Blair, 2004b). They do not share the same values as the 'decent society' (Blair, 1996: 247) and they are 'without any residual moral sense' (Blair, 2004a). For the Conservatives, offenders are part of the 'broken society', characterised by a 'slow-motion moral collapse' (Cameron, 2011b).

Indeed, for the coalition government, as for successive New Labour administrations, crime is depicted as a moral problem rather than as a structural one. It is thought to be the sole reserve of an immoral 'underclass', which is characterised by a whole host of social problems such as family breakdown, unemployment, drug and alcohol abuse and educational failure. These problems are associated almost exclusively with the poorest and most disadvantaged members of society, despite the fact that many of them also affect the wealthy and the privileged, notably marriage breakdown and drug use. As a result, social problems and crime problems come to be regarded as forming two sides of the same coin, associated with an irresponsible 'underclass' to be understood in the sense intended by the right-wing American sociologist, Charles Murray (1990). For him, as for the current British government, a rejection of traditional family values, a lack of respect for the law and unemployment and welfare dependency are seen as hallmarks of an 'underclass' or – what David Cameron might describe as – the 'broken society'. David Cameron made this attitude quite clear in his response to the English riots of the summer of 2011. Whilst denying the structural causes of the riots, such as poverty and racial discrimination, he highlighted the negative values of those involved, describing them as 'people showing indifference to right and wrong... people with a twisted moral code... people with a complete absence of self-restraint' (Cameron, 2011b). Social problems were represented as crime problems. Thus, David Cameron declared, 'Our security fightback must be matched by a social fightback' characterised by a drive to responsibilise people for their own problems by encouraging them to change their behaviour (ibid.). Consequently, on top of the 'security fightback', reinforcing police powers to tackle problem behaviour pre-emptively and making full use of dispersal and curfew powers,[4] for example, the 'social fightback' was to focus on reinforcing parental responsibility and encouraging marriage, tightening up discipline in schools and rendering access to welfare benefits even more conditional on behaviour, thus forcing people into the labour market (ibid.).

When social and crime problems are conflated in such a manner, it is unsurprising that those who find themselves the targets of criminal interventions and consequently end up in prison are disproportionately drawn from the ranks of the poor and disadvantaged. Indeed, Britain's prisons, like most other prisons throughout the world, represent a microcosm of the 'underclass'/'broken society'. The most recent Ministry of Justice statistics show that 'over 25 per cent of prisoners had been taken into care as a child compared to 2 per cent of the population', that 'one-half of male and one-third of female sentenced prisoners were excluded from school', that 'one-half of male and seven out of ten female prisoners have no qualifications', that 'two-thirds of prisoners have numeracy skills at or below the level expected of an 11-year-old', that 'two-thirds of prisoners were unemployed in the four weeks before imprisonment', that 'around 70 per cent of prisoners suffer from two or more mental disorders', compared to '5 per cent for men and 2 per cent for women in the general population', and that '5 per cent of prisoners were sleeping rough and almost one-third were not living in permanent accommodation immediately prior to imprisonment' (MoJ, 2012a: 16). Thus, it seems indisputable that 'prisoners are more likely to be socially deprived

---

[4] Dispersal orders were created by the Antisocial Behaviour Act 2003. They give senior police officers the power to disperse groups of two people or more from a public place when he or she has reasonable grounds for believing that *their presence or behaviour* has resulted in, *or is likely to result in*, one or more people being intimidated, harassed, alarmed or distressed. The police also have the power to escort young people aged under 16 home if they are found unaccompanied in the street between 9pm and 6am and if an officer considers that they are at risk of either suffering from, or engaging in, antisocial behaviour.

and harmed individuals than seriously dangerous to society' (Scott, 2008: 102).

Placing these socially deprived individuals behind bars serves to high-light their essential otherness, allowing the rest of us to feel all the more 'normal' and 'law-abiding'. Thomas Mathiesen (2000) has described this as the 'symbolic function' of the prison whereby the institution serves to draw physical and metaphorical lines between offenders and the rest of society. It therefore becomes easier to distance oneself from the criminal or socially deprived other. As Nils Christie has explained, we tend to demonise those whom we know little about (Christie, 1977: 8). Reflecting on the increased use of imprisonment in Britain, David Garland has suggested that the state is adopting a 'criminology of the other' whereby offenders are identified as being 'wicked', separate from the mainstream, thus justifying their exclusion and punishment (Garland, 2001c: 184–5). This is to the detriment of policies – more prevalent during the post-war period – which sought to reintegrate offenders into mainstream society (ibid.).

The decision to site new prisons outside city centres serves to rein-force this sense of separation. Whilst prisons may once have been built in town centres as symbolic representations of state power (Ignatieff, 1978), their contemporary location outside town centres heightens the notion of the prison as a site of othering, situated outside the boundaries of mainstream society. This may not be an express intention, financial and logistical concerns most probably being paramount (especially when some new prisons are built to house large numbers of prisoners, such as HMP Oakwood with 1,605 places), but the symbolism is undeniable: the four walls of the prison are a site of exclusion *par excellence*. Indeed, for John Pratt, locating prisons outside city centres from the end of the nineteenth century onwards helped to remove the prison from everyday life (J. Pratt, 2000; 2002: 35–59). John Pratt (2002:52) regards the desire to locate prisons 'adrift from the civilized world' as part of the 'civilizing process' identified by Norbert Elias whereby the public were gradually excluded from the spectacle of punishment and the state became recog-nised as having a legitimate monopoly in this field. The consequence was the creation of greater social distance between offenders and the general public, allowing the former to be more easily demonised as 'other' (see Scott, Chapter 15).

Whilst the desire to exclude offenders has a long history (one need only bring to mind the British practice of 'transporting' prisoners to the colonies), it is likely to be particularly marked in contemporary societies

characterised by neoliberalism. First, it is in such societies where financial rewards are especially likely to be unevenly distributed – one need
only look at levels of income inequalities in wealthy neoliberal societies
such as the USA and the UK to confirm this relationship (Wilkinson
and Pickett, 2010: 239–41; see also Scott, Chapter 15 of this volume) –
that punitive sentiments seem to be greatest. Indeed, the 'chaos of
rewards' whereby financial rewards are distributed in what appears to
be an entirely arbitrary way, with those who work the hardest often
earning the least, can encourage feelings of resentment towards both
those at the top and the bottom of the social scale (Young, 1999). This
can help to explain punitive sentiments towards 'undeserving' welfare
recipients and offenders who are seen to benefit unjustifiably from the
proceeds of crime (ibid.). These sentiments are also likely to be exacerbated in the context of the 'risk society', characterised by uncertainty
and insecurity (Beck, 1992; Giddens, 1998), the formation of which is
likely to be greatly aided by the advance of neoliberalism, which has
transformed the labour market, rendering employment insecure and
uncertain.

In addition, as highlighted above, neoliberal culture favours 'egotistic
individualism' over 'reciprocal individualism', promoting selfishness
over concern for others (Reiner, 2007: 18). The context of neoliberalism is indeed of extreme relevance, to the extent that it alters not just
the culture of a given society but also, more importantly, the fundamental role of the state. As Robert Reiner points out, it alters culture by
elevating individual responsibility over mutual responsibility and placing citizens – as free-thinking, rational individuals – in competition with
one another for access to employment and key public services. The
values of the marketplace are essentially transposed into the social
sphere. The 'good citizen' is now thought to be the 'responsible citizen'
who works to provide for him/herself and his/her family and conforms to
dominant norms (Bell, 2011). Similarly, economic logic encroaches
onto the penal sphere: Bernard Harcourt (2011) argues that, for the
neoliberals, criminal sanctions essentially exist to punish those who seek
to bypass the marketplace, which is to be understood in the widest
possible sense, including not just commercial transactions but also sex
and pleasure. Thus, even rape may be considered as bypassing the regular
'market' for sex and marriage whereby 'agents voluntarily transfer benefits to one another for compensation' (ibid.: 136). Such logic removes
punishment from the moral sphere altogether, thus conferring on punishment practices a guise of neutrality and avoiding discussion of the

need to punish the immoral behaviour of the powerful (all behaviour which corresponds to market logic being regarded as legitimate). Both legal sanctions and offenders are regarded as inherently rational. Thus, offenders are regarded as fully responsible actors and the social context of offending is ignored. Whilst individual responsibility for social problems was never denied (indeed, William Beveridge, the architect of Britain's post-war welfare state made it clear that 'the State in organising security should not stifle incentive, opportunity, responsibility' (Beveridge, 1942: 6–7)), from the 1980s onwards there has been a renewed emphasis on the individual rather than structural causes of these problems. This has further justified the exclusion of those who fail to live up to the expectations of neoliberal society and has fuelled an 'us' versus 'them' mentality.

THE DIVERSIONARY FUNCTION OF IMPRISONMENT: THE PRISON AS A TOOL OF LEGITIMACY

This cultural shift towards a more exclusive society (Young, 1999) is linked to a significant shift in the role of the state itself, which has moved from that of provider of social security for the many to that of guarantor of economic security for a small elite[5] (see Wacquant, Chapter 4). As mentioned above, rather than politics being driven by social concerns, they have instead become primarily 'market-driven' (Leys, 2003). Yet, such a project was likely to cause a crisis of legitimacy for the state, particularly as its socially catastrophic consequences became evident. It was therefore necessary for the state to emphasise individual rather than state responsibility for social problems such as crime. Paradoxically, the state actually became more interventionist in the social sphere in an attempt to enforce individual responsibility (Bell, 2011). This was particularly important for New Labour, which sought to combine a concern with social problems, offering an alternative to Thatcherism,

---

[5] Security is not just economic, in terms of job stability and high wages, for example. The elites tend to also benefit from increased protection against all forms of risk and also tend to receive enhanced forms of justice. For Barbara Hudson, the privileged middle classes of wealthy countries in Europe and North America tend to benefit from extremely large measures of security, what she regards as 'too much security' relative to less-privileged groups. As these societies have become increasingly risk-averse, they have sought to develop a whole host of precautionary measures which may protect them, not just against catastrophic events but more usually against 'the more ordinary risks which are inconveniences rather than dangers' (Hudson, 2012: 10). Justice and security are only 'selectively available' for 'those who can afford them' and pay for good insurance cover against a myriad of risks and good lawyers when they run into conflict with the law (ibid.: 14–15).

whilst continuing to embrace neoliberal economics. For David Cameron's Conservatives, tackling head on the problems of the 'broken society' has been a way to move away from their image as the 'nasty party' (May, 2002) which did not believe in society (Thatcher, 1987) and to present themselves as the 'caring' architects of the 'Big Society'. Whilst the rhetoric has changed slightly from the Thatcher years, the aim is the same: to legitimise a programme of contraction of the public sector by presenting it as being in the interests of the masses. Just as Thatcher described her project of mass privatisation as 'popular capitalism', destined to bring property ownership to the masses via the sale of council houses and the acquisition of shares in the newly privatised companies, David Cameron has sought to present the programme of massive public spending cuts and privatisation as a means of returning control and ownership to the people by enabling them to get involved in the running of local services in partnership with big business and the voluntary sector (see Cooper and Sim, Chapter 10). In terms of electoral politics, it was also imperative that neither party be seen as being 'soft on crime'. This was an image that had undeservedly haunted the Labour Party right up until the 1990s, and with which David Cameron briefly risked being associated following his so-called 'Hug a Hoodie speech' in which he spoke of the need to understand the causes of crime and antisocial behaviour and to show some understanding, 'compassion and kindness' to troubled young people (Cameron, 2006). Consequently, social interventions were often highly authoritarian in nature and sometimes even backed up by penal interventions, including prison. For example, while action intended to tackle antisocial behaviour was presented as a 'Trojan horse', allowing the government to deal with social problems 'such as child poverty, repeat homelessness, repeat offending and underattainment in schools' (Casey, 2006), these measures have instead led to the increased criminalisation of children and their parents.

Prison is perhaps the ultimate symbol of toughness, used to back up all alternative sanctions for criminal and merely antisocial behaviour. It is the ultimate institution capable of showing the strength of the capitalist state and thus enabling it to refute any accusations of 'softness' (see Scott, Chapter 15). It is also regarded as the most effective way of reinforcing individual responsibility, forcing individuals to accept severe consequences for their actions, even if in reality prisoners are deprived of the right to take responsibility over their own lives, with each minute detail of their lives being regulated by the prison regime. Perhaps more importantly, the prison has significant symbolic importance as the most effective institution for guaranteeing physical security to the population at large, even if only for the length of time that an offender may stay behind bars. Of course, this myth is only effective as long as prisoners are presented as dangerous others, regardless of the fact that the majority of them are imprisoned for non-violent offences (Berman, 2012: 4–5). But, in the public imagination it would seem that the myth prevails. Although the neoliberal state may have renounced its role as guarantor of social security, it has retained its primary regalian function: attempting to guarantee physical security to the general public. As David Garland (1996: 460) suggests, the 'willingness to deliver harsh punishments to convicted offenders magically compensates for a failure to deliver [economic] security to the population at large'. This is particularly important in a society such as Britain where people are facing all sorts of risks from neoliberal globalisation which their government is wholly unequipped (and unwilling) to protect them from. Joe Sim (2009: 128) sums this up well, commenting, 'the institution exists in the collective mind as an existential comfort blanket for the protection of the globalised citizen against the material and psychological insecurities generated by the predations of the criminal or the deviant'.

Loïc Wacquant is correct to argue that punitive crime policies are a response, not to crime and the insecurity which it engenders but rather to the social insecurity exacerbated by neoliberalism (see Wacquant, Chapter 4). Yet, it is problematic to regard welfare and crime policies as part of the same continuum of control, directed at the working-class casualties of economic deregulation, at least in the British context (Bell, 2011). Whereas the welfare system generally aims to remodel citizens in order to adapt them to flexible wage labour, the prison system fails spectacularly in this task (Piven, 2010: 115). Despite the previous Justice Secretary's attempts to oblige prisoners to work a full working week, rendering prisons 'places of hard work and industry, instead of enforced idleness' (MoJ, 2010), prisoners will continue to face extreme difficulties finding work on their release, not just on account of their lack of qualifications but also due to employer discrimination (Joseph Rowntree Foundation (JRF), 2001). Whilst both the welfare and penal systems aim to responsibilise the poor, they retain largely separate functions. The prison is in reality an extremely ineffective measure of social control, and is best understood as a vital tool of state legitimacy, diverting attention from the state's failure to provide social and economic security to the population at large. This diversionary function is undoubtedly more important than its control function.

Indeed, Thomas Mathiesen (2000) has drawn attention to the 'diverting function' of the prison whereby 'our attention [is diverted] from the dangers flowing from those in power'. The prison enables the neoliberal state to be seen to be doing something about crime, directing the gaze of the general public downwards towards those who are seen to threaten the physical and moral welfare of society whilst simultaneously diverting attention away from the failure of the state to provide social security and away from the economic elites who are the real sources of significant social harms (Tombs and Whyte, 2010). Since neoliberalism has essentially meant that the state has come to serve the economic elites rather than its electorate (Harvey, 2007), it has become imperative for it to search for scapegoats for all sorts of social problems amongst the powerless, be they those without social capital or those without legitimate residency papers. The prison is a perfect way of placing those responsible for social problems in the public gaze, holding them up as examples of all that is wrong with society and thus absolving the elites of responsibility. The problems of childhood are represented by the criminal (and hence absent) mother or father and/or the predatory paedophile; the problems of unemployment, crime and community disintegration are represented by the detained immigrant awaiting deportation who is seen to threaten the very fabric of society; the 'broken society' is represented by the criminal 'underclass'. All of these figures are 'the perfect enemies', playing to the politics of fear which enable neoliberal governments of whatever political hue to appeal to the electorate across class lines.

AUTHORITARIAN POPULISM

The British government's increasing reliance on the prison is often presented as an inherently popular policy. Indeed, the Prime Minister justified his rejection of Kenneth Clarke's proposal to reduce the length of prison sentences for those who make early guilty pleas on the grounds that such a measure would 'erode public confidence in the system' (Cameron, 2011a). Yet, whilst prison has attained 'an iconic status in public conceptions of legal punishment' and the public tends to show strong support for imprisonment, particularly as a response to crimes of violence, they significantly underestimate its use (Roberts and Hough, 2005: 89). Paradoxically, whilst they continue to support prison as a penalty, they do not believe it either punishes enough or succeeds in rehabilitating those who it incarcerates (ibid.). So, although over-reliance on prison may appear to be responding to public demand, the institution does not provide public satisfaction. In addition, it does not, in reality, act in the public interest: it is costly, ineffective in terms of rehabilitation and it fails to protect the public from harmful behaviour on account of the fact that only a very small proportion of offenders end up behind bars. This is because the vast majority of crimes remain unreported and/or unsolved and because the criminal justice system tends to focus predominantly on the crimes of the powerless, leaving the powerful to continue to cause substantial physical, psychological, financial and ecological harm with impunity.

So, rather than prison being a popular policy, it is in reality a *populist* policy. Rather than attempting to engage with public opinion in a meaningful and informed debate about criminal justice policy, the government tends instead to listen to the 'noise' of the public voice (James and Raine, 1998: 81). It invokes genuine public concerns and uses them cynically to serve its own interests, boosting its own legitimacy by appearing to 'do something' about crime and diverting public attention from the serious harms which may be perpetrated by the economic elites. In adopting an increasingly harsh stance towards working-class offenders and disenfranchised immigrants, the British government is in reality engaging in what Stuart Hall once described as 'authoritarian populism', attempting 'to impose a new regime of social discipline and leadership "from above" which had to be rooted in popular fears and anxieties "below"' (Hall, 1988). Yet, in doing so, the British government is not just promoting its own interests but also those of the economic elites whose influence over government has once again become entirely disproportionate to their actual numbers. Despite the government discourse about returning power to the people, the shift towards neoliberalism has actually resulted in profoundly anti-democratic policies which work against the interests of the vast majority of the population (see Barker, Chapter 7).

THE SECURITY-INDUSTRIAL COMPLEX

It is often asserted that there is a 'corrections-commercial complex' (Lilly and Knepper, 1993) or a 'prison-industrial complex' (Schlosser, 1998; see also Meiners, Chapter 13 and Oparah, Chapter 14 of this volume) emerging whereby the private sector exercises considerable influence over the development of penal policy, encouraging the increased use of imprisonment. The term is inspired by the notion of the 'military-industrial complex', first used in 1961 by President Eisenhower to describe the harmful influence that the defence industry can have on government. In the UK, it would certainly appear that such a complex is emerging, although it may perhaps be more appropriately described as a 'security-industrial complex' since private interests are not just involved in the supply of detention services but also the provision of policing services (Travis and Williams, 2012), forensic testing, probation services and surveillance. With regard to detention, the UK has the most privatised prison system in Europe, housing 13 per cent of its prison population in private prisons (Prison Reform Trust, 2012: 71). This figure is likely to expand significantly once the latest stage of the competition process involving nine UK prisons, announced by the government in July 2011, is completed.[6] In October 2011, HMP Birmingham became the first existing public sector prison to be handed over to a private company. This is the most significant prison privatisation project since the very first private prison, HMP The Wolds, opened its doors in Yorkshire in 1992. In addition, nine out of the twelve 'immigration removal centres' in the UK are run by private companies under contract to the UK Border Agency (see Kaufman and Bosworth, Chapter 9).

Private companies are also increasingly involved in the employment of prisoners. This is nothing particularly new. From the creation of the first Houses of Correction in the seventeenth century, prisoners were set to work, forced to perform menial tasks such as cleaning the city sewers (McConville, 1981: 33). Since the nineteenth century, convicted prisoners have been put to work, working as cleaners or cooks for example, helping with the daily running of the prison or, in the larger prisons, performing unskilled work in prison workshops. The number of prison workshops gradually increased over the course of the last century (Home Office, 1960: 26), but today only a small proportion of prisoners (less than 17 per cent) actually work in prison.[7] Prisoners are currently paid a

---

[6] In November 2012, HMP The Wolds was returned to the public sector whilst HMPs Moorland, Hatfield, Lindholme and Northumberland (which combines two prisons situated next to each other, YOI Castington and HMP Acklington) were privatised. Two brand new privately run prisons, HMP Oakwood and HMP Thameside, opened in spring 2012. In addition, all 120 public sector prisons are to have 'ancillary services' privatised.

[7] It is estimated that 9,000 prisoners per day work in public-sector prison industries in England and Wales, 1,000 work in private-sector prison industries and a further 4,400 prisoners work in catering and picking and packing services, helping with the day-to-day running of the prison (see Hansard, 20 February 2012, column 615W). In addition, approximately 450 low-risk prisoners in open prisons work in the community on individual work placements (see Hansard, 20 January 2011, column 959W).

minimum wage of just £4 per week,[8] although it is estimated that the average weekly wage is around £9.60 per week.[9] The former Justice Secretary planned to encourage the development of what he described as 'real work' in prison whereby prisoners will be obliged to work for 40 hours per week for the minimum wage, with a percentage of their earnings used to help victims of crime. Significantly, he saw the private sector as a key partner in the project:

> I intend to expand this Working Prisons programme quite dramatically. But this is not something Government can do alone. No: We need the private sector on board. And they are coming on board. This morning, eight companies – including Virgin, National Grid, Marks and Spencer give the idea their support. . . They – along with the CBI[10] – are helping us to ensure that companies can make the most of this.
>
> (Clarke, 2011)

The private sector has already been engaged with the Prison Service for some time, working under contract to provide prison workshops. It is estimated that 12 million hours are worked every year in prison industries, valued at around £30 million to businesses (Prison Labour, 2012). Current plans to extend the involvement of the private sector in prison industries would of course prove to be extremely lucrative for private business, even accounting for the fact that they may be obliged to pay the national minimum wage. Although Kenneth Clarke justified these plans principally in terms of rehabilitation, placing it at the heart of the government's 'rehabilitation revolution' (MoJ, 2010), he also appeared to be influenced by business imperatives. Indeed, when introducing the plan in the *Daily Telegraph*, he noted, 'Right now, prisoners are simply a wasted resource – thousands of hours of manpower sitting idle' (cited by Whitehead, 2012). Certainly, the rehabilitative value of work in prison is questionable: prisoners will only be able to save a small amount of the money earned to aid their reintegration on release, and the narrow focus on work as a magic solution to offending behaviour ignores the other possible problems an offender may suffer from. Indeed, prison work programmes would appear to be more about instilling personal

---

[8] Prisoners were specifically excluded from the National Minimum Wage Act 1998.

[9] Hansard, 20 January 2011, column 959W. Following the enactment of the Prisoners' Earnings Act 1996 in September 2011, prisoners working in the community will be obliged to pay a 40 per cent levy on any earnings over £20 per week to Victim Support, a charity working with victims of crime.

[10] The Confederation of British Industry is the principal professional and lobbying organisation representing business interests in the UK.

responsibility and a work ethic than about addressing the underlying causes of crime (Mathiesen, 2000). It is rather ironic that the work programme is sold as a way of reintegrating prisoners into society when prison itself actually excludes prisoners from the marketplace, not just when they are detained but also when they are released (JFR, 2001). It is therefore likely that prisons will continue instead to 'dehabilitate' as prison work policy is determined 'by the system interests attached to the prisons rather than to any interest in actual rehabilitation of the prisoners' (Mathiesen, 2006: 53). What exactly are these 'system interests' at the current time?

Certainly, budgetary concerns are a key system interest at present. Indeed, it might be thought that cost considerations have motivated the increased involvement of the private sector in both the running of prisons and the provision of work programmes – the Ministry of Justice has been forced to accept a 23 per cent budget cut (Cabinet Office, 2010). Yet, the privatisation project was already underway even before such budget cuts were imposed. Furthermore, experience of privatisation so far has failed to demonstrate that it is more cost-effective. Prisons contracted out to the private sector under the Private Finance Initiative (PFI) involve a significant number of hidden costs, which the public generally remain aware of on account of commercial confidentiality agreements (Prison Officers' Association, 2011: 9). For example, the cost of external professional advice to the government from legal, financial, insurance and technical advisors is significant (ibid.). In addition, the government has announced that significant financial incentives – the cost of which will be borne by the government – will be offered to private companies who employ ex-offenders (Warrell, 2012). Furthermore, although the privatisation programme is significant, the government will continue to support the greatest cost burden of imprisonment since it remains responsible for approximately 85 per cent of the prison estate in England and Wales and continues to assume much of the risk under PFI contracts.

The unproven cost-effectiveness of private sector involvement in prisons would suggest that privatisation is driven more by ideological considerations linked to the rolling back of the frontiers of the neoliberal state. The policy may also be motivated by a desire on the part of the government to legitimise an expansionist prison policy, which is not only seen to be protecting the public more effectively by locking more people up and making greater efforts at rehabilitation, but also seen to be offering cost savings to the already over-stretched public purse. The prison work programme, placed at the centre of the coalition government's 'rehabilitation revolution', is an excellent way of legitimating not just the prison system but the neoliberal system itself. First, it seeks to present imprisonment as an effective means of protecting the public, not just by taking offenders off the streets but also by reducing recidivism, making prisons 'work' in more ways than one. Presenting the prison as an institution that no longer 'warehouses offenders' (Clarke, 2010) but seeks to genuinely rehabilitate them can help to give it a more positive and even progressive image. For those of a more punitive disposition, prison labour can of course also be regarded as a form of punishment: 'labour as a form of punishment has had, historically, both a connotation of rehabilitation and of discipline' (Harcourt, 2011: 37). One need only think of the deliberately punitive work given to those in nineteenth-century prisons and work houses.

Second, prison work helps to legitimate the neoliberal system itself by placing such a high value on integration into the labour market. Indeed, full citizenship can only obtained through participation in the market – paid work is seen as the magic solution to a whole host of social problems. In addition, as prisons and other public institutions, such as schools, ape the values of the private sector, the latter soon become recognised as the norm throughout civil society. Private sector values are evident in the creation of competitive tendering for carceral services; in the introduction of principles of New Public Management into prison in the form of Key Performance Indicators regarding prison conditions and cost imperatives, for example; and, most latterly, in 'payment-by-results', whereby a part of the money due to private companies for the running of rehabilitation programmes, such as the work programme, is to be withheld unless the latter can prove that they have successfully reduced reoffending. That 'system' interests are being served here rather than prisoner interests is evident, especially if the recommendations of the highly influential conservative think tank, *Policy Exchange*, are to be followed: prisoners are to be hand-selected for participation in work programmes, ensuring that those offenders who may benefit most from the programme due to their lack of skills or otherwise will be excluded. A report from the think tank sets out what it describes as 'some prerequisites for a prisoner applying for work, on the grounds that prisoners who do not meet such criteria would rarely be employed in any position in the open labour market' (Geoghegan et al., 2011: 29).

It is therefore clear that 'system interests' do not just refer to government interests but also to the private sector, which seeks to gain substantial benefits from the above policy developments. G4S, the private manager of over 7,000 prisoners spread across six prisons in England and Wales, welcomes the idea of 'working prisons' and has recently published a document encouraging private companies to make full use of their prisoners, claiming that 'there is practically no business type or sector we cannot accommodate. We provide the premises and the workforce – you provide the ideas' (G4S, 2011: 2). With regard to prisoner wages, G4S declares '[w]e understand that you need to make a profit and that a partnership with us must make commercial sense' (ibid.: 1), suggesting that prisoners are to be offered to private companies as a new source of cheap labour.

According to Bernard Harcourt (2011: 237), such a development should not surprise us. Whilst the mythical 'free' market remains free from state intervention, the penal sector becomes the principal field where not only government may legitimately intervene but also a whole range of economic actors. Whilst government is limited, economics is everywhere. Harcourt notes that some American states such as Arizona are even considering handing total responsibility for incarceration over to the private sector (ibid.: 233). In Britain too, the role of private financial interests cannot be seen as negligible.

The influence of the private sector over government is evident. It exerts a certain degree of financial influence, with business lobbies contributing significant sums of money to the Conservative Party. The professional lobby, Euro RSCG Apex Communications,[11] which represents G4S and Serco, both involved in the prison privatisation programme, contributed almost £12,000 to party funds (Political Cleanup, 2012). The case for privatisation has also been put forward by influential think tanks such as *Policy Exchange*, mentioned above, which has explicitly encouraged the recruitment of prisoners by private companies (Geoghegan et al., 2011).[12] Government ministers themselves regularly meet with G4S representatives to discuss public policy (Who's Lobbying?, 2012). It would seem that government and the private sector have come to share a symbiotic relationship whereby both seek to

---

[11] The Euro RSCG Group was formed in 1991 following the merger of two French advertising agencies, Eurocom S.A. and Roux Séguéla Cayzac and Goudard. Fifteen years later, it merged with Apex, a communications firm established by Ed Owen, former political adviser to the Home Office (1997–2001) and Foreign Office (2001–5), and Pete Bowyer, a well-known leading political and media consultant. In 2011, the Group merged with Maitland, the financial and corporate communications group.

[12] Blair Gibbs, one of the authors of this report, was formerly policy adviser to the Policing and Criminal Justice Minister, Nick Herbert.

benefit from the prison industry, the government seeking to ensure its legitimacy before its electorate, and private business seeking to provide maximum profits for their shareholders. The latter may also benefit from the diversionary effect of imprisonment whereby attention is diverted from their own criminal activities as focus is placed on the powerless who find themselves behind bars. Neoliberalism does not make such a relationship imperative but it certainly creates the conditions under which government is more likely to seek legitimacy by working in the best interests of the private sector rather than in those of the general public.

CONCLUSION

The 'prison paradox' is a long-term problem, confined not just to the UK or even to countries that may be described as neoliberal. Yet, it is surely not a coincidence that the UK prison population began to increase significantly just as neoliberalism had come to establish itself in Britain following thirteen years of Thatcherism. In the specific cultural, social, political, ideological and financial conjecture created by neoliberalism, placing more people behind bars has become a useful way of boosting state legitimacy, thus constructing offenders and immigrants as conven-ient scapegoats for a whole host of social problems that have in reality been exacerbated by neoliberal economic policies (see Scott, Chapter 15). Far from responding to popular demand, the prison has become a means of diverting the public gaze away from the real culprits of these problems: government and the economic elites whose influence has grown out of all proportion to their actual numbers, posing a threat to the very nature of democracy itself. Yet, given the dominance of neoliberal market logic in contemporary society, public and private interests are often conflated. The increased involvement of the private sector in the delivery of punishment and the transposition of market values over to the prison have thus served to reinforce the legitimacy of the institution. Governed by market principles, the prison is seen to be best for the prisoner – whose rehabilitation is facilitated by their assim-ilation into the workplace – and best for the public, who is meant to be better protected by more effective 'rehabilitation' measures' and who, as a taxpayer, is meant to get better value for money. As the public become willing participants in the carceral exclusion of those who fail to live up to the standards of the neoliberal market society, the prison and the neoliberal system itself are conferred a certain democratic legitimacy.

There may be stirrings of revolt against the bankers and the politicians who are seen to be responsible for the current economic crisis, but the legitimacy of the prison and the neoliberal politics, which are currently fuelling its expansion, remain intact. The prison paradox is far from being resolved.

4

CRAFTING THE NEOLIBERAL STATE: WORKFARE, PRISONFARE AND SOCIAL INSECURITY*

Loïc Wacquant

In *Punishing the Poor* (Wacquant, 2009b), I show that the return of the prison to the institutional forefront of advanced society over the past quarter-century is a political response, not to rising criminal insecurity, but to the diffuse social insecurity wrought by the fragmentation of wage labour and the shake-up of ethnic hierarchy. The punitive slant of recent shifts in both welfare and justice policies points to a broader reconstruction of the state coupling restrictive 'workfare' and expansive 'prisonfare' under a philosophy of moral behaviourism. The paternalist penalisation of poverty aims to contain the urban disorders spawned by economic deregulation and to discipline the precarious fractions of the post-industrial working class. Diligent and belligerent programmes of 'law and order' entailing the enlargement and exaltation of the police, the courts, and the penitentiary have also spread across the First World because they enable political elites to reassert the authority of the state and shore up the deficit of legitimacy officials suffer when they abandon the mission of social and economic protection established during the Fordist-Keynesian era.

Punishing the Poor treats the USA after the acme of the civil rights movement, as the historic crucible of punitive containment as technique for the management of marginality and living laboratory of the neoliberal future, where convergent revamping of the social and penal wings of the state can be discerned with particular clarity. Its

* This chapter is a revised, shortened version of an article original published in *Sociological Forum*, 25(2), June 2010.

overarching argument unfolds in four steps. Part I maps out the accelerating decline and abiding misery of the US social state, climaxing with the replacement of protective welfare by disciplinary workfare in 1996. Part II tracks the modalities of the growth and grandeur of the penal state and finds that the coming of 'carceral big government' was driven not by trends in criminality, but by the class and racial backlash against the social advances of the 1960s. Part III heeds the communicative dimension of penality as a vehicle for symbolic boundary drawing and explains why penal activism in the USA has been aimed at two 'privileged targets': the black subproletariat trapped in the imploding ghetto and the roaming sex offender. Part IV follows recent declinations of the new politics of social insecurity in Western Europe to offer a critique of the 'scholarly myths' of the reigning law-and-order reason, prescriptions for escaping the punitive policy snare and a characterisation of the distinctive shape and missions of the neoliberal state.

Three analytic breaks proved indispensible to diagnose the invention of a new government of social insecurity wedding supervisory 'workfare' and castigatory 'prisonfare' and to account for the punitive policy turn taken by the USA and other advanced societies following its lead onto the path of economic deregulation and welfare retrenchment in the closing decades of the twentieth century. The first consists in escaping the crime-and-punishment poke, which continues to straightjacket scholarly and policy debates on incarceration, even as the divorce of this familiar couple grows ever more barefaced.[1] The second requires re-linking social welfare and penal policies, inasmuch these two strands of government action toward the poor have come to be informed by the same behaviourist philosophy relying on deterrence, surveillance, stigma and graduated sanctions to modify conduct. Welfare revamped as workfare and the prison stripped of its rehabilitative pretension now form a single organisational mesh flung at the same clientele mired in the fissures and ditches of the dualising metropolis. They work jointly to invisibilise problem populations – by forcing them off the public-aid rolls on the one side, and holding them under lock on the other – and

---

[1] A simple statistic suffices to demonstrate this disconnect and reveals the futility of trying to explain rising penal incarceration by escalating crime: the USA held 21 prisoners for every 1,000 'index crimes' in 1975 compared to 113 convicts per 1,000 crimes in 2000, for an increase of 438 per cent; for 'violent crimes', the jump is from 231 to 922 convicts per 1,000 offences, an increase of 299 per cent. This means that the country became four to five times more punitive in a quarter-century, holding crime constant (a lagged index turns up the same trend). See Wacquant (2009a: 125–33) for further elaboration and Blumstein and Wallman (2000) and Western (2006: ch. 2) for different approaches leading to the same conclusion.

eventually push them into the peripheral sectors of the booming secondary labour market. The third rupture involves overcoming the conventional opposition between materialist and symbolic approaches, descended from the emblematic figures of Karl Marx and Emile Durkheim, so as to heed and hold together the instrumental and the expressive functions of the penal apparatus. Weaving together concerns for control and communication, the management of dispossessed categories and the affirmation of salient social borders, makes it possible to go beyond an analysis couched in the language of prohibition to trace how the rolling out of the prison and its institutional tentacles (probation, parole, criminal databases, swirling discourses about crime and a virulent culture of public denigration of offenders) has reshaped the socio-symbolic landscape and remade the state itself.

A single concept sufficed to effect those three breaks simultaneously: the notion of *bureaucratic field*, developed by Pierre Bourdieu (1994) in his lecture course at the Collège de France in the early 1990s to rethink the state as the agency that monopolises the legitimate use, not only of material violence (as in Max Weber's well-known capsule), but also of symbolic violence, and shapes social space and strategies by setting the conversion rate between the various species of capital. In this chapter, I extend Bourdieu's formulation to draw out the theoretical underpinnings and implications of the model of the neoliberal government of social insecurity at century's dawn put forth in *Punishing the Poor*.

In the first section, I revise Piven and Cloward's classic thesis on the regulation of poverty via public assistance and contrast penalisation as a technique for the management of marginality in the dual metropolis with Michel Foucault's vision of the place of the prison in the 'disciplinary society' and with David Garland's account of the crystallisation of the 'culture of control' in late modernity. In the second section, I build on these contrasts to elaborate a thick sociological specification of neoliberalism that breaks with the thin economic conception of neoliberalism as market rule that effectively echoes its ideology. I argue that a proactive penal system is not a deviation from, but a constituent component of, the neoliberal Leviathan, along with variants of supervisory workfare and the cultural trope of 'individual responsibility'. This suggests that we need to theorise the prison not as a technical implement for law enforcement, but as a core organ of the state whose selective and aggressive deployment in the lower regions of social space is constitutively injurious to the ideals of democratic citizenship.

WHEN WORKFARE JOINS PRISONFARE: THEORETICAL IMPLICATIONS

In *The Weight of the World* (Bourdieu et al., 1999) and related essays, Pierre Bourdieu proposes that we construe the state not as a monolithic and coordinated ensemble, but as a splintered space of forces vying over the definition and distribution of public goods, which he calls the 'bureaucratic field'.[2] The constitution of this space is the end result of a long-term process of concentration of the various species of capital operative in a given social formation, and especially of 'juridical capital as the objectified and codified form of symbolic capital', which enables the state to monopolise the official definition of identities, the promulgation of standards of conduct and the administration of justice (Bourdieu, 1994: 4, 9). In the contemporary period, the bureaucratic field is traversed by two internecine struggles. The first pits the 'higher state nobility' of policymakers intent on promoting market-oriented reforms and the 'lower state nobility' of executants attached to the traditional missions of government. The second opposes what Bourdieu, riding off Hobbes's classic portrayal of the ruler, calls the 'Left hand' and the 'Right hand' of the state. The 'Left hand', the feminine side of Leviathan, is materialised by the 'spendthrift' ministries in charge of 'social functions' – public education, health, housing, welfare and labour law – which offer protection and succour to the social categories shorn of economic and cultural capital. The Right hand, the masculine side, is charged with enforcing the new economic discipline via budget cuts, fiscal incentives and economic deregulation. By inviting us to grasp in a single conceptual framework the various sectors of the state that administer the life conditions and chances of the working class, and to view these sectors as enmeshed in relations of antagonistic cooperation as they vie for pre-eminence inside the bureaucratic field, this conception has helped us map the ongoing shift from the social to the penal treatment of urban marginality.

In this regard, *Punishing the Poor* fills in a gap in Bourdieu's model by inserting the police, the courts and the prison as score constituents of the 'Right hand' of the state, alongside the ministries of the economy and the

---

[2] The concept is sketched analytically in Bourdieu (1994) and historically in Bourdieu (2012), illustrated in Bourdieu (1999) and deployed to probe the political production of the economy of single homes in France in Bourdieu (2005). Several issues of the journal *Actes de la recherche en sciences sociales* offer further cross-national empirical illustrations, including those on 'The history of the state' (nos. 116 and 117, March 1997), 'The genesis of the state' (no. 118, June 1997), the transition 'From social state to penal state' (no. 124, September 1998) and 'Pacify and punish' (nos. 173 and 174, June and September 2008).

budget. It suggests that we need to bring penal policies from the periphery to the centre of our analysis of the redesign and deployment of govern-ment programmes aimed at coping with the entrenched poverty and deepening disparities spawned in the polarising city by the discarding of the Fordist-Keynesian social compact (Wilson, 1996; Musterd et al., 2006; Wacquant, 2008b). The new government of social insecurity put in place in the USA and offered as a model to other advanced countries entails both a shift from the social to the penal wing of the state (detectable in the reallocation of public budgets, personnel and discursive precedence) and the colonisation of the welfare sector by the panoptic and punitive logic characteristic of the post-rehabilitation penal bureaucracy.

In their classic study *Regulating the Poor* (Piven and Cloward, 1971/ 1993), Frances Fox Piven and Richard Cloward forged a germinal model of the management of poverty in industrial capitalism. According to this model, the state expands or contracts its relief programmes cyclically to respond to the ups and downs of the economy, the corresponding slacken-ing and tightening of the labour market, and the bouts of social disruption that increased unemployment and destitution trigger periodically among the lower class. Phases of welfare expansion serve to 'mute civil disorders' that threaten established hierarchies, while phases of restriction aim to 'enforce works norms' by pushing recipients back into the labour market (Piven and Cloward, 1971/1993: xvi and *passim*). *Punishing the Poor* con-tends that, while this model worked well for the age of Fordist industrialism and accounts for the two major welfare explosions witnessed in the USA during the Great Depression and the affluent but turbulent 1960s, it has been rendered obsolete by the neoliberal remaking of the state over the past quarter-century. In the age of fragmented labour, hypermobile capital and sharpening social inequalities and anxieties, the 'central role of relief in the regulation of marginal labour and in the maintenance of social order' (Piven and Cloward, 1971/1993: xviii) is displaced and duly supplemented by the vigorous deployment of the police, the courts and the prison in the nether regions of social space. To the single oversight of the poor by the Left hand of the state succeeds in the double regulation of poverty by the joint action of punitive welfare-turned-workfare and an aggressive penal bureaucracy. The cyclical alternation of contraction and expansion of public aid is replaced by the continual contraction of welfare and the runaway expansion of prisonfare.[3]

---

[3] By analogy with 'welfare', I designate by 'prisonfare' the policy stream through which the state gives a penal response to festering urban ills and sociomoral disorders, as well as the imagery,

This organisational coupling of the Left hand and Right hand of the state under the aegis of the same disciplinary philosophy of behaviourism and moralism can be understood, first, by recalling the shared historical origins of poor relief and penal confinement in the chaotic passage from feudalism to capitalism. Both policies were devised in the long sixteenth century to 'absorb and regulate the masses of discontented people uprooted' by this epochal transition (Piven and Cloward, 1971/1993: 21). Similarly, both policies were overhauled in the last two decades of the twentieth century in response to the socioeconomic dislocations provoked by neoliberalism: in the 1980s alone, in addition to reducing public assistance, California passed nearly 1,000 laws expanding the use of prison sentences; at the federal level, the 1996 reform that 'ended welfare as we know it' was complemented by the sweeping Violent Crime Control and Law Enforcement Act of 1993 and bolstered by the No Frills Prison Act of 1995. The institutional pairing of public aid and incarceration as tools for managing the unruly poor can also be understood by paying attention to the structural, functional and cultural similarities between workfare and prisonfare as 'people-processing institutions' targeted on kindred problem populations (Hasenfeld, 1972). It has been facilitated by the transformation of welfare in a punitive direction and the activation of the penal system to handle more of the traditional clientele of assistance to the destitute – the incipient 'penalisation' of welfare matching the degraded 'welfarisation' of the prison. Their concurrent reform over the past thirty years has helped cement their organisational convergence, even as they have obeyed inverse principles. The gradual erosion of public aid and its revamping into workfare in 1996 has entailed restricting entry into the system, shortening 'stays' on the rolls and speeding up exit, resulting in a spectacular reduction of the stock of beneficiaries – it plummeted from nearly 5 million households in 1992 to under 2 million a decade later. Trends in penal policy have followed the exact opposite tack: admission into jail and prison has been greatly facilitated, sojourns behind bars lengthened and releases curtailed, which has yielded a spectacular ballooning of the population under lock (it jumped by over 1 million in the 1990s). The operant purpose of welfare has shifted from passive 'people processing' to active 'people changing' after 1988 and especially after the

discourses and bodies of lay and expert knowledge that accrete around the rolling out of the police, the courts, jails and prisons, and their extensions (probation, parole, computerised databanks of criminal files and the schemes of remote profiling and surveillance they enable). Penalisation joins socialisation and medicalisation as the three alternative strategies whereby the state can opt to treat undesirable conditions and conduct (Wacquant, 2009a: 16–17).

abolition of Aid to Families with Dependent Children (AFDC) in 1996, while the prison has travelled in the other direction, from aiming to reform inmates (under the philosophy of rehabilitation, hegemonic from the 1920s to the mid 1970s) to merely warehousing them (as the function of punishment was downgraded to retribution and neutralisation). The shared historical roots, organisational isomorphism and operational convergence of the assistential and penitential poles of the bureaucratic field in the USA are further fortified by the fact that the social profiles of their beneficiaries are virtually identical. AFDC recipients and jail inmates both live near or below 50 per cent of the federal poverty line (for one-half and two-thirds of them, respectively); both are disproportionately black and Hispanic (37 per cent and 18 per cent versus 41 per cent and 19 per cent); the majority did not finish high school and are saddled with serious physical and mental disabilities interfering with their participation in the workforce (44 per cent of AFDC mothers as against 37 per cent of prisoners). Also they are closely bound to one another by extensive kin, marital and social ties; reside overwhelmingly in the same impoverished households and barren neighbourhoods; and face the same bleak life horizon at the bottom of the class and ethnic structure.

Punishing the Poor avers not only that the USA has shifted from the single (welfare) to the double (social-cum-penal) regulation of the poor, but also that that 'the stunted development of American social policy' skilfully dissected by Piven and Cloward (1971/1993: 409) stands in close causal and functional relation to America's uniquely overgrown and hyperactive penal policy. The misery of American welfare and the grandeur of American prisonfare at the turn of the century are the two sides of the same political coin. The generosity of the latter is in direct proportion to the stinginess of the former, and it expands to the degree that both are driven by moral behaviourism. The same structural features of the US state – its bureaucratic fragmentation and ethnoracial skew, the institutional bifurcation between universalist 'social insurance' and categorical 'welfare' and the market-buttressing cast of assistance programmes – that facilitated the organised atrophy of welfare in reaction to the racial crisis of the 1960s and the economic turmoil of the 1970s have also fostered the uncontrolled hypertrophy of punishment aimed at the same precarious population. Moreover, the 'tortured impact of slavery and institutionalized racism on the construction of the American polity' has been felt, not only on the 'underdevelopment' of public aid and the 'decentralized and fragmented government and party system' that distributes it to a select segment of the dispossessed (Piven and Cloward, 1971/1993: 424–5), but also on the overdevelopment and stupendous severity of its penal wing. Ethnoracial division and the (re)activation of the stigma of blackness as dangerousness are key to explaining the initial atrophy and accelerating decay of the US social state in the post civil-rights epoch, on the one hand, and the astonishing ease and celerity with which the penal state arose on its ruins, on the other.

Reversing the historical bifurcation of the labour and crime questions achieved in the late-nineteenth century, punitive containment as a government technique for managing deepening urban marginality has effectively rejoined social and penal policy at the close of the twentieth century. It taps the diffuse social anxiety coursing through the middle and lower regions of social space in reaction to the splintering of wage, work and the resurgence of inequality and converts it into popular animus toward welfare recipients and street criminals cast as twin detached and defamed categories that sap the social order by their dissolute morality and dissipated behaviour, and must therefore be placed under severe tutelage. The new government of poverty invented by the USA to enforce the normalisation of social insecurity thus gives a whole new meaning to the notion of 'poor relief': punitive containment offers relief not to the poor but from the poor by forcibly 'disappearing' the most disruptive of them, from the shrinking welfare rolls on the one hand and into the swelling dungeons of the carceral castle on the other.

Michel Foucault (1977) has put forth the single most influential analysis of the rise and role of the prison in capitalist modernity, and it is useful to set my thesis against the rich tapestry of analyses he has stretched and stimulated. I concur with the author of *Discipline and Punish* that penality is a protean force that is eminently fertile and must be given pride of place in the study of contemporary power. While its originary medium resides in the application of legal coercion to enforce the core strictures of the sociomoral order, punishment must be viewed not through the narrow and technical prism of repression, but by recourse to the notion of production. The assertive rolling out of the penal state has indeed engendered new categories and discourses, novel administrative bodies and government policies, fresh social types and associated forms of knowledge across the criminal and social welfare domains (Wacquant, 2008a). But, from here, my argument diverges sharply from Foucault's view of the emergence and functioning of the punitive society in at least four ways.

To start with, Foucault erred in spotting the retreat of the penitentiary. Disciplines may have diversified and metastasised to thrust sinewy webs of control across the society, but the prison has not for that receded from the historical stage and 'lost its raison d'être' (Foucault, 1977: 304–5, 297–8). On the contrary, penal confinement has made a stunning comeback and reaffirmed itself among the central missions of Leviathan just as Foucault and his followers were forecasting its demise. After the founding burst of the 1600s and the consolidation of the 1800s, the turn of the present century ranks as the third 'age of confinement' that Thomas Mathiesen (1990) forewarned about in 1990. Next, whatever their uses in the eighteenth century, disciplinary technologies have not been deployed inside the overgrown and voracious carceral system of our *fin de siècle*. Hierarchical classification, elaborate time schedules, non-idleness, close-up examination and the regimentation of the body; these techniques of penal 'normalisation' have been rendered wholly impracticable by the demographic chaos spawned by overpopulation, bureaucratic rigidity, resource depletion and the studious indifference if not hostility of penal authorities toward rehabilitation. In lieu of the dressage ('training' or 'taming') intended to fashion 'docile and productive bodies' postulated by Foucault (1977), the contemporary prison is geared toward brute neutralisation, rote retribution, and simple warehousing – by default if not by design. If there are 'engineers of consciousness' and 'orthopedists of individuality' at work in the mesh of disciplinary powers today (Foucault, 1977: 301, 294), they surely are not employed by departments of corrections.

In the third place, 'devices for normalisation' anchored in the carceral institution have not spread throughout the society, in the manner of capillaries irrigating the entire body social. Rather, the widening of the penal dragnet under neoliberalism has been remarkably discriminating: in spite of conspicuous bursts of corporate crime (epitomised by the Savings and Loans scandal of the late 1980s and the folding of Enron a decade later), it has affected essentially the denizens of the lower regions of social and physical space. Indeed, the fact that the social and ethnoracial selectivity of the prison has been maintained, nay reinforced, as it vastly enlarged its intake demonstrates that penalisation is not an all-encompassing master logic that blindly traverses the social order to bend and bind its various constituents. On the contrary: it is a skewed technique proceeding along sharp gradients of class, ethnicity and place, and it operates to divide populations and to differentiate categories according to established conceptions of moral worth. America's urban (sub)proletariat lives in a 'punitive society' but its middle and upper classes certainly do not. Similarly, efforts to import and adapt US-style slogans and methods

73

of law enforcement – such as zero-tolerance policing, mandatory minimum sentencing or boot camps for juveniles – in Europe have been trained on lower-class and immigrant offenders relegated in the defamed neighbour-hoods at the centre of the panic over 'ghettoisation' that has swept across the continent over the past decade (Wacquant, 2009a).

Lastly, the crystallisation of law-and-order pornography – that is, the accelerating inflection and inflation of penal activity conceived, repre-sented and implemented for the primary purpose of being displayed in ritualised form by the authorities (the paradigm for which is the half-aborted reintroduction of chain gangs in striped uniforms) – suggests that news of the death of the 'spectacle of the scaffold' has been greatly exaggerated. The 'redistribution' of 'the whole economy of punishment' (Foucault, 1977: 13, 7) in the post-Fordist period has entailed not its disappearance from public view as proposed by Foucault, but its institu-tional relocation, symbolic elaboration and social proliferation beyond anything anyone envisioned when *Discipline and Punish* was published. In the past quarter-century, a whole galaxy of novel cultural and social forms, indeed a veritable industry trading on representations of offenders and law enforcement, has sprung forth and spread. The theatricalisation of penal-ity has migrated from the state to the commercial media and the political field *in toto*, and it has extended from the final ceremony of sanction to encompass the full penal chain, with a privileged place accorded to police operations in low-income districts and courtroom confrontations around celebrity defendants. The Place de Grève, where the regicide Damiens was famously quartered, has thus been supplanted not by the Panopticon but by Court TV and the profusion of crime-and-punishment 'reality shows' that have inundated television (*Cops, 911, America's Most Wanted, American Detective, Bounty Hunters, Inside Cell Block F*, etc.), not to mention the use of criminal justice as fodder for the daily news and dramatic series (*Law and Order, CSI, Prison Break*, etc.). So much to say that the prison did not 'replace' the 'social game of the signs of punishment and the garrulous feast that put them in motion' (Foucault, 1977: 134, 131). Rather it now serves as its institutional canopy. Everywhere the law-and-order guignol has become a core civic theatre onto whose stage elected officials prance to dramatise moral norms and display their professed capacity for decisive action, thereby reaffirming the political relevance of Leviathan at the very moment when they organise its powerlessness with respect to the market.

This brings us to the question of the political proceeds of penalisation, a theme central to David Garland's book *The Culture of Control*, the most sweeping and stimulative account of the nexus of crime and social order put forth since Foucault. According to David Garland (2001c: 139–47 and *passim*), 'the distinctive social, economic, and cultural arrangements of late modernity' have fashioned a 'new collective experience of crime and insecurity', to which the authorities have given a reactionary interpretation and a bifurcated response combining practical adaptation via 'preventative partnerships' and hysterical denial through 'punitive segregation'. The ensuing reconfiguration of crime control bespeaks the inability of rulers to regiment individuals and normalise contemporary society, and its very disjointedness has made glaring to all the 'limits of the sovereign state'. For Garland (2001c), the 'culture of control' coalescing around the 'new criminological predicament' pairing high crime rates with the acknowledged limitations of criminal justice both marks and masks a political failing. On the contrary, *Punishing the Poor* asserts that punitive containment has proved to be a remarkably successful political strategy: far from 'eroding one of the foundational myths of modern society', which holds that 'the sovereign state is capable of delivering law and order' (Garland, 2001c: 109), it has revitalised it. This is true not only in the USA, where the leaders of both parties have reached complete consensus over the benefits of punitive penal policies targeted at the inner city (Chih Lin, 1998), but also in Europe: Blair in the UK, Berlusconi in Italy and Chirac and Sarkozy in France have all parlayed their martial images of stern 'crime fighters' intent to clean up the streets into victories at the polls.

By elevating criminal safety (securité, Sicherheit, sicurezza, etc.) to the frontline of government priorities, state officials have condensed the diffuse class anxiety and simmering ethnic resentment generated by the unravelling of the Fordist-Keynesian compact and channelled them toward the (dark-skinned) street criminal, designated as guilty of sowing social and moral disorder in the city, alongside the profligate welfare recipient. Rolling out the penal state and coupling it with workfare has given the high state nobility an effective tool to both foster labour deregulation and contain the disorders that economic deregulation provokes in the lower rungs of the sociospatial hierarchy. Most importantly, it has allowed politicians to make up for the deficit of legitimacy that besets them whenever they curtail the economic support and social protections traditionally granted by Leviathan. Contra Garland (2001c) then, I find that the penalisation of urban poverty has served well as a vehicle for the ritual reassertion of the sovereignty of the state in the narrow, theatricalised domain of law enforcement that it has prioritised for that very purpose, just when the same state is conceding its incapacity to control flows of capital, bodies and signs across its borders. This divergence of diagnosis, in turn, points to three major differences between our respective dissections of the punitive drift in First World countries.

First, the fast and furious bend toward penalisation observed at the *fin de siècle* is not a response to criminal insecurity but to social insecurity. To be more precise, the currents of social anxiety that roil advanced society are rooted in objective social insecurity among the post-industrial working class, whose material conditions have deteriorated with the diffusion of unstable and underpaid wage labour shorn of the usual social 'benefits', and subjective insecurity among the middle classes, whose prospects for smooth reproduction or upward mobility have dimmed as competition for valued social positions has intensified and the state has reduced its provision of public goods. Garland's notion that 'high rates of crime have become a normal social fact – a routine part of modern consciousness, an everyday risk to be assessed and managed' by 'the population at large', and especially by the middle class (Garland, 2001c: 147), is belied by victimisation studies. Official statistics show that lawbreaking in the USA declined or stagnated for twenty years after the mid 1970s before falling precipitously in the 1990s, while exposure to violent offences varied widely by location in social and physical space (Wacquant, 2009a: 144–7). Relatedly, European countries sport crime rates similar to or higher than that of the USA (except for the two specific categories of assault and homicide, which compose but a tiny fraction of all offences), and yet they have responded quite differently to criminal activity, with rates of incarceration one-fifth to one-tenth the American rate even as they have risen.

This takes us to the second difference: for Garland, the reaction of the state to the predicament of high crime and low justice efficiency has been disjointed and even schizoid, whereas I have stressed its overall coherence. However, this coherence becomes visible only when the analytic compass is fully extended beyond the crime-punishment box and across policy realms to link penal trends to the socioeconomic restructuring of the urban order on the one side, and to join workfare to prisonfare, on the other. What Garland (2001c: 111) characterises as 'the structured ambivalence of the state's response' is not so much ambivalence as a predictable organisational division in the labour of management of the disruptive poor. Bourdieu's theory of the state is helpful here in enabling us to discern that the 'adaptive strategies' recognising the state's limited capacity to stem crime by stressing

prevention and devolution are pursued in the penal sector of the bureaucratic field, while what Garland calls the 'non-adaptive strategies' of
'denial and acting out' (Garland, 2001c: 131) to reassert that very
capacity to operate in the political field, especially in its relation to the
journalistic field.[4]

Third, like other leading analysts of contemporary punishment such as
Jock Young (1999), Franklin Zimring (Zimring et al., 2001) and Michael
Tonry (2004), Garland sees the punitive turn as the reactionary spawn of
right-wing politicians. But *Punishing the Poor* finds, first, that the penalisation of poverty is not a simple return to a past state of affairs but a
genuine institutional innovation; and, second, that it is by no means the
exclusive creature of neoconservative politics. If politicians of the Right
invented the formula, it was employed and refined by their centrist and
even 'progressive' rivals. Indeed, the president who oversaw by far the
biggest increase in incarceration in US history is not Ronald Reagan but
William Jefferson Clinton. Across the Atlantic, it is the Left of Blair in the
UK, Schröder in Germany, Jospin in France, d'Alema in Italy and
Gonzalez in Spain who negotiated the shift to proactive penalisation,
not their conservative predecessors. This is because the root cause of the
punitive turn is not late modernity but neoliberalism, a project that can be
indifferently embraced by politicians of the Right or the Left.

The jumble of trends that David Garland gathers under the umbrella
term of 'late modernity' – the 'modernising dynamic of capitalist production and market exchange', shifts in household composition and kinship
ties, changes in urban ecology and demography, the disenchanting impact
of the electronic media, the 'democratization of social and culture life'
(Garland, 2001c: 77–8) – are not only exceedingly vague and loosely
correlated; they are either not peculiar to the closing decades of the
twentieth century, specific to the USA, or show up in their most pronounced form in the social-democratic countries of Northern Europe that
have not been submerged by the international wave of penalisation.[5]

---

[4] The analytic and historical differentiation of the political from the bureaucratic field, and their
respective locations inside the field of power, are discussed in Wacquant (2005: esp. 6–7,
14–17,142–6).

[5] Read the extended analysis of the sociopolitical foundations of the 'penal exceptionalism' of
Finland, Sweden and Norway by John Pratt (2008a, 2008b), in which the cultural commitment
to social equality and welfare state security play a pivotal role, as they do in the sturdy resistance of
Scandinavia to neoliberal nostrums. Another notable anomaly for the 'culture of control' thesis is
Canada, which is as 'late modern' as the USA and yet has kept its incarceration low and stable
over the past three decades (it even decreased from 123 to 108 inmates per 100,000 residents
between 1991 and 2004, while the US rate zoomed from 360 to 710 inmates per 100,000).

Moreover, the onset of late modernity has been gradual and evolutionary, whereas the recent permutations of penality have been abrupt and revolutionary.

Punishing the Poor contends that it is not the generic 'risks and anxieties' of 'the open, porous, mobile society of strangers that is late modernity' (Garland, 2001c: 165) that have fostered retaliation against lower-class categories perceived as undeserving and deviant types seen as irrecuperable, but the specific social insecurity generated by the fragmentation of wage labour, the hardening of class divisions and the erosion of the established ethnoracial hierarchy guaranteeing an effective monopoly over collective honour to the white population in the USA and to nationals in the European Union. The sudden expansion and consensual exaltation of the penal state after the mid 1970s is not a culturally reactionary reading of 'late modernity' but a ruling-class response aiming to redefine the perimeter and missions of Leviathan so as to establish a new economic regime based on capital hypermobility and labour flexibility and to curb the social turmoil generated at the foot of the urban order by the public policies of market deregulation and social welfare retrenchment that are core building blocks of neoliberalism.

TOWARD A SOCIOLOGICAL SPECIFICATION OF NEOLIBERALISM

The invention of the double regulation of the insecure fractions of the post-industrial proletariat via the wedding of social and penal policy at the bottom of the polarised class structure is a major structural innovation that takes us beyond the model of the welfare-poverty nexus elaborated by Piven and Cloward (1971/1993) just as the Fordist-Keynesian regime was coming unglued. The birth of this institutional contraption is also not captured by Michel Foucault's vision of the 'disciplinary society' or by David Garland's notion of the 'culture of control', neither of which can account for the unforeseen timing, steep socioethnic selectivity, and peculiar organisational path of the abrupt turnaround in penal trends in the closing decades of the twentieth century. For the punitive containment of urban marginality through the simultaneous rolling back of the social safety net and the rolling out of the police-and-prison dragnet and their knitting together into a carceral-assistential lattice is not the spawn of some broad societal trend – whether it be the ascent of 'biopower' or the advent of 'late modernity' – but, at bottom, an exercise in state crafting. It partakes of the correlative revamping of the perimeter, missions and capacities of public authority on the economic, social welfare and penal fronts. This revamping has been uniquely swift, broad and deep in the USA, but it is in progress – or in question – in all advanced societies submitted to the relentless pressure to conform to the US pattern. Consider trends in France: in recent years the country has eased strictures on part-time employment as well as limitations on night-time and weekend work. Its governments of both Left and Right have actively supported the development of short-term contracts, temporary jobs and underpaid traineeships, and expanded the latitude of employers in hiring, firing and the use of overtime. The result is that the number of precarious wage earners has risen from 1.7 million in 1992 to 2.8 million in 2007 – or from 8.6 per cent to 12.4 per cent of the employed workforce (Maurin and Savidan, 2008). In June 2009, France instituted the RSA (*Revenu de solidarité active*), set to gradually replace the RMI (*Revenu minimum d'insertion*, the guaranteed minimum income grant provided to some 1.3 million), a programme designed to push public-aid recipients into the low-wage labour market via state subsidies to poor workers premised on the obligation to accept employment (Grandquillot, 2009).

Simultaneously, the oversight of unemployment benefits is being farmed out to private firms, which can terminate beneficiaries who reject two job offers and receive a financial bonus for each recipient they place in a job. On the penal front, accelerating the punitive turn taken by the Socialist government of Jospin in 1998–2002, the successive administrations of Chirac and Sarkozy have adopted sweeping measures of penal expansion (Bonelli, 2008): intensified policing centred on low-income districts, youth night curfews, enlarged recourse to incarceration for street crimes (in sharp contrast to the depenalisation of corporate crime), plea bargaining and accelerated judicial processing for low-level delinquents, mandatory minimum sentences for youth recidivists, annual targets for the expulsion of undocumented migrants and the indefinite civil commitment of certain categories of sex offenders after they have served their sentence. The country's budget for corrections jumped from 1.4 billion euros for 22,000 guards confining 48,000 inmates in 2001 to 2 billion euros for 24,000 guards and 64,000 inmates in 2009.

Tracking the roots and modalities of America's stupendous drive to hyper-incarceration opens a unique route into the sanctum of the neoliberal Leviathan. It leads us to articulate two major theoretical claims. The first is that the penal apparatus is a core organ of the state, expressive of its sovereignty and instrumental in imposing categories, upholding material and symbolic divisions, and moulding relations and behaviours through the selective penetration of social and physical space. The police, the courts and the prison are not mere technical appendages for the enforcement of lawful order (as criminology would have it) but vehicles for the political production of reality and for the oversight of deprived and defamed social categories and their reserved territories (Wacquant, 2008a). Students of early-modern state formation, from Norbert Elias to Charles Tilly to Gianfranco Poggi, fully recognised that the monopolisation of force and thus the construction of a bureaucratic machinery for policing, judging and punishing miscreants capable of minimally pacifying society was central to the building of Leviathan. It is high time that students of the neoliberal era notice that the remaking of the state after the break up of the Keynesian social compact has entailed not only renewed activity aimed at fostering international competitiveness, technological innovation and labour flexibility (R. Jessop, 1994; Streeck and Thelen, 2005; Levy 2006) but also, and most distinctively, the forceful reassertion of its penal mission henceforth set in a pornographic and managerialist key. Indeed, the second thesis advanced by *Punishing the Poor* is that the ongoing capitalist 'revolution from above', commonly called neoliberalism, entails the enlargement and exaltation of the penal sector of the bureaucratic field, so that the state may check the social reverberations caused by the diffusion of social insecurity in the lower rungs of the class and ethnic hierarchy as well as assuage popular discontent over the dereliction of its traditional economic and social duties. Neoliberalism readily resolves what for Garland's 'culture of control' remains an enigmatic paradox of late modernity, namely the fact that 'control is now being re-emphasised in every area of social life – with the singular and startling exception of the economy, from whose deregulated domain most of today's major risks routinely emerge' (Garland, 2001c: 165). The neoliberal remaking of the state also explains the steep class, ethnoracial and spatial bias stamping the simultaneous retraction of its social bosom and expansion of its penal fist: the populations most directly and adversely impacted by the convergent revamping of the labour market and public aid turn out also to be the privileged 'beneficiaries' of the penal largesse of the authorities. This is true in the USA where the carceral boom has corralled the (sub)proletarian black population trapped in the bare hyperghetto. It is also the case in Western Europe, where the primary clientele of the expanding prison is composed of precarious workers and the unemployed, postcolonial migrants and lower-class addicts and derelicts (Wacquant, 2009a: 87–102).

Finally, neoliberalism correlates closely with the international diffusion of punitive policies in both the welfare and the criminal domains. It is not by accident that the advanced countries that have imported, first, workfare measures designed to buttress the discipline of desocialised wage work and, then, variants of US-style criminal justice measures are the Commonwealth nations that also pursued aggressive policies of economic deregulation inspired by the 'free-market' nostrums, which come from the USA, whereas the countries that remained committed to a strong regulatory state curbing social insecurity have best resisted the sirens of 'zero-tolerance' policing and 'prison works'.[6] Similarly, societies of the Second World, such as Brazil, Argentina and South Africa, which adopted super-punitive penal planks inspired by developments in the USA in the 1990s and saw their prison populations soar as a result, did so not because they had at long last reached the stage of 'late modernity' but because they have taken the route of market deregulation and state retrenchment.[7] But to discern these multilevel connections between the upsurge of the punitive Leviathan and the spread of neoliberalism, it is necessary to develop a precise and broad conception of the latter. Instead of discarding neoliberalism, as Garland (2001c: 77) does, on account of it being 'rather too specific' a phenomenon to account for penal escalation, we must expand our conception of it and move from an economic to a fully sociological understanding of the phenomenon.

Neoliberalism is an elusive and contested notion, a hybrid term awkwardly suspended between the lay idiom of political debate and the technical terminology of social science, which moreover is often invoked without clear referent. Whether singular or polymorphous, evolutionary or revolutionary, the prevalent conception of neoliberalism is essentially economic: it stresses an array of market-friendly policies such as labour deregulation, capital mobility, privatisation, a monetarist agenda of

---

[6] In a major comparative study of the linkages between penal policy and political economy in twelve contemporary capitalist countries, Cavadino and Dignan (2006) find that the nations they characterise as neoliberal (as distinct from conservative corporatist, social democratic and oriental corporatist) are consistently more punitive and have become much more so in the past two decades.

[7] The international diffusion of 'made in USA' penal categories and policies and its springs are treated at length in *Prisons of Poverty* (Wacquant, 2009b). For further analyses of this near-planetary spread, read Jones and Newburn (2006), as well as Andreas and Nadelmann (2006).

deflation and financial autonomy, trade liberalisation, interplace competition and the reduction of taxation and public expenditures.[8] But this conception is thin and incomplete, as well as too closely bound up with the sermonising discourse of the advocates of neoliberalism. We need to reach beyond this economic nucleus and elaborate a thicker notion that identifies the institutional machinery and symbolic frames through which neoliberal tenets are being actualised. A minimalist sociological characterisation can now be essayed as follows. Neoliberalism is a transnational political project aiming to remake the nexus of market, state and citizenship from above. This project is carried by a new global ruling class in the making, composed of the heads and senior executives of transnational firms, high-ranking politicians, state managers and top officials of multinational organisations (the Organisation for Economic Co-operation and Development, World Trade Organisation, Internal Monetary Fund, World Bank and the European Union) and cultural-technical experts in their employ (chief among them economists, lawyers and communications professionals with germane training and mental categories in the different countries). It entails not simply the reassertion of the prerogatives of capital and the promotion of the marketplace but the close articulation of four institutional logics:

1. Economic deregulation – that is, reregulation aimed at promoting 'the market' or market-like mechanisms as the optimal device not only for guiding corporate strategies and economic transactions (under the aegis of the shareholder-value conception of the firm), but for organising the gamut of human activities, including the private provision of core public goods, on putative grounds of efficiency (implying deliberate disregard for distributive issues of justice and equality).
2. Welfare state devolution, retraction and recomposition designed to facilitate the expansion and support the intensification of commodification and, in particular, to submit reticent individuals to desocialised wage labour via variants of 'workfare' establishing a quasi-contractual relationship between the state and lower-class recipients, treated not as citizens but as clients or subjects (stipulating their behavioural obligations as condition for continued public assistance).

---

[8] This is the common core one can extract from a vast (and uneven) literature on the topic across the disciplines, among which can be singled out the pointed analyses of Fligstein (2001) for sociology, Campbell and Pedersen (2001) for political economy, Comaroff and Comaroff (2001) for anthropology, Brenner and Theodore (2002) for geography and Duménil and Lévy (2004) for economics.

3. An expansive, intrusive and proactive penal apparatus that pene-trates the nether regions of social and physical space to contain the disorders and disarray generated by diffusing social insecurity and deepening inequality, to unfurl disciplinary supervision over the precarious fractions of the post-industrial proletariat and to reassert the authority of Leviathan so as to bolster the evaporating legitimacy of elected officials.
4. The cultural trope of individual responsibility, which invades all spheres of life to provide a 'vocabulary of motive' – as C. Wright Mills would say – for the construction of the self (on the model of the entrepreneur), the spread of markets and legitimisation for the wid-ened competition it subtends, the counterpart of which is the evasion of corporate liability and the proclamation of state irresponsibility (or sharply reduced accountability in matters social and economic).

A central ideological tenet of neoliberalism is that it entails the coming of 'small government': the shrinking of the allegedly flaccid and over-grown Keynesian welfare state and its makeover into a lean and nimble workfare state, which 'invests' in human capital and 'activates' commu-nal springs and individual appetites for work and civic participation through 'partnerships' stressing self-reliance, commitment to paid work and managerialism.

Punishing the Poor demonstrates that that the neoliberal state turns out to be quite different in actuality: while it embraces laissez-faire at the top, releasing restraints on capital and expanding the life chances of the holders of economic and cultural capital, it is anything but laissez-faire at the bottom. Indeed, when it comes to handling the social turbulence generated by deregulation and to impressing the discipline of precarious labour, the new Leviathan reveals itself to be fiercely interventionist, bossy and pricey. The soft touch of libertarian proclivities favouring the upper class gives way to the hard edge of authoritarian oversight, as it endeavours to direct, nay dictate, the behaviour of the lower class. 'Small government' in the economic register thus begets 'big government' on the twofold front of workfare and criminal justice. Between 1982 and 2001, the USA increased its public expenditures for police, criminal courts and corrections by 364 per cent (from $36 to $167 billion, or 165 per cent in constant dollars of 2000) and added nearly 1 million justice staff. In 1996, when 'welfare reform' replaced the right to public aid by the obligation to accept insecure employment as a condition of support, the budget for corrections exceeded the overall sums allocated to AFDC and food stamps, the country's two main assistance programmes. That same year, corrections vaulted to the third largest employment in the land after Manpower Incorporated and Wal-Mart (see Wacquant, 2009b: 152–61). The results of America's grand experiment in creating the first society of advanced insecurity in history are in: the invasive, expansive, and expensive penal state is not a deviation from neoliberalism but one of its constituent ingredients.

CONCLUSION: PENALITY IN THE BUILDING OF A CENTAUR STATE

It bears stressing in closing that the building of a Janus-faced Leviathan practising liberal paternalism has not proceeded according to some master scheme concocted by omniscient rulers. Nor does it spring mechanically from the systemic necessities of some grand structure such as late capitalism, racism or panopticism (as in various neo-Marxist and neo-Foucauldian approaches, as well as in the activist demonology of the 'prison-industrial complex'). Rather, it arises from struggles over and within the bureaucratic field, aiming to redefine the perimeter, missions, priorities and modalities of action of public authorities with respect to definite problem territories and categories. These struggles involve, crucially, not only battles pitting organisations stemming from civil society and state agencies, but also internecine contests between the various sectors of the bureaucratic field, which vie to gain 'ownership' of the social problem at hand and thus valorise the specific forms of authority and expertise they anchor (medical, educational, social welfare, penal, economic, etc., and within the penal domain, the police, courts and confinement institutions and post-custodial means of control). The overall fitness of punitive containment to regulating urban marginality at century's dawn is a rough post hoc functionality born of a mix of initial policy intent, sequential bureaucratic adjustment, political trial and error and electoral profit-seeking at the point of confluence of three relatively autonomous streams of public measures concerning the low-skill employment market, public aid and criminal justice. The complementarity and interlocking of state programmes in these three realms is partly designed and partly an emergent property, fostered by the practical need to handle correlated contingencies, their common framing through the lens of moral behaviourism and the shared ethnoracial bias stamping their routine operations – with the (sub)proletarian black population from the hyperghetto figuring at the point of maximum impact where market deregulation, welfare retrenchment and penal penetration meet.

Whatever the modalities of their advent, it is indisputable that the linked stinginess of the welfare wing and munificence of the penal wing under the guidance of moralism have altered the make-up of the bureaucratic field in ways that are profoundly injurious to democratic ideals. As their sights converge on the same marginal populations and districts, deterrent workfare and the neutralising prison foster vastly different profiles and experiences of citizenship across the class and ethnic spectrum. They not only contravene the fundamental principle of equality of treatment by the state and routinely abridge the individual freedoms of the dispossessed, they also undermine the consent of the governed through the aggressive deployment of involuntary programmes stipulating personal responsibilities just as the state is withdrawing the institutional supports necessary to shoulder these and shirking its own social and economic charges. And they stamp the precarious fractions of the proletariat from which public-aid recipients and convicts issue with the indelible seal of unworthiness. In short, the penalisation of poverty splinters citizenship along class lines, saps civic trust at the bottom and saws the degradation of republican tenets. The establishment of the new government of social insecurity discloses, *in fine*, that neoliberalism is constitutively corrosive of democracy.

By enabling us to break out of the crime-and-punishment box to re-link welfare and justice while fully attending to both the material and symbolic dimensions of public policy, Bourdieu's concept of bureaucratic field offers a powerful tool for dissecting the anatomy and assembly of the neoliberal Leviathan. It suggests that some of the pivotal political struggles of this century's turn – if not the most visible or salient ones – involve not the confrontation between the mobilised organisations representing subaltern categories and the state, but battles internal to the hierarchical and dynamic ensemble of public bureaucracies that compete to socialise, medicalise or penalise urban marginality and its correlates. Elucidating the nexus of workfare, prisonfare and social insecurity, in turn, reveals that the study of incarceration is not a technical section in the criminological catalogue but a key chapter in the sociology of the state and social inequality in the bloom of neoliberalism.

PART II

PUBLIC PARTICIPATION

5

PLEASURE, PUNISHMENT
AND THE PROFESSIONAL MIDDLE CLASS

Magnus Hörnqvist

Introducing the problem of middle-class punitivity, Svend Ranulf wrote that the 'disposition to assist in the punishment of criminals' is 'an important factor in the constitution of human societies', and particularly intriguing as the disposition can be considered disinterested 'since no direct personal advantage is achieved by the act of punishing another person' (Ranulf, 1938: 1). The lower middle class seemed to have little to gain from the exacted punishment yet was the main actor in all the countries considered in his *Moral Indignation and Middle Class Psychology*. When David Garland later returned to the theme of a specific punitivity of the middle class, its role was seen to be the reverse. Historically the professional middle class was less punitive and more civilised than the rest of the population, although it had adopted more punitive attitudes in recent years, becoming 'the dog that did not bark' faced with high crime, social change and populist sentiments (Garland, 2000; Garland, 2001c: 152). Garland's claim has since been discussed in empirical studies by Cesaroni and Doob (2003) and E. Brown (2006). By and large, however, one cannot avoid the impression that the puzzle posed in the 1930s by Ranulf (1938) has been a non-issue. The class that acts in and through the prison has been remarkably invisible in the sociology of punishment.

When social class is theorised in relation to the prison, the focus has tended to rest exclusively on the receiving end. In particular, critical prison studies have prolonged the orientation towards the social strata – race, gender and class – that populates the prison. What happens to the impoverished, superfluous and potentially disruptive individuals in this particular institutional setting, and why they were put there in the first place, have been central preoccupations. The impact on the receiving end could then be used to account for the central role of the prison – how it preserved social order under capitalism. The effect has been analysed in terms of deterring, disciplining and warehousing (Rusche and Kirchheimer, 1939/2003; De Giorgi, 2006; Wacquant, 2009b). By incapacitating variable numbers of the working class, the rebellious instincts are quelled among the class as a whole, making it work for productive ends. In a move that would found cultural criminology, Emile Durkheim turned the perspective around to the audience. The punished themselves, their crimes and what may become of them upon release was secondary. Instead, it reinforced social solidarity by staging an underlying unity, shared collective sentiments and values (Durkheim, 1893/1933). Punishment practices were seen to be communicative acts 'through which a society could come to understand itself' (P. Smith, 2008: 20). The focus on the audience and societal self-understanding did not include sensitivity to social divisions and material inequality. The categories of the Durkheimian tradition effectively excluded social class. This chapter takes the opposite tacks of both critical and cultural criminology. It has been long overdue to interrogate the social class that acts in and through the prison. We need to look at the prison from the perspective of class formation – what it displays and what it accomplishes in relation to the middle class. That has so far been largely neglected.

The question of class and agency is absolutely essential to pose if we are to understand the prison. Someone designs prisons, someone reforms them, categorises offenders, writes about them, makes films, invents treatment programmes and formulates administrative routines. Who is doing that? The short answer is the professional middle class. Whereas 'society' or the audience in general has had little to say about the design and narratives of punishing practices, this is where the professional middle class rules supreme. Prison practices and discourses is an entrenched domain of social scientists, clinical psychologists, lawyers, auditors, prison managers, journalists, authors, film-makers and architects. Their social positioning cannot be left out when accounting for the concrete institutional design as well as the central societal function of the prison.

I therefore analyse the prison against the background of class relations. Those who punish and those who are being punished come from different social classes. The large majority of prisoners are underclass, or superfluous workers, whereas prison designers, reformers, governors and commentators belong to the professional middle class. That is the fairly trivial observation that provides the point of departure for this chapter. In accordance with this observation, the prison will be conceived of as a venue for a punishing encounter between social classes. Essentially, the prison is a punishing encounter, which takes place under conditions where members of one class are subjected to the physical disposal and ― classificatory power of another class. The responses of those on the receiving and resisting end in the penal encounter will be left out. I am exclusively interested in the social class that acts in and through the prison, how this particular institution contributes to its self-formation. Through the prison, the professional middle class distinguishes its social being in relation to all other classes: the underclass, which is being punished; the dominant classes, which have little to do with punishing practices; and the working class, which provides the bulk of the prison personnel executing the punishment.

In what follows, class formation is approached from a Bourdieu-inspired perspective, understanding the process of distinction in relation to other social classes by focusing on desires, fears and fantasies through the particular lens of penal institutions. We are looking for the underlying subject position, the basic categories organising the social world. In this respect, the middle class may be read as an open book. Foucault´s remark on the bourgeoisie of the nineteenth century – going through the archives, he was surprised to see that it expressed in great detail and with much cynicism what it wanted and why it wanted it (Foucault, 1976: · 52) – can be transferred to the current situation. The prison-related documents reveal what the professional middle class wants to be, what it is afraid of, what it enjoys, what it believes in and why. Its strong attachment to this particular form of punishment moreover requires a discussion of the specific pleasures and thrills associated with the prison, what Slavoj Žižek would call 'the underlying economy of *jouissance*' (Žižek, 1997: 53). This dimension is speculative and allows for several interpretations, yet I believe it is crucial.

CLASS FORMATION IN THE PUNISHING ENCOUNTER

Attractive, contested and imprecise, the concept of 'the middle class' has played a central role in public discourse ever since the eighteenth century (Kocka, 2004). Attempts have been made to uncover the defining characteristics of the middle class – squeezed between capitalists and workers – in workplace autonomy, supervisory functions, organisational assets and specialised skills (Poulantzas, 1975; Wright, 1985). Yet no single bundle of structural features defines the middle class. It cannot be reduced to its position in the social structure (Wacquant, 1991). The most promising approaches to class are sensitive to historical context and multidimensional. That is, they emphasise various aspects of agency – subjectivity, mobilisation and contestation – in addition to structural position. Whereas the concept of class is inextricably linked to the uneven distribution of material resources and its origin in the economic structure (Crompton, 2008), class *formation* denotes complex historical processes including further dimensions. The middle class depends on state policies, employment structure, interest-group formation and informal networks, and appears as a distinguishable entity only in the interaction with other social classes (Kocka, 1981; Boltanski, 1987; Lockwood, 1995; Savage, 2000; Kocka, 2004). Particular institutions, in the narrow sense, are also conducive. The educational system for instance is one much-studied arena for middle-class formation (Ball, 2003). By implication, other institutions – such as the prison – may also be of importance. Further, fundamental desires must be taken into consideration. John Frow (1995: 111) has suggested that 'processes of class formation' are 'played out through particular institutional forms and balances of power' as well as 'through desires, and fears, and fantasies'. In particular, the latter lead is to be pursued in this chapter as I focus on how the professional middle class constitutes itself as a class in and through the 'desires, and fears, and fantasies' played out within the institutional domain of the prison. The prison is not the only, nor the most import, arena for middle-class formation. But it is one important arena.

The link between the prison and the middle class goes back to the birth of the modern prison in the late-eighteenth century. 'With a few exceptions, the impetus to reform was traceable to the merchants, the factory owners, the managers of resources and labour, whose sons tended to move into the professions or, like John Howard himself, into the new gentry' (J. Bender, 1987: 30f.). For a bourgeoisie with cultural and economic capital and limited political influence, the prison was a means to distinguish itself from the dominant classes. The institution was formulated in conscious opposition to the aristocracy, which favoured corporeal punishments and the old houses of correction. As such, the prison was part of 'a reaction against the military mentality and honour culture of the old ruling class' (Garland, 2010: 145). The

Enlightenment bourgeoisie thought of itself as civilised, industrious and healthy, and would arrange prison punishment accordingly. Like other parts of the expanding state administration, the prison was organised bureaucratically and provided a platform for class formation. During the entire nineteenth century, the contours of a new bourgeois social stratum took shape all over Europe. It was non-entrepreneurial, rooted outside of the commercial sector, in the growing spheres of state administration and higher education, which rendered individuals 'a distinctive cultural capital linked to professional position' (Savage et al., 1992: 39).[1] This was the professional middle class, the class that subsequently would dictate conditions in the penal domain.

Through the prison, the professional middle class positions itself symbolically in relation to other classes. In the very beginning it manifested bourgeois norms as opposed to the feudal culture of *l'ancien régime*. However, since the middle of the nineteenth century, when the main adversary of the European middle classes, according to their own perceptions, shifted from the aristocracy to the lower classes (Kocka, 2004), one process of distinction stands out: that towards the working class. Within the prison, the professional middle class is given free range to express its specific tastes and interpretative frames in relation to all other classes and in particular the working class. It is an active positioning, in which the subject sets itself apart from the social other, thereby chiselling out its own specific features. The prison expresses the classificatory grid organising the social world of the middle class. As Pierre Bourdieu (1984: 468) has argued, by classifying the other according to 'a network of oppositions between high (sublime, elevated, pure) and low (vulgar, low, modest)', individuals order the social world, including their own position within it. The play of oppositions establishes differences between social classes on the most fundamental level. The classificatory grid not only maps the social structure but is slighted towards an approval of actions and dispositions from members of the same class and a projection of negative qualities onto other classes. As Barbara Herrnstein Smith (1988: 38) stresses, 'the privileging of the self and the pathologising of the Other remains the key move and defining objective of axiology'.[2] Displaying oneself as good (elevated and pure) by associating the other with the vulgar and low could be seen as an expression of self-interest or a mere justification of class privilege. Bourdieu, however, wanted to make a different point.

[1] See also Kocka (1981) and Boltanski (1987).   [2] See also Skeggs (2004).

The active ordering of the social world cannot be reduced to class interest.

> What individuals and group invest in the particular meaning they give to common classificatory systems by the use they make of them is infinitely more than their 'interest' in the usual sense of the term; it is their whole social being, everything which defines their own idea of themselves, the primordial, tacit contract whereby they define 'us' as opposed to 'them'.
>
> (Bourdieu, 1984: 478)

When transferred to the prison, this means that the professional middle class can be assumed to distinguish itself in all aspects of its social existence in the punishing encounter. Prisons provide one institutional arena on which desires, fears and fantasies of the professional middle class are enacted. Through the prison practices and discourses it comes to know itself as a social group with distinctive characteristics and desires. It constitutes itself dialectically in relation to other social classes as the active subject in a dual fundamental fantasy, which corresponds to the specific duality of imprisonment.

In a form sharper than in perhaps any other social institution, the prison expresses a duality, which at first sight may appear as a contradiction. The self-constitution of the professional middle class in the punishing encounter is marked by a fundamental tension between humanitarianism and sovereignty. Since its inception, the prison has been a venue for both humanitarianism and sovereignty. Imprisonment introduced the idea of human betterment as part of the punishment (Foucault, 1977). Historically, this feature sets the prison apart from all other forms of punishment. Through the vehicle of rehabilitation, the offender was to be made into a subject capable of exerting the rights and responsibilities that come with citizenship. At the same time the state would not dispense with its core sovereign prerogative. As a harsh punishment for transgressions, the prison incarnates a sovereign right to brute force, reinforcing the state´s ideological position as standing above the classes charged with the overall responsibility of maintaining order (Jessop, 2008). As a consequence, the prison is inevitably torn between humanitarian and sovereign concerns. The two ambitions are basically limitless; there is literally no end to the efforts to construct as well as to disintegrate subaltern agency inside the prison. Humanitarianism and sovereignty are neither easily reconcilable nor immediately contradictory. In what follows, we will see how the tension plays out in contemporary prison practices and shapes the professional middle class. Further, the split between humanitarianism and sovereignty – reform of the underprivileged other and violence to affirm social order – characterises the prison at every level, ranging from concrete practices over planning documents and scientific studies to the underlying pleasure economy. In terms of middle-class formation, the prison has two basic dimensions: (i) a narrative dimension, the 'ways of world-making' (Goodman, 1978) and the ways of home-making in the made world (Bourdieu, 1984); and (ii) the dimension of drives, pleasures and fears (Žižek, 1997; Lacan, 1999). Each dimension is discussed separately, even though they are intimately connected. Prison narratives, exemplified by current rehabilitation programmes and risk assessments, are analysed in the next section, followed by a closer look at the extracted pleasures and pains.

HUMANITARIAN NARRATIVES AND SOVEREIGN FANTASIES

The prison as an institution for the transformation of offenders into citizens, from the early days of religious contemplation in isolation to the contemporary cognitive behavioural programmes in a classroom setting, has been thoroughly analysed in the Foucauldian tradition. Considered as a vehicle of productive power, the prison is elaborate in terms of organisation. Scientific theories are translated into administrative routines and treatment practices, which are followed up in rituals of affirmation, giving rise to imaginary penalties where everybody acts as if the goals were attainable when in fact they are not (Carlen, 2008; Hörnqvist, 2010). The productive power is remarkably unsuccessful in changing offenders' behaviour. Its effects are, however, not ephemeral on those who exercise the same power. In fact, the lack of productivity at one end is compensated by a wealth of creativity at the other end. If we are looking for lasting effects of power, I would argue, such effects are produced predominantly on those who exercise the power. By modelling prisoners after their own fears, desires and fantasies, the professional middle class constitutes itself and creates the coordinates to navigate the social world.

The class to which prisoners belong is the working class. A more precise typology would perhaps locate them in the lower sections. In general, however, and in particular given 'the slippage from working-class to "underclass"' in contemporary middle-class discourse (Lawler, 2005: 435), precise sociological distinctions between higher and lower segments of the working class are not always relevant. Moral and psychological typologies are more pertinent. Inside the prison, the routine assessments according to prevailing typologies involve moral devaluation or scientific pathologisation of the imprisoned individuals and, by extension, of the class to which they belong. The physical disposal of the members of lower social strata is linked to their classification. As such, classification is a basic operation of class formation as well as a core characteristic of the punishing encounter in the prison. From a Bourdieuan perspective, the prison represents a condensed and highly ritualised form of this general mechanism of class formation. The assessments differentiate the categorising subject from the social other. The professional middle class articulates its own tastes and beliefs in its attempt to reform the social other while at the same time positioning itself hierarchically. This is a double movement. The prisoners are made to become just like the reformers, while establishing the difference.

The prison projects a mirror image of traditional middle-class values and habits. As I have argued elsewhere (Hörnqvist, 2010), the risk assessment instruments, along with the manuals of cognitive behavioural programmes, delineate a common conception of what constitutes the proper target for correctional intervention. The underlying theory operates by means of a frequent use of the adjective 'antisocial', positioned interchangeably in front of nouns such as 'attitudes', 'values', 'cognition' and 'personality'. Fulfilment of the mundane obligations of social life is absolutely central. This preoccupation is, for instance, spelled out in item 15 in the psychopathy checklist:

> Item 15 describes an individual who habitually fails to fulfil or honour obligations and commitments to others. He has little sense or no sense of duty or loyalty to family, friends, employers, society, ideas, or causes. His irresponsibility is evident in a variety of areas including: financial dealings (a poor credit rating, defaulting on loans, failure to discharge debts, etc.); behaviour that puts others at risk (drunk driving, recurrent speeding, etc.); work behaviour (frequently late or absent, careless or sloppy performance not attributable to lack of ability, etc.); business relationships (violating contractual arrangements, not paying bills, etc.); and relationships with family and friends (failing to provide financial support for spouse or children, causing them unnecessary hardship, etc.).
>
> (Hare, 1991: 25)

Inside the prison everything is organised according to a series of prosocial–antisocial dichotomies. Fundamental to the evaluation of behaviour as one or the other are specific conceptions of self-control and responsibility. The social features associated with an imagined model citizen – or the self-understanding of programme designers – can be laid bare by inverting the postulated indicators. The above description of item 15 in the psychopathy checklist provides an insight into the norms of responsibility – the ability to take on responsibilities, fulfil commitments, pay the bills, be on time, have a good credit rating, respect speed limits, maintain steady employment, provide financial support for children and accept responsibility for one's own actions. Other indicators of risk provide similar insights. It appears that instrument designers attach great value to the ability to plan ahead, consider consequences, a structured way of living, ability to accept frustration and resist strong emotions. The indicators point towards an individual embodying all the values, sentiments, thought patterns and predispositions associated with the professional middle class, and the very opposite of the antisocial personality of the typical offender. It differs from most prisoners, not simply in terms of law abidingness but who they are as persons, how they think and the values they hold.

Self-control and responsibility are the principles organising correctional assessments as well as the construction of the subject's social world as a whole. They help explain how the world works. The perceived impulsivity and irresponsibility equally account for the moral shortcomings of prisoners as well as their subordinate social position. This aspect of middle-class formation involves a double movement of affirmations and denials. As a prerequisite for desistance, the prisoner must become a mirror image of the middle class. At the same time prisoners can never become like it. Even though middle-class values and practices are invoked as an all-pervasive standard, prisoners will not and should not acquire them. On the one hand, the relevance of material circumstances is systematically denied. For instance, the introductory one-to-one meeting of the cognitive skills programme conveys the message that 'successful individuals' have been able to 'master a set of thinking and reasoning skills' and that such skills can outweigh the impact of class background and career opportunities (KVV, 2000: 17). On the other hand, the weight of the social structure is embraced. It is taken for granted that the position is subordinate and that the relevant situations are filled with conflicts and frustration. Consequently, the cognitive skills programme includes role-playing scenarios such as:

> You want to ask your boss about a day off, but you notice that he seems tired and irritated when he arrives in the morning.

'You' refers to the prisoner, who needs to get something important done on that particular day, but this depends on being given permission, as well as on the skills to handle the moodiness of 'your boss' (ibid.: 192). Besides 'your boss', three further figures recur in the scenarios, which are always fraught with trouble: 'your parole officer', 'your partner' and 'a friend'. Hence, the prisoner will learn to handle everyday frustration in the workplace, negotiate conflicts with superiors, manage stress in close relationships and say 'no' to old friends. Successful completion of the treatment entails a social status at a safe distance from that of the professional middle class, characterised by employment opportunities in the low-wage sector, the ability to follow instructions of superiors, hold a relationship together, pay bills on time and raise children. They are taught to be self-controlled, responsible, flexible and reliable while being barred from other parts of the cultural capital of the professional middle class involving purposefulness, integrity, independence and expertise.

This is a way of doing class, where the programme designers stage their 'whole social being' and the super ordinate status of the class to which they belong in role-playing scenarios and other disciplinary techniques where prisoners enact their subordination. At the same time, they stage their moral superiority. By undertaking to reform the underprivileged 'Other' despite previous transgressions and present obstacles, the professional middle class distinguishes itself as good. This distinction is implied in the rehabilitation practices themselves and, as Michelle Brown and Caleb Smith have shown, made explicit in prison-related cultural practices such as prison movies, television shows, novels and tourism (C. Smith, 2009; see also Michelle Brown, Chapter 6 of this volume). The enlightened subject demonstrates its goodness by being responsive to the misery of the underprivileged other. Using a prison setting, a drama of salvation, civilisation and high moral ground is enacted where the professional middle class occupies the centre place (Michelle Brown, 2009; C. Smith, 2009).

The other, sovereign pole of the punishing encounter acts as a corrective to the self-stylisation of the professional middle class as humanitarian and well meaning. Penal practices and discourses associated with institutional order interpellate a quite different subject, who is called on to display necessary cruelty, steadfastness and character in the face of forces capable of dissolving its existence. This prison tells a story of an invested subject who is confronted with the break up of social order. Violence is the driving force – both the embrace and the suppression of the violence of the prison. As Austin Sarat and Thomas Kearns have argued, the law suppresses its own violence, the violence of the punishment meted out, while feeding on images 'of an even greater violence outside, or before, the law', thereby 'fueling our worst fears and nightmarish beliefs about ourselves and one another' (Sarat and Kearns, 1993: 221–2). The Hobbesian state of nature supplies the sounding board. The punishing encounter between social classes is shot through with fear and violence. The fundamental fear is the social threat from below. This threat has a thousand names in the penal discourse on institutional order, each equally associated with uncivilised nature and ungovernable at heart (Hörnqvist, 2010). I will give just one example, which in recent years has attracted attention from both prison administrators and researchers: prison gangs.

The danger emanating from prison gangs is explicitly socially coded. For example, in threat assessments produced by the Swedish Prison Service, the topic of prison gangs is imbedded in a vivid narrative about young male offenders from immigrant backgrounds who have grown up in poverty-stricken neighbourhoods. This particular group is described as being 'without standards, dependent on gangs, violent and hateful' (KVS, 2002: 5). The social threat from local suburbs is super-imposed on the transnational threat posed by organised crime. The prison is conceived to be the physical location where this union takes place. Local prison governors were concerned and one of the surveys summarised their fears in the following manner:

> Most prisons mention that the gang members 'try to take over power in the prison and to control fellow inmates and the staff'. Other elements that are emphasized include threats and violence; solidarity among the inmates; that they are orderly, but 'you don't know what they are really doing'; that they influence staff decisions, file complaints, etc.; organized criminality; the recruitment of new members; the domination of fellow inmates; that they are young; that they have foreign background; and that they spread their message.
>
> (KVS, 2000: 11)

This somewhat rhapsodic characterisation leaves no doubt as to why prison gangs are dangerous. Young male prisoners from poor circum-stances and 'without standards' join forces with more seasoned criminals from other countries and become an alternative centre of authority, threatening to disturb prison order in the most fundamental sense, by challenging the sovereign power of the prison administration. By exten-sion, the order of the social world to which prisoner managers and

forensic psychologists are firmly attached is at stake, necessitating violence, determination and proper administrative procedures. The use of
force, in the form of high-security prisons and administrative segregation, often goes beyond what is necessary to maintain institutional order.
The excessive violence in the contemporary prison system has been
attributed to an idea of civil death, according to which any vestiges of
the former subject must be eradicated, echoing past institutions such as
colonial slavery and the soul's salvation. The prisoner will then be
reborn: 'in the fiction of civil death', Colin Dayan writes, 'the state
reinvents what happens after literal death' (Dayan, 2011: 70).
Consequently, even the most recalcitrant offender will gradually be
broken down and transformed into an ordinary citizen (C. Smith,
2009). Whether the conditions constitute cruel and unusual punishment in legal terms, they sustain the underlying order by manifesting the
ability of the professional middle class to take action, faced with the
threat of a wider social breakdown. The sovereign prison thus inscribes
the social threat from below in a narrative of pacification where prisoners pass through a stage of civil death and are reborn in the hands of
designers, reformers and managers, who figure as chief engineers in the
maintenance of social order.

The underlying social antagonism is thus simultaneously demonised
and domesticated. While the concrete manifestations of the social
threat are purged by violence, more opaque forms are simultaneously
summoned by the same violence. This ambiguity is typical for tran-
scendental fantasies. 'Fantasy', says Žižek, conceals the horror for social
antagonism, 'yet at the same time it creates what it purports to conceal,
its "repressed" point of reference' (Žižek, 1997: 7). The violence feeds
fantasies of what goes on at the other end, escaping the punishing agent
and fuelling the very fears it should have erased. Further, the same
fantasies help us orient in the world. In the Lacanian tradition, fantasy
gives direction to existence and supports the subject's sense of reality.
This is different from – and complementary to – the social sense of place
in the world emphasised by Bourdieu. Fantasy 'takes the subject beyond
his or her nothingness', Bruce Fink argues, 'and supplies a sense of being'
(Fink, 1995: 60). Without fantasy, the existence would disintegrate.
Given that 'a fantasy constitutes our desire, provides its co-ordinates'
(Žižek, 1997: 7) or makes objects and practices desirable in the first
place, the subject would not know what to do. The fantasies implicated
in the excessive violence are vital for the world-making capacity of
representations and for their ability to guide the desire. Consequently,

they secure the existence in the most fundamental sense – sustaining social order while securing personal existence.

SENTIMENTAL PLEASURES AND OBSCENE EXCITEMENT

The recent revival of Durkheim in the sociology of punishment strives to understand the narratives communicated through the prison. Just like in the section above, the focus rests on the cognitive aspect. Philip Smith (2008: 8) formulates the basic assumption that punishment must be conceived of as 'communicative acts in which messages are being sent'. Yet imprisonment is not only about meaning and messages but also, and perhaps more fundamentally, about desires, fears and fantasies. Durkheim himself was not insensitive to the emotional aspect. On the contrary: 'Passion', he said, 'is the soul of punishment' (Durkheim, 1893/ 1933: 86). However, for Durkheim the passions involved were tied to the crime. Vengeance, satisfaction and other emotions accompanying the punishment were seen to be provoked by the transgression. There was no room for the passions of punishment itself, independent from desires provoked by transgressions.

To account for the full scale of passions involved, we need to move beyond the cultural turn. I will pick up on Nietzsche's observation that 'in punishment there is so much *festive!*' (Nietzsche, 1989: 67; emphasis in original). Nietzsche brought attention to the mix of pleasure, fear and excitement, which was traceable to specificities of the punishing encounter rather than to a crime. There is much more involved than revenge and redress. The prison-related desires and emotions cover contempt for otherness, desire for order, identification with suffering, lust for transgressions and pleasure in unbounded power. It will be assumed that the emotions affect 'the entire social being', just like the classifications and narratives discussed in the last section; and just like them, desires and emotions are caught in the fundamental tension between humanitarianism and sovereignty.

To understand the pleasure that can be drawn from the act of punishment, we must take a closer look at the relationship between the punisher and the punished. The specificities of the punishing encounter are essential: that it takes place under conditions where the latter is subjected to the former's physical disposal and classificatory power. The punishing subject has a temporary hold over the convicted body, being given the right to inflict pain, suspending conventional considerations of morality and utility. This is not simply the barbaric pleasure in cruelty emphasised by Nietzsche, but also the right and the safe position from which cruelty can be exercised and pleasure extracted. Jacques Lacan later elaborated on this pleasure through the concept of *jouissance*. Jouissance denotes human enjoyment unbounded by rational and moral considerations. It is not pleasure pure and simple; jouissance is pleasure inextricably mixed with excitement and suffering.

In opposition to the Freudian *Lustprinzip*, which is preoccupied with avoiding pain and obtaining a safe amount of pleasure, Lacan (1992) maintained that the subject strives to go beyond every limitation to enjoyment, even if that involves suffering and destruction. The drive is manifested in love, sexuality, crime, religion or wherever the subject encounters 'the intensity of the real' (Žižek, 1997: 61). Punishment is one such area. As noted by Klaus Mladek (2004: 215), jouissance is 'intimately tied to the field of pain, death and suffering – the results of punishment'. For this reason, to the extent that pleasure is involved in punishment, this notion appears well placed to account for it. Lacan made jouissance to the central point of the law: 'That is clearly the essence of law – to divide up, distribute, or reattribute everything that counts as jouissance' (Lacan, 1999: 3). The law regulates everything that can give rise to unbounded pleasure, in particular punishments. To explain the law's regulatory function, Lacan turns to the concept of usufruct. Usufruct refers to the right of using and enjoying something without being its proper owner. Conventionally, it regulates access to property and not, as in this case, the temporary disposal of another person's body. The law transfers the right to enjoy the other's body to the punishing subject, which can use it unrestrained by considerations of utility (Lacan, 1999: 2f.).[3] On condition that the body is returned relatively unscathed when the sentence is served, the punishing subject is free to extract jouissance from the other.

Just as punishments change over time, so too do the concomitant pleasures and excitements. The prison corresponded to a new economy of jouissance, a shift in pleasures and excitements on the part of the punishing subject. The pleasure economy evolved around the same two poles as the prison narratives: the humanitarian and the sovereign. The prison was heralded as a humanitarian reform by a bourgeoisie appalled by public mutilations (Foucault, 1977). Nietzsche (2011: 49), commenting on the history of punishment, spoke of an ongoing

[3] See also Fink (1995) and Mladek (2004).

sublimation – or literally *Vergeistigung* – of cruelty, evolving from base blood thirst to more intricate refinement. With the birth of the prison, John Bender (1987: 35) remarks, '"sentences" came to be served rather than executed'. The infliction of pain was implicated in a future-oriented story and extended over time, rather than a drama ending on the town square, followed by a rapid diminution of excitement once justice had been done. The placid pleasures of the bourgeoisie came to be expressed in the panoptical principle. Writing on his never-realised model prison, Jeremy Bentham (1995: 48) emphasised that the gates of Panopticon should be 'thrown wide open to the body of the curious at large'. Everybody would have free access to the facilities and be attracted by their own voyeuristic curiosity. Bentham (1995: 45) thought of the observation of the prisoners as a 'great and constant fund of entertainment', a pastime in which even family members could participate. Joshua Jebb, who designed Pentonville, one of the very first modern prisons, envisioned that his prison would attract well-dressed visitors, strolling and conversing in the prison halls, reminiscent of a contemporary shopping mall (P. Smith, 2008: 71).

The prison was thus originally conceived as a form of amusement park for the enlightened classes, where the sight of the punished would satisfy and edify spectators. But the prison would never be opened to the public, and little is known about how these refined sentiments were satisfied (see Michelle Brown, Chapter 6). Caleb Smith (2009) has argued that the humanitarian emotions surrounding the prison were expressed in the sentimental novel, which was one of the most popular literary genres of the nineteenth century. The sentimental evolved around the socially conditioned meeting with the other. 'In the sentimental mode, the free middle-class subject embraces a suffering other', Smith writes, 'and draws the victim into the community of the human, producing an affective charge of tearful sympathy' (C. Smith, 2009: 57f.). The sentimental pleasure presupposes a suffering other. Yet it is not essentially the identification with the suffering object that causes the pleasure. As Lynn Festa (2006: 175) argues, in the sentimental mode the readers primarily identify with each other and the pleasure stems from 'the image of oneself enjoying the image of the suffering object'. That is, while the readers think that they identify with the suffering object, what they in fact enjoy is their own self-image. Transferred to the prison, once again we are confronted with the same circular character of the encounter. In the humanitarian-minded literature the imagined prisoners help stage a self-image of the punishing subject, with which it can identify and enjoy, just like real prisoners served as walk-ons enacting middle-class narratives of themselves in the treatment programmes.

In the repressive mode, the pleasure is linked to violence and transgression. The jouissance of the prison involves a kind of civilised excess – where the violence is both civilised and excessive. On the one hand, the prison represents a perfect order of violence distributed according to careful administrative assessments, grounded in well-established risk factors and fundamentally restrained by the law. The imaginary of the prison as a punishment based on the twin authorities of law and science appealed to the humanitarian sentiments of the Enlightenment bourgeoisie, positioning itself against the bloodthirsty old aristocracy. It indicated self-restraint and rendered the violence invisible. On the other hand, the prison represents excessive violence tied to an obscene pleasure. This feature, Žižek (1997: 73) argues, is endemic in all forms of organised violence; 'the obscene "nightly" law (superego) necessarily accompanies, as its shadowy double, the "public" Law'. The obscene pleasure is implicated in the enunciation of regular law. The desire for transgression is generated by the instal-lation of prohibition, signalling enjoyment beyond the imposed restraint. The promise of such enjoyment is vital, as 'the law can sustain its authority only if the subjects hear in it the echo of the obscene unconditional self-assertion' (Žižek, 2006: 337). The obscene authorises the law and makes it acceptable.

The attraction of unbounded enjoyment can be felt from both sides of the law, by those who are set to enforce it as well as by those who are potentially punished. Yet the subjects best positioned to hear 'the echo of the obscene unconditional self-assertion' belong to the former category. Individuals in dominant social positions tend to have a higher morality, in the sense of standing above the law, and a more relaxed relationship to existing laws compared to other social groups (Boltanski, 2011: 151). Both qualities, the instrumental relationship and the deserved entitlement, are connected, as the restrained violence can turn into excess whenever the regular law is perceived to stand in the way of a higher law, which condones transgressions. Further, the very element of transgression serves to reinforce the pleasure. Lacan speaks of 'the jouissance of transgression' excited by the fact that the subject knows that the action is forbidden (Lacan, 1992: 195). It is moreover a secret violence in that it is officially denied. Perhaps more than anything else, that circumstance contributes to the cohesion of the punishing agent. The obscene law condoning transgressions is 'the primordial lie that founds a community' (Žižek, 1994: 57). Every member of the social group must relate to the collective injustices committed, and to the collective disavowal of the same injustices. This lie founds the community by forging bonds of 'solidarity-in-guilt' (Žižek, 1994: 58). Consequently there is no need to take actual part in the violence to experience the obscene supplement of the prison regulations. Everyone knows, and what one does not know the imagination compensates for (see Michelle Brown, Chapter 6).

There is no contradiction between excesses of sovereignty and the placid pleasures associated with humanitarianism. Instead, the obscene and the sentimental form different poles in the underlying economy of jouissance and rely on the same basic mechanisms. In both cases, the pleasure stems from core features of the punishing encounter and is extracted from the other´s body. And in both cases, the pleasure is mediated by the imagination and further reinforced by the institutional form of the prison. The punishment is a realisation of state directives in a dense web of routines. From a psychoanalytic perspective, punishment involving bureaucratisation and selfless duty provides additional excitement. Exacting punishment not for one's own sake but as a cog in a complex administrative machinery for abstract goals provides surplus pleasure for the participants. For this reason it has been maintained that Marquis de Sade's 'pleasure palaces resemble penitentiaries rather than brothels' (Mladek, 2004: 218). With regard to the example of historical Nazism, Žižek (1997: 55) argues that 'the basic lesson of the perverse ritual also applies here: this "bureaucratization" was in itself a source of an additional *jouissance*'. The excessive violence organised in the institutional form of imprisonment thus enhances the pleasure. Similarly, by ordering the efforts in a bureaucratic scheme for a higher cause rather than for the subject's own satisfaction, the jouissance drawn from the compassionate self-image is further reinforced. In the sentimental mode, like in the sovereign mode, the administrative rationality facilitates the punishing agents' identification with each other.

CLASS-SPECIFIC OR HUMAN, ALL TOO HUMAN?

This chapter has probed into the links between the prison and class formation. For the professional middle class, the prison provides a venue on which it enacts desires, fears and fantasies in a punishing encounter with the working class. In the encounter, the professional middle class distinguishes itself in all aspects of its social existence and not only in relation to crime and desistance from crime. It constitutes itself as a social class – and as individuals. Through the desires, fears and fantasies enacted in the prison practices and discourses, the professional middle class comes to know itself – letting every member of the class know what to desire, what to fear and what the world looks like and what their own role is, thereby constituting it in relation to other social classes.

Much the same mechanisms of middle-class formation are presumably at work in a range of institutions other than the prison. If so, is there anything special about the punishing encounter from the perspective of class formation? The specific contribution of the prison should be sought in *the composition* of categories and fantasies, fears and pleasures. The self-constitution of the professional middle class in the punishing encounter is marked by the fundamental tension between humanitarianism and sovereignty. In the humanitarian narratives evolving around the improvement of the underprivileged other, self-control and responsibility are the principles organising the subject's social world. Self-control and responsibility account for the social trajectory of individuals and why the middle classes are relatively well off and form the backbone of society, whereas the lack of self-control and responsibility account for the assortment of moral and social shortcomings typical of prisoners and, by extension, the working class. Sovereign prison practices and discourses rely on other categories to describe the world and the necessity to take action, articulating the underlying fear for the break up of social order. An entire universe of security risk signifiers disassembles the prison collective and reassembles a unitary middle-class subject willing to exercise violence. Further, compared to earlier forms of punishment, the prison corresponds to a new economy of jouissance, a shift in pleasures and excitements on side of the punishing subject. It springs not simply from exercising violence and watching the suffering of the social other: the pleasure economy of the prison revolves around the sentimental and the obscene, where the former is associated with compassionate goodness and the latter with sovereign display. In the face of a suffering other, the humanitarian efforts involve sentimental pleasure deriving from a self-image of cultural refinement. The sovereign regulation, on the other hand, entails obscene pleasure beyond legal limitations. Yet both the sentimental and the obscene pleasures rely on the same characteristics of the punishing encounter: the temporary disposal of the other's body, the suspension of notions of utility and the bureaucratisation and selfless realisation of state interests.

The question remains whether the narratives and jouissance of the prison punishment are class-specific rather than, as Nietzsche (1986) would have it, 'human, all too human'. The prison is firmly rooted in desires and fantasies that transcend class boundaries, and this is arguably what accounts for its enduring political popularity. The narratives of humanitarianism and sovereignty – the sentimental and obscene pleasures – are by no means confined to the professional middle class. No single desire, fear, fantasy or pleasure is class-specific. As it became the dominant form of punishment, the narratives and pleasures associated with the prison spread to other social classes and came to structure the attachment of the subject to the social world, not only for the immediate actors but for everyone who could share the fantasies and draw jouissance from the punishing encounter. The audience in general, or 'the penal spectator' (Michelle Brown, 2009: 21; see also Michelle Brown, Chapter 6 of this volume), could also tap into the circulating economy of pleasure. Consequently, the prison would have a role to play in the formation of *other* social classes. Yet is it the same role? Available studies suggest that the working class relates to the prison through different categories than the middle class. With regard to the former, the prison primarily appeals to notions of respectability, conventional morality and straightforward punitivity (Lamont, 2000; Skeggs, 2004; Svallfors, 2006). Respectability and punitivity rather than humanitarianism and sovereignty would thus be the main categories for the working class. Although the question cannot be pursued further here, one hypothesis is that every class makes use of the prison in specific ways. Then, should the class differences in the use made of the prison turn out to be less pronounced than expected, there will always be a difference in terms of authorship; the circumstance that the professional middle class is the class that acts in and through the prison. It was conceived by the Enlightenment bourgeoisie, and all parts of the punishing encounter – rehabilitation, security, placement, assessment, architecture – are designed by the professional middle class, which accounts for the circular character of the relationship between this particular class and the prison. Whereas the prison shapes the desires, fears and fantasies of all social classes, in the case of the professional middle class – and only in the case of the professional middle class – its desires, fears and fantasies went into shaping the prison. For other classes, the creative moment is missing. Hence no other class could be said to create *itself* through the prison.

6

PENAL SPECTATORSHIP AND THE CULTURE OF PUNISHMENT

Michelle Brown

As penal spectators, we watch across vast culture-scapes where penality flourishes explicitly and implicitly in narratives and commentaries structured through penal correlates of prison, detention, surveillance, judgment and accusation. We screen execution chambers and prison tiers. We tour defunct prisons. We look toward prisons near and far, at our borders and across war zones, vicariously exploring the meanings and limits of acts rendered both visible and invisible within them. In this way, we live our everyday lives amid complex, but often fleeting, anecdotal appearances of the penal, even as punishment emerges as a structuring force in globalising frameworks. In these contexts, we could benefit profoundly from a structure of critique (Butler, 2004, 2005, 2009), a framework from which to challenge our distanced selves in relation to our own place in the culture of punishment.

In this chapter, I explore how punitive understandings of the prison circulate across culture in a manner that depends upon a troubling distance between the punisher and the punished. Because the axis of penal incarceration in the USA extends along distinct race and class lines, a privileged group of citizens (white, middle-class and politically powerful) have remained carefully removed from the experience of penal incarceration even as they have supported and sustained the largest punitive political turn in history. These penal spectators – citizens who have no necessity to address the problem of hyper-incarceration – develop cultural meanings and understandings about punishment by way of what is available in popular discourse, including media representations, prison tourism and political debates about new war and immigration prisons

(Michelle Brown, 2009). In its attention to the meanings and imaginative processes of ordinary citizens, the concept of penal spectatorship affords us a site from which to analyse why prison persists. In such contexts, where individuals only know penal incarceration at a distance, the dynamics of penal participation are slippery and can quickly devolve into complex, often voyeuristic, frameworks which privilege various kinds of punitive, individualistic judgment and the practice of imprisonment. As penal spectators, who sanction – in our approval and witnessing – the infliction of pain from a distance, we risk overlooking the reasons for democratic oversight of the project of punishment and, more broadly, justifications for the prohibition of pain (see Barker, Chapter 7; McBride, Chapter 11).

PENAL SPECTATORSHIP

To conceive of ourselves as penal spectators asks us to consider a rarely remarked-upon set of aspects about punishment's practice. First, it fore-grounds the fact that for those of us without direct connections to formal institutions of punishment, a kind of experiential distance defines our relationship to its practice (see Barker, Chapter 7). Such distance shields us from the most fundamental feature of punishment: its infliction of pain. The remoteness of the penal spectator guarantees that his or her imagining of punishment is haunted by abstract potentialities of danger and insecurity against surprisingly rigid logics of retribution, making spectators a cultural agent and formidable force in the construction of pain. In gossip and conversational chat, leisure and recreation, as well as media and political commentary, the exploration of inflicted pain as nothing other than an appropriate and desirable response to other people's pain and violence is in many ways a naturalised part of the contemporary American landscape of punishment. Part of my argument is that this kind of imagining has taken on dangerous propensities in recent times, disconnected from the aims of crime control and most evident in the scale of penal incarceration in the USA and its global exportation of prisons. Alongside this, the terms of debate surrounding the meanings of punishment in culture are less varied and increasingly difficult to alter. Rather, we see a case in which the very need to conceal law's violence and the pain of punishment erodes, where accountability in authority and legitimacy is presented as without need of democratic check and where the pain of punishment is foregrounded as a new and acceptable currency for public exchange – even as the practice and experience of punishment by prisoners, detainees and the stateless remain remarkably removed from public life (see Barker, Chapter 7). Importantly, this is a dangerous discursive and rhetorical manoeuvre because it is an acceptance of the infliction of pain with no oversight or civic engagement with punishment's practice. As criminologist Nils Christie (2000; 2007: 103) argues, punishment – or 'pain delivery in western society' – is 'expressed through representation'. If punishment were brought close,

> a whole row of new questions would have to be raised: Was the punishment one where ordinary people – including the victim – took part in all aspects of the decision? Did they take part in the actual execution of the punishment? Did they all – one after the other – carry out the work inside the penal establishments? How much did everybody in society know about all the details? What could be done to increase knowledge? If one hesitated about bringing in local TV, ought they not instead to hesitate to bring in punishment? If pain is too bad to be executed by everybody, and seen by everybody, is it not because it is too bad? If the purpose of pain was pain, was it then arranged so that this becomes crystal clear to everybody?
>
> (Christie, 2007: 104)

The very outlandishness of this transaction in a contemporary framework reveals that it is the pain of a distant punishment that is argued to speak most powerfully and effectively for citizens, spanning in its authority as the voice for victims of crime and a new global platform from which to define human worth and citizenship against constructions of criminality, including prisoners, detainees, 'enemy combatants', the 'undocumented', 'bogus refugees', and the otherwise 'non-citizen'. In this way, penal spectatorship achieves ideological dominance.

Such processes and propensities point fundamentally to what occurs in societies where frameworks of punishment are foundationally privileged – at a distance. Such distance also shields us from the democratic burden of punishment as a kind of cultural work: something we do that requires intention, deliberation and human check, that has effects both intended and unintended – and can and should be interrogated relentlessly. Although public works and projects of democracy, prisons are not frequented like libraries, highways, memorials, parks or state houses, but rather are carefully concealed, making the cultural imaginary that much more formative in our understandings of punishment. The penal spectator thus makes decisions about punishment in a manner that denies any real democratic engagement in interrogating the project of punishment and overlooks the power to punish as a special aspect of human agency, always fundamentally chained in its assertion to the production of human pain and its restraint.

This foreclosure depends upon a complex kind of penal subjectivity manifest in the rise of penal spectatorship. Here, subjectivity can be understood 'as both an empirical reality and an analytic category: the agonistic and practical activity of engaging identity and fate, patterned and felt in historically contingent settings and mediated by institutional processes and cultural forms... a strategy of existence and a material means of governance' (Biehl et al., 2007: 5). The penal spectator then is not to be misconstrued as an individualised identity, monolithic and static in its appearance, or as a pathology, but rather as a temporal possibility and proclivity, a logic which expresses durability and prevalence in a contemporary framework amid particular sets of cultural conditions. Penal spectatorship is a subjectivity in which we all engage. In this respect, its very breadth and contradictory qualities open up key points of contest, resistance and the possibility of transformation.

> Subjectivity is not just the outcome of social control or the unconscious; it also provides the ground for subjects to think through their circumstances and to feel through their contradictions, and in doing so, to inwardly endure experiences that would otherwise be outwardly unbearable. Subjectivity is the means of shaping sensibility. It is fear and optimism, anger and forgiveness, lamentation and pragmatism, chaos and order. It is the anticipation and articulation of self-criticism and renewal.
>
> (Biehl et al., 2007: 14)

Because subjectivity is the ground from which we think through our lives and relations to others, it is a critical source for alternative ways of being. More often, it is a process through which to engage the ambiguities of our subject positions. For instance, it is quite possible that citizens see themselves as the targets of surveillance in a culture of control – at school, work, home, etc. (T. Monahan, 2010) – even as they see themselves in other contexts as potential crime victims (Simon, 2007). Such complex orientations open up room for contesting hegemonic discourses and building empathy with groups, like the incarcerated, who are state targets in a far more dramatic physical and material way (Michelle Brown, 2012). The penal spectator, nonetheless, is a kind of dominant subjectivity practice that denies or prohibits this kind of reflection, which is in part how the prison risks permanence.

For instance, penal spectatorship includes practices and engagements that we ordinarily do not conceive of as caught up within the spectrum of punishment at all – moments where cultural scripts and meanings about punishment are invoked in everyday conversation, ordinary events and popular performances distanced from the formal institutions of punishment. Daily we engage in institutions that map our experiences and decision-making through penal frameworks. We watch from within and across a massive mediascape in which films, television dramas, the internet, video games and news commentary all lay out scenarios and events from which we try out punishment – and theorise its correlate judgment, blame, pain and accountability (Rafter, 2006; Michelle Brown, 2009). We navigate institutions designed increasingly and commonly through penal architecture, now mundane security features of everyday life – gated buildings and communities and a wide array of new surveillance techniques at home, school and work, as well as in our leisure and travel (Simon, 2007). We witness the transformation of public space through spatial exclusion policies that merge civil and criminal law, leaving the homeless, the poor, the mentally ill and addicts in exile (Beckett and Herbert, 2010; Beckett and Murakawa, 2012). We weigh in on political debates about immigration, detention and economic crisis that legitimise penal responses and impact the lives of distant others (Aas, 2011; Bosworth, 2012; see also Kaufman and Bosworth, Chapter 9 of this volume). Daily the relationships between punishment and social control materialise around us – but often in a manner that obscures the nature of this practice as anything more than a distant look or fleeting glance. Practices of punishment are strategic sites for democratic and critical inquiry, and they serve uniquely to depict the ways in which collective action – the social – is fundamentally and with intentionality directed at creating exclusion and suffering. And yet punishment performs this work in ways that are largely invisible. When individuals explore the meaning of punishment in popular culture, television news, recreational tours, immigration debates and military service at faraway prisons, they ultimately are exploring and trying out justifications for the infliction of pain or its prohibition. In this regard, we are encouraged to consider just how far, by way of culture, our penal gaze may carry.

PENAL CULTURE

Penal iconography has a salient role in the formation of cultural understandings about punishment, particularly for citizens who remain fundamentally distanced from the day-to-day practice of punishment. In order to understand punishment broadly and at work in culture, as sociologist David Garland insists, 'we need to study not just the grandiloquent public statements which are occasionally made but also the pragmatic repetitive routines of daily practice, for these routines contain within them distinctive patterns of meaning and symbolic forms which are enacted and expressed every time a particular procedure is adopted, a technical language used, or a specific sanction imposed' (Garland 1990: 255).[1] Sites of entertainment and leisure, the performances and images of popular culture present us with the most powerful place in which the practice of imprisonment has been re-enacted to the largest audience. Films, television, video games and the internet often serve as our first access points and cultural resources from which to make sense of punishment and its proper place in the social order. Punishment remains a site of discursive fascination and proliferation across media genres and platforms precisely because of its distance and invisibility. The prison tour, even as it brings visitors into contact with the original architecture and machinery of the penitentiary, acts carefully to distance us as outsiders in its privileging of cultural associations and stereotypical images of criminals over a more thoughtful structure, which links history with the unprecedented contemporary dimensions and sociology of imprisonment. Similarly, the scandalous photos at Abu Ghraib, the public debate about detention and interrogation practices at Guantánamo and the moral outrage that has led to the criminalisation of immigration and the rise of detention and deportation regimes are possible in part due to the privilege of distance. These are acts, practices, performances and institutions that occur in conjunction with hyper-incarceration; have institutional roots at state and federal prisons in the USA (including domestic efforts at isolation like the supermax prisons); and are juridical outcomes of the pursuit of a new legal architecture post-9/11 which openly privileges exception, executive power and securitisation efforts around non-crime-related problems.

In each of these cases, distance affords spectators a space in which they need not do many things, including engage the complexities, contradictions and tragic qualities of punishment nor reflect upon their own role in its formation. This is critical because, at such a distance, direct deliberation and interrogation of punishment rarely materialises in the everyday life of the spectator; instead, the prison is naturalised in social life. Spectatorship normalises what should be cause

[1] On culture, see also Garland (2001c, 2005a, 2005b, 2006) and Ferrell et al. (2008).

for concern across cultural life in a manner that is extensive and portentous. I explore these possibilities by way of the examples discussed above, each a brief glimpse of culture in action. These three cases include: (i) the historically most prominent site for prison iconography: media representations; (ii) the rise of prison tourism; and (iii) the exportation of prisons and securitisation of displacement.

PRISON ICONOGRAPHY

In American culture, citizens are much more likely to screen the prison rather than visit it. They are consequently familiar with imprisonment, not through its institutional practice but through its cultural representation, and this is an important site for the construction of a cultural memory that is largely iconic. Images build narratives of punishment that perhaps began historically at the cinema but now end at an infinite number of points across social life, where image and practice blur. In many of these settings we see the prison through a deeply structured cinematic legacy with specific tendencies, long-standing conventions and its own cinematic vocabulary. For instance, 'prison films' have historically operated as primers in prison sociology, introducing their viewers to the mechanical daily routines and bureaucratic processes of imprisonment typically through the entry of a central character into the overwhelming subculture of the institution. Fantasies of wrongful conviction, violence, escape and redemption are central elements of these films that rarely engage the contemporary dynamics of hyperincarceration in its foundations or effects.

More broadly, penality circulates in many of the daily declarations that make up film and television's most popular programming: prisons, prisoners and prison guards make brief, spectacular appearances. Documentary and docu-drama, two of the most prolific and accessible genres of penal representation, illustrate many of popular culture's tendencies in the depiction of punishment. Prime-time drama, ranging from Hollywood Box Office's *Oz* to the British *Bad Girls*, blurs convention with Microsoft and National Broadcasting Company's (MSNBC) *Lock-Up* series, Arts and Entertainment Network's (A&E) *Investigative Reports*, History Channel's *Big House* and National Geographic's *Lockdown*, all of which rely sensationally upon penal structures and motifs: the titillating promise to take their viewers 'inside' the real world of gangs, drugs, violence, women behind bars, death row and maximum security. The documentary programmes privilege the notion of a normalised empirical reality, often beginning with the stark statistics of prison demographics and expansion. The spectatorial enters in as producers point to the extraordinary (which is now quite ordinary and redundant across television) circumstances under which they were able to gain access to the most hidden and dangerous institutions. With reliance upon prison workers, inmates and experts, producers construct a narrative that is presented in its objectives as an effort to inform its audience by revealing the realities of prison life. However, in their reliance upon ominous soundtracks against often repetitive or mundane footage of prison spaces, converted into fast-paced zooms, pans and dissolves, producers strain to create a coherent narrative that is framed as a documentary but is steeped in sensationalism. Through a heavy dependence upon individualised frameworks, often following a prisoner or guard through the daily routine of incarceration, the films rarely effectively create sociological connections between structure and agency, but instead pivot precariously from the mundane conditions of prison life to pure spectacle. Episodic in structure, such treatments are also discrete, brief and emphasise the most sensational aspects of prison life – violence and its potentiality – in a manner that rarely interrogates any of the social conditions driving violence, penal incarceration or its social effects (see Hörnqvist, Chapter 5).

Nonetheless, such engagements prove seductive environments from which penal spectators may peek into the world of imprisonment – and claim legitimacy and authority simultaneously. Within such a context, a less reflexive, far more accusatory space emerges in which a kind of perpetual judgment and authority is given privilege. Here, prisons are still places where a disproportionate focus upon guards and victims often leads to the reproduction of stereotypes and a pathologisation of the individual – as these settings become universalised in a manner where ordinary actors engage in extraordinary violence, thereby closing off discussions of the political, social and cultural conditions in which violence takes a startlingly specific form. Here, the key actor is not the prisoner, nor his or her custodian, but the moral spectator invested with juridical authority, imagining punishment. Punishment is then most often, in late modernity, an imagined exercise of judgment. Recent discourse on the representation of pain increasingly insists that from this imagining must emerge some consideration of the nature of responsibilisation (Butler, 2004; Das, 2007). Consequently, part of the peculiarity of punishment as a cultural form derives from the relationship of this very specific kind of looking with a politics of affect

(Bandes, 1999; Berlant, 2011; Karstedt et al., 2011). Recent work on penal representation claims that there is a power to films about prison in their ability to reveal, benchmark, defend, keep alive and humanise prisoners as people (Tzanelli et al., 2005; Wilson and O'Sullivan, 2005; Rafter and Brown, 2011). Cinema remains, from this perspective, a viable resource in the pursuit of penal reform. Socio-legal scholar Austin Sarat (2000) argues, similarly, that cinema has an ethical pedagogy to it, one in which the viewer may actively choose positions, in that:

> Film gives testimony to the fact that, as Morson... says about narrative, time is always 'a field of possibilities, (and that) each moment has a set of possible events... that could take place in it'. It quite literally restores vision and brings the field of possibility into view. It 'recreates the fullness of time...' When we watch the moving image, we have the chance to confront what was, what is, what might be, multiply, fluidly, and often in ways that are hard for us to grasp.
>
> (Sarat, 2000: 40)

In this conceptualisation, an alternative discourse, one that denies the permanence of the prison, is one in which the field of vision is disrupted, together with the identities that depend upon that structure. Images that ignite, provoke and mobilise are often both penal and disruptive – historically they are images that have 'pointed somewhere else, beyond themselves, to a life and to a precariousness that they could not show' (Butler, 2004: 150). For penal representation to do a more critical work, when invoking these images it must open up a set of questions that it cannot (and does not) close off. As Judith Butler writes, 'For representation to convey the human, then, representation must not only fail, but it must *show* its failure. There is something unrepresentable that we nevertheless seek to represent, and that paradox must be retained in the representation we give' (ibid.: 144). The irony, then, is that the position of critique, challenge and interrogation that must be struggled for, depends, in the end, upon representation. Such strategies carry over into other kinds of cultural engagement with punishment.

PRISON TOURISM

Another cultural arena in which penal spectatorship is achieving new and unprecedented possibility lies in the realm of prison tourism. Across the USA, commercialised tours of defunct prisons are gaining in popularity, attracting hundreds of thousands of visitors annually. These sites include such recognisable institutions as Alcatraz and Eastern State Penitentiary, but also feature a wide range of lesser-known former state penitentiaries in nearly every state. Tourists walk through tier blocks, casually exploring the decaying remains of the cells, wandering in and out of them and sometimes being locked up for a few titillating seconds. They stand in empty mess halls, examine left-over medical equipment in hospital wards, gaze curiously into showers, climb up into guard towers, stroll through the exercise yard and linger at death row. Their wanderings take them through former cafeterias, libraries, classrooms and industrial quarters. Stops are made along the way at various points where stabbings, assaults, rapes and murders occurred. These are some of most descriptive and prolonged moments of the guided tours, where escorts engage in complex narrative constructions, much like a good ghost story, emphasising at the conclusion that all of this took place 'right where we are standing'.

Two kinds of penitentiary tours have achieved unusual levels of popularity: the prison haunted house and the overnight prison ghost hunt. Both now run annually across the USA from spring into late fall, with ticket sales the largest factor in preservation budgets. These tours are unique in a variety of ways, but also simply convert conventional aspects of the basic day tour into what Eastern State describes in its promotional ads as 'cellblocks of terror'. For ghost hunts, groups arrive late in the evening and are given a quick tour of the premises, with special attention to 'haunted' sites – spaces where assaults, murders and executions occurred. Along the way, some experience the thrill of being locked into cells or encountering ghastly re-enactments of executions. Everyone is eventually left on their own, locked in with flashlights and curiosity, allowed complete freedom to roam the dilapidated premises, searching for ghosts, exploring the empty space and periodically scaring one another. In the early morning hours, tired and cold, participants assemble in the souvenir shop, make their purchases and begin the long trek home. In the case of the prison haunted house, the penitentiary tour takes on many theme park characteristics, modelling the event after the most stereotypical and, of course, frightening aspects of imprisonment in a carefully controlled setting (see Hörnqvist, Chapter 5). Across the Halloween haunted prison sites, tourists enter and initially take on the role of prisoners, with tour staff posing as guards in a simulation of intake processes, yelling and playfully harassing visitors, forcing them into lines along dark corridors of the prison. As visitors wind their way through reconstructed blocks of the prison, they are surrounded by prisoner-actors, all of whom take on a stereotypical portrayal of the psychotic prisoner, reaching out from cells and jumping out of hidden corners. Medical wards are peopled with 'mad' doctors who are performing experiments upon prisoners. Physical space is depicted as an industrial ruin: toxic, damp, mist-enshrouded and electrified. The prison is configured as an empty historical and haunted space, informed vaguely by the design of institutional daily life, where you are 'abandoned, but you may not be alone. Scared straight?'[2]

Significantly, prison tourism exists within a set of larger sociological patterns in relation to late-modern tourism, one that demonstrates a growing interest among consumers with the spectacle of death, disaster and atrocity. Dark tourism is directed at assessing the manner in which these kinds of limited experiences have become patterned into consumption, how such a phenomenon is itself a product of late modernity and how social life, in turn, is transformed by such economies. These bodies of literature include Seaton's *thanatourism* (1999), Rojek's 'black spot' tourism (1993), and even 'grief tourism', where individuals and groups travel to the site of terrible events (Foley and Lennon, 2000; Sturken, 2007; Sharpley and Stone, 2009). The spectator in these circumstances, the 'dark tourist', is not someone who comes because of some sort of specialised interest – a personal historical connection, a need to witness, a research or informational project (significantly, this group is argued to be the minority of most tourists at these sites) – but rather shows up out of serendipity, the direction of the tourism industry or simple curiosity on a cursory outing. They are then the otherwise distanced spectators who are just passing through. Among these tours, 'former sites of incarceration – places where the intentional state-sanctioned infliction of punishment, pain and privation took place – are among the most popular' (Strange and Kempa, 2003: 389).

This complex intersection of popularity and penality deserves careful theoretical interrogation and empirical attention as new life is given to dead prisons in a society that imprisons on an unprecedented scale with unforeseeable long-term consequences. As tempting as it is to disregard sites of penal leisure and entertainment as pure or morbid spectacle, such practices serve as important sources of evidence about how citizens attempt, or fail to attempt, to understand and process the meanings surrounding punishment. Even more significantly, because they

[2] Based upon Eastern State Penitentiary 2006 promotional brochure: 'Terror behind the walls: Halloween at Eastern State Penitentiary'.

function often as primary engagements by citizens with punishment, the nature of this engagement – its distance, its easy comfort, its sustenance of cultural fantasy – demands a deeper consideration of the ways in which punishers are linked to the punished. Connections exist, but they are dependent upon a deep cultural imaginary that actively shapes any sociality or solidarity derived from penal practice. In the context of the prison tour, distance from the project of punishment is key – and belies the manner in which emptiness, absence and silence are fundamental to its unchallenged practice. Looking away from punishment's present to its imagined, ghostly past is one way in which the project of imprisonment persists, dependent upon cultural proclivities and a preferred distance to any acknowledgement of the violence of punishment itself. Another more critical perspective is one which forever traces the everyday configurations of penality to its most overt instance: the infliction of pain in order to remind all that with every look, we have a choice. For this reason, on the great American prison tour, the possibility of producing 'a visitor capable of critique' remains of profound and vital consequence (G. Rose, 2007: 183).

PRISON ARCHIPELAGO

Penal spectatorship in the above contexts foregrounds the necessity of not simply critical engagement but the very need for a space of critique, for the possibility of something more than a popular spectator. Certain kinds of prisons, because of their history, function and framing, foreclose these kinds of possibilities and the questions they raise even as they increasingly open their doors to visitors. Others remain off limits and yet are subject to this same kind of dangerous cultural imaginary, the majority of them situated at border zones and, increasingly, off-shore sites. Detention, immigration and new war prisons offer only highly controlled tours for journalists, researchers and human rights organisations (many of whom have had no access to detainees) with only occasional video material released by state departments to supplement public oversight.

This distance, of course, is an energetic structuring force that lends the prison a mystical quality, further feeding the reproduction and growth of cultural fantasy. As sociologist Philip Smith (2008) carefully demonstrates, efforts at bureaucratic closure and restrictions in accessing punishment have, in fact, made the prison's symbolism via fantasy more vigorously attractive. Guantánamo, as the central detention facility in the war on terror, the one that has, by and large, achieved the most international attention, still remains largely invisible. The images that originated there are iconic but largely built around a central event: the arrival of the first wave of detainees to the site. Images of detainees kneeling below razor wire fence lines are exemplary in their communication of the closed-off, secretive nature of the camp. Most of these shots in fact are shot through the fence, physically detailing the removal of external oversight. The transfer of prisoners visualised beneath an American flag in the belly of a transport plane, arranged in orange jumpsuits, hoods, goggles and ear muffs upon arrival and positioned in outside cages mark much of the extent of visual coverage outside of a few sterile newscasts from inside Camp X-Ray and Delta. Much of the visualisation of Guantánamo has occurred from a distance and via the cultural imaginary.

More significantly, amid these new modes of punishment, a new penal subject emerges as well, one that is juxtaposed to that of the penal spectator – bare life as embodied in the figure at the limits of the law: the refugee (Arendt, 1973; Agamben, 1995, 2005). At Guantánamo, being caught in legal limbo – in the conditional state of being either a threat (potential danger) or of intelligence value without legal status – maintains one's detention. In immigrant detention, as criminologist Mary Bosworth (2012: 134) writes, 'detainees are clearly at a disadvantage since their lack of citizenship is both the cause and the effect of their detention'. Because legal status in these contexts is intentionally open-ended and ill-defined, detainees are subject to the cultural imaginary and are especially susceptible to abuse. Political philosopher Giorgio Agamben (2005: 4) writes, 'in the detainee at Guantánamo, bare life reaches its maximum indeterminacy'. The detained then constitute a crucial kind of subjectivity, and the newness of this identity, Agamben argues, is based upon its radical erasure of 'any legal status of the individual, thus producing a legally unnamable and unclassifiable being' (ibid.: 4). Here, in a protracted legal limbo, we encounter another category that depends upon extreme distance: the life that is moved outside of the juridical order – the life deemed unworthy of living. Bare life speaks to the ways in which state practices render types of individuals and groups foundationally excluded from the political and social orders, those who are exposed to the ever-present vulnerability of being killed or disappeared as they exist invisibly in exile with no political rights. For Agamben, it is this potentiality that all citizens now carry within them – with refugees, illegal combatants and the undocumented as exemplars of this possibility. These threshold experiences and identities materialise only by way of a profound form of distancing that, again, is penal in many respects. Penal spectatorship is part of a larger process of aversion and denial that positions beings beyond the pale (Bauman, 2000; S. Cohen, 2001). As sociologist Zygmunt Bauman (2000: 155) argues in his extrapolation of the Milgram experiments, 'inhumanity is a matter of social relationships' and social distance is inevitably defined by a lack of moral relationship and responsibility. In that bare-life formation, 'it is quite easy to be cruel towards a person we neither see nor hear' (ibid.: 155), and that is in itself, regardless of distance, a relation of violence.

The move toward incapacitation in the USA with its consequent prison expansion and hyper-incarceration has positioned it as a 'global archetype' and cultural force for imprisonment and bare-life configurations throughout the world (Hallett, 2008). In its managerialist, populist and punitive proclivities, imprisonment in the USA is now a primary practice through which to regulate a variety of international insecurities built upon class, race, economy, immigration and nationalism. In these contexts, security justifications and actuarial methods become arbiters for the use of incarceration and deportation to securitise migration and occupy conflict zones, with a massive and growing economic investment. This takes on a distinctly racialised and postcolonialist form in contemporary world settings, as the USA continues to shrink the space of asylum through a larger enforcement archipelago located around military bases and island detention centres even as it remains, ironically, the largest host and resettlement country for refugees. This unprecedented use of imprisonment, what some are calling an 'immigration penality' (A. Pratt, 2006) and others a 'deportation regime' (De Genova and Peutz, 2010), has largely taken place outside of democratic checks and public oversight even as it has depended upon an active cultural imaginary built upon outrage and affect. At the heart of contemporary debates about migration in the USA are nationalist cultural narratives that criminalise the broad and varied contours of immigration, reducing migrants and refugees to figures of economic and security threat.

The unprecedented penal expenditures surrounding these formations mark the global emergence of a new discourse of punishment, one whose racial divisions and abusive practices are revised into a technical, legal language of acceptability, one in which Americans are conveniently further distanced from the social realities of punishment through strategies of isolation and exclusion, all conducted in a manner and on a scale which exacerbates the fundamental class, race and gender contradictions and divisions of democracy. In this respect, 'detention' is constituted by both material practices and cultural discourses that sustain the expansion and intensification of protracted spaces of border and off-shore incarceration. These locations are strategic as they carefully circumvent the spaces of protection embedded in human rights law. They are also portentous of how the global North may invoke incarceration to respond to the continued and increasing mega-trends of mobility and migration across the planet. As populations encounter greater economic, environmental and conflict displacement, to name only a few, the prison sits at the intersection of the 'crisis of asylum' and processes of securitisation, with the world's most vulnerable populations its new political and economic target.[3] Actors caught within these processes – refugees and asylum seekers at the crux of detention and deportation – engage in the most fundamental assertions of visibility, proximity and existence. Hunger strikes and lip-sewing, for instance, expose 'the radical relationality of state and refugee': 'In taking on their life as bare life, the protestors call for a direct, unmediated, visceral response, life to life' (Edkins and Pin-Fat, 2005: 23). Amid cultural fantasies of outrage and insecurity, the mode of critique that can or will check the state's power on such a global scale – that will bring actors, the pain they produce and the people in pain in direct relation – remains an open question.

CONCLUSION: A WAY OUT?

It is with the luxury of distance that much of the popular knowledge about punishment is constructed – in spaces far from the social realities, social facts and social suffering that define hyper-incarceration and detention. Consequently, the turn away from imprisonment, if and when it occurs, will only be meaningful if we know something beyond the political, economic and structural forces that contribute to its decreased use. We will need to know something about the ways in which people who are removed from punishment imagine it – and why certain kinds of political rhetorics and cultural meanings are given so much privilege at particular historical moments. We will need to know how ordinary citizens use imprisonment, what they find

[3] As experts have argued concerning mass incarceration domestically and its exportation, such investments are both incredible and illogical when poised against alternative and less-costly political solutions of restoration, resettlement, and repatriation (Nyers, 2009; Mountz, 2010).

fascinating about it, why it emerges at key moments in particular kinds of representational frameworks and public discourse and finally, and perhaps most importantly, what kinds of penal subjectivities develop out of these interactions.

Recent accounts of penal restraint make important contributions to how a decreased reliance upon imprisonment and a cessation of hyper-incarceration might develop. For instance, many penal commentators point to the limits of state and federal budgets in a dramatic time of economic downturn, where crises in other social institutions – economy, health care, education – have assumed centre stage over crime and punishment (Gottschalk, 2006). Similarly, others point to styles of governance and the role of political contest in the historical transformation of punishment. Attention to the political dimensions of culture has demonstrated that openings in public decision-making emerge under specific conditions of governance (Whitman, 2003; Barker, 2009; see also Barker, Chapter 7 of this volume). Of course, fiscal, pragmatic, political and proceduralist reforms do not necessarily challenge or force an interrogation of cultural values and the dangerous convergences of democracy and punishment.

The project of punishment, as idealised in democratic political philosophy, always depends on internal limits, critique and a deep self-doubt. Such commitments are largely lost in the era of hyper-incarceration. A new kind of intervention will not only revisit these principles but will evolve out of a struggle to understand the cultural conditions under which political fatigue and fervour in relation to punitiveness arise. A critical self-awareness of the role of law and institutions in the production of pain and violence amid democratic contexts is crucial in such a pursuit. This turn would seek not only to bring back and render more transparent the deliberative qualities, the checks and balances, that are required in any invocation of punishment, but also would simply remind us that deliberation, critique and open-endedness are essential cultural values in themselves. Such a perspective would strive to build a deepening sensitivity and thorough understanding of the stakes, scope and inevitably troubled character of punishment in local and global contexts in times of safety and danger, austerity and plenty.

For these reasons, criminologists must look for the fissures in penal culture, potential sites to disrupt patterns of spectatorship, invoking every opportunity to think and act beyond the prison. The exploration depends upon developing alternative ways to think both more broadly and more thoroughly about our social commitments and cultural investments in punishment (see Oparah, Chapter 14). This approach includes examining what these commitments reveal about our understandings of social obligation in relationship to the predominant role of pain and exclusion in our world. Exclusion always passes through institutions. It is generated through the family, economy, health care, educational and political systems. We work hard in the USA to make those exclusions appear self-generated, products of individual action, deserving of punishment and the removal of rights. Such strategies and logic produce new and darker regimes of exclusion that extend well beyond the punished to those who are assigned little or no worth across a broad and increasingly global network of social institutions and settings. In this way, punishment and the punished are always our closest witnesses of the ways in which the social destinies of our most vulnerable are ordered. When these narratives and lives take precedence in the cultural imagination, perhaps the prison will become something otherwise.

7

PRISON AND THE PUBLIC SPHERE: TOWARD A DEMOCRATIC THEORY OF PENAL ORDER*

Vanessa Barker

This chapter argues that the breakdown of American democracy parti-ally accounts for the unprecedented rise in incarceration over the past thirty years. Americans by and large have retreated into the private sphere and eroded the quality and character of the public sphere. These dual processes have major implications for the rise of state coercion against marginalised social groups. By becoming detached from the public sphere, by being 'alone together' as Sherry Turkle (2011) explains it, Americans have become detached from a sense of mutual obligation and civic responsibility, instead experiencing social isolation and social polarisation, exacerbated by the growing economic crisis. This social reality has weakened the emotional and political support necessary to sustain inclusive public policies and instead has unleashed the corrosive powers of the state, particularly against those most vulnerable – the poor, the under-educated and racial and ethnic minorities.

At the same time, however, there has been a significant counter-movement to mass imprisonment: de-escalation and reintegration. By bucking the national trend, some American states have maintained relatively low imprisonment rates and have done so not by insulating public policy from public demands, but rather by engaging ordinary people in a more open and participatory democratic process – a process oriented toward public welfare rather than private self-interest. A more

* My sincere thanks to David Scott for putting the compendium together and for asking the question 'why prison?' with a sense of urgency and purpose – his editorial insights and suggestions are also appreciated.

vibrant civic life can support mild penal sanctioning, contrary to conventional claims about punitive populism. A reinvigorated public sphere may provide a way out of such excessive and repressive crime control policies.

MASS INCARCERATION / HYPER-INCARCERATION

American domestic policy has been radically transformed over the past thirty years. The dramatic expansion of penal incarceration and the simultaneous retraction of social welfare together have left over 2 million Americans imprisoned, where one out of every 100 adults is currently imprisoned (Bureau of Justice Statistics, 2011), and has left many more living day to day in highly precarious circumstances battling under-employment, low wages, poor housing and even food shortages. These policies have been especially hard hitting on the poor and under-educated white and black populations and have been heavily concentrated in cities, especially in disadvantaged African American neighbourhoods (Sampson and Loeffler, 2010). Loïc Wacquant (2010a) has aptly renamed 'mass incarceration' as 'hyper-incarceration' to capture its class and race effects on a specific rather than general population. Over-reliance on penal incarceration and its continued aftermath on prisoners' families and neighbourhoods (Clear, 2008) has reintroduced such extreme levels of inequality that it now threatens to undermine the very basis of citizenship in the USA (Western, 2006). Based on de facto and de jure exclusion of socially marginalised groups, hyper-incarceration has not only blocked members' full social, economic and political participation in American public life but also limited their life chances. Our democracy is truly broken if we accept such unequal treatment for any member of the polity.

WHY PRISON?

Why prison? Why such heavy reliance on what was once thought to be an ineffective and brutalising institution? Despite the well-developed literature on the topic and widespread agreement about the historic nature of the phenomenon, there is less agreement about the immediate or deep-seated causes, let alone how to change it. Some analysts such as Loïc Wacquant (2009b, 2010a; see also Wacquant, Chapter 4 of this volume) argue that the rise of neoliberalism with its emphasis on deregulation and flexible labour and its associated smaller, leaner and meaner welfare state have come to rely on the penal state as a new form of racial social control, the functional equivalent of the ghetto as it maintains racial hierarchies and social inequality. Michelle Alexander (2010) calls the contemporary era of black incarceration *The New Jim Crow*. Still others such as David Garland (2001c) have focused on the underlying structural changes in late-modern societies as generative of existential angst, ontological insecurity and a 'culture of control' that needs, wants and demands an insatiable sense of security, control and containment of any sign of social disorder, especially crime. Similarly, Michael Tonry (2004) has traced mass incarceration to the cycle of moral panics and 'fierce overreactions' to rising crime as a driving force behind these movements. Jonathan Simon (2007) has provocatively pronounced these shifts as the era of 'governing through crime', explaining how the logic, rationale and practices of crime control have seeped into and transformed large swaths of seemingly unrelated public policy such as education and family life. By excavating the deep origins of the carceral state, Marie Gottschalk (2006; see also Gottschalk, Chapter 12 of this volume) has argued that mass imprisonment should be understood as a bipartisan project of state building: state capacity grew in response to an unexpected set of liberal and conservative interest groups, an expansion that stretches back to the beginning to the twentieth century. Each approach, sophisticated in its understanding of how complex social structures created the conditions conducive to repressive crime control, has provided a persuasive although different explanation of one of the most momentous changes in the twentieth century, and has consequently inspired a generation of new research in the field. This author and present volume included.

Yet, there are two unresolved analytical and empirical issues in these leading accounts: uniformity and agency. First, on uniformity: each approach, to a certain degree, treats this period of increased incarceration as a uniform, coherent and seamless process that occurred in all places at all times under shared conditions, in spite of significant counter-trends that suggest a different set of causal dynamics. The growing literature on comparative penal sanctioning (Savelsberg, 1994; Cavadino and Dignan, 2006; Lacey, 2008) and subnational crime control (Miller, 2008; Barker, 2009; Lynch, 2009; Schoenfeld, 2010; Page, 2011; Campbell, 2012) all emphasise degrees of divergence and variation and point to alternative explanations rooted in the political process. Second, on agency: each approach with its emphasis on structural factors presents an underdeveloped view of agency and does not sufficiently account for the reality or impact of counter-movements such as penal moderation, decarceration, restorative justice and abolition, each of which has kept imprisonment rates down in some places over the same period (Bosworth, 2010a; Gartner et al., 2011; Gottschalk, 2012b; see also Oparah, Chapter 14 of this volume).

TOWARD A DEMOCRATIC THEORY OF PENAL ORDER

These analytical and empirical gaps can be partially resolved if we turn to a more basic account of punishment: democracy. By making democracy more central to our analysis, we might be able to see that it is not only the retraction of the welfare state that drives penal expansion but that the breakdown of democracy itself has led to both. I make four claims about democracy and punishment below that are drawn from my prior conceptual and empirical work in The Politics of Imprisonment (Barker, 2009) and relevant secondary literature. This work was based on a comparative and historical analysis of three representative American states with varying democratic traditions and varying penal orders: California, Washington State and New York. In the original study, the highly punitive southern states were excluded in part because they were under-democratised and dominated by the legacies and policies of racial social control; the book sought to examine how the democratic process, including the political incorporation of African Americans and not just their exclusion, influenced crime control policies from the 1960s to the present. Today, there are several rich case studies on Southern states that point to similar political configurations and political institutions that drive penal development in these states (Lynch, 2009; Schoenfeld, 2009; Campbell, 2012).

The democratic approach to punishment emphasises human agency (how ordinary people get involved in politics) and it emphasises variation – not only how penal sanctioning varies but how public participation differs by institutional context, with varying effects on penal sanctioning. By taking these steps, this approach develops an account of counterfactual cases: when and where penal moderation can occur, providing insight into possible pathways out of mass incarceration / hyper-incarceration. This comes at a critical moment when some American state governments, national politicians, grassroots organisations and critical scholars have all questioned the moral, economic and social costs associated with the massive prison build up over the past thirty years, especially as the prison has created more social problems than it has resolved: unemployment, family break-up, recidivism, difficulty with 're-entry', second-class citizenship tainted with social stigma and dishonour (Petersilia, 2003; Western, 2006; Clear, 2008; Wacquant, 2010a).

This chapter is organised around the following claims:

1. Crime and punishment are inherently political issues since they involve the distribution of public goods (safety, security), the recognition and limits on the rights of others (victims and offenders) and limits on state authority (how much internal force is legitimate in democratic societies). As such, we need a democratic theory of punishment to explain recent events.
2. Civic engagement – how people get involved in politics – is a critical determinant of the degree to which states infringe upon the rights and freedoms of others to realise public goods.
3. De-democratisation – the breakdown of democracy – can lead to more repressive penal sanctioning.
4. Democratisation – the expansion of public participation and civic engagement – can lead to more moderate penal sanctioning.

Why democracy?

Crime and punishment are highly charged emotional and moral issues that are deeply connected to the democratic process. There are no easy answers to crime and punishment as they involve what are essentially irresolvable dilemmas about pain, suffering, life, liberty and death, and hinge upon the delicate balance between repairing the harm done by crime and infringing on the rights and liberties of others. Herbert Packer (1968) framed this dilemma as competing values in criminal justice between due process and crime control. Democratic states must sanction crime (even when it is driven by economic inequality), understood as a violation of the social contract to maintain the rule of law, civil peace and social order, but they must do so without undermining freedom or relying on too much force. Crime and punishment invoke core questions about the limits of state authority and the rights of others, and as such they are inherently political in nature. And we know from the sociology of punishment that democracy and imprisonment have had a long, intertwined history (Foucault, 1977; Beaumont and de Tocqueville, 1979; Garland, 1985). These social institutions are mutually constitutive: democratic reforms in the late-eighteenth and early-nineteenth century built the prison (buried the bloody scaffold, sign and symbol of absolute monarchy and its military might) while imprisonment – the deprivation of liberty and liberty alone, the ideal principle in a free and equal society – ensured democracy, creating self-regulating, disciplined but free subjects (Foucault, 1977; Dumm, 1987). Democratisation through the nineteenth and early-twentieth century provided the foundation for the rehabilitative ideal (Rothman, 1971; Garland, 1985). Democracy and imprisonment are tightly nested institutions; they form a type of first-order relationship, and as one changes, the other is likely to follow. Moreover, penal sanctioning provides the means to define the nature of social relations in complex political communities; it provides the symbolic and material resources to establish the conditions of citizenship, collective identity and other forms of social classification, affirming social ties of mutual reciprocity as well as solidifying social hierarchies and social exclusion. A more nuanced understanding of the democratic process can help us understand and explain how these processes are resolved, if only temporarily and almost never satisfactorily.

Civic engagement

Civic engagement is a significant factor in shaping the degree to which states infringe upon the rights and freedoms of others to realise public goods. Civic engagement provides the legitimacy, social meaning and checks and balances on the use of state power in criminal sanctioning; it acts as a break on or accelerator of punishment in the realisation of public goods such as safety, security and the reassertion of the rule of law. This is a lesson we learned from Émile Durkheim (1933/1984): punishment is made meaningful through the expression of collective sentiment. Penal sanctioning is not exclusively a top-down imposition of power relations, social stratification or racial social control; it must and does involve some measure of public support to be at all meaningful, packed with cultural resonance and emotional weight. As Nils Christie (1981) explained in his classic Limits to Pain, values are expressed through the gradation of pain infliction while participatory justice would help to clarify these values. Penal sanctioning must, and does, involve public participation to maintain its resilience and legitimacy in democratic societies.

In terms of democratic theory, public participation is necessary for accountability. Here, accountability does not mean elected officials' knee-jerk response to public demands, but rather an interactive process of communicative action. Accountability encourages more 'flexible balanced thinkers' who rely less on emotion to make more informed decisions through discussion and deliberation.[1] Accountability not only holds policymakers responsible for public policies but also provides a space for those affected by crime control – especially as it involves the loss of liberty, one of the most basic organising principles of democratic societies – to influence shape, support or reject limits on freedom to realise public safety. Ian Loader and Richard Sparks (2012:32) have called this process 'participatory parity,' invoking Nancy Fraser's termi-nology, in which those most affected by crime control policies have an equal chance to impact the distribution of these public goods. To Loader and Sparks, crime control is a central site in democratic societies where conflict is regulated, resources allocated and the nature and character of social relations ordered (Loader and Sparks, 2012: 33). As such, public participation is necessary for democratic validity. Crime control is a site of 'democratic responsibility', as they explain, a part of social life in which public goods depend upon ongoing 'public work' (Boyte cited in Loader and Sparks, 2012: 33).

De-democratisation

What has happened, however, in the USA over the past thirty years is the abject failure of the parity principle. Not only are those who are most affected by crime control policies not adequately represented in decision-making, but there has been a general breakdown of public participation in the political process. Despite claims about punitive populism and the rise of a loud, boisterous, irrational and vengeful public, there is more empirical evidence to suggest a more general decline in public participation in all areas of collective life, including voting and political participation (Putnam, 2000). In his internationally acclaimed Bowling Alone, Robert Putnam (2000) documented the steady decline of civic engagement in which fewer people turn out to vote on election-day; fewer people regularly attend local community meetings; fewer people volunteer; and fewer people belong to a range of social and civic associations. On average with about 53 per cent voter turn-out for presidential elections and about 42 per cent during mid-term elections since the mid 1970s (United States Census Bureau, 2012: table 397), it is difficult to see how runaway democracy is the problem. Michael Tonry (2007) is equally sceptical of the reality and force of penal populism. In Diminished Democracy, Theda Skocpol (2002) similarly documents

---

[1] See discussion by Taslitz (2012: 177) for further details.

the wholesale transformation of how Americans participate or no longer participate in the political process, as professionalised and managerial lobbyists have replaced grassroots civic engagement. The once highly public Americans have retreated into the private sphere where they are essentially 'alone together', as Sherry Turkle (2011) explains, as they sit side by side absorbed by social media rather than have face-to-face conversation and interconnection. Likewise, Thomas Mathiesen (2001) explains how infotainment, the commodification of public space for entertainment and sensationalism, has deteriorated the quality and character of public life, eroding the quality of 'communicative rationality', debate principles based on sincerity and truthfulness. For Mathiesen (2001: 35), the decline of the public sphere 'corrodes values like civil rights, the rule of law and humanity'.

This decline in public life, apart from conjuring images of an idealised past or preferred future, has had real world consequences by decreasing social capital, thereby decreasing the ties that bind people together in complex communities, making both small- and large-scale coopera-tion on public works more difficult and possibly more corrosive (see Foreword). In *Making Democracy Work*, a comparative study on Italian governance, Putnam (1993) found that locales with a higher degree of social capital – that is, how well people connect and cooperate with one another – tended toward a higher degree of economic prosperity and more generous and less coercive public policies. Subsequent and related research has found that the ability to make ties across social groups – what Putnam calls 'bridging' social capital, rather than thick ties within a group or 'bonding' social capital – is more effective in generating inclusionary public policies. In his analysis of Durkheim on social solid-arity, David Garland (2012) makes a similar point: societies with organic solidarity based on inter-group cooperation and respect for individual-ism rather than strong group identity tend to promote generous welfare states and less punitive policies. The ability to make connections with neighbours or across communities has declined in the USA. This has troubling consequences for the development of public policy, especially policies revolving around such heated issues as crime and punishment.

If we return to the parity principle and decline in participation, then we can see how this configuration is particularly devastating for former offenders. In Jeff Manza and Christopher Uggen's (2006) breakthrough study on felon disenfranchisement and their follow-up study with Melissa Thompson on citizenship and civic reintegration (Uggen et al., 2006), they explain how felons and former felons are effectively denied the ability to participate in public life. The civil penalties that can be imposed on those with felony convictions include: the loss of voting rights, employment opportunities and parental rights; deportation in the case of resident aliens; and restrictions on holding public office, access to public housing and student loans (Uggen et al., 2006: table 4: 297; Manza and Uggen, 2006: table A3.2: 247). These civil penalties imposed after imprisonment seriously undermine the quality and character of citizenship for anyone with a felony conviction, and they fundamentally alter the shape of the electorate itself. By blocking the participation of felons and former offenders, those most affected by crime and punishment are not able to fully participate in the political process. These restrictions (which vary by state) have a particularly negative impact on racial and ethnic minorities and the poor and under-educated population, who are clearly over-represented in the criminal justice system but under-represented in the political sphere. Their absence, as Uggen et al. (2006: 298) insightfully note, changes the terms of the debate: 'The major political parties need not attend to the concerns of more than five million citizens – mostly poor and people of color – who are currently locked out of the democratic process.' Their absence in public life seriously undermines former felons' ability to make connections or develop social ties across groups. Without this kind of bridging capital, it may be difficult to build the social support and social solidarity necessary to reform punitive and regressive penal policies. Such a lack of civic reintegration for former offenders has serious implications for race and democracy in the USA. Mass incarceration's denial of full civic participation for thousands of former felons, especially racial and ethnic minorities in Southern states, is reproducing what Bruce Western (2006) has forcefully called second-class citizenship, an antiquated social hierarchy that should have been long gone with the Fourteenth and Fifteenth Amendments to the US Constitution.

Taken together, these trends have diminished the quality and character of democracy across the USA, a key finding that has been supported by subsequent research and solidified by the 2010 United States Supreme Court ruling on *Citizens United* that upheld big spending by private corporations on political campaign contributions, essentially allowing affluent corporations to out-spend and out-influence nearly everyone else in the political field (Supreme Court of the United States, 2010).

The reported frenzy of electoral politics concerning crime control certainly involved a degree of public participation, but the *politicisation* of this issue does not mean it has become democratised. Quite the contrary: the politicisation of crime and punishment may have had the opposite effect of shutting down discussion and participation, driving away middle-of-the-road voters and leaving elections open to highly mobilised groups with more dogmatic positions than pragmatic and moderate positions of most Americans on crime control. Populist politics of crime control runs counter to democratisation, with too few people participating, no accountability and public policies directed against socially marginalised groups, moves that undermine the equality principle in democracy. The breakdown of American democracy has failed to protect minorities against the excesses of state coercion and, in some cases, has led to increased coercion against the most vulnerable for private self-interest. This result is not meant to suggest that the public should not be involved in crime control, but rather to suggest that the public needs to be more involved through more effective mechanisms, specifically through deliberative democracy, discussed below.

Mechanisms of civic engagement and penal policy

Even if we can agree that civic engagement may be vital to crime control policies, we still need a more developed account of the mechanisms by which civic engagement impacts public policy and how it may vary by historical conditions or political context. Here I locate civic engagement as a form of collective agency that operates within specific political institutional contexts. The democratic process is conceptualised as a varying set of *political structures* and *collective agency*: it captures varying patterns of institutionalised decision-making (the rules of the game that enable or disable certain paths of action and varying forms of civic engagement), how ordinary people get involved in the political process and how they make demands, trying to realise public goods, material interests or a particular moral vision of a good and just society (Barker, 2009: 37–40). This conceptualisation was developed with the American federalist system in mind but, with some modification, the basic points could be used to map other democratic polities such as France, Sweden or the UK.

Political institutions establish legitimate channels of action and patterns of decision-making and, as such, they channel flows of information and exchange. They establish power relations within a particular field in ways that often determine budgets, legislation and even rationalities of governance. The institutional environment exerts a kind of gravitational pull, attracting certain kinds of actions and repelling others, exerting influence in a way that goes beyond the interests or desires of any one particular person or actor. Joshua Page (2011) conceptualises the *penal field* in a similar way as a relatively bounded set of actions and taken-for-granted assumptions that shape how actors struggle to realise their will and attain more capital. Like institutional configurations, collective agency significantly shapes the possibilities of action in the political field: it shapes how people understand the very possibilities of action, how they make and realise meaning. As Charles Tilly (1997, cited in Barker, 2009: 39) explains, social mobilisation 'relies on and transforms shared understandings concerning what forms and ends of action are desirable, feasible and efficacious; collective learning and memory strongly limit the claims that people make and how they make them'. Collective agency can take on a range of deep or shallow forms, ranging from voting in national elections, signing a petition, attending a rally, speaking at a community board meeting, participating in a town hall meeting, writing a letter to a local representative, running for office, or volunteering for a grassroots organisation, for example (see Barker, 2009: 39–41). Taken together, political structures and collective agency shape the underlying texture of politics in a particular place; they shape debates about the distribution of public goods, the nature of state authority and the limits and responsibilities of both state and citizen.

To be able to make more systematic comparisons across different types of democratic processes, I follow conventional typologies among political sociologists and political scientists: I map political structures according to the degree to which political systems distribute or share power across or between branches of government and between state actors and civil society. The degree of decentralisation is a key indicator of decision-making power and structure: open polities with more bottom-up decision-making and multiple access points for public input are considered decentralised; closed polities with more top-down decision-making and limited public access are considered centralised. In a decentralised system, decision-making power is shared across and between levels of government and may include forms of 'direct democracy', a mechanism by which non-elected people make legally binding decisions through the ballot box, voting on initiatives, referendums or recall measures. In decentralised systems the power and right to rule is invested across multiple branches of government and incorporates ordinary, non-elected, people to govern. By contrast, in more centralised systems, the right to rule is invested in state actors, including the executive, civil servants and politicians, without much direct input from ordinary people or civil society organisations.

To map civic engagement, I return to the work of Robert Putnam and others who have developed the concept of *social capital* to capture how well people connect and cooperate with one another through civic engagement to bring about public goods (Putnam, 1993). In societies, regions or locales with a high degree of social capital, Putnam explains, people tend to be active in politics and community life, creating both thick and thin networks of social ties that can then increase cooperation, social cohesion and mutual trust. As noted, he found that regions with a higher degree of social capital tended toward higher economic prosperity, more generous and efficient social policies and less coercive social control.

In terms of crime and punishment, where we see a higher degree of civic engagement and social capital, we might expect to see more restorative and less punitive penal policies, policies that limit state coercion against individuals and are dependent on mutual trust and social reciprocity. A restorative or more moderate approach recognises the harm done to crime victims and holds offenders responsible for the pain and suffering of victims and the emotional and economic costs to communities but does so without resorting to excessive uses of repressive state power (Braithwaite and Petit, 1990). When people share a sense of civic duty, responsibility for self-governance and social connectedness, they may be less willing to inflict on one another the violence of penal sanctioning. By contrast, in political environments with a low degree of civic engagement and high degree of social polarisation, we are likely to see a more retributive approach to criminal victimisation. Here the polity members' antipathy and resentment toward one another, especially toward marginalised social groups such as criminal offenders, can be easily expressed through penal sanctioning without much concern for the social reintegration of offenders.

Together, as mapped along these indices, varying forms of political structures and collective agency construct four ideal types of democratic process: deliberative democracy, polarised populism, elite pragmatism and corporatism (see Table 7.1).

Polities with a high degree of decentralisation and high degree of civic engagement form a deliberative mode with the most open and most participatory form and are likely to depress state coercion; polities with a high degree of decentralisation but low degree of civic engagement form polarised populism with ineffective government and more reliance on

TABLE 7.1   Democratic processes by decentralisation and civic engagement

Civic engagement	Decentralisation	
	High	Low
High	Deliberative democracy	Corporatism
Low	Polarised populism	Elite pragmatism

TABLE 7.2   Democratic process by penal order

Case	Democratic process	Penal order
California	Polarised populism	Retributive
Washington	Deliberative democracy	Moderation
New York	Elite pragmatism	Managerial

state coercion; polities with a high degree of centralisation but low degree of civic engagement take on a pragmatic mode dominated by state elites that are likely to moderate but strategically deploy state coercion without much public oversight – when this mode is dominated by its elitist tendencies, private interest reigns and tends to lead to more restrictive penal policies, but when the more pragmatic and bureaucratic mode dominates, we see more concern with distributing public goods and more moderate penal sanctioning. The fourth type, the corporatist mode with a high degree of civic engagement and centralisation was not examined in the case studies but is predicted to lead to more moderate penal sanctioning.[2] Polities with lower levels of civic engagement, more so than the degree of centralisation, are likely to lead to more repressive penal sanctioning (see Table 7.2).

Because this approach seeks to document and identify more precise mechanisms by which democratic institutions shape penal outcomes, it can move us beyond the conventional view that democracy always undercuts rational crime control policies. The democratic process is not a unitary or even a coherent process. This democratic approach provides a differentiated analysis of how people participate in public debates about

---

[2] For more on the case studies, logic and secondary literature these arguments are based on, see Barker (2009: chs. 3, 4 and 5).

crime and punishment, specifying particular conditions under which civic engagement can lead to harsh or mild penal sanctioning. 'The public', which hardly exists as such, holds complex views of crime and punishment: these views are often less severe than current penalties; are sometimes inconsistent as they advocate both rehabilitation and retribution; tend to change when given more information (Green, 2006); vary by socioeconomic status; tend to be more holistic than subnational or national policymaking allow (Miller, 2008); and tend to vary in their understanding of the causes of crime – ranging from moral depravity to social depravity, from ecological to pathological or as an environmental or public health contagion that needs to be classified and quarantined (Barker, 2009). The public's views on crime and punishment are far from uniform or necessarily vengeful; they depend much more on the particular institutional mechanisms that put their views into play to shape public policy and penal outcomes (see Michelle Brown, Chapter 6).

RACE AND DEMOCRACY: BLACK INCORPORATION

We should note here that the public also includes African Americans who were not passive victims but active participants in the making and unmaking of mass incarceration. Black political incorporation – that is how African Americans participated in public debate about crime control – and not just their exclusion is key to understanding the development of penal policy in the USA. In the case study of New York, for example, I examine how black activists in Harlem were on the forefront demanding state protection and standing against what they perceived to be a 'reign of criminal terror' in their communities (Barker, 2009: 150). In the late 1960s, the National Association for the Advancement of Colored People (NAACP) Citizens' Mobilisation against Crime pushed for stronger law enforcement in black neighbourhoods. This is a demand to be treated and recognised as full citizenships worthy of state protection rather than as second-class citizens relegated to neglect or abandonment. Lisa Miller (2008) similarly documents the key role of black participation in driving gun control legislation in local politics. In *The Golden Gulag*, Ruth Gilmore (2007) documents how African American and Latino women's grassroots organising has been at the forefront opposing the prison boom in California. Marie Gottschalk (2012b) critically notes a recent shift by the NAACP to actively oppose the war on drugs and expansion of the carceral state, a major breakthrough by connecting civil rights discourse to opposition to mass incarceration.

POLARISED PUBLIC AND HARSH JUSTICE

The relationship between public participation and harsh penal sanctioning is dependent upon specific historical conditions such as high crime rates and social insecurity (Garland, 2001c) and specific institutional frameworks such as open or decentralised polities (Savelsberg, 1994). Consider the case of California in the 1980s and 1990s in which conditions were set for 'punitive populism' – that is, public involvement that resulted in more punitive and harsh sanctioning. The rise of the crime victims movement with its more conservative law-and-order allies and grassroots campaigns against sex offenders that culminated in the 'Three Strikes and You're Out' legislation with extraordinarily long prison terms for (violent and non-violent) repeat offenders (Zimring et al., 2001) both involved public participation that tapped into the state's longer history of social conflict and social insecurity mediated and resolved through crime control.[3] Populism in this case did include public participation through direct democracy measures such as the initiative process, making it a decentralised polity with multiple access points for public input.

It is absolutely critical to grasp here, however, that it was the *contentious* character of California's public participation, particularly its use of the initiative process, coupled with its surprisingly low rates of civic engagement that shaped its more retributive approach to penal sanctioning. California's populist tradition has been shaped by a high degree of social polarisation and winner-takes-all politics where mutual obligation and reciprocity are downplayed. These features magnified by specific institutional channels, such as the initiative process, tended to polarise public debate, forcing complex social issues into simple 'yes' or 'no' policy choices. This style of politics had the effect of forcing the general public out of the debate and out of the vote, making the policy process captive to highly mobilised people with special interests (who, of course, claim to act in the name of the public good). The reliance on populist mechanisms such as direct democracy had the unintended consequence of decreasing public participation, decreasing opportunities for a diverse set of views and opinions on crime control, diminishing

---

[3] On 'governing through crime', see Simon (2007).

opportunities for compromise and decreasing opportunities to build social trust across diverse groups. Populism here functioned similarly as an under-democratised polity with relatively low rates of civic engagement, low rates of social capital and high rates of coercive public policies (Putnam, 1993; Barker, 2009), creating restrictive and exclusionary conditions of citizenship, often in the name of the public good at the expense of racial and ethnic minority groups.[4]

DELIBERATIVE DEMOCRACY AND PENAL MODERATION

By taking democratic differentiation seriously, this approach can provide insight into counterfactual cases: when civic engagement drives down incarceration. Here democratisation – the expansion of participation – can lead to moderate penal sanctioning. Penal moderation is dependent upon the agency of actors to change the current course of events. We know from the history of the Civil Rights Movement in the USA that sustained collective action based on the moral principles of democracy can bring about radical social change. There is an emerging movement toward penal moderation in the USA that similarly presses the civil rights violations of mass incarceration. Likewise, there is a movement in the UK for penal parsimony that seeks to restore eroded civil liberties, a principal organising feature of the society (Bosworth, 2010b). Since 2009, more than half of the American states have reduced their prison populations (Greene and Mauer, 2010). Abolitionist groups such as Critical Resistance (see Oparah, Chapter 14), activists groups such as Families against Mandatory Minimums (FAMM), Mothers Reclaiming Our Children (R. Gilmore, 2007) and the Drop the Rock campaign in New York, as well as responsive politicians and criminal justice actors such as prosecutors and judges, along with local residents fed up with crime and mass incarceration have all played a role in pushing for reform (Gottschalk, 2012b: 225). Judith Greene and Marc Mauer (2010) of the Sentencing Project (a non-profit research and advocacy organisation) detail penal reforms in four states, many based on diversion, reduction of time served, increased release and legislative reform; they found that FAMM played a vital role in the repeal of Michigan's mandatory minimum drug statutes.

---

[4] For more on the specific legislative process, political institutions and social history in California, see Barker (2009: ch. 3).

Likewise, in her study of crime politics in Pennsylvania, Lisa Miller (2008) found that public participation tended toward penal moderation rather than law-and-order politics, contrary to conventional claims about too much democracy. Miller shows how African American residents in Philadelphia actively participated in local-level debates demanding a more holistic approach to crime control, an approach that included gun control and reflected the social realities of inner city life. But with the federalisation of crime control, she explains, as crime control moved to the national stage, public participation and holistic responses declined in favour of more professional special interest lobbyists, the kind described by Skocpol (2002) as indicative of diminished democracy. In the Pennsylvania case, a broader spectrum of participants who were actively involved in policy debates tended to favour penal moderation. When crime control is taken out of the hands of local residents, in violation of the parity principle, managerial and special interests take hold, promoting more simplistic and sometimes more punitive responses to crime control.

There is growing empirical evidence and theoretical developments that support a more nuanced and complicated view of democratic participation (Braithwaite and Petit, 1990; Gutman and Thompson, 2004; Green, 2006; Miller, 2008; Loader and Sparks, 2012; Taslitz, 2012). The case study of Washington State builds on and develops this finding.

In Washington State, democratisation, particularly as it was part of a deliberative process and communicative action, defused growing social conflict and social insecurities and suppressed reactionary calls for punitive penal sanctioning. Public participation included a wide range of forums including more conventional voting, volunteering and public hearings, and more deliberative forums such as state-wide community meetings, citizen advisory boards and hybrid state-citizen commissions. Direct democracies, although used less frequently, are also available in the state as Washington shares a similar but more cooperative populist tradition as California. Local community meetings, also referred to as town hall meetings, are critical to getting people involved in the business and work of government in small-scale, face-to-face settings where non-state actors can actually talk to and hold state agents accountable for public policy. These small-scale face-to-face settings allow people to bypass special interests that dominate electoral politics and may have the long-term effect of improving trust in government, which can improve the delivery of public policies. Under certain conditions,

these forums can bring about what Jürgen Habermas (1981) conceptualised as 'communicative action', a type of collective agency based on
deliberation and cooperation. Deliberative forums allow for an open
exchange of ideas and arguments and enable individuals to discuss their
own viewpoints and opinions without representing or being limited by
special or organised interests. It can encourage the expression of different and conflicting opinions but can push these differences toward
compromise (de Haan, 1990). As Amy Gutman and Dennis
Thompson (2004) explain in *Why Deliberative Democracy*, deliberative
forums operate under the expectation of compromise rather than domination, where 'free and equal persons' seek 'fair terms of cooperation'
(Taslitz, 2012: 135). It operates under the principle of 'participatory
parity', where people directly impacted by public policies have a say on
the substance and trajectory of those policies (and the broader issues
they represent), returning to Loader and Sparks' (2012) concerns about
public input.

Of course, these forums can be co-opted by special interests or by
politicians who use public input to advance his or her agenda in ways
that may be incompatible with the outcome generated by the forum.
Officials can use community meetings to defuse potential conflict without actually doing anything about the sources of the conflict. Politicians
can advance their own interests while pacifying demands for public
inclusion but take no action. Because deliberative forums are based on
discussion rather than voting, they can lack a tangible policy result,
leaving participants feeling once again excluded from the business of
government. The degree to which deliberative forums are effective
participatory mechanisms or instruments of state control is an empirical
question and most likely varies by political and cultural context. In
Washington State during the thirty years under investigation, deliberative forums and other avenues of public participation were vital to
maintaining and sustaining the state's relatively low and more moderate
penal sanctioning.

The growing body of research on deliberative forums provides further
support for this historical case. Given the opportunity, public participants can make more informed, rational and pragmatic decisions about
public policy. David Green (2006) found that citizens' participation led
to more 'liberalising' views on crime and punishment and decreased
their demands for vengeance and custodial sanctions. Likewise, Gerry
Johnstone (2000) has argued that public participation can increase
public knowledge and understanding of the negative effects of penal

sanctioning and change their perspective on public interest. Jason Barabas (2004) has shown how deliberative forums can change a person's deeply held views, even on sensitive policy issues such as social security. In Washington State, deliberative democracy not only expanded public participation and increased ordinary citizens' ability to influence decision-making; it set a tone and texture of political debate, contra California, that encouraged open discussion, dialogue and compromise, features that over time would make decision making (even about contentious issues like crime and punishment and race relations) more inclusive, rational and less dogmatic.

Andrew Taslitz (2012) has written about the inclusionary nature of deliberative forums that simultaneously promote the inclusion of a wide range of social groups and promote inclusionary public policies that require a 'strong commitment to individual liberties'. In Washington State, policymakers and public participants consistently demonstrated a strong commitment to the individual rights and liberties of criminal offenders (Barker, 2009: ch. 4). This inclusive stance on the rights of offenders provided a key counterweight to calls for more punitive or harsh penal sanctioning; the rights and liberties of offenders could be infringed upon to repair the harm caused by crime but they could not be summarily dismissed or degraded to appease concerns for retribution or public safety. James Whitman (2003), in his comparative analysis of American, French and German penal orders, found that the continental legal systems afford much more weight to rights and dignity of criminal offenders, providing legal and cultural mechanisms that inhibit more repressive sanctioning and tend to favour milder penal sanctioning. A similar dynamic seems to have been operating in Washington State that was at least in part achieved and sustained through public participation.

Taslitz (2012) makes an interesting connection between deliberative forums and the research on empathy and happiness, arguing that increased public participation improves wellbeing, accountability and the rule of law and leads to less coercive public policies. These are interesting connections and worth pursuing in future research. For now, I return to the connections between deliberative forums, social capital and social trust, mentioned earlier, as critical to supporting milder or more moderate penal sanctioning. Following Putnam, I connect civic engagement with social trust, as the underlying mechanism that facilitates more effective and less coercive public policies. Deliberative forums and the willingness to participate in them most likely require a certain degree of social capital and social trust, but once in operation can generate social trust. Washington State scored relatively high on various levels of civic engagement, volunteering, voting and attending community meetings, and ranked relatively high on social capital and social trust, ranking tenth in the nation according to Putnam's index (Putnam, 2000). A high rate of social capital suggests that people are relatively well connected and have well-developed norms of reciprocity. Reciprocity – the mutual exchange to support, gifts, favours and goods – goes beyond the exchange of contractual obligations with its threat of force. Reciprocity indicates a desire to maintain and build rather than break down social ties, and a willingness to take a chance on others. Social trust indicates a social group's ability and capacity to recognise and acknowledge others and treat them with mutual respect, even those who are different (S. Cohen, 2001). It indicates a social group's willingness to try to solve the problem of order with the least amount of repression.

CONCLUDING REMARKS

This chapter has sought to make the case that democracy is central to our understanding of 'why prison?' based on four key claims: (i) imprisonment is inherently political as it engenders key issues concerning state authority, the power to punish, the legitimacy of pain infliction and the intractable dilemma of public order in democratic societies; (ii) civic engagement – the manner in which people become involved in political activity, particularly how they mobilise social capital – is critical to understanding how social groups cooperate or fail to cooperate to realise public goods like safety and security; (iii) how de-democratisation weakens social bonds, leads to greater political rigidity and sum-zero politics, detachment and more entrenched political positions; and (iv) how more democracy can reduce penal excess through civic engagement and deliberative forms of participation.

If lower levels of participation and social trust tend to foster social exclusion, enabling majorities to dominate minorities, the key is finding mechanisms that generate bridging social capital and generate social trust, which of course can be difficult in unequal societies such as the USA, but not impossible. This drift toward penal moderation is propelled by an emerging social movement made up of mothers protecting their sons and daughters, families devastated by collateral damage, ethnic and racial minorities demanding full participation, local residents fed up with crime and the prison boom, and key actors in the criminal justice system, including but limited to long-term prosecutors and judges. This movement represents a formative example of inter-group cooperation based on communicative action and a strong desire to change the course of events to find a more inclusionary and parsimonious solution to the problem of order. The success or failure of this movement will depend upon genuine public engagement with these critical issues, rather than retreat.

PART III

STATE DETENTION

8

THE IRON CAGE OF PRISON STUDIES

Mark Brown

In the mill of academia it is within prison studies and penology that the 'issue' or 'problem' of imprisonment is addressed. That makes perfect sense in many respects. It promotes specialisation and expertise, it clarifies the demarcations between different academic specialities (such as psychiatry on the one hand, or population studies on the other) and it introduces a certain level of efficiency and predictability into universities' academic endeavour. Occasionally these separations are breached. This was the case, for example, with Bernard Harcourt's (2006) analysis of aggregate institutionalisation figures in the USA since 1928. Penologists and penal theorists have tended to look only at imprisonment figures and thus have spoken in recent times of a new 'hyper-incarceration' phenomenon. Yet if incarceration (involuntary detention) is taken to include mental health detainees also, the run-up in prisoner numbers of the last twenty years or so – this so-called imprisonment boom, or 'mass imprisonment' – barely brings levels of aggregate incarceration back to the rates of the 1940s and 50s. Yet the singular focus on punishment and imprisonment continues. Ironically, then, we might agree with Aldous Huxley's (1936: 122) character Anthony in *Eyeless in Gaza* who, in defending completeness over single mindedness, observes: 'That's the trouble of all single minded activity; it costs you your liberty. You find yourself driven into a corner. You're a prisoner.' Is this, then, the final irony of prison studies and penology, that they came eventually to embody precisely that which they studied?

For Mariana Valverde (2012), the question would perhaps seem irrelevant since in her view penology, at least, is 'moribund, perhaps even dead'. The only residual question, she suggests, is 'who/what killed penology'? (ibid.: 246). Much contemporary study of the prison, Valverde (2012: 245) suggests, is in fact a nascent 'post-penological criminology' linking prisons and punishment not to moribund questions of penal effectiveness but rather to a more expansive set of questions about state power. At the same time, however, Valverde identifies in the new post-penological approach a fixation upon practices of state that arguably work as an evasion of some of the key (and now neglected) questions about offending and human nature that also gave penology (and perhaps, too, criminology) its vitality and direction. In introducing the special issue on punishment to which Valverde's comments are directed, Kelly Hannah-Moffat and Mona Lynch (2012: 119) are more inclined to describe this contemporary literature as 'punishment and society', something lying 'at the juncture of the interdisciplinary fields of criminology and law and society'. Part of what is new about these approaches is the application of what we might term a punishment analytic into spheres not previously associated with punishment studies, such as in Mary Bosworth's work on immigration detention (Bosworth and Kaufman, 2011; Bosworth, 2012; see also Kaufman and Bosworth, Chapter 9 of this volume) or Katherine Beckett's on civil penalties (Beckett and Herbert, 2010; Beckett and Murakawa, 2012). What these studies reveal are punitive tactics much more widely distributed and inflected in the practices of state than was visible within the old confines of penological criminology.

In this chapter I propose to take the question posed by prisons in a second and, hopefully, equally productive new direction. Rather than examining the extensiveness and form of new punitive practices, I suggest that another important way of escaping the confines and myopias of prison specialism is to look at prison as *but one form* of involuntary detention (cf. Birkbeck, 2011). Moreover, I suggest that if the 'main game' of the last two decades was the apparently limitless rises in imprisonment rates – theorised variously as mass imprisonment (Garland, 2001b) or hyper-incarceration (Wacquant, 2010a) – then the main problems of this decade and the near future will be new forms of involuntary confinement and detention and new restrictions upon civil liberties that are fashioned specifically so as to be not prison-as-we-know-it. Thus, if the new literature on punishment works to create a kind of post-penological criminology, then it might be hoped that a wider examination of places and practices of confinement and detention will escape the iron cage of prison studies to create another new criminological offspring. The notion of an iron cage is invoked here both in a literal sense as 'an iron cage that imprisons' (Feeley and Rubin, 1999: 284) but also in its traditional Weberian sense of an institutional form within the academic bureaucracy, something which will 'tend to form habits, vest interests and to channel thinking. . . they become part of the scheme of things, continuing long after the original reasons for their creation have faded' (Garland, 2001a: 179). Part of the argument to be developed in this chapter, therefore, is that contemporary practices of confinement and detention require more for their theoretical and practical understanding than can be delivered by a simple, and perhaps simplistic, focus upon prisons.

The remainder of the chapter is divided into three sections. The first briefly provides a theoretical rationale for transforming prison studies into a wider study of detention and confinement. It is followed by a look at some key sites of detention which either mimic the prison, extend the prison's normative frame to new domains or, through methods and narratives of dissemblance, reproduce the prison while disavowing its relationship. Finally, the chapter takes up Jonathan Simon's (2010) challenge to understand imprisonment, or in this case prison-like forms, using a wider set of theoretical and conceptual devices than are typically found within mainstream criminological thought.

RATIONALE: WHY GO BEYOND THE PENAL INSTITUTION?

It might eventually be felt that the examples of new domains and forms of detention and confinement described in section two of this chapter provide, in and of themselves, a rationale or justification for breaking down the traditional barriers erected around prison studies. Yet there are at least four *a priori* reasons for doing so as well. First, if the study of confinement is to be a critical endeavour, it must recognise that prison is not detention *sui generis* but rather intimately connected to a whole raft of detention practices. This is not to invoke Michel Foucault's (1977) argument from *Discipline and Punish* that the prison is the archetypal disciplinary institution, part of a carceral archipelago, although that argument certainly holds some force. Rather it is to argue that to focus on prison is to focus on precisely that group of involuntary detainees whose rights, status and corporeal safety are most protected, since, despite its harms and privations, punishment is ultimately an inclusive exercise. R. A. Duff (2003) aptly puts this view when he argues that the act of judicial punishment, through which an individual is rendered into prison:

is consistent with, indeed expressive of, the defining values of liberal political community. It addresses offenders, not as outlaws who have forfeited their standing as citizens, but as full members of the normative political community: it is inclusionary rather than exclusionary. It treats them as citizens who are both bound and protected by the central liberal values of autonomy, freedom and privacy.

(Duff, 2003: 129–30)

It is therefore to forms of involuntary detention that exist outside normally regulated judicial procedure – or other long-established and regulated forms of law, such as mental health law (Harcourt, 2006) – that our attention should turn. In the new world of confinement and detention, a number of examples of such practices exist, but criminologists have not always found an easy place for them within existing frameworks. In examining the case of immigration detention, Mary Bosworth (2012: 124) asks of detention centres, '[g]iven their administrative rationale, should they even fall into the purview of criminology?' Yet she concludes her analysis with immigration detention enfolded within critical penal discourse as a form of 'penal power' and 'practices of state power' (ibid.: 135) in which it is citizenship (or the lack thereof) that fundamentally undermines liberty rights and ordinary judicial protections enjoyed by prisoners. In what follows, it may emerge that the proliferation of sites and practices of involuntary detention are such that this notion of penal power itself needs to be opened up to further reflexive analysis.

Yet the penal is often not too far from these new sites of detention. A second *a priori* justification for extending our analysis of detention beyond the prison is the expansion of the prison industry itself into new notionally non-penal domains. To look again to immigration detention, it is clear that private prison providers have expanded into this new area of confinement, creating a multi-billion dollar industry (New York Daily News, 2011; New York Times, 2011) that far out-sizes, in proportionate terms, the privatisation of prisons within the penal estate that so captured criminological debate during the 1990s and 2000s. The model upon which immigration detention facilities are designed and constructed is the prison, as opposed, for instance, to other institutional forms such as the hospital or the aged-care facility. Moreover, wherever these institutions are privately operated, they are increasingly run by private prison companies (Corporate Watch, 2012). Yet, again, the rights and protections afforded prisoners often fail to materialise within the immigration domain. Children and babies are routinely imprisoned and often within high-security detention facilities (National Inquiry into Children in Immigration Detention, 2004; *Popov* v. *France*[1]); detention often occurs not just by (legal) executive fiat but through administrative and sometimes private (corporate) decisions that have no basis in law (*Amuur* v. *France*[2]); protests or difficult behaviour that would not constitute a criminal offence can lead to transfer to a penal prison (Australian Human Rights Commission, 2002); visibility of detention conditions is hampered by the absence of community oversight – detainees may have property confiscated arbitrarily or may be forced to pay for 'services' (such as using the toilet) within less well-regulated facilities (MigrEurope, 2010); and private detention facility staff, unlike prison officers, may begin work with no previous custodial experience or relevant qualifications (Senate Joint Select Committee on Australia's Immigration Detention Network, 2012). Together, this assemblage of conditions provides an *a priori* case for breaking down the walls of the prison studies specialism to consider the prison form and its material effects in new, supposedly non-penal environments.

Judith Butler (2004: 53) recognised the emergence of new prison-like forms and domains, framed within tightly bounded legal, or arguably non-legal, regimes when she coined the phrase the 'new war prison'. Taking Guantanamo Bay as the example par excellence, Butler observed that:

> [its] prisoners are not considered 'prisoners' and receive no protection from international law. Although the US claims that its imprisonment methods are consistent with the Geneva Convention, it does not consider itself bound to those accords, and offers none of the legal rights stipulated by that accord. As a result, the humans who are imprisoned in Guantanamo do not count as human; they are not subjects protected by international law. They are not subjects in any legal or normative sense.
> (Butler, 2004: xv–xvi)

A key theme running through analyses of these new modalities of detention, whether it be of immigrants or 'unlawful combatants', is the suspension of law or the exclusion of the detained from access to law. Butler argues that these new forms of state power reintroduce archaic forms of sovereignty wherein sovereign, executive and managerial power is enfolded and the modern state reprises a pre-modern form. Yet the form of the new war prison itself is distinctly modern, as Michelle Brown

---

[1] *Popov* v. *France* [2012] ECtHR Application Nos. 39472/07 and 39474/07, Judgment of 19 January 2012.

[2] *Amuur* v. *France* [1996] ECtHR Application No. 19776/92, Judgment of 25 June 1996.

(2005) has observed, not only modelled on the prison institution but also drawing upon and replicating the life experiences and subjectivities of those bound into the lower working class habitus of modern correctional work. In her review of the abuses at Abu Ghraib prison in Iraq, Brown cites evidence given by Sgt Joseph Darby, the whistleblower in the case, to a military hearing: a fellow soldier, he reports, said of the abuses: 'The Christian in me knows it was wrong, but the corrections officer in me can't help but want to make a grown man piss himself' (Michelle Brown, 2005: 982). Eschewing an account that telescopes focus onto the direct perpetrators of the abuses at Abu Ghraib, however, Brown speaks of a 'primary narrative' that is 'based upon voyeuristic sadism, the fascination and relentless public speculation concerning how average Americans come to be private, now public, torturers' (ibid.: 983). More broadly, though, what Abu Ghraib reveals is the way the 'prison-industrial complex and military-industrial complex converge' through the importation of the skills, logics, structures, architectures and, finally, abuses, of modern American imprisonment into the lightly regulated and seldom-seen world of military detention. Together with immigration detention, the new world of military detention destabilises the neat boundaries that allowed penology and prison studies to confine and isolate the domestic civilian prison as an object worthy of special attention (see Michelle Brown, Chapter 6).

Finally, we may turn to the broader international community's understanding of imprisonment, confinement and detention as a source of justification for breaking down these walls around the prison. The United Nations (UN) specifically conjoins these sites, refusing to distinguish the manner by which individuals arrive in involuntary detention from the character of that detention itself. The UN *Body of Principles for the Protection of All Persons under Any Form of Detention or Imprisonment*, adopted by the General Assembly in 1988, seeks to uphold the rights of all individuals under involuntary confinement (United Nations, 1988). The UN Working Group on Arbitrary Detention similarly fails to distinguish the means by which detention occurs. Although the Working Group does not develop jurisprudence (in the manner, for example, of the UN Human Rights Committee), it does actively pursue a definition of what constitutes 'arbitrary' detention and seeks to influence contracting states in their exercise of state power. In 2005 the Working Group extended its review of arbitrary detention to the worldwide problem of 'over-incarceration'. Here it noted that it was 'fully cognizant of the fact that States enjoy a wide margin of discretion in the choice of their penal policies' and that in individual cases, therefore, it was not possible to compare a prison sentence received in one country with that which might be expected in another (United Nations, 2005: 19). Yet the Working Group also observed, that states' obligations under international human rights conventions to respect the liberty and security of their citizens and others meant that '[s]tates should have recourse to deprivation of liberty only insofar as it is necessary to meet a pressing societal need, and in a manner proportionate to that need' (ibid.). The whole phenomenon of 'mass imprisonment', which the Working Group observed had lead to massive disparities between countries, meant it was 'doubtful therefore' that high-imprisonment states, or those with extremely high rates of imprisonment of social or ethnic minorities, 'can find an objective and acceptable explanation' that would satisfy those states' international obligations in respect of fair and proportional use of confinement (ibid.). This analysis of 'mass imprisonment' occurred within the Working Group's broader practice of each year examining 'issues of concern', placing it next to matters such as the arbitrary detention of immigrants and refugee claimants, detentions associated with counter-terrorism measures, the detention of non-citizens and the question of psychiatric detention. Together, these concerns conjoin the prison and a variety of other, oftentimes new, sites of involuntary detention. It is to some examples of these phenomena that we now turn.

EXAMPLES: VARIETIES OF IMPRISONMENT

The expanding prison estate takes many forms and raises a multitude of questions about the proper place and use of detention in modern states. The aim of this section is not to provide an exhaustive catalogue of these various elements, but rather to point to some key examples that raise particular issues for prison studies. I begin in the prison itself, with the re-inscription of prison space as suitable for 'non-penal' preventive detention of socially undesirable characters. These are schemes using either civil law or some form of civil/criminal hybrid to detain, often indefinitely, suspect characters who, although not having committed any offence, are felt to pose a risk to public safety. Next I turn to immigration detention to consider the way that 'administrative detention' turns back the clock, placing detainees in an almost pre-modern era when the prisoner, like the slave or the 'impressed' sailor, had few, if any, rights and was restricted in access to the law. Generally this reduced status of the detainee *vis-à-vis* the prisoner is achieved through direct recourse to ideas like the 'alien' whom a sovereign (state) may rightfully eject from its territory. Finally, then, I will look at the restructuring of territory itself as a means of denying specific classes of prisoner – principally migrants, refugees and terror suspects – access to law that would challenge both the fact and the conditions of their imprisonment.

Post-sentence detention

Systems of post-prison detention for those considered dangerous due to mental abnormality or character defect have existed in a number of countries for many years (cf. mental illness – see European Commission, 2005). There is a long history of such laws in the USA (Janus, 2010), and in Europe countries like Belgium and Germany have had such measures on their statute books for decades. In Belgium, for instance, the Social Protection Act 1964, a law providing 'social protection' to the Belgian public 'against abnormal behaviour, delinquency and certain sexual offences', allows a prison sentence to be followed by up to ten years' preventive detention at the discretion of the government. The European Court of Human Rights has found this sort of detention consistent with the European Convention for the Protection of Human Rights and Fundamental Freedoms (hereafter 'the Convention') because the preventive element is connected directly with an offence and subsequent conviction, and as such can be construed as part of the penalty for the offence (*Van Droogenbroeck* v. *Belgium*[3]).

But in the last decade a number of Western countries have developed post-sentence detention schemes wherein preventive detention is retroactive, which is to say determined at the conclusion of a prison sentence rather than at the time of sentencing, and in which prisoners who have expiated their sentence in full are detained, either indefinitely or potentially so, in a prison for purposes of social protection and/or further rehabilitation. In Australia such laws are now found in Queensland (2003), New South Wales (2005), Victoria (2010) and Western Australia (2005), and a version of these similar statutes also applies in South Australia (2005) (see generally, McSherry and Keyzer, 2009). Those detained are called 'prisoners' and held in a prison or prison annex. Yet the High Court of Australia has held these laws constitutional

---

[3] *Van Droogenbroeck* v. *Belgium* [1982] ECtHR Application No. 7906/77, Judgment of 24 June 1982.

despite their apparent violation of the common-law principle, restated as recently as 1992 in the case of *Chu Kheng Lim* v. *Minister for Immigration Local Government and Ethnic Affairs*,[4] that 'the involuntary detention of a citizen in custody by the State is penal or punitive in character and, under our system of government, exists only as an incident of the exclusively judicial function of adjudging and punishing criminal guilt' (at 23). In a series of Australian cases, the 'non-penal' imprisonment of 'dangerous' individuals without conviction has been drawn together with the detention of illegal aliens, stateless people and indigenous children in a new jurisprudence of social protection that elevates governmental intentions over the material experience of imprisonment (Michelle Brown, 2011a, 2011b,). This refashioning of imprisonment as an apparatus of civil social protection was succinctly described by McHugh J. in *Al-Kateb* v. *Godwin*,[5] the case of a stateless man facing indefinite immigration detention, thus: 'a law authorising detention will not be characterised as imposing punishment if its object is purely protective' (at 44; see also *Re Woolley*[6] at 61).

In Europe also there has been a recent expansion in the use of this kind of detention, imprisoning so-called dangerous offenders post-sentence and without further offence or conviction. In Switzerland, a citizen-initiated referendum conducted on 8 February 2004 led to an amendment of the Swiss Constitution to allow lifelong indefinite detention, with limited avenue for appeal or release, of certain offenders whose behaviour seems resistant to treatment. The resulting Article 123a of the Swiss Constitution dictates that where the 'condition [of a sexual or violent offender is] assessed as untreatable, he or she must be incarcerated until the end of his or her life due to the high risk of reoffending. Early release and release on temporary licence are not permitted.' The only circumstances where release might be considered would be 'if new scientific findings prove that the offender can be cured'. Since the offender by definition constitutes a risk to the public, Articles 64.4 and 76.2 of the Swiss Criminal Code provide that the lifelong indefinite detention shall be in a prison.

In France, Decree No. 2008–361 of 16 April 2008 provides for *Rétention de sûreté*, a form of post-sentence detention for violent offenders that imprisons an individual in a 'centre of socio-medico-legal security' for a potentially indefinite period (Code de Procédure Pénale, Article

---

[4] *Chu Kheng Lim* v. *Minister for Immigration Local Government and Ethnic Affairs* [1992] HCA 64.
[5] *Al-Kateb* v. *Godwin* [2004] HCA 37.   [6] *Re Woolley* [2004] 225 CLR 1.

706–53–13). It is unclear whether the measure will withstand scrutiny by the European Court of Human Rights, since although it requires judgment at the point of sentencing, the French Constitutional Council has proclaimed that it does not constitute 'punishment' within the meaning of French law and can thus also be applied retrospectively (Council of Europe, 2008). In two recent cases, the European Court has declared German laws of a similar character as in violation of the European Human Rights Convention. In M v. Germany[7] and Haidn v. Germany[8] the Court held that German preventive detention law, which captures around 500 individuals at any one moment (Detention Watch, 2009), breached Convention Articles 5 (concerning right to liberty) and 7 (concerning additional and retroactive penalties). In the case of M, the Court declined to accept Germany's contention that the indefinite preventive detention did not constitute a punishment since, as in the Australian cases cited above, it had a protective intent, and ruled that in order not to constitute a penalty, any protective order must neither look nor feel like prison and must be focused on securing safety through return to the community and not penal isolation from it (see Michelle Brown, 2011b; Merkel, 2011; Janus et al., 2012). This has led the German Constitutional Court to declare preventive detention laws operating at various levels as unconstitutional and to require their overhaul by May 2013 at the latest (Constitutional Court of Germany, 2011).[9]

Immigration detention

The recent expansion of immigration detention, its mandatory character in many countries, the influence of private prison operators within the new industry and its many other problematic features has been well documented (Grewcock, 2009; American Civil Liberties Union, 2012; Bosworth, 2012). Rather than detailing these over again, the aim in this section will be to give some examples of the way the study of immigration detention provides opportunities for analytic development within a re-envisioned prison study.

---

[7] M v. Germany [2009] ECtHR Application No. 19359/04, Judgment of 17 December 2009.

[8] Haidn v. Germany [2011] ECtHR Application No. 6587/04, Judgment of 12 January 2011.

[9] Interim changes to the preventive regime following the case of M v. Germany [2009] ECtHR Application No. 19359/04, Judgment of 17 December 2009 have failed to alter the character of the detention sufficiently for it to be regarded by the European Court as not in the nature of a penality. See K v. Germany [2012] ECtHR Application No. 61827/09, Judgment of 7 June 2012 and G v. Germany [2012] ECtHR Application No. 65210/09, Judgment of 7 June 2012. These judgments follow the original case of M and do not develop the Court's jurisprudence on the matter, as did Haidn.

A staple of prison studies has been comparative research on punishment and imprisonment (Young and Brown, 1993; Cavadino and Dignan, 2006; Cunneen at al., 2013). Yet one important difficulty faced in such exercises is the lack of any substantive criteria or principle against which to judge the various approaches to punishment: there is not even agreement on what might constitute 'mass imprisonment' or 'hyper-incarceration' – is it headline numbers, or disproportionate use, or offence focus? – let alone what is the right amount of imprisonment. The potential of a broader approach to detention to contribute to this debate was hinted at earlier in this chapter when reference was made to the UN Working Group on Arbitrary Detention's decision to examine what they term 'over-incarceration'. At the same time as recognising states' prerogative to set domestic policy, the Working Group also observed that it was 'not entirely indifferent to the sentencing policies of States', since 'Article 9 of the International Covenant on Civil and Political Rights starts with the fundamental principle that "Everyone has the right to liberty and security of person"' (United Nations, 2005: 19). On that basis, the Working Group noted that the massive cross-national disparities currently found in imprisonment rates posed a problem that high-imprisonment states would have difficulty finding 'an objective and acceptable explanation' for (ibid.: 19).

In the realm of involuntary detention, it is possible to observe strong contrasts between the behaviour of states that have enshrined such human rights principles in domestic or supra-national law and those that have not. One example may suffice. The Australian case of *Al-Kateb*, it will be recalled, concerned the question of whether or not the continued mandatory detention of a stateless person was permissible when, due to an inability to find a safe receiving country, there was no reasonable prospect of deportation in the foreseeable future. Detention was thus rendered potentially indefinite. In *Al-Kateb*, the High Court of Australia, which is bound by no overarching framework or vision of human rights, resolved the question in two ways. First, it simply observed that the mandatory character of detention legislation meant that, 'tragic as the position of the appellant certainly is' (at 32), no reference to individual circumstances of a detainee was possible. But second, and to foreclose the only remaining avenue of claim, being that indefinite detention would be of such a character as to render it punitive, the Court developed the legal fiction of 'protective intent'. What this meant was that 'a law whose object is purely protective will not have a punitive purpose' (at 44) and thus will not infringe the Constitution's Chapter III separation of powers that reserves powers of punishment solely to the judiciary.[10]

In two recent cases, the European Court of Human Rights has investigated questions of a similar nature. The difference, of course, is that the two states concerned – Belgium and the UK – are governed by the European Convention for the Protection of Human Rights and Fundamental Freedoms. In M.S. v. Belgium,[11] the Court held that the detention of an Iraqi man pending deportation breached Article 5(1) of the Convention, which protects the right to liberty and security and, by implication, guards against unfair or arbitrary detention. The Court in M.S. held that the man's continued detention breached his right to liberty because, with the stalling of diplomatic efforts to find a receiving state that would guarantee his safety, the necessary link between the detention and deportation (one of the listed exceptions under Article 5(1) to the inherent right to liberty) was broken. Thus the Court was forced to 'note the lack of connection between the detention of the applicant and the possibility of departing from the Belgian territory' (at 179),[12] and thus the contravention of Article 5(1) of the Convention.

In the case of A and Ors v. United Kingdom,[13] the Court considered the question in the context of individuals whose continued detention was justified not only by the lack of a suitable receiving country but also (in a way similar to the Australian element of mandatoryness in the detention legislation) by the national security risk they were felt to pose. In light of such risks, the UK had issued a notice of derogation from Article 5(1) of the Convention. The Court, however, did 'not accept the Government's argument that Article 5 §1 permits a balance to be struck between the individual's right to liberty and the State's interest in protecting its population from terrorist threat'. Moreover, it held that the limited exceptions to the right to liberty listed in Article 5(1) is exhaustive and '[i]f detention does not fit within the confines of the paragraphs as interpreted by the Court, it cannot be made to fit by an appeal to the need to balance the interests of the State against those of the detainee' (at 171).

---

[10] In 2012 the case of M47/2012 v. Director General of Security and Ors [2012] HCA 46 sought to challenge the Al-Kateb ruling on indefinite detention, which in late 2012 was estimated to affect at least fifty detainees. In fact, the court declined to consider the question of indefinite detention, although two judges offered the view that Al-Kateb needed to be revisited, even if the circumstances of this case did not allow it.

[11] M.S. v. Belgium [2012] ECtHR Application No. 50012/08, Judgment of 31 January 2012.

[12] The judgment in M.S. v. Belgium is available only in French. This is my translation.

[13] A and Ors v. United Kingdom [2009] ECtHR Application No. 3455/05, Judgment of 19 January 2009.

The point of this comparison is not simply to suggest that different views of human rights are possible, though that is surely the case. Rather it is to observe that just as punishment practices change 'due to larger trends and fashions in governance' (Valverde, 2012: 246), the instrument of formal human rights law (the European Convention in contrast, for example, to Australia's notional ascription to the International Covenant on Civil and Political Rights) has the effect of restricting the capacity of governments to blow with those winds of popular opinion and governmental fashion.[14] This opens up a series of questions within prison studies as to what might be achieved by examining punishment practices, cultures of punishment, punishment sensibilities and contemporary governmentality more broadly through the lens of arguments developed here within the context of involuntary detention (see Michelle Brown, Chapter 6).

International zones

The sovereign power to expel an alien from its territory has, in recent times, been seen by some states to be undermined by the alien's physical location on national soil, which places them within grasp of certain rights and privileges, particularly access to the law. It has produced proposals for pre-emptive interdiction, such as the proposal by the Greek Foreign Minister in June 2009 for 'a ship of sufficient tonnage' to ply the Aegean sea, collecting up 'illegal migrants' for processing and assessment before repatriating or forwarding them on to EU transit or detention centres (*Clandestina*, 2009). Elsewhere it has led to efforts, such as those in Australia, to excise certain portions of remote territory (mainly coastlines and islands) from domestic legal jurisdiction, in the sense that physical presence in the annexed areas does not confer the right of access to Australian domestic law (see Chambers, 2011).

Perhaps the starkest and most complex form of this de-territorialisation, or the de-linking of the ancient relationship between territory and sovereignty, is the creation of 'international zones' at airports and other embarkation points. Among these, the international zone at France's Roissy-Charles deGaulle Airport, the busiest in Europe (Makaremi, 2009), is most notorious and well studied. Termed *Zone d'Attentes pour Personnes en Instance* (ZAPIs), these liminal areas were created as a zone

---

[14] See also the European Court's refusal to allow states to determine what constitutes a preventive versus punitive measure, the distinction invoked by the Australian High Court in *Al-Kateb*. This is achieved through the Court's anti-subversion doctrine of 'autonomous meaning': see M v. *Germany* (at 120).

of international jurisdiction located within French domestic territory, meaning that although a person housed therein was physically on French territory, they had no right of access to French law or, indeed, to the ordinary mechanisms by which those making asylum applications would present their case. The case of a Somali family is instructive. In 1992, four Somali brothers and sisters arrived at Charles de Gaulle Airport via Cairo. At the international border they attempted to register a claim for asylum but, due to border officials' concern that their passports were not valid, they were detained in the ZAPI waiting zone, which, in this case, included part of the Hôtel Arcade where they were interned at night, while during the day they were left in the airport's Espace pre-departure lounge. Ordinarily, asylum seekers would be granted a temporary visa in order to enter France and from there access French authorities responsible for registering and assessing asylum claims.

In a case later brought before the European Court of Human Rights, it was revealed that the Amuur family had been held virtually incommunicado while efforts were made to persuade them to accept deportation. They arrived on 14 March and attempted to register a claim for asylum with the French Office for the Protection of Refugees and Stateless Persons on 25 March, but the claim was rejected for lack of jurisdiction, since the family was located in the ZAPI and thus outside French territory. When finally a legal representative gained access to them, an emergency case was brought before the Créteil Tribunal de Grande Instance demanding their release from detention. However, the Tribunal's 31 March decision that their detention was arbitrary and not sanctioned by any law came too late, for on 29 March they had been summarily deported to Syria. In the case of *Amuur v. France*,[15] the Court heard that France had previously been warned of the dubious legal basis of such non-territorial zones. In September 1991 the Council of Europe had reviewed the ZAPI arrangement and declared that '[t]he international zone has no legal background and must be considered as a device to avoid obligations' (at 26). Further, on 25 March 1992, during the imprisonment of the Amuur family in the international zone, the Paris Tribunal de Grande Instance had ruled in relation to another group of detainees that the zone had no basis in French nor indeed international law:

---

[15] *Amuur v. France* [1996] ECtHR Application No. 19776/92, Judgment of 25 June 1996.

we reject as ill-founded the [government]'s submission that the complaint of an interference with personal liberty should be dismissed because the alien was merely prevented from entering France, as he was detained in a place which had to be regarded as an 'extension' of the airport's international zone. No evidence has been adduced of the existence of any provision of national or international law conferring any extraterritorial status on all or part of the premises of the Hôtel Arcade – which lies, moreover, outside the airport's perimeter and the area under customs control.

    ... [A]s matters stand, this zone, which is a legal fiction, cannot be exempted from the fundamental principles of personal liberty.

(Amuur: at 22)

Despite these rulings in national and supra-national tribunals, the device of non-territorial jurisdiction has been developed and extended in France and elsewhere (Council of Europe, 2008; Makaremi, 2009; Gammeltoft-Hansen, 2011). It raises questions for prison studies on a number of levels. It problematises, for example, the equation of imprisonment with involuntary detention and the reasonableness of choices which might lead a person to stay in detention, since both the French government and the Australian High Court have argued that such confinement cannot be punitive or involuntary when the restriction is only upon *entry* into a territory, not upon voluntary *exit* from it. As the French Minister of the Interior declared to Parliament in 1991, 'aliens in that situation are not detained (retenus), since they are not on French territory, as they are free to leave at any time' (*Amuur*: at 20). Similarly, the disabilities placed upon non-citizens link with a whole series of civil disabilities meted out upon offenders, ranging from restriction of voting rights while in prison to post-prison disenfranchisement, withdrawal of access to benefits, educational support, social housing and the like (Mele and Miller, 2005), and further to the proliferation of sub-criminal sanctions that impinge upon basic liberty rights (Ashworth and Zedner, 2010).

THEORISATION: TOWARD A POST-PENAL ACCOUNT OF IMPRISONMENT?

How might we make sense of developments such as these? How, in other words, does a post-penal study of imprisonment create a structure of meaning, explanation and understanding around the new field of confinement it reveals? There seem to be two avenues to pursue. First, we might look to extant frameworks within criminology and criminal law to aid us. There is much to be recommended in this approach. Lucia Zedner (2003: 176), for example, has suggested 'harvesting. . . analogous principles' from criminal justice as a means of regulating the potential excesses of a discourse of security. An example of this kind of transfer can be found in the adoption of the principle of proportionality in respect of involuntary detention. It will be recalled that the UN Working Group on Arbitrary Detention invoked the principle as a general measure of the reasonableness of a detention measure. Similarly, proportionality has been adopted as a guiding principle by the United Nations High Commissioner for Refugees in the *Revised Guidelines on Applicable Criteria and Standards Relating to the Detention of Asylum-Seekers* (United Nations High Commissioner for Refugees, 1999) and the Council of Europe in its *Twenty Guidelines on Forced Return* (Council of Europe, 2005). Moreover, Flynn (2011) has suggested that proportionality may serve as an index of reasonableness not just in individual cases but also more broadly in terms of detention centre design and system performance.

Yet we are also faced with the fact that this wider set of imprisonment practices speaks to a broader and perhaps even more fundamental set of tendencies within the interior dynamics of state power and public desire. Jonathan Simon (2010) has recently lamented the lack of wider critical enquiry of the 'mass imprisonment'/'hyper-incarceration' phenomenon, suggesting the approach taken by recent scholars of the death penalty and post-9/11 detention centres be replicated in respect of this. Rather than repeating the sort of analysis given to military detention, dark sites and secret prisons (see also Council of Europe, 2007; United Nations High Commissioner for Refugees, 2010), places that have in recent times seen almost medieval practices of atrocity meted out upon prisoners designated 'high value detainees', I would prefer to see the two discourses brought together. I would thus differ from Simon by suggesting we move to a wider frame of reference rather than fetishise not only the domestic prison but also, even more narrowly, the practices of 'mass imprisonment' that characterise just a small number of jurisdictions. The second avenue I suggest we pursue, therefore, is to try to think more expansively about imprisonment, developing a post-penal analysis of confinement albeit perhaps with the prison at its centre. Following from the cases discussed thus far, I will touch very briefly upon three thematic possibilities that link the theoretical notions characteristic of the social and humanities scholarship pointed to by Simon with features of the modern detention project.

1. The subject of imprisonment: from errant citizens to alien minds

> Moral Insanity, or madness consisting in a morbid perversion of the natural feelings, affections, inclinations, temper, habits, moral dispositions, and natural impulses, without any remarkable disorder or defect of the intellect or knowing and reasoning faculties, and particularly without any insane illusion or hallucination.
>
> Intellectual Insanity, in contradistinction to the preceding form. . .
>
> (Prichard, 1835: 16, emphasis in original)

Far from being a distant character, the figure of the prisoner has traditionally taken a central role in debate and principle formulated in respect of the limits of state power. Blackstone (1766/1979: 132) in his Commentaries argued that '[t]he confinement of the person, in any wise, is an imprisonment. So that the keeping [of] a man against his will. . . is an imprisonment' and further that 'no subject of the realm. . . shall be sent prisoner. . . where they cannot have the benefit and protection of the common law' (ibid.: 133). Of course, the equally ancient exception to such protections lay in the mentally disordered person, the sufferer of intellectual insanity who, together with the alien to be deported from the realm, constituted some of the strictly limited exceptions to the universal principle of right to liberty articulated by Blackstone and reflected most recently in the European Convention on Human Rights.

Yet contemporary developments in detention reveal a return to something like the nineteenth-century vision of alienism, the sufferer of Pritchard's moral insanity or what Etienne-Jean Georget, a student of Pinel, would describe at about the same time as 'lesion of the will' (Augustine, 1996; Eigen, 1999: 435). The sex offender indefinitely detained upon completion of his sentence, or terror suspects confined under special legislation or by executive order due to their suspect beliefs, do not suffer any recognisable intellectual disorder, nor have they committed any crime. They do not fit the long-standing division between sanity, free volition and liberty on the one hand, and insanity, reduced responsibility and a circumscribed right to liberty and access to law on the other. One important line of investigation for future work into the expanded realm of imprisonment will be better to understand newly evolving notions and narratives of incomprehensible conduct outside the domain of mental illness, and a return to thinking about the concept of the alien and alienism may offer a way into that.

2. The motivation to imprison: from penal populism to the politics of hate

> The paradox involved in the loss of human rights is that such loss coincides with the instant in which the person becomes a human being in general... *and* different in general, representing nothing but his own unique individuality which, deprived of expression within and action upon a common world, loses all significance.
>
> (Arendt, 1951: 302, emphasis in original)

Criminology, and prison studies in particular, has done a rather poor job of accounting for the energy lying behind the desire to imprison and exact pain (cf. Karstedt, 2002; Freiberg and Carson, 2010; see also Hörnqvist, Chapter 5 of this volume). Imprisonment is widely recognised in surveys as supported by the public, together with a desire for sentences to be longer, more painful and austere, but from whence does the emotional or psychic energy for such desires come? As governments trample fundamental human rights (imprisoning migrant children, sequestering individuals in indefinite post-sentence detention and 'rendering' terror suspects for interrogation in secret prisons), they rely upon what appears to be a widespread support for the systematic reduction of certain types of individuals. We may use the term 'reduction' in the sense of a removal, abrogation or effacement of an individual's status as a rights-bearing subject, their reduction to a kind of simple humanity which, in its naked individuality and thus perhaps perplexity, appears at once barbaric and superfluous.

Here we might profitably move from a general discussion of emotion in criminal justice to a more complex understanding of what I will term *enabling* emotions, such as hate. Sarah Ahmed (2001: 346), for instance, has suggested that the 'emotion of hate works to animate the ordinary subject', bringing 'that fantasy to life' through the constitution of normality, ordinariness, as 'already' and perpetually in crisis and under threat. But although hate works through figures like the 'child molester or rapist, aliens and foreigners', it is not stuck to them but rather constitutive of a field that is at once intimate, working to fix the identity of the other, while also aligning 'bodily space with social space' (ibid.: 349). How does an emotion like hate, therefore, support or provide the conditions under which certain classes of human beings are reduced to a kind of base or abject humanity?

3. The claim to imprison: from proportionality to degradation

> [I went into] these warrens where three brothels might be in one building and not all the sandal-oils of Lucknow would hide the stench of gutters

and latrines... Men with clubs stood guard at the entrances. Guarding whom from what? In the dim, stinking corridors sat expressionless women, very old, very dirty, shrivelled almost to futility; and already one had the feeling people were negligible: these were the sweepers, the servants of the gay girls of the Bombay poor, doubtless lucky because employed: a frightening glimpse of India's ever receding degrees of degradation. Degrees of degradation because gradually one discovers... [it] is charted... answering [a] need: definition, distinction. To define is to begin to separate oneself, to assure oneself of one's position, to be withdrawn from... the abyss at whose edge the sweeper of the gay girl sits.

(Naipaul, 1964: 44)

If proportionality has been the favoured device by which claims to a just measure of pain are apportioned, in what way do contemporary practices of imprisonment and detention speak to deeper cultural practices of hierarchy and order? Yet in contradistinction to what we might suppose from the operation of enabling emotions like hate, is it possible that degradation or reduction also find support in this need for carefully charted definition and distinction? Is it possible that degradation or reduction is not a categorical relationship of inside/outside, but instead finely and intricately measured and balanced? How do we understand a contemporary Western social order in which prison officers 'guard at the entrances' of razor-wired detention facilities imprisoning children and families, 'doubtless lucky' because they have reached Western shores? In what way do we perceive these people as 'negligible'? Against the threat of what abyss does the open field of contemporary imprisonment operate, and why does it seem so much more suitable that a detention centre should look and feel like a prison, rather than, for example, a hospital or aged-care village?

CONCLUSION

In ordering the release of a Jamaican slave from confinement aboard his master's ship on the Thames in 1772, Lord Mansfield is said to have remarked '[t]he air of England has long been too pure for a slave and every man is free who breathes it' (Riddell, 1923: 249). The slave, James Somerset, had been produced upon a writ of habeas corpus and the case of *Somerset* v. *Stewart*[16] is often linked with the broad writ of liberty that attaches to any subject found upon British soil. Yet neither personal

---

[16] *Somerset* v. *Stewart* [1772] Lofft 1; [1772] 20 St. Trials 1.

liberty nor security from arbitrary and degrading detention come as a given today, as many of the cases discussed in this chapter have revealed. It has been the point of the chapter to argue that criminology's longstanding investment in the study of prisons as the key location of that diminished liberty associated with confinement is, if not misplaced, then at least increasingly out of step with contemporary events.

Recent decades have seen a massive expansion in the scope and scale of involuntary confinement, and it has been possible in this chapter to touch on just a few of these places. As I noted in the introduction to the chapter, some criminologists have suggested that this reflects an expansion of state penal practices, constituting perhaps what Beckett and Murakawa (2012: 222) term a 'shadow carceral state', in which both the pathways into prison are transformed and the prison institution is buttressed by a range of new hybrid civil-criminal or administrative penalties (see also De Giorgi, 2006). Others have looked upon such expansions as reflective of long-standing tendencies within criminal law to provide preventive protection (Ashworth and Zedner, 2011), while still others have attempted to develop a jurisprudential base via what has been termed 'enemy penology' or 'enemy criminal law' (Krasmann, 2007; Gómez-Jara Díez, 2008). Finding a suitable analytic and theoretical frame for these new forms of involuntary confinement is no easy task. Yet to draw them all within an expansive penality seems to present at least two problems. To begin, it seems a potentially boundless exercise in which any form of confinement, however temporary or delimited, may be called punishment. This was precisely the difficulty Michel Foucault (1977) avoided in *Discipline and Punish* when he teased out the genealogical relation between those two concepts in matrices of modern power, else we would be left discussing the temporary imprisonment of children in school rooms and workers in factories. Second, to encompass airport international zones or indeed secret Central Intelligence Agency prisons and black sites as simple acts of punishment works both to stretch excessively the notion of penal punishment while at the same time ignoring the wider social and political context within which such confinement occurs. It is for this reason that I have attempted in the closing section of this chapter to suggest ways of theorising and making sense of new forms of confinement that do not fall back on old criminological categories – like punishment and penality – that work to enfold the world within the comfortable classifications of a domestic criminal science.

If prison studies is to re-invent itself for the modern world, it will thus need to take cognisance of the extensiveness and variety of modern forms of confinement, its often non-disciplinary character and its linkages into wider social phenomena than just crime and punishment. It will need to find a theoretical framework that can both connect the airport international zone to the domestic prison, while at the same time explaining the role of that local prison as a kind of ideal type of the confinement milieu, providing important inspiration and guide to form while at the same time being not quite suitable for the diversity of confining impulses abounding in the contemporary world. A reinvigorated prison studies will need also to return to those forgotten questions of penology concerning human nature, the impulses that drive behaviour and perhaps now also the impulses and emotions that drive, support and make meaningful the degradations and reductions that are so much a feature of modern involuntary confinement.

9

THE PRISON AND NATIONAL IDENTITY: CITIZENSHIP, PUNISHMENT AND THE SOVEREIGN STATE*

Emma Kaufman and Mary Bosworth

Settler countries have always built prisons as one of their first orders of business, not only to hold offenders but also to mark out the symbolic and actual limits of the nation state. In periods of conflict, new institutions of confinement spring up to hold enemy combatants, displaced refugees and prisoners of war. As immigration and crime control measures have intersected over the last decade (Stumpf, 2007, 2011), prisons in a number of countries have ended up housing a growing population of foreign national offenders and immigration detainees. Today, in the USA and in England and Wales, foreign national prisoners whose criminal sentences have expired can be held indefinitely in prisons and detention centres as they await deportation (Bosworth, 2011a; Bosworth and Kaufman, 2011; Kaufman, 2012a, 2012b).

Given this range of examples, it is somewhat surprising that criminologists have spent so little time exploring the relationship between imprisonment and national identity. With notable exceptions (Simon, 1998; Sudbury, 2005c; Bhui, 2007; Cain 2009), scholars almost universally treat the prison as an institution bounded by and contained within the nation state. This chapter seeks to disrupt that tradition of prison studies by drawing on testimonies gathered from a range of custodial institutions in England and Wales. Comparing accounts from foreign

* The research for this article was funded by the Marshall Scholarship Fund and the Oxford University Clarendon Fund (EK), and by the Nuffield Foundation, the British Academy and the Oxford University Press John Fell Fund at the University of Oxford (MB). We would like to thank those prisoners and detainees who spoke with us, as well as the staff who facilitated the research.

national prisoners and immigration detainees, we explore the implica-tions of the global and transnational reach of the prison. Ultimately, we argue that the prison is a site for the construction and contestation of the late-modern nation state.

Our claim is both theoretical and empirical. The prison is not only a projection of national sovereignty and an expression of state power. It is also a concrete space where global inequalities play out. Aiming to capture both of these dimensions of imprisonment, this chapter weaves together policy analysis and first-hand narratives. We begin with an account of incarceration trends in Britain, which in the last decade has witnessed significant increases in the foreign national prisoner popula-tion and a rapid expansion of the immigration detention estate. The first two sections of the chapter trace these structural developments and highlight some of the many convergences between immigration and criminal imprisonment. The next section examines these systems of incarceration in the context of feminist and post-colonial theory. Using interviews we conducted in prison and detention centres, we draw out the voices and experiences of incarcerated 'foreigners' to explore how the practice of imprisonment creates an exclusionary vision of British national identity.[1] In the end, this chapter argues that any answer to the question 'why prison?' must begin from critical assessment of the relationship between punishment, citizenship and sovereignty.

A CHANGING PENAL ESTATE

Over the last two decades, and particularly in the last several years, questions about foreignness and citizenship have come to the fore in debates about prison management. Such questions have arisen, in part because of the growing population of foreign national offenders. At the time of writing, foreign nationals constitute 13 per cent of the total prison population in England and Wales (MoJ, 2011). In actual num-bers, there are somewhere between 10,500 and 13,500 non-citizens in

---

[1] This chapter draws on interviews and observations from our separate studies of incarceration in England and Wales. Mary Bosworth, working in concert with two research officers, Blerina Kellezi and Gavin Slade, conducted twenty-four months of research in six immigration removal centres for a forthcoming book on British immigration detention practices (for more on that project, see Bosworth, 2011b, 2012, in press (a), in press (b); Bosworth and Kellezi, 2012; in press). Emma Kaufman conducted twelve months of interviews with foreign national prisoners in five men's prisons for her doctoral thesis (Kaufman, 2012a, 2012b, in press).

the penal estate (ibid.).[2] This statistic marks a significant (more than 100 per cent) increase from a decade ago, when British prisons held only 5,400 non-citizens (Banks, 2011).[3] While uneven reporting practices and deportation trends make it difficult to calculate the precise numbers of foreigners behind bars on any given day, especially when those numbers are compared over time, it is clear that the population of imprisoned non-citizens has expanded rapidly since the turn of the twenty-first century.

There are a number of different explanations for this growth (see De Giorgi, Chapter 2). Criminologist James Banks (2011: 187) attributes the expansion of the foreign national prisoner population to 'substantial increases' in the use of custody for non-citizens in recent years. Banks points out that foreign nationals are sentenced to imprisonment more frequently than they were a decade ago and at increasingly disproportionate rates relative to British citizens (ibid.). This is not because foreign nationals commit more or more-serious crimes than their British counterparts; there is little evidence to support that claim. Rather, foreign nationals appear to commit criminal offences at roughly the same rates as British nationals (MoJ, 2011; Vine, 2012). The two exceptions to this rule are immigration offences and drug offences, the latter of which tend to receive particularly harsh penalties (Allen et al., 2003). According to Banks and several other criminologists, these sentencing trends contribute to a penal estate in which foreign nationals serve longer criminal terms than their British counterparts (ibid.; Banks, 2011).

While compelling, this explanation for the growth of the foreign prison population requires further context and several caveats. For one, it is not entirely clear that there are more foreign nationals in prisons solely (or even primarily) because immigration has been recast as a criminal offence. Evidence from court-based research suggests that, with the exception of passport fraud, few immigration offences are

---

[2] The exact number of foreign nationals in the penal estate is difficult to calculate and is always changing. As of year-end 2010, the prisons in England and Wales held 10,866 prisoners identified as foreign nationals, and another 1,794 prisoners listed as 'nationality not recorded' (MoJ, 2011). Hindpal Bhui's research suggests that many of these 'unrecorded' prisoners are, in fact foreign nationals (Bhui, 2004). According to the Vine Report (2012), which was published in early 2012, there are also 760 ex-prisoners currently being detained in prisons under immigration (rather than criminal) powers. Taken together, these statistics put the population of imprisoned foreign nationals as high as 13,420.

[3] In 1999, the recorded population of foreign nationals imprisoned in England and Wales was 5,388 (Banks, 2011).

actually prosecuted under criminal law powers (Aliverti, 2012). Instead, the British government prefers to 'manage' foreigners through the use of detention and deportation, both of which are technically administrative processes (ibid.). People who have been given deportation orders can be held in immigration 'removal' centres (IRCs) rather than imprisoned, while those who are prosecuted are imprisoned and then detained after the conclusion of their criminal terms. There is, in other words, a nuanced and symbiotic relationship between immigration detention and imprisonment and, more broadly, between criminal and administrative law (see Mark Brown, Chapter 8). That relationship complicates a straightforward narrative about the criminalisation of immigration.

Trends in the foreign national prisoner population in England and Wales must also be placed in a broader geographic perspective. Relative to other European states, for instance, where the rate of incarcerated foreign nationals can reach heights of 70 per cent and commonly hover between 25 to 40 per cent, the numbers of non-citizens locked up in Britain are not particularly high (Van Kalmthout et al., 2007; see also De Giorgi, Chapter 2 of this volume). These numbers are, however, disproportionate to the percentage of foreign citizens living in the wider community, which is the more illuminating trend (Van Kalmthout et al., 2007; Global Detention Project, 2011). Foreign nationals are over-represented in the penal estate and, at least in terms of the non-EU population, share many characteristics with black or minority ethnic (BME) British citizen prisoners whose parents migrated to Britain.[4] These parallels suggest that the line between foreigners and citizens is less clear than it can seem in prison statistics. That line is also crucially related to the meaning of race and ethnicity in contemporary British society. Claims about the 'foreign' prison population often obscure this socio-cultural context.

Statistics on incarcerated foreigners can also suppress the wide variation within the foreign national prisoner population. While imprisoned non-citizens do have distinct and identifiable needs (they tend to face greater language and cultural barriers than British prisoners; they often have difficulty maintaining family ties; and some studies suggest that

---

[4] This is different, for example, from the USA, where Dario Melossi (2011) points out that there are fewer foreigners than you might expect in the state and federal prison systems (though their numbers do rise significantly once local and county jails are included) (see also Bosworth and Kaufman, 2011). African Americans, the largest 'minority' community behind bars in the USA, are typically not foreign nationals. The growing number of Latino prisoners in the USA would be more analogous to the foreign national population in England and Wales.

they have higher rates of self-harm and suicide than British nationals), these prisoners cannot be lumped into a single homogenous group (Bhui, 2004, 2007; Borrill and Taylor, 2009). According to the Prison Service, foreign national prisoners hail from as many as 161 different countries (or 'disputed territories' such as Western Sahara, which is counted as a distinct region in Ministry of Justice polls) (MoJ, 2011). Some of these countries are more represented than others in the penal estate: Jamaica, Ireland and Poland were the top three in the most recent count, while nearly half of all foreign national prisoners were born in countries with colonial ties to the British state (ibid.).[5] These figures hint at the wider historical context – and the enduring legacies of colonialism – in the constitution of today's 'foreign' prisoner population.

The more immediate context for debates about 'foreign' prisoners is a highly publicised political scandal. No discussion of the incarceration of foreigners in Britain would be complete without an account of the foreign national prisoner 'crisis', which is often cited by prison officials and staff as a turning point in the approach to non-citizens behind bars. That 'crisis' began in April of 2006 when, prompted by partisan campaigning, Home Secretary Charles Clarke announced that over the preceding decade more than 1,000 foreign nationals had been released from prison without first being considered for deportation.[6] Clarke's claim initiated a media storm – 'Home Office Blunders Left Foreign Rapists in the UK', one headline read – and eventually led to his dismissal from the government (Daily Mail, 2006). Clarke's revelation also catalysed legislative and policy shifts regarding the treatment of foreign national prisoners in England and Wales.

In the months after the foreign national prisoner 'crisis' emerged, the British government made a series of public overtures aimed at quelling public anxieties about the 'threat' of 'foreign criminals'. Several weeks

---

[5] Foreign nationals born in countries with colonial ties to Britain that formally ended in the twentieth century constitute 45 per cent of the total foreign national prisoner population and 8 per cent of the total prison population (MoJ, 2011). This number includes both remand and sentenced prisoners and excludes those prisoners whose nationalities are 'not recorded' or recorded as 'other', as well as those prisoners from nations whose colonial relations with Britain formally concluded before the twentieth century (such as the USA) or were never formally colonial (such as Somalia). Hindpal Singh Bhui has noted that the unrecorded prison population likely includes foreign nationals (Bhui, 2004). That claim – not to mention a more expansive definition of nations that have 'colonial' relations with Britain – suggests that the estimate of 45 per cent is low (see Kaufman, 2012b).

[6] Emma Kaufman's doctoral dissertation (2012b) describes in detail how the foreign national prisoner scandal emerged from an East Anglian election, during which the Conservative MP Richard Bacon sought to make deporting 'foreign criminals' a key theme of his re-election campaign.

after the scandal broke, the Blair administration petitioned the European Court of Human Rights to reconsider the absolute ban on deporting people to countries where they could face torture or death (BBC, 2006). Parliament then passed the UK Borders Act 2007, which provides immigration officers with police powers of detention, search and seizure and significantly expands the use of deportation for foreign national prisoners (Bosworth, 2008; Gibney, 2008; Harper and Symonds, 2009). Under this new legislation, all non-citizen prisoners are automatically considered for deportation, while non-European nationals sentenced to at least one year and European Economic Area (EEA) nationals sentenced to at least two years face mandatory deportation.[7]

The UK Borders Act 2007 radically alters the impact of custodial punishment for non-citizens. Whereas before foreign nationals were released onto British soil at the conclusion of their criminal sentences, now they are punished, arguably doubly, by being deported as well. Prior to their deportation, moreover, some foreign nationals endure a second custodial sentence in either a prison or an immigration 'removal' centre – this time without a fixed end date, due to the indefinite nature of immigration detention (Bosworth, 2011a). In essence, this new piece of legislation makes imprisonment the beginning of a separate incarceration experience, one that can extend well beyond a prisoner's criminal term.

These public attempts at border control were met with equally broad shifts in bureaucratic practice. In the wake of the foreign prisoner scandal, the Ministry of Justice began to restructure the penal estate around the goals of migration control. Over the three years following the foreign prisoner 'crisis', the Prison Service released a series of new policies on how to handle non-citizens (HM Prison Service, 2006, 2007, 2008). These policies were the first Prison Service documents to engage with citizenship in explicit terms; before the scandal, the Prison Service classed immigration and nationality under the heading of race relations (HM Prison Service, 2006, 2007, 2008). Newly focused on 'the problem of foreigners', the Prison Service also entered into negotiations with the UK Border Agency (UKBA), which was at the time – and under the same political pressures – rapidly expanding its criminal

[7] These sentence lengths – one year for non-European nationals and two years for EEA nationals – are both cumulative and retroactive. This means, for instance, that a non-European foreign national with a prior record of nine months in prison would face 'removal' based on a three-month sentence, regardless of when the original nine months was served.

casework division.[8] Those negotiations resulted in a Service Level Agreement between the two agencies, which is typically referred to by prison and immigration officials as the 'hubs and spokes' policy (Ministry of Justice and UK Border Agency, 2009).

At least in theory, this new penal policy creates a holistic model for the management of 'foreign criminals' in England and Wales. Under the hubs and spokes policy, which has been revised slightly since its introduction in 2009, the approximately 11,000 foreign national prisoners in the British penal estate are concentrated in and around prisons known as hubs, each of which is 'embedded' with full-time immigration staff (MoJ and UKBA, 2009). The policy also created two 'dedicated foreign national-only' prisons (this number has since risen to three). These facilities are supposed to hold foreign nationals facing deportation who are within five years of the end of their criminal sentences (ibid.).[9] Prisoners identified as 'foreigners' were transferred into these hub and foreign national-only institutions en masse, in some cases overnight, the day after the new policy went into effect.

In addition to reorganising the penal estate, the hubs and spokes policy also lays out guidelines for the interactions between prison and immigration staff. Among those guidelines is a mandate: where UKBA representatives are not actually 'embedded' within the prison, prison staff are responsible for identifying all the foreign nationals in the prison's population to immigration authorities (MoJ and UKBA, 2009). This directive means that in many cases prison officers are working as quasi-immigration agents and, more to the point, are working toward the aims of migration control rather than criminal punishment. From day to day, prison staff members also do a number of other jobs for the UKBA: they regularly search prisoners' cells for passports and identity documents; they communicate between prisoners and the UKBA; they manage prisoners' immigration casework and reach

---

[8] In the wake of the foreign prisoner scandal, the UKBA's Criminal Casework Directorate expanded to thirty-five times its original size and saw a £40 million increase in its annual budget (MoJ, 2007a).

[9] Thomas Ugelvik has written about a similar phenomenon in Norway, where the creation of 'foreign-only' prisons has contributed to what he calls a 'two-tier' system, with better service and treatment for Norwegian nationals (Ugelvik, 2012). While there are parallels between that model and the British one, Ugelvik found consistently worse conditions in prisons for 'foreigners'. In contrast, the 'foreign-only' prisons in Britain are contradictory places, with worse conditions in some respects and better treatment in others. See Kaufman (2012b) for a full analysis of the 'all foreign national' prisons in England and Wales.

out to solicitors; and, at least in some instances, they deliver immigration information to prisoners on the UKBA's behalf (Kaufman, 2012b).

In these ways and many others, both prison workers and the prison itself have been redirected toward the project of migration control. In the six years since the start of the foreign prisoner scandal, the British penal estate has shifted dramatically. Or rather, to be more accurate, fuelled by a political furore over the dual 'problems' of immigration and crime, changes that were in motion prior to the 2006 scandal have accelerated since that 'crisis'. The cumulative result of these developments is that today's prisons are decreasingly distinct from other sites of border control, such as airports, police stations and detention centres. Both on paper and in practice, the prison has become a key site for border control. Nationality and citizenship, meanwhile, have become central issues in British incarceration practices. This trend is clear not only in British penal institutions but also in the country's rapidly expanding collection of immigration 'removal' centres.

A NEW DETENTION APPARATUS

Purpose-built immigration detention centres have existed in the UK since 1970, when a forty-bed immigration detention unit was opened adjacent to Heathrow Airport on the site of the former roadworks department at Harmondsworth. Still there today, though much larger, Harmondsworth was originally designed to hold Commonwealth citizens who had been denied entry at the border but were granted in-country right of appeal under the Immigrant Appeals Act of 1969. In the 1970s and 80s, Harmondsworth was just one possible destination for foreigners who entered the UK. Non-Commonwealth citizens had no rights to in-country appeal and hence faced immediate deportation, while asylum seekers and immigrants caught on British soil without documents were placed in prisons. The British immigration estate was thus intertwined with the prison system from the start.

While these historical roots are important, particularly for the enduring relationship they reveal between colonialism and border control, the current scale and purpose of immigration detention is a more recent development. Like many crime control measures in the UK, the expansion of the British detention apparatus began in the 1990s and intensified under the New Labour Government (1997–2010). During that period, the government passed numerous pieces of immigration legislation which targeted so-called 'bogus asylum seekers', 'terrorists' and 'economic migrants' (Bosworth, 2008; Bosworth and Guild, 2008; Wilsher, 2011). The effect of this legislation (and more broadly, of the New Labour commitment to 'securing the borders') was evident in the expansion of the detention estate from a capacity of 250 in 1993 to more than 10 times that number in 2012 (Bacon, 2005; Home Office, 2012).

Today, around 3,000 foreign nationals are detained under Immigration Act powers at any given time (Home Office, 2012). Most of these people are held in 1 of 10 IRCs, while about 100 are placed in short-term holding facilities at ports. These 'removal' centres are typically located in the south of the country, near Gatwick and Heathrow airports, though there is one centre in Scotland and another, the sole women's establishment, sits outside Bedford. Most of the people in these detention centres are held awaiting deportation or administrative removal. A smaller number are confined while the government processes their asylum claims or establishes their identities. Male detainees may be moved around the detention estate at any time if they become 'disruptive' or if their transfer is convenient for the UKBA (Gill, 2009). Since there is only one women's establishment, female detainees do not circulate between facilities unless they are sent to prison.[10] Over the course of the year, the total figure of men, women and children 'arriving in detention' expands ten-fold to approximately 30,000 (Home Office, 2012).

Despite its size and scope, immigration detention is in many ways a localised practice. There is a national immigration detention system, yet there is no single service provider for the detention estate. Instead, the institutions are divided between the Prison Service and a series of private security companies, and each is run according to terms set out in a confidential legal contract. Within every centre, moreover, there are different levels of administration and accountability. While custodial staff members are responsible for the day-to-day running of 'removal' centres, they report to an on-site UKBA 'contract monitor' whose job is to check that the facility's legal contract is followed. That UKBA contract monitor also line-manages a number of local immigration officers who mediate between detainees and their 'case-owners', who are based elsewhere. These local immigration officers are the face of the UKBA in detention – they serve removal directions, give detainees

---

[10] There are a handful of short-term holding rooms for women in Colnbrook and Dungavel, though I (MB) am unaware of women being moved to these spaces from Yarl's Wood.

documents and information, and communicate decisions about bail, temporary admission and asylum. They do not, however, make those decisions, leaving that task to the off-site caseworkers. This arrangement means that detainees have no human contact with the people who determine whether and when they will be deported.

While this management structure distinguishes the detention apparatus from the prison estate, there is significant convergence between the two systems of incarceration. Since the foreign national prisoner scandal in 2006, the numbers of ex-prisoners in immigration 'removal' centres has grown exponentially. Today, formerly incarcerated people constitute around 50 per cent of the total detainee population (Vine, 2012). Many 'removal' centre managers are former prison governors from both the public and private sectors, as are a number of the civil servants within the UKBA. Several detention facilities, particularly those run by HM Prison Service, are former or presently operating penal institutions. The IRCs Brook House and Colnbrook, for instance, are both built to the model of a Category B prison, as are the new wings of Harmondsworth.[11] The IRCs Dover, Lindholme, Haslar and Morton Hall each occupy part or all of former or current prisons.[12]

Beyond this architectural overlap, there is also considerable conceptual parity between prisons and IRCs. Key policies in the detention centre are based on those from prison (Bosworth, 2007). As in prisons, daily life in 'removal' centres is increasingly directed by concerns about 'safer custody' and security. Detainees, for instance, are allocated to rooms in IRCs only after they undergo 'room share and risk assessments'. Those considered to be at risk of suicide or self-harm are placed on the Assessment, Care in Detention and Teamwork system, which draws heavily on the Prison Service's Assessment, Care in Custody, and Teamwork model. Both sets of institutions have designated security staff whose job is to monitor potential illegal or harmful activity. These staff members pay particular attention to 'high-risk' detainees, who are referred to within the detention centres as 'development nominals'. Removal centres also encourage staff to submit 'security incident report' forms for any kind of behaviour or incident that strikes them as

---

[11] Brook House sits alongside the Gatwick Airport runway, while Colnbrook is based next to Heathrow Airport's Terminal 5.

[12] Dover IRC, for instance, along with Haslar and Morton Hall, occupy the entire sites of former prisons, with Morton Hall 're-roled' from a women's prison to a male IRC only in January 2012. IRC Lindholme, in contrast, shares its site with a functioning prison.

suspicious. Each of these policies uses the prison and its security measures as a reference point.

There are also similarities between detainees and foreign national prisoners in terms of national origin. While there are sizable detainee populations from China, Vietnam and recent war zones like Afghanistan, the majority of those in detention migrated from former British colonies, most notably India, Pakistan, Bangladesh, Jamaica and Nigeria (Vine, 2012; Bosworth, 2012). As in the prison population, such people end up in the UK for a variety of reasons, including family ties, violence in their homeland and economic opportunity. Moreover, like foreign national prisoners, immigration detainees have a range of feelings about their national identities. Some want to return 'home'; others identify as British and resist their ejection from the country. The high number of ex-prisoners in the detention estate, not to mention the transfer of detainees between prisons and detention centres, means that these issues of national identity and origin affect both institutions.

Despite these parallels, there are notable legal differences between imprisonment and immigration detention. Detainees are held under administrative rather than criminal powers, and as such are not afforded the same due process rights as prisoners (Wilsher, 2011). Immigration detainees can be held indefinitely and there is significantly less oversight of the detention estate. In these ways and others, incarcerated migrants are in a far more vulnerable position than prisoners, whose ties to the criminal justice system come with the rights and protections of the criminal law (Bosworth, 2011b). Moreover, while many detainees describe and experience their detention as a form of punishment (Leerkes and Broeders, 2010; Bosworth, 2012), immigration imprisonment is not technically a criminal sanction. Detainees cannot cite the criminal law to explain their incarceration. As a result they are often left wondering why they are in cells and behind bars, particularly given the number of migrants living in the wider British community.[13]

Comparisons like these capture the significant tension underlying the practice of immigration detention. They also compel further examination of the relationship between the prison and the detention centre. These two modes of incarceration are theoretically distinct but practically aligned. They are different in key ways, especially at a conceptual

---

[13] While statistics on migrants are notoriously difficult to collect, the Global Detention Project estimated that by year-end 2007, somewhere between 525,000 and 950,000 'irregular migrants' resided in the UK (Global Detention Project, 2011). Those numbers, which may well have risen in the past five years, compare to the 3,000 people held in detention at any given time.

level, yet they share goals – most obviously, migration control – and do a similar kind of socio-cultural work around the concept of British citizenship. This cultural dimension of incarcerations is crucial and is too often overlooked in scholarship on the prison (Kaufman, 2012b). It becomes particularly clear when we examine the testimonies of those held in Britain's incarceration regimes.

NARRATIVES OF NATIONAL BELONGING

Despite the legal distinctions between immigration and criminal imprisonment, detainees and foreign national prisoners often articulate their experiences in similar terms. Many immigration detainees, for example, compare their surroundings to the prison. As one detainee wryly observed in regards to his living quarters:

> It's not a room; it's a cell. Anything without a window and a ventilator, would you call that a room? Anything to do with you being locked up and you can't even see what is outside, somebody has to check from the outside on you with light on, to see if you're still alive, that's a cell. It qualifies as a cell.
>
> (Barbados, BH)[14]

When another detainee raised these concerns with an officer in the detention centre, the following exchange ensued:

Detainee (Taiwan, YW):	I am a prisoner.
Officer:	No you are not. You are a resident.
Detainee:	I feel like a prisoner.
Officer:	You are not. [Slowly and loudly, insistently.] You. Are. A. Resident!
Detainee:	But there are walls here. I am trapped.

This conversation captures the belief, expressed by a number of immigration detainees, that the 'removal' centre is a kind of prison. Yet, while many detainees compare these two institutions, others distinguish detention centres from prisons in order to assert their greater suffering. Inside the detention centre, it is not unusual to hear variants of the claim 'the British treat us worse than their own criminals' (Pakistan, CH) or 'this place is worse than Guantanamo' (Rwanda, CB). These comments help detainees highlight their particular struggles and

---

[14] See also Bosworth (2012).

underscore the racialised nature of their experiences. As one Jamaican woman put it, 'Why *we* always got to be in *prison?*' (Jamaica, YW). For others, comparing prisons and detention centres illuminates the gendered precarity of life in Britain, as well as the gendered nature of many people's desires to migrate. 'This place is prison', one Pakistan woman said in Yarl's Wood. 'But it's better than my house.'

In actual prisons, meanwhile, a similar logic unfolds as foreign nationals compare their imprisonment to detention. George, a migrant from Rwanda, spoke at length about his time in IRC Harmondsworth, where he had been detained before being transferred into the prison system. 'They say it's a detention centre, but no difference to prison except more time out and the internet', he explained. In other interviews, foreign national prisoners invoked the idea of the detention centre to challenge the legitimacy of their imprisonment. Several prisoners held in an all-foreign national prison argued that they were being imprisoned for their foreignness rather than for their criminal offence. 'We're here for being foreign', one man said. 'I think all 300 prisoners here would say they're being punished because they're foreign.' Another man in the same prison expanded upon this claim: 'It does feel like punishment for being foreign a bit... I felt, yeah, I was being punished because I was tagged as a foreign national' (Kaufman, 2012b: 260).

As in the 'removal' estate, these testimonies compete with a set of claims about the distinctions between prisons and detention centres. While foreign national prisoners often note the overlap between criminal and immigration incarceration, they tend at the very same time to differentiate their experiences from those in detention. 'It's worse here than in detention centres', one foreign national prisoner said. Another man argued:

> This facility ain't here to figure out immigration cases. You're just sitting, like a duck. You need fax machines, access to solicitors, paperwork. It ain't here. It's harder to do everything here.
>
> (Kaufman, 2012b: 260)

Yet in the 'removal' facilities with those fax machines, detainees often believe that life would be better in a prison. A man from Eritrea put this sentiment in simple terms: 'I'd rather be in prison' (Eritrea, CH). Similarly, a detainee from Uganda argued:

> You know, they should put everyone in one of these places, first, before prison. Then they'd have no troubles, no one would re-offend. These places are hard man.
>
> (Uganda, CB)

In general, both detainees and foreign national prisoners facing deportation say that their lives would improve if they were in the other type of custodial institution. These claims are one way of imagining the possibility of a better life. In this sense, they constitute an important coping mechanism for those held in prisons and detention centres.

The fact that both detainees and prisoners make such claims leaves unclear whether prisons or detention centres are in fact 'better' or 'easier' places to be incarcerated as a foreigner. The real insight that emerges from these testimonies, particularly when they are assessed together, is that the prison and the detention centre exist in reference to one another. These two custodial systems are not just connected in theory, through architecture, policy and their role in migration control. They are also related in the minds and experiences of those held within them. Though they are not typically examined in the context of border control, at least by criminologists, prisons are linked at a fundamental level to immigration detention centres. For the 'non-citizens' who inhabit them, these custodial spaces are part of the same effort to punish foreigners for their presence in the UK.[15]

This lived connection between prisons and detention centres begs a series of questions about the effects of Britain's different incarceration regimes. Can scholars understand prisons and detention centres as part of the same effort to 'shore up' Britain's borders (Bosworth and Guild, 2008; Kaufman, 2012b)? Should we be studying these custodial institutions separately if they are doing shared cultural work? What do we lose when we view prisons in isolation, outside the context of migration control? Again, the answers to these questions lie (at least in part) in the experiences of those behind bars. Notwithstanding the significant legal differences between imprisonment and detention, it is evident from the voices inside them that detention centres and prisons have shared social effects. Both custodial institutions work to draw the

---

[15] There is considerable debate about whether detention can be called a form of punishment (Leerkes and Brodeurs, 2010; Bosworth, 2012). The affective element of punishment – that is, the fact that detainees believe they are being punished, or that foreign national prisoners believe their punishment is aimed at their foreignness – contrasts with the legal definition of punishment as the outcome of a criminal sanction. Scholars like Antony Duff (2010) and Lucia Zedner (2009) argue that calling detention punishment dilutes the connection between punishment and the criminal law, and in the process makes it more difficult to challenge the legitimacy of immigration detention. In this view, detention is illegitimate precisely because it is *not* a form of punishment. The contrasting argument is that detention is experienced as punishment by detainees and that calling it anything else obscures and delegitimises this lived experience.

line between foreigners and citizens and, in the process, to produce an exclusionary vision of British citizenship.

In the prisons where many foreign nationals are identified, for instance, prisoners often say that incarceration creates a newfound feeling of foreignness. 'Would you say you're British?' one interview began. 'I understand them more, but I don't feel British', replied Michael, a prisoner who had been incarcerated for more than ten years. 'I could never feel British in a place like this' (Kaufman, 2012b: 260). Another foreign national prisoner, Damian, had a parallel experience of imprisonment. Damian had lived in the UK for decades and had identified as British until he was incarcerated for a drug offence. 'It wasn't until I got to prison that I realized I wasn't British', he explained. 'When all this started, they made me realize I wasn't British' (Kaufman, 2012b). In both of these narratives, the feeling of incarceration shifted prisoners' senses of who they were.

Detainees in 'removal' centres reported similar transformations in their understanding of themselves. One Ugandan detainee, for example, offered this account (Bosworth, 2012):

> It's embarrassing being in detention. I don't want to tell my friends. When I called them and told them where I was, there were like 'really man? With all those immigrants?!' I guess I am an immigrant.
>
> (Uganda, CB).

For this man, detention was not simply a punishment for 'illegal' immigration or a route to deportation. It was also a means by which he came to understand himself as a different kind of person – namely, as 'an immigrant'. From this perspective, immigration detention appears to be much more than a new mode of custody or particularly 'tough' approach to border control. On a deeper level, it is a vehicle through which the nation state revises its relationship to its subjects. Through the experience of incarceration, detainees, like foreign national prisoners, learn that the law determines who they are and where they belong.

Often, this lesson about the force of the law conflicts with foreigners' personal senses of national identity. Time and again, both foreign national prisoners and detainees protested that, whatever their legal citizenship status, they felt and lived their lives as British people. Many of the prisoners categorised as foreigners under the new hubs and spokes policy have lived in the UK for years or even decades, have British citizen family members, have thick British accents and have few if any cultural or linguistic ties to the countries in which they were born.

Similarly, many detainees think of themselves as British despite facing what the government describes as necessary and 'imminent' deportation. As Patrick, a prisoner who migrated from the Congo as an infant put it, 'I don't know what they're thinking. If I went to the Congo, they'd call me a foreigner. Here I'm a foreigner; there I'm a foreigner. I don't know' (Kaufman, 2012b: 164).

While family ties and cultural connections to the UK do not preclude deportation, they do create palpable tension between the lived and legal definitions of foreignness. This tension is felt by foreign national prisoners and detainees alike, and it motivates acts of resistance in both incarceration estates. One Jamaican man held in Brook House, for instance, straightforwardly refused to acknowledge his status as a 'non-citizen': 'I am a British citizen. I just don't have a passport. I did primary school, middle school, high school. I am British' (Jamaica, BH). Less audibly but no less forcefully, another detainee, a woman in Yarl's Wood, crafted and wore a t-shirt that read '100% British' (Bosworth, 2012). Meanwhile, in the penal estate, prisoners who contest their status as foreign nationals refuse to produce their passports, employ fake British accents to avoid immigration authorities and even threaten to commit suicide if they are given removal orders (Kaufman, 2012b; see also Borrill and Taylor, 2009).

Within the UKBA lexicon, these acts of resistance are called 'non-compliance'. In criminology, however, scholars might understand them as a window into the relationship between incarceration, globalisation and mobility. Prisoners and detainees who resist their categorisation as foreigners illustrate that imprisonment involves a highly contested negotiation about the meaning of individual and national identity. Imprisonment is one way that the government determines what it means to be British or to be foreign. Whether criminal or administrative, the practice of incarceration is doing a particular kind of cultural work: it is delineating the borders of citizenship in an increasingly globalised world.

This is the point at which the detention centre and the prison meet. While these systems of incarceration are distinct, in some cases diametrically, they are operating in tandem to identify a class of vulnerable, deportable people who are implicitly less 'worthy' of the rights accorded to British citizens. To borrow Judith Butler's language (2004; 2009), these regimes are working together to render certain people 'unrecognisable', and as a consequence, 'ungrievable'. 'Part of the very problem of contemporary political life', Butler observes, 'is that not everyone counts as a subject' (2009: 31). Those who do not count are literally and metaphorically 'unrecognisable'. They live precarious lives, out of sight and often outside the protections of the law.

While Butler's writing is directed at American foreign policy, her critique resonates with our fieldwork in British prisons and detention centres. Both of these custodial institutions mark out the 'foreigners' among us and make clear that 'outsiders' are liable to exclusion from the British nation state. Together, these incarceration regimes work to make particular groups of people 'unrecognisable' in the eyes of the sovereign state. In this sense, the prison and the detention centre set the terms of twenty-first century political recognition (see Michelle Brown, Chapter 6).

This is a stark shift away from the past, at least for the penal institution. Traditionally, the prison has created the delinquent subject, one who was suspect yet implicitly capable of reform and return to the community (Foucault, 1977). Today, in contrast, the prison joins the detention centre in producing a group of 'non-citizens' whose precarity places them outside our usual expectations of decent practice and legal accountability. Although the 'foreigners' behind bars resist their detention and removal, they have few tools to combat this entrenched social framework. Detainees can appeal their deportation but they alone cannot undo the presumptions upon which global inequalities depend. These presumptions – that foreigners do not belong or that they do not deserve rights – are increasingly relevant to the management of British custodial regimes. We appear to have entered a new age of exclusion in the practice of imprisonment.

Yet, while the particularly exclusionary bent of incarceration seems new, its strategies flow directly from the past. There is a long tradition of revisiting and recasting the relationship between sovereign and subject in British history. In the twentieth century, Britain routinely reworked the boundaries of citizenship in relation to its former colonies. Since the 1970s, successive immigration laws have limited the rights and benefits that accord to membership in the British Commonwealth (Hall et al., 1978; Gilroy, 1987; Wilsher, 2011). While British subjects born in Nigeria, Jamaica or India once had the right to migrate and reside in Britain, today they are being deported from the UK at record rates. In Britain, the precariousness of citizenship is inextricably related to a colonial past and to the country's effort to carve out a 'post'-colonial present (Kaufman, 2012a).

The systematic push to detain and deport foreign nationals draws on this long history of excluding certain classes of people, including those who identify with the UK or who were at one time British subjects. The patterns of the last half-century demonstrate that British citizenship is a contingent and constantly changing idea. In 2012, this idea is more confined than ever before. With the help of the detention centre and penal policies like hubs and spokes, citizenship has been recast as an earned and easily lost privilege. As a result, the rights of political membership appear to flow from citizenship rather than from our shared humanity or from a supra-national space. Contemporary imprisonment practices are thus part of a larger effort to reify the link between citizenship and rights. In an era of mass mobility, incarceration affirms a territorial notion of citizenship, and with it, the boundaries and sovereignty of the nation state.

CONCLUSION

This account of imprisonment is necessarily incomplete. The narratives presented in this chapter do not begin to capture the variety in prisoners' and detainees' feelings about their incarceration and the questions we have raised are only a few of those that surface from the testimonies behind bars. Detainees and foreign national prisoners are not universally opposed to their deportation. In England and Wales alone, there are more than 13,000 people incarcerated as foreigners on any given day; each has his or her own story, goals and struggles. The views of staff, detention centre managers and policymakers also complicate an analysis of migration control. There is much more work to be done on these issues.

Even a brief exploration of the links between prisons and detention centres, however, suggests that criminologists could be thinking more about the relationships between punishment and sovereignty, rights and recognition. In the twenty-first century, scholars cannot assess prisons as if they derive from, rather than producing, the bounded nation-state. Prisons are places where the meaning of citizenship is crafted and where the practice of liberty deprivation is increasingly shaped by the goals of migration control. They are also institutions that depend upon and enable legally dubious incarceration regimes like immigration detention. In this context, the traditional concepts of prison theory – decency, legitimacy, rehabilitation, even punishment – may look different or may no longer apply.

To answer the question 'why prison?', scholars must thus test and trouble these concepts. Criminologists and legal scholars should be mapping out the connections and disjunctions between criminal and administrative law. We should be exploring the lived experiences in different incarceration regimes, especially places that are typically considered in isolation, and we should be asking what those experiences can tell us about the late-modern penal institution. That line of thought will almost certainly raise other questions, some of which we have hinted at in this chapter. What is punishment, given the overlap between theoretically discrete custodial institutions and legal realms? Where do first-person narratives fit in criminological accounts of the prison's purpose? Where do questions about race, gender and colonialism come into prison theory? These questions can help scholars connect the prison to other structures of global inequality. In doing so, they might generate new and provocative ways to challenge the practice of incarceration.

10

PUNISHING THE DETRITUS AND THE DAMNED: PENAL AND SEMI-PENAL INSTITUTIONS IN LIVERPOOL AND THE NORTH WEST

Vickie Cooper and Joe Sim

> *The more the so-called minorities accept themselves as such, and close off from one another, the sounder the only real minority – the dominant class – will sleep. All through history, among the self-proclaimed rights of power, power has always arrogated the right, as an intrinsic condition of its very being, to paint the portrait of those who have no power. And the picture the powerful paint of the powerless, to be incarnated by them, obviously will reinforce the power of those who have power, by reason of which they do their portrait painting.* (Friere, 1992: 131)

The reproduction of the social residuum in the 1880s, the cycle of deprivation debate in the 1970s and the discourses of the underclass and social exclusion in the 1980s and 1990s, historically, have evoked a 'shadowy category of persons, living perpetually off the labour of others, relegated to the social margins by their inability to acculturate to the work ethic' (Welshman cited in Estreich, 2011: 133). Those who have fallen into these categories have been disdainfully caricatured as 'bodies without brains', whose very existence is intolerable to 'urban, entrepreneurial governance' (Wilson and Anderson, 2011: 56). Their punishment has been normalised and legitimated through recession economics as well as cutbacks and austerity inflicted through welfare reform. The evidence suggests that welfare polices and penal institutions have converged 'to form a system of governance over socially marginalized groups' (Wheelock et al., 2012: 1). This, in turn, has shaped public and political views that a high penal incarceration rate is a rational solution to counteract problems of crime, and that welfare support should be withdrawn from those who commit crime (Wheelock et al., 2012). Put differently, successive governments have legitimated a political ideology that the poor and socially excluded populations deserve to be punished *and*, moreover, are undeserving of welfare support (ibid.).

This vision of the undeserving poor is most evident in the treatment of the homeless and their struggle with neoliberal state responses to their poverty, the objectification of the risk they pose and the identification of their 'criminogenic needs'. Irresponsive to consumerism, work, time and space, the homeless embody a mythical profile of poverty that is inherently criminal, where they are seen to be 'delinquent or deviant rather than displaced' (Adlam and Scanlon, 2005: 454). They are constant targets of moral regulation exercised through health, housing, shelter and welfare programmes, and their 'everyday' activities are criminalised through the privatisation and militarisation of public space, involving zero-tolerance crime control strategies and new techniques of banishment (Beckett and Herbert, 2010: 61).

Seen as inherently deviant, the homeless have historically been locked out, locked up and quarantined (Beckett and Herbert, 2010), and although they are subject to far- and wide-reaching mechanisms of disciplinary control, they continue to pose a threat to the moral and social order as they are seen as 'unpromising partners in coerced "responsibilization" contracts with the state' (Carlen, 2002: 119). According to DeClerk (2006: 162):

> The plight of the homeless is compounded by the insidious sadism of a society that needs to punish those that live on its fringes and which, to this end, ensures that the health and welfare provisions made for the homeless are structurally inadequate.

In considering the punishment of the poor, this chapter utilises data from a study on homelessness and imprisonment carried out in Liverpool and the North West in 2011.[1]

First, it explores the direct experiences of the homeless, where we make the argument that the biggest obstacle for offenders and ex-offenders experiencing homelessness is not simply imprisonment but the *process* of punishment across a range of penal and semi-penal institutions, orientated towards the targeting and incarceration of the unhoused. Second, the chapter critically analyses the different programmes operating in HMP Liverpool designed, in theory, to normalise the petty short-term male offender, including the homeless, as well as exploring the contradictions within and between these programmes. Third, the chapter explores the contradictions within and between these programmes.

---

[1] The study was based on 34 interviews: 31 people experiencing homelessness and 3 practitioners working in the field of homelessness and resettlement.

Fourth, we consider the differential experiences of homeless women and the normalisation programmes they are confronted with both in penal and semi-penal institutions. Finally, the chapter analyses these developments in the context of an austere, converging penal/welfare complex which, in turn, raises some key political questions not only concerning 'why prison?' but also, following Pat Carlen (1993), 'why not utopianism, abolitionism and socialism?'

HOMELESSNESS AND IMPRISONMENT IN LIVERPOOL

In 2010, in the Index of Multiple Deprivation Liverpool was ranked highest in England (JRF, 2012). In 2007 nearly 56 per cent of the city's inhabitants lived in the 10 per cent most deprived areas of England (Liverpool City Council, 2009). Most of those who were homeless came from 'the lower super output areas, which [were] the 10% most deprived across England' (Liverpool City Council, 2012: 47). According to Liverpool City Council, in 2010/2011 there were 1,887 people who were presented as homeless, and four people were identified as becoming statutorily homeless as a result of 'leaving prison' (Liverpool City Council, 2012: 38). Given this small figure, the council suggested that 'there has been a significant reduction in the number of people becoming statutorily homeless from prison in the last two years' (ibid.). However, based on postcode data research, gathered from Liverpool Prison, it was found that of the 550 prisoners who originated from the Liverpool area, 32 per cent were recorded as having no fixed abode (NFA).[2] This indicates a greater representation of homelessness in HMP Liverpool compared to that suggested by Liverpool City Council. Disproportionate levels of homeless groups in Liverpool Prison should come as little surprise, given that the Social Exclusion Unit (2002) estimated that 32 per cent of the national prison population were homeless. Why is this the case?

The 'flight risk': housing the unhoused

People experiencing homelessness are over-represented in prison not as a result of their recidivist, compulsive and pathological behaviour but as a result of the risks constructed and associated with people who deviate from normative ideologies surrounding domesticity and the home.

[2] These data were obtained from the prison by the two authors. Thanks to Jim Hollinshead for his help in analysing the data.

Simon (2001: 16) argues that the construction of risk allows the wider society to 'valorize certain people while mobilizing disdain for other people and behaviours'. Those who deviate from discourses around the home are socially constructed as the 'other' within the criminal justice system, whereby homeless people are managed and governed according to pre-ordained institutional values that identify risk with behaviour that is not so much dangerous, as different.

Nowhere is this social construction more evident than in the risk associated with the 'fear of flight'. 'Fear of flight' describes the judicial decision for remanding homeless people to custody based on the risk that they will fail to surrender to custody and abscond. According to the Bail Act 1976, decisions determining pre-trial imprisonment all hinge upon a series of *risks*, including that of failing to surrender to court and custody (Player, 2007). Judicial decision-making guidelines, therefore, hinge upon the defendant having a house, which stands as a determining factor when passing key decisions in granting bail, sentencing to community punishment or granting parole. Without a house, surveillance is compromised because homeless defendants/offenders are perceived to be 'chaotic' and 'difficult to track down' (ibid.: 422). Furthermore, '[t]he fewer ties an individual has to conventional society the easier it is to slip from social surveillance' (ibid.). Therefore, to prevent the risk of homeless defendants failing to appear in court, magistrates are more likely to detain them on remand, as opposed to granting bail (ibid.). As one interviewee from the Liverpool study noted:

> I did a four month remand that if I'd have had an address I wouldn't have had to have done, because I had nowhere to live, there was nowhere to bail me too. They always say at court, 'due to fear of flight', because I don't have a stable address, they say, 'due to fear of flight, Miss [x] must be remanded into custody' for things that I wouldn't be remanded for. I get sentences for things that I wouldn't get sentences for because I'm not deemed appropriate for any probation or community sentence orders because of the fact that I'm homeless.
>
> (Shirelle, probation hostel)

This experience is not uncommon for homeless people within the criminal justice system. Due to the 'flight risk' (specifically the failure to appear in court), the circumstances surrounding their homelessness can impair a defendant's right to be granted bail, or be given a community punishment. Homeless defendants and offenders are acutely aware of this obstacle and, as a survival strategy, will often provide a false address and/or give their parents' address in order to be granted bail or parole. Recognising this, Baldry (2001) and Seymour and Costello (2005) suggest that 'official statistics generally grossly under-represent the number of homeless individuals in the criminal justice system' (Seymour and Costello, 2005: vii). The experiences related below describe how respondents felt compelled to lie in court about having an address so as to avoid either being remanded or sentenced to custody:

Researcher: When you went to court in [name of city] did they talk about your housing situation?

Kenny: Yeah and I lied. I said I was living in the Salvation Army... I lied to save my own neck basically, so I could stay outside rather than be inside. I would have got six months on the spot otherwise. Then I would have missed summer out again. I would have come out at the same time in winter again in December and what am I going to find then? At least I have got a chance now to find somewhere, haven't we ... and try and put things right. It's been going on for years and years this now and it's wearing me down.

(Kenny, centre for rough sleepers)

Researcher: So what happened when you came out of [name of recent prison]?

Belinda: I just go back to my mum's for the week; she doesn't like it but... just for an address you know, to get out on my licence.

Researcher: So according to the prison then, they think you've got...

Belinda: ... an address, yes.

(Belinda, homeless hostel)

Therefore, far from being passive and docile subjects of the state, people experiencing homelessness are active social agents who frequently adopt strategies of survival (Carlen, 1996; Wardhaugh, 2000) and, through transgression, exploit flawed systems of power and control (Doron, 2000). In the particular instances above, participants lied about having an address in court to avoid pre-trial imprisonment, and they also lie when inside prison in order to maximise their chances of being released on parole.

Semi-penal disciplinary practices

According to Mehta (2008: 192), 'if the offender does not have identified suitable housing on release, then consideration is given to the suitability of an approved probation hostel'. However, releasing homeless offenders into probationary accommodation is problematic. For

193

example, people under probationary supervision *and* accommodated in probation hostel premises (approved premises) are subject to more rules and regulations compared to domiciled parolees (Padfield, 2012). They must adhere to probationary licence terms and conditions, in addition to individual probation hostel residence licences (MoJ, 2007b). Rules and regulations stipulated in the residence licence can involve room searches, signing-in, no visitors, drug testing, the prohibition of alcohol, curfews, treatment (around domestic violence issues, mental health and substance misuse) as well as regular contact with the police as part of joint management schemes (MoJ, 2007b). To that end, 'probation hostels can be actually more restrictive than open prison for some' (ibid.: 9) and the omnipresence of social control can make it difficult for offenders *not to* breach the terms and conditions of their licence (Padfield, 2012). According to the Ministry of Justice (2007b: 37), failure to meet the residence licence can 'warrant eviction' where offenders 'will be returned to court or prison'. This is further compounded by the fact that, since the introduction of the Criminal Justice Act 2003, there has been an increase in powers given to the Probation Service to recall parolees back to custody for breaching the terms and conditions of their licence, making it increasingly difficult for homeless offenders to complete their licence period in the community. Also known as 'back-door sentencing' (Padfield and Maruna, 2006), recalling prisoners to custody increased almost threefold between 2000–1 and 2004–5, rising to 11,081 in 2004–5 (HM Inspectorate of Prisons, 2005: 7). According to the Ministry of Justice (2007c), recalls contributed to a 16 per cent rise in the overall increase in the prison population between 1995 and 2007.

The study conducted in Liverpool highlighted the links connecting back-door sentencing, probationary accommodation and homeless offenders' experiences of probationary accommodation. This study indicated that respondents who were homeless when released from prison, and were accommodated in probation accommodation, were likely to breach their licence terms and conditions and thus be recalled to prison. The difficulties in negotiating the boundaries of disciplinary control for those sentenced to community punishment were described by a number of respondents in the Liverpool study:

> When they tell you what to do, you've got to: if you breach it, they put you back in here [prison]. To be quite honest with you, you are better off in here [prison]. That housing association, don't ask me how they get paid

for that accommodation. Then I had to go into a different probation one. That was horrible. They put you in a shared room you have to go into a shared room first. It sounds petty. That's a probation run hostel, all they are doing in those places is giving you enough rope to hang yourself.

(Martin, prisoner)

I started going into hostels and then I got recalled in last January, not this January gone, last year January I got recalled and I was in for five months then. I got out went back to a hostel and again and this is basically non-residing that I'm coming in for because I don't want to stay in a probation hostel. . . when people say to me sum it up what it's like there I say it's like a strict decap prison, it's like a strict open prison.

(Callum, prisoner)

The first time that I went away they sorted out my Salvation Army. I was on warrant for breaching my licence and I went back on a twenty three day recall. I came out on licence but I didn't keep up with it so I went back to court and then back to the Farms. It's just like probation, I would rather go to jail and do my time rather than get another order.

(Jamie, homeless rough sleeper)

Thus, the experiences of poor-quality probation accommodation, combined with disciplinary regimes of control, can result in those living in semi-penal institutions such as hostels being recalled to custody. In many respects, community punishment was not perceived as an alternative to imprisonment but as a *different* type of punishment, whereby stringent terms and conditions made it difficult for men and women to live in the community.[3] Additionally, the constant threat of being recalled subverted their agency and power to negotiate boundaries of control and order. To that end, unattainable expectations of male offenders in the community – combined with their social, political and economic marginalisation – made prison, from their perspective, a comprehensible method of punishment, whereby recall 'felt almost like a relief' (Padfield, 2012: 41).

However, as we illustrate below, this sense of 'relief' is strongly mediated by a series of formal and informal processes of punishment that operate within penal and semi-penal institutions and which provide, in practice, little relief or rehabilitation to male and female offenders. It is to a critical consideration of these processes that this chapter will now turn.

---

[3] This punitive mentality in Liverpool was reflected in the broader drive towards punishment in the community to the point where, in 2012, the Prison Reform Trust noted that a government consultation paper on community sentences, which was 46 pages long, 'was littered with 42 uses of "punitive" and 48 references to "punishment" with far less emphasis on rehabilitation and reform' (Prison Reform Trust, 2012: 3).

A CRITICAL READING OF PENAL AND SEMI-PENAL PROGRAMMES

When New Labour came to power in 1997, a central theme in the government's agenda was that prisons could be made to work. Under the auspices of the Crime and Disorder Act 1998, a range of programmes were developed via, at least in theory, a joined-up partnership approach to offending behaviour. 'What Works' became the government's repetitive, recycled, law-and-order mantra (Sim, 2004). This in turn led to the introduction of programmes such as Reason and Rehabilitation, Enhanced Thinking Skills, Problem Solving and CALM (Controlling Anger and Learning to Manage it) (Stewart, cited in ibid.: 253). For offenders in general, and short-term prisoners in particular, these programmes were designed to alter their cognitive thinking and by extension normalise their behaviour. How can this development be explained?

Following Michel Foucault (1977), the development of partnerships and joined-up government responses to crime and deviance can be understood as relying upon numerous and diverse discursive practices that compel individuals to act within, and upon, their own subjugation. Lynne Haney (2004) has made the point that this has not only led to 'the convergence of discourses of responsibility, dependency, and empowerment in the welfare and penal systems' but has also generated a 'devolution and decentralization' in the power of the state which has diversified into 'a multiplication of actors now playing the role of the state' (Haney, 2004: 348 and 352). This development has occurred under the ideological camouflage of the entrepreneurial alliances between the central state, the local state, private companies and the third sector, legitimated by a national and local media network, schooled and disciplined in the fine art of 'defining in' acceptable views and conversely 'defining out' (Mathiesen, 1980) those individuals and groups whose views and attitudes conflict with the dominant discourses of entrepreneurial city governance. Crucially, this coalition of the willing has generated new layers of social control, involving not only traditional state institutions and private companies such as Group 4/Securicor and Serco but also voluntary sector organisations who have become 'proactively competitive' in their orientation to the point where:

> Neoliberal social capitalist discourse has entered British voluntary sector politics through the activities of politically well-connected lobbyists

within the sector who aim to reposition it as an exemplar of entrepreneurial flexibility and to alter perceptions of its 'well meaning and unbusinesslike amateur[ism]'.

(Corcoran, 2011: 43)

In the UK, approximately 180,000 registered charities and thousands of smaller voluntary organisations currently deliver '£13 billion worth of public services annually' (Association of Chief Executives of Voluntary Organisations (ACEVO), 2011: 4). This sector's involvement in constructing the welfare agenda should not be underrated, because those involved in the business of welfare and criminal justice share a 'correspondence of interests' (Hall and Scraton, 1981: 474), where 'each group of actors tends to seek strategic alliances with the other to fulfill their own goals, but the goals themselves are also homologous' (Davies, 2011: 91). They have an impact upon how social problems are understood, how responses to these problems are framed and mobilised and how further strategies can be developed, emanating from the reductive ideological frame of reference they operate within to ensure conformity, control and order. Corcoran (2011) has also noted that different interest and pressure groups – including ACEVO, the Social Market Foundation, the Confederation of British Industry and the Rainer Foundation – are involved in the process of control and regulation. ACEVO, in particular, 'envisages altering the state's role in public expenditure to that of a "market maker"' (ibid.: 43). Crucially, the various inquiries commissioned, and research conducted, by a number of these organisations 'have concluded in favour of increasing prison capacity' (ibid.: 44).

Penal programmes and state power

Bob Jessop has pointed out that it is possible, through utilising a critical reading of Foucault's later work, to develop a theoretical framework that transgresses, we would argue, the increasingly tired debate between Foucauldian theory and Marxist theory. In this work:

> Foucault began to analyse state(s) as a crucial site for the strategic (re)-codification of power relations linked to new governmental projects and modes of calculation. These operate on something called the state; but the latter is something that is not only pre-given as an object of governance but is also being (re)constructed through changing practices of government.

(B. Jessop, 2008: 150)

Indeed, as Jessop notes, Foucault's 'later work [shows] some interesting, if generally unacknowledged and perhaps unintentional, convergences toward more sophisticated Marxist positions, including those of Gramsci and Poulantzas' (ibid.: 145). Utilising a Gramscian theoretical framework, with its emphasis on the consolidation of power differentials within an 'integral state' form, illustrates how networks (as well as partnerships) operate as 'a dimension of neoliberal hegemonic strategy' (Davies, 2011: 101). This strategy is itself 'part of the "regulative cultural work of producing ideal neo-liberal subjects"' (Johnston cited in Davies, 2011). Thus, the rebuilding of deviant subjectivities, in penal and semi-penal environments, is being articulated through different state-sanctioned interventionist programmes involving a constellation of old and new 'judges of normality' (Foucault, 1977: 304; Sim, 2005). They are orientated towards the same goal, namely the programming and reprogramming of the deviant, ranging from the single-parent welfare claimant to the short-term, petty recidivist, including the homeless.

Furthermore, what is emerging is a disciplinary penal logic *and* a disciplinary welfare logic increasingly propelled forward by private and third-sector interests, which, taken together, are concerned with reconfiguring the deviant subjectivities of the poor into enterprising and responsibilising subjects of the free market; hence the link between the penal 'judges of normality' (Foucault, 1977: 304) and their welfare counterparts (see Wacquant, Chapter 4). It is in this context that state control has intensified under the Conservative/Liberal Democratic coalition government, who have built on the authoritarian legacy of New Labour, whose 'mantra' of '"no rights, without responsibilities"' has become [for the coalition] "few rights with lots of responsibilities"' (Grover, 2011: 2).

The issue of violence
Additionally, from a neo-Marxist perspective, there is the ongoing issue of violence, as well as the threat of violence embedded in state practices (Coleman et al., 2009), an issue which transcends the stated rehabilitative aims of the different programmes. According to Dario Melossi (2008), twenty-first century penal discourses of 'rehabilitation', along with the discourses of 'correction', 're-education' and 'resocialisation', should be deconstructed due to the competing definitions and meanings attributed to them. For the state, rehabilitation means 'teaching the lesson of subordination' (Melossi, 2008: 241); in other words, it is 'about learning to lower one's head and execute orders, understanding that one

is on the receiving end of the deal' (ibid.: 242). Melossi notes that for those at the sharp end of the process of subordination (that is, those who have 'nothing to expect but a hiding'), punishment is not about rehabilitation but is:

> a powerful instrument of government which teaches discipline. This has nothing to do with the kind of 'labor' that goes on inside prisons or with 'rehabilitation' as commonly intended. Or, if it is a kind of 'rehabilitation', it is a peculiar type. It has much more to do with *maintaining* a social stratum of the canaille.
>
> (Melossi, 2008: 242, emphasis in original)

Or to put the argument in Gramscian terms, 'coercion is the ever-present condition of consent' (Davies, 2011: 105). Davies points out that it is possible to analyse current political developments around partnerships not as progressive and positive but rather as intrinsic to an 'integral state' form where consent and coercion are dialectically interrelated:

> The difference between consent and coercion is not, therefore, adequately captured by a simple distinction between governmentality and armed violence. The distinction is rather that between internal or biopolitical regulation (governmentality) and external regulation (disciplinary power), which includes but is not limited to violence. Just as consent operates on a continuum from passive and grudging to active and enthusiastic, so compulsion is a continuum from bureaucratic obstruction to armoured force... Hegemony or consent in civil society is always mediated by coercion or tacit threat – the 'shadow of hierarchy'.
>
> (Davies, 2011:105–6)

In 2011, this 'shadow of hierarchy' was articulated in Liverpool prison through an informal network of punishment that, crucially, remained unaccountable. The Prison Inspectorate found that the Incentives and Earned Privileges Scheme, operating in the prison, was 'too focused on repression':

> Moves to basic were used when it was not possible to establish guilt at an adjudication which was a subversion of proper disciplinary procedures. Men spent too much time locked in cells in conditions similar to cellular confinement, which was particularly inappropriate for those identified as at risk of suicide or self-harm... In some cases moves to basic seemed to be a subversion of formal disciplinary procedures and prisoners were held in conditions similar to cellular confinement without the normal safeguards that would apply.
>
> (HM Chief Inspector of Prisons, 2012a: 11 and 66)

This was reinforced by a wider disciplinary process where power was exercised with maximum discretion given to prison managers and, conversely, with minimum accountability in terms of the construction of a bureaucratic paper trail detailing how decisions were made when prisoners were disciplined:

> Many records indicated insufficient enquiry into charges and some guilty verdicts were reached with no explanation of how the adjudicator had reached that conclusion. There were no quality assurance arrangements to identify and address such deficiencies... In a number of cases, authorisation for segregation did not give sufficient reasons to justify it and were often signed by the manager responsible for the segregation unit rather than the manager who had made the operational decision to relocate the prisoner.
>
> (HM Chief Inspector of Prisons, 2012a: 64–5)

The Inspectorate was equally explicit about the use of force which 'had risen significantly from 100 incidents in the six months before the last inspection to 147 incidents in the six months before this one and there has been a steady increase from 2009' (ibid.: 64). Of most concern:

> were the levels of vulnerability demonstrated by some prisoners located in the reintegration unit... Some... prisoners described carrying out extreme acts such as jumping on netting and barricading in cells as a way of extricating themselves from what they saw as dangerous circumstances and as a last resort following a lack of support from wing staff. Not only had the zero tolerance approach blinded managers from exploring the circumstances behind such actions but the regime was also far too restrictive for such vulnerable prisoners. Despite the unit's stated aim of reintegration there was a lack of multidisciplinary input and support for prisoners.
>
> (HM Chief Inspector of Prisons, 2012a: 66)

In practice, therefore, the rehabilitation programmes that have been developed in Liverpool prison (and elsewhere) continue to be confronted by a historical legacy and a set of deeply institutionalised daily practices, which emphasise the delivery of pain and punishment in a coercive environment. In that sense, the idea that prisoners voluntarily engage with the programmes (where they exist), and to which they give their consent, is an ideological mystification. The domination of the offender in penal and semi-penal institutions remains paramount. In other words, 'new state initiatives, no matter how they are represented, are always underpinned by the coercive capacities of states' (Coleman et al., 2009: 13).

PROGRAMMES IN PRACTICE: CONTRADICTIONS AND
CONTINGENCIES IN LIVERPOOL

In December 2011, Liverpool Prison maintained its role in warehousing short-term and remand prisoners. For over 63 per cent of the population, the 'length of stay', as Her Majesty's Inspectorate of Prisons euphemistically expressed it, was 12 months and under (HM Chief Inspector of Prisons, 2012a: appendix 2). In other words, the prison continued to confine those engaging in a 'localized criminality' which was 'politically harmless and economically negligible', a group whose 'controlled illegality. . . [was] an agent for the illegality of. . . dominant groups' (Foucault, 1977: 278–9).

Furthermore, where programmes of responsibilisation were being pursued in the prison, and heralded as the panacea for the elimination of the criminality and deviance of the 'economically negligible', they were not being seamlessly put into practice, if at all. The Prison Inspectorate found a range of issues affecting the reintegration of these '"anomalies" back into the social body' (Rabinow, 1984: 21). As they noted:

> [R]esettlement resources were not adequate to meet the needs of the population held. There were significant backlogs of the reviews necessary to address prisoners' offending behaviour and little planning for remand or short-term prisoners. Housing services were stretched and some prisoners did not have accommodation confirmed until the day they were released; during the inspection just before Christmas, some prisoners genuinely expressed great anxiety that they would be homeless after release.
>
> (HM Chief Inspector of Prisons, 2012a: 6)

In terms of purposeful activities, and the resettlement programmes themselves, the Inspectorate was equally critical:

> Implementation of the learning skills strategy had been slow and few skills acquired at work were recognised or led to qualifications. There were very few vocational trading places. . . More offending behaviour programmes had been introduced but the range of courses was too limited to meet the prison's aim of becoming a community prison. Gaps had been identified for alcohol-related offending, anger management, domestic violence and victim awareness. Prisoners were unable to be assessed for programmes not run at Liverpool.
>
> (HM Chief Inspector of Prisons, 2012a: 14 and 16)

Despite the 'rehabilitation revolution' endlessly articulated by the coalition government, the reality of penal power remained as debilitating and disempowering as ever for the short-term, petty recidivist. Furthermore, even if the programmes were accepted as offering some form of rehabilitation to offenders, there is the broader question about what prisoners are being rehabilitated *to*. For Pat Carlen, 'rehabilitation programmes in capitalist societies have tended to be reserved for poorer prisoners' and therefore 'have not been designed for corporate criminals' (Carlen, 2012: 8). Furthermore:

> [R]e-integration, re-settlement or re-entry are often used instead of re-habilitation. Yet all of these terms, with their English prefix 're', imply that the law breakers or ex-prisoners, who are to be 're-habilitated'/'re-integrated'/'re-settled' or 're-stored', previously occupied a social state or status to which it is desirable they should be returned. Not so. The majority of prisoners worldwide have, prior to their imprisonment, usually been so economically and/or socially disadvantaged that they have nothing to which they can be advantageously rehabilitated.
>
> (Carlen, 2012: 3).

Even on their own terms, the accredited programmes do not meet the needs of prisoners. In June 2012, only 36 per cent of those released went on to education, training or employment, while 'very many [others were] homeless and in debt on release' (Prison Reform Trust, 2012: 3). Thus, the state's rehabilitative discourse based on 'what works' can be understood as an 'imaginary penality' (Carlen, 2008) in that:

> [the] 'what works', neo-liberal governmental discourse on reducing crime has gradually erased the citizen-subjects of the welfare state from the penal frame, replacing them with the risk-laden, techno-entities of surveillance and security fetishism. Moreover, whatever the official claims regarding 'what works', criminal prisons in most jurisdictions are still primarily for the poor, the mentally-ill, the homeless, ethnic minorities and the stateless – and yet!!! the belief in rehabilitation as a panacea for all penal ills lives on!
>
> (Carlen, 2012: 7)

While we concur with the view that the rehabilitation model of punishment provides little by way of prisoners' development beyond their release (as this chapter previously evidenced, offenders frequently return to prison through the 'back-door'), women-centred models of rehabilitation can also be criticised for their reliance upon discursive practices of the self in particular – and the principles of the self-esteem movement in general – that are geared towards enticing women to reflect upon their individual failures and to take full responsibility for their offending behaviour. Such a reductive analysis is detrimental to a critical consideration of the wider structural processes that induce their powerlessness, and by extension their criminalisation. It is to this critical consideration of the genderised phenomenon of rehabilitation in semi-penal institutions that the chapter now turns.

WOMEN-CENTRED MODELS OF PUNISHMENT

> Through their exposure to education, work and training, they progressively developed good economic potential and social well-being, which provided an excellent platform for helping them to reintegrate into society on release.
>
> (HM Chief Inspector of Prisons, 2012b: 61)

The complex relationship between homelessness and imprisonment is a highly gendered social phenomenon (Barton and Cooper, 2012). Where some male participants perceived imprisonment to be a solution to insufficient and repressive probationary accommodation, women highlighted their positive experiences of probationary accommodation. This involved routinised activities that encouraged them to critically reflect upon their offending behaviour and domestic abuse, as well as improving their self-esteem. Group work was a key conduit through which self-knowledge and individual experiences were mobilised:

> When you sign up to come to here you do groups every day and it's like stress awareness, anger management, drug awareness and we are actually doing one today and it's about women empowerment, you know about domestic violence and stuff.
>
> (Nicola, probation hostel, North West)

Group work also encouraged women to confess and empathise with other confined women, which facilitated collective empowerment and 'institutional intimacy' (Barton and Cooper, 2012). 'Institutional intimacy' describes the extent to which female residents relied upon the semi-penal institution for friendship and emotional and moral support, as well as a sense of belonging, which in turn helped to create a harmonious and respectful environment:

> I know it sounds weird, because I have just wanted to get out of [this] place, but you get loads of support here and I've got no family. And the friends I've got, they are all in this house. I didn't know anybody when I came, at all.
>
> (Nicola, probation hostel, North West)

Some of the respondents also testified that they had reached turning points in their lives as a result of receiving institutional support:

> Yeah, since I've been here. . . how can I put it, I've never felt so stable in the whole of the drug life that I've had, than I've had being in here. I could honestly say that it has got its good points about it in the end.
>
> (Vivienne, probation hostel, North West)

> I had to do a drink detox [before arriving here] because I was a bad alcoholic and I was taking Crack and Smack all the time but I'm off all that now. Since I've been here it's sorted my head right out.
>
> (Shirelle, probation hostel, North West)

Others suggested that their individual failings were due to their own irresponsible conduct and flawed decision-making:

> You see it's down to you, you're the individual person, if you want to make a go of something then you'll make a go of it. . . if you're determined to get off the drugs. You see, people don't realise, they just don't, it's *you*. You have got to want the help. [There's] no point in people helping you if you're not going to help yourself and you're not prepared to help. Because at the end of the day if you make a go of it, this place can help you.
>
> (Vivienne, probation hostel, North West, emphasis added)

Some analyses of women-centred models of punishment suggest they are useful as women can 'gain sufficient self-esteem to directly engage in problem solving themselves, and feel motivated to seek appropriate employment' (Gelsthorpe et al., 2007: 54). However, it has also been argued that these models are so socially and culturally entrenched in the 'self-esteem' movement that not only have they become synonymous with confidence building (Cruikshank, 1999; Haney, 2010) but they are also gendered and class-specific as they routinely coerce female offenders into reflecting upon their own individual failures without taking into account their wider experiences of economic and gender inequalities (Hannah-Moffat, 2002; Carlen, 2003).

Furthermore, they rely upon discursive practices that encourage individuals to act *within* their own subjugation in order to reconstruct themselves as responsible and empowered agents (Cruikshank, 1999; Haney, 2010). Semi-penal institutions are crucial sites for this rebuilding process. They are sites where 'social problems are narratively produced' under 'the auspices of the needs and necessities of the agencies' (Marvasti, 2003: 89). 'Needs talk' and behavioural programming play a crucial role in these narratives as they function to encourage women to talk about their failures, hopes and desires so that institutional pro-grammes can equip them with the necessary 'life skills' to 'become independent and self-sufficient' (Haney, 2010: 10). The programmes construct a set of categories, discourses and knowledges 'for the produc-tion of clients' (Marvasti, 2003: 89) that aim to redirect immoral con-duct amongst populations of the poor. In this case, poor women are steered through discursive practices, away from their deviance and towards becoming empowered and responsible agents. Empowerment models, therefore, involve a diverse process of programme training that can take various forms, but mostly comprise of 'needs talk', group work, behavioural programmes and pedagogies of life skills. Women's partic-ipation in these programmes is coercive. Probation hostels must ensure that the confined keep up with their offending behaviour programmes, since failure to attend and engage with such programmes may result in a breach of the rules, which in turn can result in 'either eviction; a return to court or their immediate re-call to prison' (MoJ, 2012b: 1).

According to Carlen and Worrall (2004:75), the empowerment model of punishment has been adopted by prison managers to help women make real life choices about 'how they live their lives in prison and in preparation for their release'. Barton and Cooper (2012) have also noted that this model has been adopted in community-based, semi-penal hostels, where women are taught how to develop strong self-esteem and routinely 'confess and empathize with each other' (ibid.: 147). Crucially, however, both Carlen and Worrall (2004) and Barton and Cooper argue that this 'happy ideology of empower-ment' (2012: 146) mystifies the exercise of gendered power relations whereby female offenders are punished via surveillance strategies of regulation and control where they must critically reflect upon their esteem issues and resolve their pathological pleasures and 'dangerous desires' through confidence training (Haney, 2010). In other words, individual women are held responsible for their own failures both in group work and through the compulsion to concentrate on the dis-courses of the irresponsible self, which were then confessed to the other women.

Crucially, while the respondents made the connection between being supported and addressing their individual problems, the confessional process decontextualised their socioeconomic problems in order to foren-sically focus on their own individual personal failures and experiences of victimisation. Despite the economic and structural inequalities they experienced, they considered the will to change as being independent of their poverty-related circumstances, including their homelessness, thereby isolating their offending-related needs from these wider inequalities. This, Carlen (2003: 34) points out, is problematic because women offenders are still discharged into the same, if not greater, conditions of economic and structural inequality. As such, empowerment training can be seen as 'irresponsible', whereby women are made to believe that 'they have many choices about how they live their lives when they do not even have a roof over their heads'. Or, as she noted in another piece, these programmes see the problem of women's deviance as 'being in the [women's heads], not their social circumstances' (Carlen, 2002: 169).

For poor women in Liverpool exiting from the criminal justice system's various responsibilisation programmes, the environment they were returning to was grim. While over 91,000 children in the Liverpool City Region were living in poverty in August 2009, future projections suggested that there would be 'a significant increase in relative and absolute poverty through to 2020' (Liverpool City Region, 2012: 9). The vast majority of these children were living in households with no work, with 'particularly high rates of out-of-work poverty amongst lone parent families' (ibid.: 29). Of these families, 97 per cent were headed by women. Additionally, 'the level of female claimant count in the City Region [was] the highest that it ha[d] been since September 1995' (ibid.: 9).

STATE PUNISHMENT IN AUSTERE TIMES

The increasing convergence of penal, semi-penal and welfare systems, despite the contradictions and contingencies within and between them, means that as *state* institutions they retain a central role in containing and punishing the poor, as well as disproportionate numbers of subaltern groups within this general category – the sexually abused, the mentally ill, the unemployed and the homeless (Prison Reform Trust, 2012). They are also integral to the wider struggle to maintain moral and social order, based on a deeply embedded configuration of 'neoliberal ideas, policies and strategies' which 'are incrementally gaining ground, re-defining the political social and economic model, governing the strategies and setting the pace' (Hall, 2011: 12). This redefinition is clearly evident in the state's response to the poor through the punishing attacks on welfare claimants and their morally stained characters as they eke out a precarious, insecure and often degrading living on the edges of a brutal and brutalising social order. At the same time, the wider social order remains brittle, fragmented and open to contestation, as the disturbances throughout England in August 2011 demonstrated. More specifically, the penal/welfare complex also remains open to contestation. This complex is not an expression in the exercise of unrestrained power. Following Foucault, Bob Jessop (1990b) has noted that:

> Resistance is rooted in the first instance in the availability of alternative meanings... and in agents' attachment to meanings which are contrary to those which are being imposed through particular meaning systems. There is no primal source of resistance, whether in plebeian or class instincts: resistance is always a contingent effect of contrary or contradictory attempts at specifying subjects, their identities and interests.
>
> (B. Jessop, 1990b: 244)

Those who are the objectified targets in the exercise of criminal justice and penal power subjectively remain attached to alternative meanings and definitions of reality that lie outside of the state's unrelenting, but fragmented, attempts to create docile bodies and capture reconstructed minds. From providing false addresses through to the hostility of many prisoners towards the judgments made by prison psychologists regarding their prison lives (as the pages of the prisoners' newspaper *Inside Time* demonstrates), the power of the state remains constrained and contested with respect to moulding an obsequious penal class, obedient and obligated to the rationalities and demands of the norms and values of neoliberalism. This is not to idealise the behaviour of those involved with the criminal justice and penal system, nor is it to attribute a political consciousness to those living on the economic and political margins of the society where daily survival predominates over thinking about the politics of broader social change. However, it *is* to suggest that, despite the ideological power and material resources available to the state, achieving hegemony, both for the implementation of a law-and-order response to offenders in general and for the unrestricted unfolding of disciplinary programmes and policies within and without penal and semi-penal institutions in particular, remains problematic and elusive. In short, practices which contest the dominant discourses can be understood as 'oppos[ing] those very mechanisms which compel individuals to accept pre-constituted categorical identities and to behave coherently' (De Giorgi, 2006: 143). Despite this, the explosive, social fall-out resulting from the brutal atavism inherent in free-market neoliberalism is likely to be profound and will remain central to ensuring that the prison population will either continue to rise or is unlikely to fall much beyond the current rates of imprisonment (see Bell, Chapter 3). Prison population figures, projected up to June 2017, indicate that the average daily population in England and Wales could be as 'low' as 83,100, or as high as 94,800, with a medium figure of 88,900 (MoJ, 2011).

CONCLUSION

Physically displaced and economically marginalised, the criminal justice system has become 'the last safety net' for homeless individuals (Beckett and Herbert, 2010: 146). Beckett and Herbert (2010) argue that the increasing criminalisation of social problems, such as homelessness, reflects the individualising effects of neoliberalism, whereby homelessness is perceived by the criminal justice system as an individual affliction, *un mode de vie*, that can be deterred by a multitude of crime-control strategies and imprisonment. However, 'social problems are not individual matters' (Beckett and Herbert, 2010: 143), but are structural socio-economic problems of the state, generated by the 'conjoint erosion of the low-wage and low-income housing markets, and the scandalous apathy of government in dealing with these derelict populations' (Wacquant, 2009b: 284). For Loïc Wacquant, this development can be explained via the elision of the penal state and the welfare state where both have:

> come to be informed by the same behaviorist philosophy relying on deterrence, surveillance, stigma and graduated sanctions to modify conduct. . . They work jointly to invisibilize problem populations – by forcing them off public aid rolls, on the one side, and holding them under lock, on the other – and eventually push them into the peripheral sectors of the booming secondary labor market.
>
> (Wacquant, 2009b: 288)

In England and Wales, this process has intensified since the election of the coalition government in May 2010. The government's relentless attacks on welfare recipients, and the retrenchment of the welfare state more generally, is a paradigmatic example of this process. By June 2012, according to the Institute for Fiscal Studies, the £18 billion in cuts to welfare benefits, implemented by the government, were 'without historical or international precedent' (Toynbee, 2012: 28). These cuts were only the beginning of the assault on welfare recipients:

> Few people realize that 88 per cent of the cuts are still to come, with two thirds of disabled children to lose large sums. Housing benefit cuts driving thousands of families miles from their homes and children from their schools, have only just begun. Cameron's plan to peg housing benefit to prices, not to inflation, will be devastating. Shelter reports that if prices rose as fast as rents since 1971, a chicken would now cost £47.51.
>
> (Toynbee, 2012: 28)

According to Corporate Watch (2012), private companies that deliver Welfare to Work schemes such as Serco, Seetec, Working Links and A4E have 'been even more eager to sanction people than the government' (Corporate Watch, 2012: 1). Between June 2001 and January 2012, these companies referred over 110,000 cases for sanctioning to the Department of Work and Pensions (DWP). The DWP approved sanctioning in 40,000 of these referrals (ibid.: 2). This was happening against a background which saw the number of sanctions imposed on those seeking Jobseeker's Allowance more than tripling to 508,000 over the first calendar year of the coalition's time in government (ibid.).

Challenging this punitive welfare and penal trend remains extremely difficult, but not impossible, as has been shown in the USA with the closure of prisons in a number of states, closures not necessarily resulting from a sudden benevolent turn towards abolitionism but because of the fiscal crisis faced by the governing authorities (see McBride, Chapter 11). Despite this welcome development, it is still necessary to visualise radical alternatives to the prison that transcend the purely economic in terms of cost–benefit analysis, alternatives which are located in the realm of the political, ideological and cultural and which are underpinned by the principles of 'utopianism, abolitionism and socialism' (Carlen, 1993). These principles remain entirely applicable today – perhaps even more so than when they were identified by Pat Carlen two decades ago in a lecture in memory of Willem Bonger. This is particularly relevant with respect to transgressing the endless – increasingly redundant – recycling of the liberal reform agenda and, instead, constructing a critical praxis that contests the apparently unrelenting growth of the repressive penal/welfare complex and the morally dubious, private and third-sector interests that are adding a further, sanctimonious layer to the power of this complex to target and discipline the poor and the powerless (see Oparah, Chapter 14). As she noted at the time:

> [A]lthough the existence of social inequality cannot be allowed to licence crime, – (even although in some circumstances it might both explain and

justify it!) – strategies to decrease crime must be made subservient to integrated policies to reduce economic inequality and increase participatory citizenship. As Bonger himself wrote in 1916: 'The question of crime and the social question are inseparable; he [or she] who examines the first without the second will not do much toward solving it...' Some people might call it a truism! I would insist that it is a truth which cannot be repeated too often.

(Carlen, 1993: 18)

Therefore, instead of confronting those who support more prisons and less welfare as the panacea for state-defined criminality with the question 'why prison?', following Carlen, a better question might be 'why *not* utopianism, abolitionism and socialism?' Removing the prison from the popular and political imagination and, ultimately, from the landscape of the wider society could therefore begin by removing the institution from the very language itself, whenever crime and punishment is discussed. In that sense, the prison should become the end point and not the starting point in the debate about what is to be done about law and order. Such a course of action, in itself, would help to contest and perhaps eventually banish the endless 'reactivation of the penitentiary techniques' (Foucault, 1977: 268) that have dominated and distorted the debate around law and order for the last 200 years.

PART IV

PENAL REFORM

11

WHY PRISON? INCARCERATION
AND THE GREAT RECESSION

Keally McBride

> And as in private life one differentiates between what a man thinks and
> says of himself and what he really is and does, so in historical struggles one
> must distinguish still more the phrases and fancies of parties from their real
> organism and real interests, their conception of themselves, from their
> reality. (Marx, 1963: 47)

The title of this collection is 'Why Prison?' The question was presented
as a general framing device for essays from varied disciplinary perspectives on issues of penal incarceration. However, I found that it haunted
me. I realised I had not heard anyone ask that question since my children
had passed the age of six or seven. Penal incarceration impacts an
unprecedented portion of the population of the USA and consumes a
significant allocation of national and state budgets, yet there is a conspicuous lack of debate about its fundamental premise. The US public
sphere is not known for well-reasoned discourse, but nonetheless I have
seen some debate mustered about issues such as the purpose of public
education, the meaning of marriage, vaccinations and public health, the
nature of homeland security and the rationale behind military intervention. Though conversations are not as robust and nuanced as one might
hope, there is a tendency to question why the state pursues particular
policies. But even scholars of the penal industry and its practices do not
seem to dwell upon *why* we send people to prison in the first place.
Instead we focus upon who gets sent there, what the conditions are like
in prisons and what happens when people are let out of prisons.

The average American is even less inclined to do so, though we do
spend time watching television shows about prison and televised trials,
following particular cases, and seem generally fascinated with crime and
punishment (see Michelle Brown, Chapter 6). We can debate whether
three strikes should mean you are 'out', or the legalisation of drugs, but
question the actual practice of imprisonment? Virtually never. The logic
of sending people to prison is taken as *a priori*. The conspicuous absence

of consideration of this question begs for analysis, which is what I begin this chapter by doing. I then move on to propose that asking this question now might provoke significant – dare I say revolutionary – alterations in current practices of 'mass incarceration'. It seems there is a realignment stirring. This is not to argue that we have had a philosophical shift in our views of crime, punishment or penal incarceration. Instead, finances are driving shifts in practice. But reconsidering the principles of imprisonment can help accelerate and potentially solidify the shifts in penal practice that are happening, often without much attention, or intention even.

The task of this chapter is difficult: I am tracing the evolution from one poorly thought out and relatively incoherent penal policy to a different incoherent and illogical penal policy. Yet, it is a shift nonetheless, albeit one driven by economic necessity. The epigraph by Marx strikes me as the best description of penal policy over the past five years, as there is a growing distinction between the stated goals of penal policy, the social and political impulses that drive that policy and the implementation of that policy. The disjunction between what we think we are doing and what we are actually doing becomes greater all the time.

INCAPACITATION

Frank Zimring and Gordon Hawkins (1995) noted in their book, *Incapacitation: Penal Confinement and the Restraint of Crime*, that there was virtually no research, consideration or investigation of the rationale which had become central for imprisonment: incapacitation. 'All of the other objectives of incarceration are ancillary to the basic structure of the modern prison and jail: incapacitation is central. . . This function of confinement is too obvious to be visible or important to scholars' (Zimring and Hawkins, 1995: v). Their book is one of the few that takes the logic of prison at face value. We lock people up in order to have them locked up.

This was not always the case in the USA. As I explored in *Punishment and Political Order* (McBride, 2007), the penitentiary was embraced as a spiritual tool, whereby those who had lost their way in the social and moral confusion of the early American Republic were given the opportunity to be removed from contagion and have their souls recalibrate themselves. One observer, Robert Turnbull (1796: 58–9) waxed enthusiastically about the effects of the first penitentiary in Philadelphia, the Walnut Street Jail: 'It is in this state of seclusion from the world that the mind can be brought to contemplate itself – to judge of its powers – and thence to acquire the resolution and energy necessary to protect its avenues from the intrusion of vicious thoughts.' Developing an institution that would keep wayward citizens within the fold of democracy was central in the development of American principles (McBride, 2007).[1] Embracing the principle of self-rule in the early Republic meant maintaining faith in the abilities of the average citizen to be moral and reasonable, or to at the very least be educable and normative. This impulse to see imprisonment as rehabilitation persisted until the 1970s, even as the prison as an institution morphed from its origins as Benjamin Rush's sanitarium where the soul could 'recalibrate itself' to gain an almost unrecognisable mass institutional harshness. Nonetheless, for almost 200 years, the *stated* reason we put people in prison in the USA was to change them for the better, so they could rejoin the world outside.

From the very start, it was dubious whether penitentiaries had the effects they were supposed to. Even Tocqueville and Beaumont (1833/ 1970) debated whether true transformation could be effected in a person's soul and whether mere obedience might be the most an institution could create. Critics of rehabilitation shadowed its dominance as the justification for imprisonment, providing an interesting contrast to the current era. During the 1970s the rehabilitation model became widely discredited by critics of social work within penology, prisoner rights advocates, prison guards unions and administrators. Zimring and Hawkins (1995) note the necessity for a new logic of imprisonment to emerge as rehabilitation was discarded.

Two other alternatives for *why* we incarcerate were obvious candidates to replace rehabilitation: deterrence and desert. Perhaps we put people in prison to warn others not to break the law, or perhaps we put bad people in prison because they deserve it. Both of these justifications would more closely match the philosophical justifications for punishment that have been circulating since the ancient Greeks. However, the impact of deterrence is ambiguous; how do we know other people were deterred from committing crimes, and doesn't prison also somewhat *hide* the practice of punishment? Desert does not explain why incarceration is the answer to what bad people deserve. Why not publicly shame, fine, torture or kill people if they are bad? Why put them in prison? Neither of

---

[1] See also Dumm (1987), Meranze (1996) and the original Tocqueville and Beaumont (1833/1970).

these logics have a clear applicability to prison as an institution (Zimring and Hawkins, 1995: 14–15).

In 1973, there was widespread agreement that prisons failed to reha-bilitate prisoners. However, the varied groups involved at this turning point in penality interpreted the apparent failure of prison as a rehabil-itative institution differently. Leftist critics of the prison who formed the National Council on Crime and Delinquency assumed that only the most hardened and violent criminals would be sent to prison. The majority of people who did not pose public risk would be given alter-natives in the criminal justice system, such as medical treatment, edu-cation and counselling. They estimated in 1973 that 'in any state [in America] no more than one hundred persons would have to be confined in a single maximum security institution' (cited in Zimring and Hawkins, 1995: 10). On the other hand, critics of rehabilitation on the right assumed that the more people that were locked up, the more significant the reduction in crime. They saw the logic of incapacitation as an invitation to put as many offenders as possible in prison. One does not need to carefully examine the most recent prison population statis-tics to know whose vision carried the day.

The fact that incapacitation emerged as the winning logic for impris-onment at this juncture proved far more momentous than its complete obviousness would suggest. Incapacitation directly reverses the rehabil-itative model of individual malleability. It assumes that people cannot be changed. Hence, people who have committed crimes are always destined to commit more crimes, so the longer they stay in prison the better. This logic helps explain the sudden lengthening of sentences over the past thirty years. Furthermore, if we do not expect prison to have changed anyone's criminal habits, it naturally follows that society would choose to ostracise those who have been released from prison. It is not surprising to see the elaboration of more legislation that targeted ex-offender rights and opportunities following the adoption of the logic of incapacitation. The real conundrum becomes 'why would we ever let anyone out of prison at all?'

Sharon Dolovich (2011, 2012) has pointed out how the logic of incapacitation has developed penal policy in her recent work. She details the illogic behind incapacitation in inhumane conditions, instead of prison as a system of reform: 'What one finds instead is a system both inhumane and self-defeating, in which the most disadvan-taged and marginalized citizens are targeted for exclusion under harsh conditions certain only to exacerbate whatever incapacities and antisocial tendencies already consigned them to social marginalisation even prior to their incarceration' (Dolvich, 2011: 262). The current system of incapacitation simply breeds the need for more incapacitation.

Interestingly, Dolovich (2011) links the relatively sudden expansion of supermax confinement and the growing instance of the sentence of life in prison without parole (LWOP). Both of these innovations in punishment can be directly traced to the basic logic of incapacitation.[2] LWOP assumes that some people can never be trusted to leave prison– whilst supermax confinement assumes that prison itself is not incapacitating enough for some inmates. The mental disorders that result from supermax confinement make inmates subjected to it fragile, unpredictable and dangerous to themselves and others (Rhodes, 2004). Both are policies that reflect a slippery slope – once a society embraces the idea that some people need to be removed indefinitely and that it is within our collective rights to debilitate other human beings, it becomes difficult to know where to draw the line, or how to bring anyone back from this form of exclusion. This extreme form of incapacitation in supermax confinement, which truly pushes the boundaries of what can be considered human existence and the proliferation of LWOP sentencing, has placed ever greater numbers of people outside of the bounds of society.

Others have written about the experience of supermax confinement, and LWOP is now receiving the attention it deserves.[3] What I want to do is look more closely at the naturalisation of the logic of incapacitation outside of prisons. After all, Eighth Amendment jurisprudence is based upon the evolving standards of society – what we deem to be cruel and unusual. Therefore, the way we think about incapacitation serves an important role in legally and politically justifying mass incarceration.

Loïc Wacquant (2010a) has pointed out that the term 'mass incarceration' is not entirely accurate. After all, penal incarceration does not impact the entire population randomly. If it did we most likely would have had a discussion about the logic of incapacitation by now. Instead, as Wacquant argues, '[T]he stupendous expansion and intensification of the activities of the American police, criminal courts, and prison over the past thirty years have been finely targeted, first by class, second by

---

[2] Dolovich (2011) calls this 'exclusion' in her argument. Although she also includes some discussion of incapacitation, the emphasis is slightly different in her work. Dolovich is emphasising the segregation from society which seems to be the only logic that drives current confinement practices, while I have chosen to use the term 'incapacitation' instead in order to signal the physical, mental and social debilitation of those who are put into prison. Clearly these two aspects of current confinement practices are related.

[3] See the many fine essays in Ogletree and Sarat (2012).

race, and third by place, leading not to *mass* incarceration but to the *hyper*-incarceration of (sub)proletarian African American men from the imploding ghetto' (Wacquant, 2010a: 74). Therefore, because hyper-incarceration is aimed disproportionately at poor, minority males, the logic of incapacitation appears so self-evident as to become invisible. The assumed character of those in prison makes arguing the case for incapacitation unnecessary.

Even scholars who are critical of mass incarceration/hyper-incarceration unwittingly play into this naturalisation of incapacitation by not taking it as seriously as we should. It is not that we exactly disbelieve the incapacitation hypothesis; we just assume that this rationale is not sufficient to truly explain the phenomenon of mass incarceration. We have looked for the underlying real interest behind the phenomenon of mass incarceration; the stated intent – to incapacitate – does not seem to justify the extent and expense of the endeavour. We look to neoliberal economics, racial structures, fear, deindustrialisation, state legitimisation and corporate profits to help explain the real, unstated reason we lock such a proportion of our population in prison. Many of us have sought to undermine the logic of incapacitation by revealing it to be driven by ulterior motives, to reveal the ugly truth behind the banal. But perhaps we need also to focus on the illogic of imprisonment in the first place, not just its unjust application.

Although I agree with Wacquant's analysis of hyper-incarceration in the USA, I am going to use the term 'mass incarceration' in this chapter because I believe that this term more accurately captures the shift that I see happening in debates about the prison population in California and elsewhere. The number of those in prison, and the expense required to keep them there, is starting to challenge the unquestioned presumption that every prisoner needs to be there in the name of increased security for the rest of us. Though the population in prisons is not random, what I want to emphasise is the debate about sheer numbers that is emerging. Another manifestation of this shift is that the character of those in prison is starting to be questioned, as I will detail below.

THE END OF THE NEOLIBERAL EXCEPTION?

Since the advent of the Great Recession, there seems to be a willingness on the part of policymakers to begin to question the expense of mass incarceration, if not the logic of incapacitation. As I mentioned, I cannot detect a philosophical shift in the American public or policymakers; it is more a turn to pragmatism. Simply, prison stands out as a glaring anomaly in the era of neoliberal governance, which has seen the state exit a great many of the social functions that it used to perform. As David Garland (2002) and Marie Gottschalk (2006) have pointed out in their work, both the UK and the USA embarked upon an incarceration boom at the same time they presumably started 'shrinking the state'. Such discrepancy cries for some sort of explanation. The state, taking up ideologies of free choice and individual responsibility, rolled back some forms of regulation, outsourced some of its functions and noisily scaled back its own ambitions.

Of course, as Bernard Harcourt (and others) point out, the rhetoric of neoliberalism does not match the reality (Harcourt, 2011). Neoliberal states *are* interventionist and have grown their budgets over the course of the past thirty years. Some forms of government spending and regulation were 'naturalised' by neoliberal ideology, and others were repudiated by that same ideology. Thus as the state was declaring its own impotence in some areas such as creating employment demand, it was simultaneously taking on the complete administration of the lives – not the welfare, mind you – of an increasing percentage of citizens through mass incarceration.

Mass incarceration was a huge state-run endeavour in the era that presumably eschewed state-run endeavours, which is why I call it a 'neoliberal exception'. Why do legislators and citizens who supposedly hate government spending make an exception for mass incarceration? Another way to think about this problem is to say that mass incarceration is a glaring, expensive anomaly on the neoliberal political landscape, and the fact that such a programme is not *seen* as exceptional should give us all pause. Somehow this exceptional spending is naturalised; or in David Harvey's language, there is a 'fix' that allows mass incarceration to coexist peacefully with the rhetoric of a minimal state (Harvey, 2007).

On the deepest level, it is a marker of a particularly bleak period in social and political history when we stopped believing in state projects and society's ability to mould better citizens. Instead, we take individuals as what they are and then we build institutions around them. Perfectibility be damned, the past forty years has been marked by a relative dearth of overt social engineering.[4] The individual is sacrosanct,

---

[4] Of course, eschewing the possibility that society can shape individuals is a covert form of social engineering and has reshaped every aspect of contemporary life.

but what this logic requires is that the individual behave in only very particular ways; if they do not become the economically driven creature envisioned by neoliberals, prison appears as the only alternative. In the USA, we have abolished most other state interventions, mostly because we do not believe that the state can do anything that is worthwhile or make a positive impact. The most it can do is restrain, not produce. For this reason, it makes sense that the prison takes on a certain logic of inevitability and that it is difficult to see alternatives to it, given the current way of imagining the state, the market, individual malleability and freedom. This view of limited state capacity and a focus upon individual responsibility neatly ties in with the logic of incapacitation as well.

It took the Great Recession to start debate about the inherent wisdom of mass incarceration in circles beyond prison activists. To call what is currently happening a 'debate', however, would give it more credence than it deserves. Instead, states are struggling to balance budgets and prisons now appear as an unacceptable weight on an already unbalanced ledger. Is the prison-industrial bubble going to pop? Even though build-ing prisons provides contractor employment, rural development and 'good jobs' for guards, suddenly legislators are suddenly awake to the fact that this is a massive transfer of wealth from the state. Once the beds have been built, you need to keep paying to have them filled. The costs of incarceration, now that they are put in relief by dollars and cents rather than those fuzzy ideas about human suffering, look like they just may be unacceptable.

One group, Right on Crime, is an excellent example of how con-servatives that embraced law-and-order politics are now reconsidering the logic of prison without any concurrent re-examination of our pun-ishment philosophy. Led by Grover Norquist, the group observes exactly what I have called 'the neoliberal exception' of law-and-order politics:

> Conservatives correctly insist that government services be evaluated on whether they produce the best possible results at the lowest possible cost, but too often this lens of accountability has not focused as much on public safety policies as other areas of government. As such, corrections spending has expanded to become the second fastest growing area of state budgets – trailing only Medicaid.
>
> (Right on Crime, 2012)

As an alternative, Right on Crime suggests that the USA reconsider mass incarceration during this era of fiscal downsizing.

Conservatives are known for being tough on crime, but we must also be tough on criminal justice spending. That means demanding more cost-effective approaches that enhance public safety. A clear example is our reliance on prisons, which serve a critical role by incapacitating dangerous offenders and career criminals but are not the solution for every type of offender. And in some instances, they have the unintended consequence of hardening nonviolent, low-risk offenders – making them a greater risk to the public than when they entered.

(Right on Crime, 2012)

What is missing from this discussion is whether they seek to redefine practices of punishment or confinement. The intent is to make it less expensive with standard neoliberal practices such as outsourcing (to jails), privatisation (community groups and non-profits can take over reform) and mechanisation (surveillance technologies) (Right on Crime, 2012).

Sentencing reform is one of the very few issues that receive cross-party support in the politically polarised USA. In the past six months, two major reports have been issued about the cost of penal incarceration in the USA. Their timing is excellent since both have made their way onto the editorial pages of major newspapers such as the *New York Times*, which has been printing an increasingly steady call for sentencing reform on their editorial pages over the past eight months. The Vera Institute of Justice released 'The price of prisons: what incarceration costs taxpayers' (Henrichson and Delany, 2012). This report points out that many of the costs of mass incarceration are actually under-reported, involving pensions, medical costs and offloading prisoners to local jails. The Vera Institute calculated that in the forty states that they surveyed, costs were on average 13.9 per cent higher than the official corrections figures. This brought the cost of penal incarceration to $39 billion in the forty states surveyed.

In June 2012, The Pew Report on the States released 'Time served: the high cost, low return of longer prison terms' that takes a slightly different approach to accounting mass incarceration expenditures (Pew Center for Research on the States, 2012). This report focuses on the creeping sentence length for all crimes over the past twenty years. They surveyed sentencing practices between 1990 and 2009 and saw that sentences for drug crimes had increased by 36 per cent, property crimes were up 24 per cent and violent crimes were up 37 per cent. This means that the average offender being released from prison has been there on average nine months longer than she/he would have been twenty years earlier. Rather than speculate on the inherent wisdom of this, the report points out that this additional time amounts to a cost of $23,300 per person. The goal of the report is to encourage policymakers to reduce the time of sentences: 'The analysis in this study shows that longer prison terms have been a key driver of prison populations and costs and the study highlights new opportunities for state leaders to generate greater public safety with fewer taxpayer dollars' (Pew Center for Research on the States, 2012: 1–2).

These two reports can be read complementarily, both emphasising that today, more than ever, it is time to reconsider the cost/benefit ratio of penal incarceration. States, in the interest of budgets, need to scale back which offenders they put in prison and for how long. One commonalty is that there is agreement that prison is necessary for 'the most hardened' criminals, while others do not need to be incarcerated, at least not for as long. Now, rather than making a stark division between those who are law-abiding and those who are criminal, we move towards drawing a line within the previously monolithic criminal group. This may be considered progress of sorts that the line of exclusion is being moved, softened. But imagine for a moment if the debate was different: what if policy analysts were asking which offenders would be reformed by putting them in prison? This would be the result if we could have a public debate about *why* we imprison people in the first place.

Of course, one can also see another Keynesian possibility in play. The Great Recession may encourage states to maintain their penal industries as a stabilising force in their local economies. On 5 January 2011, Andrew Cuomo declared in his State of the State speech: 'An incarceration program is not an employment program. . . If people need jobs, let's get people jobs. Don't put other people in prison to give some people jobs' (Hakim and Confessore, 2011). Crushed by upstate lobbyists and 'small government' Republican legislators, by 27 January, Cuomo later backed off his ambitious plans to scale back the penal apparatus in New York considerably (Hakim and Kaplan, 2011). It seemed upstate prisons were indeed a viable jobs plan. As Cavadino and Dignan (2006) observed, 'In a perverse variation of Keynes's hypothetical cure for recession – get the state to hire large numbers of people to dig holes and then fill them in again – the USA has hired one lot of people to keep another lot locked up' (cited in Gottschalk, 2010).

The USA is not alone in its reconsideration of the cost of mass incarceration. Nor its confusion about whether it should think of mass incarceration as a jobs programme or simply a drain on state budgets.

Interestingly, during the 2011 election for Prime Minister in the UK in the televised debate between Nick Clegg, David Cameron and Gordon Brown, David Cameron was quick to say that law-and-order politics had failed and that it was time to scale back on incarceration. Gordon Brown rejoined by pointing out that scaling back on law and order would mean losing more jobs for public sector employees.

I must again cite Marx's *Eighteenth Brumaire* (Marx, 1963) as I research current budget crises. A few years ago I surveyed policies of mass incarceration and saw the needless devastation of human lives, communities, families, systemic racism and classism, and saw mass incarceration as a tragedy. I do not want to make it seem any less a tragedy today. However, watching different governing bodies try to figure out a way to reduce the costs of mass incarceration without questioning its logic makes it seem that we have now moved into the era of farce. It is not clear that the entities who are engaged in implementing mass incarceration believe their own rhetoric or logic any more than the prisoners; they are actors spinning more and more outrageous yarns, trying to make adjustments and reduce costs at the margins without examining the logic of imprisonment.

The closest thing I can find to a debate about mass incarceration is a new uncertainty about the character of those in prison. For instance, in opposition to California's adaptation of early release policies, a political consultant who works for the California Correctional Peace Officers Association and Crime Victims United of California (which incidentally is funded by the correctional officers' union) made the following statement: 'The legislation was based on a lie that the prisons are filled with low-level offenders who pose no real threat to public safety, and that is absolutely not true. When you release dangerous people, other people get hurt' (Furillo, 2010). Once the character of those in prison starts to become ambiguous, the incarceration of this population becomes evident as a choice. Like all government expenditures, then, such a choice needs to be weighed by its costs and benefits.

However, we are looking at a crisis of governance, not governability. What I mean by this is that the policy of mass incarceration was naturalised and had garnered political support by a government that focused exclusively on the character of those who are incarcerated. These ungovernable deviants posed such a risk to public and private safety that the government presumably had no other choice than to lock them away. But now the government simply cannot afford to maintain the mass incarceration apparatus that it established. If mass incarceration can be debated as a question of governance rather than posed as a solution to ungovernability, then a true opening in our penal environment will have occurred. As the Vera Report on the Price of Prisons stated, 'The cost of state corrections budgets has largely been the result of policy choices, rather than broad social or economic trends beyond policy makers' influence' (Henrichson and Delaney, 2012: 11). Apparently, no longer are we faced with a population that simply needs to be neutralised; rather, we have been *choosing* to neutralise an ever increasing segment of the population (see Bell, Chapter 3; Wacquant, Chapter 4).

CALIFORNIA

California gave rise to the popular tax revolt and the backlash against the political radicalism of the 1960s in the form of Richard Nixon and Ronald Reagan. At the cutting edge of so many governmental disasters and the political innovations that these spawn, it is worthwhile to consider California as a case study in what I believe is the fiscal unravelling of mass incarceration institutions. Note that I do not say the penal philosophies are unravelling, because even in the face of abundantly clear evidence that mass incarceration is a budget item that California can no longer afford, there has not been a clear debate, shift or reconsideration of these policies.

The stalemate in California is the result of a broken constitution that mandates a two-thirds vote (by either the legislature or direct referendum) to pass any tax increases combined with a minority Republican party that has pledged to never increase taxes of any kind for any reason. This means that by a margin of four to five seats, the legislature has been unable to pass any new taxes. California's 'Three Strikes and You're Out' legislation mandated life in prison for anyone caught committing a third felony, thereby creating the country's largest prison population that was also systemically, egregiously, underfunded. California's prisons have been operating at 200 per cent capacity for much of the twenty-first century. One would think the difficult choice between hiring school teachers and prison guards would make lawmakers reconsider some sentencing strategies. In fact, in 2009 the deal that Governor Schwarzenegger and the California State Legislature brokered to pass the new budget specifically removed the proposed panel on sentencing reform (*LA Times*, 2009). Republican legislators would only pass the austerity budget, including changing the conditions of parole and threshold for grand larceny, if reconsidering mass incarceration was *not* on the table. They assented to a slight reduction in prisoners, but only if all the sentencing provisions that got them there in the first place remained in place, thus insisting upon adherence to mass incarceration *in principle*, if not in practice.

Since California has specifically stated that it will not consider sentencing reform, it was unclear whether the budget stalemate would ever impact penal policy. After all, the state of California has been struggling for decades; public education has been cut in favour of prisons for thirty years now. Ultimately the catalyst came from elsewhere: the Supreme Court ruling in 2011 in *Plata* v. *Brown*, which generated the largest prisoner release order (PRO) in history.[5]

California's state government has worked itself into a unique bind, which is a magnified version of much of the developed world's state budgets. How do you pay for state expenditures if you have stopped taxing corporations and the wealthiest people? How do you balance a budget in a time of economic recession? The political system could not seem to find any solution to the issue, having been caught in the bind created by both of its narratives – no new taxes and zero-tolerance policies. The two conflicting strands finally became such a disaster in California that the US Supreme Court stepped in.

In 1995, the US Congress passed the Prison Litigation Reform Act in order to deal with the growing number of cases due to prison overcrowding as the nation's prison population continued its exponential growth. Though it did leave the very slim possibility of some court interference in prison management, the Act was intended to establish the authority of prison administrators to deal with overcrowding as they saw fit, without the undue interference of black robes. To this end, the Act established a series of conditions that must be met in order for the court to mandate either population caps or PROs. There are six preconditions that must be met for a PRO to be valid:

1. PROs can only be issued by a specially convened three-judge court.
2. Before this court may be convened, a district court must have first given an order for less intrusive relief.
3. Sufficient time for this relief to be successful must be allowed and only if it fails can the court be convened.
4. The three-judge court must find overcrowding the primary reason of the violation of Federal rights.

[5] *Plata* v. *Brown*, 131 S.Ct. 1910, 1923 (2011).

5. The three-judge court must have as narrow a PRO as will be sufficient to deal with the problem.
6. The impact upon public safety must be given serious weight before any decision can be made.

While these relatively stringent guidelines were designed to make a PRO the least likely outcome of court investigations into prison conditions, California's prison system was in such disarray that the majority opinion in *Plata* ruled that all six of these conditions had been met.[6]

There were two cases that had been plaguing the California corrections system for twenty years. The first, *Coleman v. Brown* had been filed in 1990 on behalf of inmates with mental health problems, charging that they were systematically denied adequate care.[7] An overseer was appointed in 1995 to develop a solution for the problem. Twelve years later, the current overseer filed a report admitting that any progress in the issue had been erased by the growing population and that prisoners often had to wait months and even years for mental health treatment. His report proved to be central in the three-judge court's finding that a reduction of population was absolutely necessary.

The other case was the already mentioned *Plata v. Brown*, which charged Eighth Amendment violations due to lack of medical care for California's prison population. In 2005, the court appointed a receiver to oversee efforts to reform the medical system. Three years later the receiver reported this back on the state's efforts to cope with the problem:

> Timely access is not assured. The number of medical personnel has been inadequate, and competence has not been assured. . . Adequate housing for the disabled and aged does not exist. The medical facilities when they exist at all, are in an abysmal state of disrepair. Basic medical equipment is often not available or used. . . Indeed it is a misnomer to call the existing chaos a 'medical delivery system' – it is more an act of desperation than a system.[8]

Much of the Opinion takes pains to establish that all six of the preconditions had been met, outlining how overcrowding exacerbates any efforts to provide basic care. 'For years the medical and mental health care provided by California's prisons has fallen short of minimum constitutional requirements and has failed to meet prisoners' basic health

---

[6] I want to thank Sharon Dolovich for sharing her notes on the *Plata* decision with me.
[7] *Coleman v. Brown* PC-CA-0002.   [8] See *Plata v. Brown*, 563 U.S. (2011) 11.

needs. Needless suffering and death have been the well documented result.'[9] In 2006, then-Governor Schwarzenegger had declared a 'state of emergency' in California's prisons as the suicide rate was near one per week – eighty times the average for prison populations elsewhere. California's prisons were filled to 200 per cent capacity for more than eleven years. What this meant was every available space was filled with bodies – imagine 100 beds in a gymnasium with 2 guards and 50 prisoners sharing one toilet. Conditions shocked even seasoned veterans such as Doyle Wayne Scott, former head of corrections in Texas. The court cited his report, describing 'conditions in California's prisons as "appalling", "inhumane" and "unacceptable"' and stated that 'in more than 35 years of prison work experience, I have never seen anything like it'.[10]

The three-judge court concluded that the population needed to be reduced to 137.5 per cent of operating capacity, splitting the difference between two different estimates of reform: one at 130 per cent and another at 145 per cent. What this amounted to was a release of 46,000 prisoners in the next few years. The Supreme Court affirmed this target, noting that it was left up to the discretion of prison officials how best to achieve it.

Aside from the scope of the PRO and the significant turn towards being willing to enforce prison population targets on the part of the court, there are two other aspects of the decision worth noting in this context. The first is that California's fiscal crisis plays a significant role in the case. Particularly in light of California's ongoing fiscal crisis, the three-judge court deemed 'chimerical' any 'remedy that requires additional spending by the state'.[11] The receiver in charge of overseeing revisions to the medical care in California's prisons estimated that providing adequate care 'would "all but bankrupt" the state'.[12] The court estimated that earlier reform efforts had failed because of inadequate resources, not because of intent. Remarkably, the court notes that California's resources will not improve any time in the immediate future:

> The common thread connecting the State's proposed remedial efforts is that they would require the State to expend large amounts of money absent a reduction in overcrowding. The Court cannot ignore the political and fiscal reality behind this case. California's Legislature has not been willing or able to allocate the resources necessary to meet this crisis absent a reduction in overcrowding. There is no reason to believe it will

---

[9] Ibid., 3.   [10] Ibid., n. 1.   [11] Ibid., 30.   [12] Ibid., 18.

begin to do so now, when the State of California is facing an unprecedented budgetary shortfall.[13]

Interestingly, Justice Kennedy, who authored this opinion, had earlier suggested that California could simply not afford its incarceral habit. One year before the ruling was announced, Justice Kennedy gave a speech at Pepperdine University, addressing the status of California's penal policies:

> The overall tone of Justice Kennedy's address to the Pepperdine University School of Law was 'courtly and humorous,' according to the *Los Angeles Times*. He turned more serious, however, on the subject of incarceration. Sentences in the United States are eight times longer than those handed out in Europe, Justice Kennedy said. California has 185,000 people in prison at a cost of $32,500 each per year, he said. He urged voters and elected officials to compare taxpayer spending on prisons with spending on elementary education.
>
> (*New York Times*, 2010)

There are two separate dissenting opinions in the ruling. By examining the majority opinion and the dissenting ones, the nature of the disagreements becomes clear. First, you see two different conceptions of who is in California's prisons. There is a remarkable moment in the majority opinion when they address prisoners who have not directly had health or mental health problems but who would be in danger were they to develop them while in California's prison system. 'Prisoners who are not sick or mentally ill do not yet have a claim that they have been subjected to care that violates the Eighth Amendment, but in no sense are they remote bystanders in California's medical care system. They are that system's next potential victims.'[14] An ironic twist when the rhetoric of victim's rights is now applied to an entire prison population.

In contrast, Justice Scalia wrote a scathing dissent to the *Plata* decision, arguing – correctly – that this is a significant shift in Eighth Amendment jurisprudence that has been based upon 'individualized showing of mistreatment'. 'Whether procedurally wrong or substantively wrong the notion that the plaintiff class can allege an Eighth Amendment violation based upon "system wide deficiencies" is assuredly wrong.'[15] Most telling is when Scalia describes the 46,000 prisoners who will be decarcerated under the PRO: 'Most of them will not be prisoners with medical conditions or severe mental illness; and many

---

[13] Ibid., 32. [14] Ibid., 35. [15] Ibid., Scalia J., dissenting, 5.

will undoubtedly be fine physical specimens who have developed intimidating muscles pumping iron in the prison gym.'[16] A far cry from the potential victims of the California penal system described by Kennedy, instead prison has honed Scalia's imaginary convict into an even more dangerous presence.

Scalia's vision of the prisoner is more in line with popular culture and past jurisprudence and political debates, which is why the opinion in *Plata* is such a momentous shift in the way the court envisions the character of those in prison. Along with this split in the law's image of the prisoner is another polarised vision of the relationship between public safety and prisons. Both dissenting opinions reinscribe the basic idea that increased incarceration decreases crime and hence have dark premonitions about the bloodshed and suffering that will be caused by the PRO. The court's action will result in 'inevitable murders, robberies and rapes to be committed by the released inmates' according to Scalia, while Alito concludes his dissent with an equally bleak prognosis: 'I fear that today's decision, like prior PROs, will lead to a grim roster of victims. I hope that I am wrong. In a few years, we will see.'[17]

In contrast, the majority opinion argues that public safety will be better served by reducing overcrowding. They cite these remarks: 'The former warden of San Quentin and acting secretary of the California prison system testified that she "absolutely believe[s] that we make people worse, and that we are not meeting public safety by the way we treat people."'[18] The opinion also cites the finding of the three-judge court: 'any negative impact on public safety would be "substantially offset, and perhaps entirely eliminated, by the public safety benefits" of a reduction of overcrowding'.[19]

The difference between these two visions of public safety is that the dissent envisions prisoners as a danger to an innocent public, while the majority opinion includes prisons and their populations as part of the public. If prisons and prisoners are unsafe and unhealthy, this in itself constitutes a detriment to public safety. Therefore, the *Plata* decision marks a momentous shift, not in policy but in the way that the courts are now willing to imagine prisoners, as part of the public, as potential victims in their own right. The absolute wall between those in prison and those outside of it seems to have a crack in its structure.

The decarceration in California has been remarkably uneventful thus far. Tellingly, the government does not call it decarceration because that

[16] Ibid. [17] Ibid., Alito J., dissenting, 17. [18] Ibid., 38. [19] Ibid., 40.

would be too clear to its constituents; instead it is called 'realignment'. Most residents do not follow Supreme Court news and there has been no sentencing reform that might garner public attention or at least attention during the election season. There has been no visible policy shift in mass incarceration: only a relatively invisible shift in practices.

Decarceration has been achieved in two ways. First, the Department of Corrections has changed the structure of parole. Nearly half of all people placed in prison in California were there because of parole violations, including testing positive for drugs or missing a scheduled appointment with a parole officer. Now most released prisoners are placed on probation, which means they must break a law before they are returned to prison. In order to reduce the load on parole officers around the state, now low-risk ex-offenders will no longer need to go through any sort of parole process. Oscar Hidalgo, spokesperson for California Department of Corrections, argued for the shift: 'What you really have is a changing California parole structure that is really unprecedented. It allows our agents to focus on the highest risk parolees, which increases public safety' (Furillo, 2010). A few weeks earlier, Hidalgo indicated that the shift in parole structure would also work to eliminate petty recidivism as well. 'We think ultimately this will allow our agents to keep their eye on more serious individuals. You start changing your prison population to the people who need to be in there rather than just rotating people in for four months at a time' (Stanton, 2010). This may not be a wholesale debate, but if California's correctional officials are publically admitting that they are engaging in unnecessary incarceration, we might have some hope for a reconsideration of sentencing practices sometime soon.

Second, non-violent offenders are now referred to county jail facilities. Counties have more freedom to use alternative forms of sentencing and punishment, including in-home monitoring and probation instead of jail time. In his 2011–12 California State Budget, Jerry Brown stated that 'offenders convicted of non-violent, non-serious, non-sex offenses, and without any previous convictions for such offenses, would fall under local jurisdiction, while the state would be responsible for inmates convicted of the most serious offenses' (Governor's Budget Summary, 2012). Remarkably, this budget provision does not question the logic of incarcerating 'non-serious offenders'; it just establishes that the state is unable to do so and passes the buck to counties. But county facilities are already overcrowded, and local governments are just as cash strapped as the state. Yolo County Sheriff Ed Prieto told reporters, 'We're maxed out pretty much all the time, the only thing we could do is release county inmates to make room for state inmates' (Brannan, 2011: A13). Federal consent decree requires jails to release prisoners when they are at 90 per cent capacity. This would mean half to three-quarters of the forty-five jails with such population caps would routinely release prisoners (Brannan, 2011).

While these might sound like relatively minor shifts in practice, the result has been a 16.5 per cent drop in California's prison population in one year from July 2011 to July 2012. The prison population is shrinking at a rate of approximately 2,000 prisoners per month. Since the *Plata* ruling, the California prisoner population has shrunk by 27,000. Now 9,000 prisoners that were housed around the country due to overcrowding will return to California in the next few years.

In one more example of how state budgets are creating some change, but not yet loosening the naturalisation of incarceration, the death penalty appeared on the state ballot in November 2012 in California as a cost-cutting measure. In a surprise defeat, the public voted to keep the death penalty as an option. This was the third time in the last forty years that the citizens of California have voted on the death penalty. In the previous two elections, impassioned arguments about justice, judicial fallibility, proportionality and redemption were rebuffed in favour of maintaining death row and the execution chamber. This year, the issue was encapsulated briefly on the front page of the *San Francisco Chronicle* of 24 September 2012: 'This time, death penalty debate about cost'. Two reports have been issued since the advent of the Great Recession, emphasising the cost of the death penalty in the Golden State:

> A 2008 study by a state commission headed by former Attorney General John Van de Kamp concluded that the death penalty was costing California $137 million a year for trials and appeals – far more than other types of cases – and the maintenance of Death Row. Substituting life without parole would reduce the cost to $11.5 million, it said. A study last year by Arthur Alarcon, a federal appeals court judge, and Professor Paula Mitchell of Loyola Los Angeles law school put the death penalty cost even higher, at $184 million. Since California reinstated the death penalty in 1977, the report said, it has spent more than $4 billion, which works out to $308 million for each of the 13 executions carried out since 1992.
>
> (Egelko, 2012)

Life in prison without parole is being sold as the humane and less expensive option to the death penalty, demonstrating the pressing need for the logic of incarceration to be actively questioned.

231

I have been waiting for the stories of robbery, rape and murder from a released prisoner that could be used to generate a public outcry about these quiet changes that have been implemented. I suspect they might be out there, but no politician as yet feels that he or she can insist that the state can afford to go back to those practices of the past. Nor has there been the predicted spike in crime rates either. This brings us back to the original question: 'why prison?' It just might be possible that strapped budgets will allow us to ask that question again and arrive at a different answer to it than the USA did forty years ago. But only if we start to ask what penal incarceration does in the first place, instead of accepting it as inevitable.

12

THE POLITICS OF THE CARCERAL STATE: YESTERDAY, TODAY AND TOMORROW

Marie Gottschalk

Throughout American history, politicians and public officials have exploited public anxieties about crime and disorder for political gain. Beginning in the 1970s, these political strategies and public anxieties came together in the perfect storm in the USA. They radically transformed US penal policies, spurring an unprecedented prison boom. Today the USA is the world's warden, incarcerating more people and a higher proportion of its population than any other country.

How did this happen? Why didn't politicians from Republican Barry Goldwater to Democrat Bill Clinton face more public opposition to the proliferation of harsh talk and harsh penalties, like mandatory minimums, three-strikes laws, life sentences and capital punishment? After all, public opinion polls show that Americans' views on crime and punishment are not uniformly harsh. Indeed, it wasn't until the early 1990s – two decades into the prison boom and just as the crime rate was plummeting – that the public identified crime as a leading national problem (Beckett, 1997a: 23–5; Chambliss, 1999: 20; Frase, 2001: 268).

Liberal disillusionment with rehabilitation, beginning in the 1970s, together with attacks from the right and left on sentencing policy (notably indeterminate sentences) certainly provided major openings for penal policy to shift radically in the USA. The profitable prison-industrial complex and powerful conservative groups like the National Rifle Association were also key players in promoting hardline policies. But the picture is more complex than that.

Other groups, some of which are not the usual suspects, helped facilitate, often unwittingly, a more punitive environment. Four movements in particular mediated the construction of the carceral state in important ways: the victims' rights movement, the women's movement, the prisoners' rights movement and opponents of capital punishment. An examination of the distinctive origins and development of these movements helps explain why such a massive carceral state took root in the USA. It also illuminates why an apparent change of heart today prompted by the bottom-line budgetary concerns of some leading politicians and other public figures in the USA in the wake of the Great Recession will not be enough to dismantle the carceral state (see McBride, Chapter 11). And finally, it sheds light on why some other industrialised countries may be increasingly vulnerable to a 'burst for the worst' (Brodeur, 2007: 84). In Europe and elsewhere, incarceration rates are slowly but steadily marching upwards, as David Scott discusses in Chapter 1 of this volume. Nonetheless, the USA remains in a league all its own when it comes to punitiveness. As Franklin Zimring once remarked, comparing increases in incarceration rates over the last three decades in Europe to those in the USA is like comparing a haircut to a beheading (cited in Downes, 2007: 103). But it does raise the question: 'Is the United States an outlier or a harbinger of things to come elsewhere?' Or, in other words: 'Is a haircut the prelude to a beheading?' (Downes, 2007: 103).

THE VICTIMS' RIGHTS MOVEMENT

Four decades ago, the USA gave birth to a formidable victims' movement that was highly retributive and punitive. Victims became a powerful weapon in the arsenal of proponents of tougher penal policies. In a way not seen in other Western countries, penal conservatives successfully framed the issue as a zero-sum game that pitted the rights of victims against the rights of offenders. This movement was remarkably in sync with the country's growing penal conservatism and relatively immune from critical examination.

A highly retributive victims' movement centred on meting out tougher penalties to offenders originally coalesced in the USA, but not elsewhere, for several reasons. The greater development of and public support for social welfare programmes in other Western countries help explain why Britain and New Zealand, not the USA, were pioneers in making the plight of crime victims a public issue. British interest in victims first took root in the 1950s when confidence in the welfare state, and sympathy for offenders, was still high, and law and order was not yet a major factor in national politics. Elite penal reformers with extensive experience in helping offenders were at the forefront of drawing public attention to victim-related issues. Victims themselves did not wage a mass campaign. Indeed, they were largely silent and unorganised (Weeks, 1970; Childres, 1975: 368–70; Elias, 1983: 26; Mawby and Gill, 1987: 39–40; Rock, 1990: 48–53).

The British government sought to avoid galvanising a broad victims' movement. At each stage in the debate over crime victims, the British Home Office was reasonably successful in steering and co-opting the growing public concern for victims. This made it tougher for law-and-order penal conservatives to exploit the victims issue for political gain.

With the passage of landmark victims' compensation schemes in the 1960s, reformers in Britain and New Zealand sought to bestow compensation on crime victims much as the expanding welfare state bestowed housing, education and medical services on its clients. In doing so, penal reformers denied crime victims a powerful political identity independent from that of other victims of misfortune. This undermined the political salience of the crime victim issue. It opened up an important avenue to be supportive of crime victims by bolstering the welfare state rather than by expanding the criminal justice system.

This issue developed quite differently in the USA. In the late 1960s and 1970s, the USA became a pioneer in the use of large-scale victimisation surveys (Maguire and Pointing, 1988: 7–8). The US surveys discovered that the level of victimisation was much higher than previously indicated by the FBI's Uniform Crime Reports. This fostered the belief that much crime went unreported and thus unprosecuted (Sparks, 1982: 54–7; Elias, 1983: 3; Mawby and Gill, 1987: 115–18; Zedner, 1994: 1208–10). Concern grew that uncooperative victims and witnesses were undermining the efficiency and operations of the criminal justice system. These narrow surveys did not investigate a wide range of other issues related to victimisation. The accepted conventional wisdom was that crime victims were punitive, even though the limited psychological evidence available at the time suggested that retribution and tougher law enforcement did not address victims' primary needs (Gottschalk, 2006: 303, nn. 52–5).

Largely because of the victimisation surveys, improving the efficiency of the criminal justice system became the main goal of hundreds of new government-funded victim and witness programmes in the USA. These programmes became the nucleus of the victims' rights movement. The

Law Enforcement Assistance Administration (LEAA), created by Congress in the mid 1960s as an arm of the US Department of Justice, was pivotal in creating a victims' movement that viewed the rights of victims as a zero-sum game predicated on tougher penalties for offenders. The LEAA funded some of the leading victimisation studies. It also provided crucial support for key victims' organisations, like the National Organization for Victim Assistance (NOVA) and hundreds of victim and witness programmes designed to increase cooperation with prosecutors and the police.

By the early 1980s, interest in the plight of crime victims was intense in the USA. There was a flurry of legislative and other political activity thanks in part to government-supported organisations like NOVA. Victim advocacy groups played a prominent role in the formation and passage of measures that enlarged victims' rights and toughened penalties for offenders at the federal, state and local levels.

Governmental organisations were not the only ones that exploited the victims' issue to promote hardline penal policies. So did many law enforcement groups. For example, the California Correctional Peace Officers Association, the state's powerful prison guards' union, provided office space and virtually all the funding for the Doris Tate Crime Victims Bureau (renamed the Crime Victims Action Alliance), a fierce advocate of three-strikes legislation and other tough measures (Page, 2011).

Many so-called victims' advocates drew a stark line in the public mind between crime victims and criminals, even though many perpetrators have themselves been victims of violent crime. The US victims' movement also largely ignored the fact that incarcerated men and women are regularly victimised by a brutal penal system in which prison rape, assaults by correctional officers and unsanitary, even life-threatening, living conditions are commonplace.

The all-powerful prosecutor
The relative weakness of the US welfare state, the proliferation of victimisation surveys and strong government support for victims' rights organisations were not the only reasons why a punitive victims' movement initially took hold here but not elsewhere. Another important difference is the unique role of the public prosecutor in the US legal system. The USA made the transformation from private prosecution to public prosecution earlier on and more extensively than many European countries (Gottschalk, 2006: 91–8). As a consequence, the government

historically has monopolised the prosecution process to a much greater extent, leaving victims far more marginalised in the US legal system.

US prosecutors possess huge discretionary powers that the courts have consistently left largely unchecked in key areas, including the initial decision to press charges, what level to charge a suspect and when to terminate prosecution. Attempts by victims and other private individuals to compel prosecution are usually not successful. Until the advent of the victims' rights movement, the victim's role in the US legal process was largely confined to that of a witness in a criminal proceeding. By contrast, victims in many other Western countries traditionally have enjoyed considerable rights to participate in the prosecution of a case.

The common-law judicial system that prevails in the USA further compounded the marginalisation of victims and ignited calls for victims' rights. This accusatorial legal system demands more of victims and incites greater animosities than the inquisitorial, less adversarial legal system that prevails in continental Europe. In the USA, the prosecution and the defence have equal standing before the courts, which are relatively passive in developing the case. Defence attorneys go to war with prosecutors as they attempt to tear apart the state's case. In the process, victims and their claims often are put on trial as well.

In the common-law system, the focus is on eliciting the facts relevant to determining guilt or innocence. Elsewhere, for example in the Netherlands, the public trial mainly serves as a check on whether the investigations have been carried out properly, as a greater portion of the trial is devoted to understanding the personal circumstances and why the offence occurred. In the European continental system, judges play a more active role in shaping the case by controlling the legal proceedings, including the calling and questioning of witnesses.

Differences in the legal training, professional norms and career paths of prosecutors and judges are another reason why victims' rights became such a flashpoint in the US war on crime. Most prosecutors and many judges in the USA are either elected or nominated and confirmed through a political process, which makes them highly dependent on public approval and more vulnerable to political pressures. By contrast, many other Western countries rely on career prosecutors and career judges with special training and education to run their legal systems. Once the victims' rights movement burst forth, US prosecutors and judges were forced to respond to its punitive demands or risk being voted out of office.

THE WOMEN'S MOVEMENT

Politicians of all stripes, including Barry Goldwater, Governor George Wallace of Alabama and Presidents Lyndon Johnson and Richard Nixon, promulgated the politically potent – but highly misleading – image of white women, preyed on by strangers, as the most likely victims of violent crime. But leading politicians had considerable help from women's groups in feminising the crime issue and taking it in a more punitive direction.

Women's groups and feminists in the USA have a long and conflicted history on questions related to crime, punishment and law and order (Gottschalk, 2006: 116–21). Periodically, they have played central roles in defining violence as a major threat to society and uncritically pushing for more policing powers. The US victims' rights movement coalesced at about the same time that women's groups were mobilising against rape and domestic violence. This had important consequences for the growth of the carceral state.

The contemporary women's movement in the USA was among the first to draw widespread attention to the issue of violence against women in the 1970s. By some measures, the US anti-rape and domestic violence movements were remarkably successful. Nearly every state enacted legislation designed to make it easier to convict and punish people accused of sexual assault or domestic violence. These reforms had significant effects on public attitudes. On the positive side, more services became available for victims of sexual assault and domestic violence. Public officials and members of law enforcement were sensitised to these issues in ways they had not been before. On the negative side, these movements, with their emphasis on law enforcement solutions, bolstered a more punitive climate.

Feminists allied themselves with law-and-order groups to secure rape reform and domestic violence legislation. If they had not, the simmering backlash against the women's movement in the 1970s likely would have derailed their efforts in many state legislatures. The cost of these alliances was high. In Washington State, for example, the women's lobby marketed a rape reform bill to the legislature as a law-and-order bill. The measure was eventually enacted in July 1975, in part by riding on the coat-tails of a new, mandatory death penalty statute (Loh, 1981). In California, the rape shield statute was named the Robbins Rape Evidence Law in honour of its co-sponsor, conservative state senator Alan Robbins (McDermott, 1975; Henderson, 1985).

Mainstream national women's organisations, notably the National Organistion for Women, are credited with putting rape and, later, domestic violence on the national agenda. But the original rape crisis centres and shelters for battered women in the USA had strong local and radical origins (O'Neill, 1969; Ferree, 1987: 183; Dobash and Dobash, 1992: 23; Matthews, 1994: xii–xiv). Over the years, many of these centres and shelters were dramatically transformed (Gornick et al., 1985: 260; Smith and Freinkel, 1988: 81–2).

Apolitical professionals replaced many of the highly politicised volunteers and staff members who had established these facilities. Shelters and centres cast aside their initial concerns about being too closely associated with the government, and developed formal and informal ties with police, prosecutors, hospitals and social service agencies (Matthews, 1994). They became more dependent on government money and more supportive of law enforcement solutions, like stiffer penalties, mandatory arrests and no-drop policies. Shelters in the USA faced greater pressure to secure government funding because the US welfare state is comparatively less developed. British shelters could fund themselves, primarily by charging rent to their residents, many of whom received financial support from the government.

Many US shelters and centres had modest goals that turned out to be quite compatible with the growing conservative law-and-order movement. They sought to press public officials to manage violence and eschewed any broader critique of the government's role in the war against crime. In the process, rape and domestic violence were increasingly redefined as individual, psychological traumas. This seemingly apolitical view of violence against women complemented the conservative view that attributed the increase in crime to the pathologies of individual criminals and not to deeper social, economic and political problems in the USA. It also was compatible with the proliferation of dehumanised images of black criminals preying on innocent white victims, best exemplified by the infamous Willie Horton commercials of the 1988 presidential campaign (Matthews, 1994: 154–9; Madriz, 1997).[1]

As the victims' rights movement took shape, anti-rape activists mimicked some of its key tactics in order to secure legislation and funding. For example, they used storytelling tactics that dramatised accounts of a

---

[1] These ads featured the mug shot of a black man who attacked a white couple while on a furlough from a Massachusetts prison and became a centerpiece of George H. W. Bush's presidential campaign that year.

rape victim's experience (Schmitt and Martin, 1999). By framing the rape issue around horror stories and victimhood, they fed into the victims' movement's compelling image of a society held hostage by a growing number of depraved, marauding criminals.

The main vehicle for greater state involvement in the cause of violence against women was the US Department of Justice, which funnelled money, expertise and philosophy into the emerging movement. The patchwork, incoherent, means-tested US welfare state had neither the will nor the way to help women who were victims of violence. Instead, the US Department of Justice became the champion of abused women. It was a leading critic of the government's response to domestic violence, including the failure of law enforcement to protect women from further abuse. Law enforcement solutions filled a vacuum created by an underdeveloped and much maligned welfare state.

By contrast, Britain's Home Office and police maintained their distance from women's groups fighting rape and domestic violence (Rock, 1990: 44). By the time the women's movement in Britain sought to politicise the issue of violence against women in the early-to-mid 1970s, the needs of crime victims had been an ongoing, though not leading, concern in elite British politics for nearly two decades. The anti-rape and domestic violence movements in Britain emerged at a time when the politics of victims was already on a relatively settled course that emphasised social welfare solutions and that did not pit victims against offenders.

The presence of a more developed welfare state in Britain predisposed British feminists and public officials to view social policy as the most promising arena to address violence against women. State officials in Britain were responsive to calls from women's groups for more housing, social services and welfare benefits to help them escape violence by achieving economic independence. They were far less receptive than US officials to criticisms of policing and other law enforcement practices in dealing with domestic violence and rape. By not legitimising feminists' criticisms of law enforcement's unresponsiveness to violence against women, the British government reduced the likelihood that feminists would become accomplices in the brewing 'get-tough' movement in Britain. In essence, it neutralised the salience of violence against women as a law-and-order rallying point.[2]

---

[2] For a more extensive discussion of the differences in the origins and development of the victims' and women's movements in the USA, Britain and elsewhere, and of their differential impact on penal policy, see Gottschalk, 2006: chs. 4, 5 and 6.

The US women's movement embraced the cause of violence against women at a moment when the politics of victimhood was still very embryonic, fluid and volatile in the USA (Gottschalk, 2006: 124–30). Attention to the needs and rights of rape victims and abused women helped to ignite and politicise a broader interest in victims that stressed victims' rights and that denigrated offenders. In the USA, the victims' movement and the women's movement increasingly converged, which helped to embolden penal conservatives. In Britain they remained largely at arm's length from one another.

Women's groups in the USA worked closely with state officials and government agencies at a time when the voice of penal conservatives was growing louder in local and national politics. As a consequence, they were not well positioned to resist the rising tide of penal conservatism. Indeed, they ended up supporting policies that emboldened it.

The most notorious example is the federal Violence Against Women Act (VAWA) of 1994. The VAWA was a considerable achievement in many ways. It heightened public awareness of violence against women, promoted greater cooperation between agencies with vastly different perspectives on the issue and provided states with new resources to tackle this problem. But the VAWA also strongly emphasised law enforcement remedies.

The VAWA was part of the landmark $30 billion Violent Crime Control and Law Enforcement Act signed into law by President Clinton, which allocated nearly $10 billion for new prison construction, expanded the federal death penalty and created a federal 'three-strikes' law. In the name of protecting women and children, it contained several measures that challenged established privacy protections, including a mandate that all states establish a registry for sex offenders or risk losing federal money. The crime bill also permitted prosecutors in federal cases to introduce a defendant's previous history of sexual offences into court proceedings.

The consolidation of the VAWA into the crime bill solidified the understanding of domestic violence and other violence against women as primarily criminal matters. The VAWA became yet another way for congressional leaders to show they were tough on crime. Although women's groups had some concerns about the VAWA as it wound its way through Congress and became attached to the crime bill, they nonetheless spearheaded the effort to pass it. The VAWA's supporters ended up aligning themselves with conservative political forces that had been prosecuting the war on crime so zealously.

At the time, few feminists and women's groups considered that, by relying so heavily on the criminal justice system to combat violence against women, they might be fostering a punitive political environment conducive to a prison boom. The enormous expansion of the carceral state in the decades since may finally bring about a day of reckoning for feminists and women's groups. With more than 2 million people behind bars, the overwhelmingly majority of them men, millions of women are the mothers, daughters, wives, partners and sisters of men entombed in the carceral state. Moreover, since 1995, women have been the fastest growing segment of the US prison population.

The chorus of doubts about relying on penal solutions to address violence against women has been growing louder in the USA. Across a broad range of feminists, crime experts, academics and social workers, concerns have been mounting about mandatory arrest, presumptive arrest and no-drop policies, and about tougher sentencing. The belief is growing that these legal remedies do not necessarily reduce violence against women and have contributed to greater state control of women, especially poor women.[3] In recent years, women's groups in the USA have emerged as some of the fiercest critics of the widening net of registration, community notification, residency and civil commitment laws that ensnare sexual offenders.

THE PRISONERS' RIGHTS MOVEMENT IN THE USA

The US women's movement was exceptional. So was its prisoners' rights movement that burst forth in the 1960s. A forerunner in the prisoners' rights revolution, the USA ended up being a forerunner in the construction of the carceral state. For a time, the USA experienced a considerably more open and progressive public debate about prisoners' rights and penal policy. But law-and-order conservatives waving the bloody shirt of victims' rights eventually captured the public debate, helped along by the distinctiveness of the US prisoners' rights movement.

The US prisoners' rights movement emerged earlier and had deeper roots both inside and outside of prison than prisoners' movements elsewhere.[4] Several important developments explain why, including the

---

[3] See, for example, Minow (1998), Coker (2001), Sontag (2002) and Bumiller (2008).
[4] For more on the exceptional nature of the US prisoners' rights movement, see Gottschalk, 2006: ch. 7.

rising proportion of the black population behind bars, the government's initial efforts to desegregate federal penitentiaries and the emergence of the black Muslims as a formidable organisation inside USA prisons. The Nation of Islam and the civil rights movement pried open the courts, rendering them important arenas for prison activism. In the process, prisons were pried open and subjected to intense public scrutiny. The racially charged political atmosphere in which the prisoners' rights movement emerged provided an opportunity for race and imprisonment to become tightly linked issues. Some black prisoners and other minorities became celebrities with significant bases of support on the outside. With the help of the New Left and other outside groups, they made powerful and highly publicised claims that they were the true victims. They promoted the idea that lawbreaking should be seen primarily as a political act aimed at a racially, economically and politically repressive system.

These claims to victimhood together with the high-profile nature of the prisoners' rights issue helped foreclose any role for the state in brokering a détente between offenders, their sympathisers and the emerging victims' movement. Indeed, these claims served to push the US victims' movement in a more punitive direction as women and other victims of violent crime sought to wrestle the status of victim away from the prisoners' rights movement and its allies. This helps explain why the backlash against prison activism was so strident in the USA and why the government was so effective at decimating the movement once it sought to impose a lockdown on political activism behind bars. It also helps to explain why penal conservatives ultimately won the day.

The new black majority

Between the 1930s and 1970s, the prison population in the USA was racially transformed. In the 1920s, fewer than one in three prisoners were black. By the late 1980s, for the first time in US history the majority of prisoners were black. The presence of a growing and disproportionate number of the black population in US prisons at a time of rising political mobilisation and tension around racial issues focused government and public attention from the 1950s to 1980s on prisons in a way not seen in other countries. For a time, prisons became an important part of the political fabric and the touchstone for debates about fundamental political questions involving race, justice and oppression.

World War II had a transformative effect on US prisons, as it did on many other institutions in the USA (King, 1995). The war brought an influx of new types of prisoners into federal penitentiaries for violations of the 1940 Selective Service Act, including Elijah Muhammad, the founder of the Nation of Islam, who was sent to a federal facility in Minnesota in 1942 after refusing to be drafted. These conscientious objectors, many of whom were sentenced to lengthy terms, tended to be more educated, politically active and ready to challenge prison authorities on a number of fronts, especially race relations (S. Walker, 1999).

World War II also focused national and international attention on segregation in the US armed forces, which spurred a wider debate about segregation in other government institutions. In the 1940s, the leadership of the US Bureau of Prisons set out to challenge the deeply entrenched segregationist practices in federal penitentiaries. The Bureau's director pushed to end discrimination in federal penitentiaries and grant black prisoners the same opportunities and privileges that white prisoners enjoyed (King, 1995: 150–70; King, 1998).

The Bureau sought to end segregation, but in its own time and in its own way. It stridently resisted efforts by prisoners themselves to lay claim to the race issue, be they politicised conscientious objectors who challenged the colour line or, later, black Muslims who organised their own tightly knit groups. With their commitment to desegregate, federal prison administrators, wittingly or unwittingly, put race at the centre of prison life, changing the very nature of prison protest.

In other ways, government authorities fostered the creation of a highly politicised prisoners' rights movement that had deep roots behind bars and significant ties and political notoriety outside. The growing confidence in the 1940s about the constructive role that government and education could play in remaking society infused penal policy in many states. Belief was widespread that incarcerated people could be remade into constructive citizens through education and closer contact with the world outside prison gates.

California took the rehabilitative ideal most to heart in the post-war years. Republican Governor Earl Warren and other public officials portrayed California's prisons as places to reform minds rather than punish bodies (Cummins, 1994). Group counselling, family picnics, greater access to reading materials through 'bibliotherapy' and more contact with the outside world were cornerstones of this new approach. Experts and new ideas streamed into prisons, courtesy of the state, helping to politicise prison life and to pull aside the iron curtain that had shrouded prisons from the public. By making prisons less closed institutions, state authorities provided an opening for people in prison to develop and retain identities imported from outside. Their primary identity was no longer just their status as a prisoner.

California's zeal for rehabilitation helped to create the first in a long line of US prisoners who became celebrities in the post-war years. Caryl Chessman, sentenced to death in 1948, became a prolific and best-selling author. For penal reformers, Chessman was exhibit A in defence of the rehabilitative ideal as he challenged his death sentence on the basis of his writings and his contributions as a legendary jailhouse lawyer.

Chessman became a national and international *cause célèbre* – he was a model of how a prisoner could be empowered through writing and could subvert San Quentin's controls on reading and writing. He inspired a worldwide movement opposed to his execution and capital punishment. His May 1960 execution in the gas chamber spurred angry demonstrations around the world. With his death, US prisoners and their supporters became increasingly disaffected from the promised land of rehabilitation, for his execution exposed the apparent hollowness of the promise that rehabilitation would bring, if not release, at least reprieve (Hamm, 2001).

Emergence of the Nation of Islam

This disaffection coincided with the emergence of the Nation of Islam as a powerful force within prisons and beyond their walls in the early 1960s. The black Muslims set in motion a radical transformation in how prisoners viewed themselves and in how society viewed them. They introduced the idea of prisoners as victims of the system rather than as transgressors of the system, which had major consequences that lasted long after the Nation of Islam ceased to be a major factor in penal politics by the mid 1960s.

The black Muslims established a collective and disciplined organisation that was unprecedented in prison politics. In doing so, they provided a model for other groups to organise in prison. By introducing a new ethos of group solidarity into prison life, they upended the prison norm of 'do your own time' that had defined prison subculture. Furthermore, once they went above ground with their strikes and lawsuits, the black Muslims became an important window through which prisons became visible to the wider public (Berkman, 1979: 50–5; Jacobs, 1979: 8; Irwin, 1980: 68–9; Jacobs, 1980: 431). The barrage of litigation they instigated in the 1950s and 1960s prompted the media and the public to focus intently for the first time on the inhumane conditions in many prisons. The black Muslims, despite their small numbers, engineered a dramatic shift in how prisoners viewed themselves and how society viewed them. With their emphasis on group identity and collective oppression, they laid claim to the idea that members of the black population were society's victims and that the difficulties they faced were not primarily the result of their own personal deficiencies.

From rights to revolution

Once the Nation of Islam sought salvation through court challenges, the legal profession and other prison reform groups streamed in. The black Muslims were aided and abetted by a potent civil rights movement that had established important precedents for using the courts to challenge the colour line. The civil rights movement initially focused on the racial ills of the Jim Crow South. It primed the public to take a hard and sympathetic look first at penal farms in the South and then at penal facilities elsewhere. The movement also provided important legal and other resources for the prisoners' rights movement that emboldened it.

With the fitful abolition of formal segregation in prisons in the 1960s and the barrage of legal challenges to prison administration and penal conditions, a void in prison structures and authority opened up. Prisons in the USA exploded, paralleling wider political unrest and rioting in many cities (Useem and Kimball, 1989). For much of the 1960s, relations between the black and white prisoners were highly antagonistic (Berkman, 1979: 58; Irwin, 1980: 72–6). The massive race riot at California's San Quentin Prison in January 1967 exemplified this antagonism and was a major turning point for the prison movement (Pallas and Barber, 1972: 11).

Many prisoners acknowledged the self-defeating nature of the San Quentin riot. Following that upheaval, underground prison publications and radical ones on the outside began to emphasise the need for cross-racial struggles centred on economic issues. They began to challenge the basic legitimacy of prisons, portraying them as an extension of an oppressive racial and class structure. This was a direct rebuke to the Nation of Islam, which emphasised strict racial segregation. It also was a rebuke to the civil rights movement, which attacked explicitly racist practices like Jim Crow laws, but appeared unable or unwilling to indict larger social and economic structures like class (Skolnick, 1969: 129; Berkman, 1979: 101).

By the late 1960s, prison activism in the USA became enmeshed in revolutionary causes in a way not seen elsewhere. The activities of the more radical strands of the prison movement began to overshadow the efforts of civil rights lawyers and other legal groups working on behalf of prisoners. The US prisoners' movement came to be seen in the USA and abroad as a vanguard of a worldwide liberation movement for oppressed people, especially people of color.

Black prisoners began to eschew the separatist stance of the Nation of Islam and started forging direct ties with the white radicals associated with the New Left in California and elsewhere. The writings and charismatic leadership of Eldridge Cleaver, George Jackson, Huey Newton, Martín Sostre and other black and Latino prisoners prompted the New Left to view prison issues as central to wider struggles against political and economic oppression. Some members of the New Left became obsessed with the place of the prison in larger political struggles and began to idealise prisoners (Cummins, 1994).

The 1968 unity strikes at San Quentin and the 1970 rebellion at California's Folsom Prison were dramatic expressions of the new political and interracial foundations of the emerging radical prison movement. The San Quentin and Folsom uprisings had significant outside support and depended on interracial coalitions within. In their wake, incarcerated people across the country became highly politicised (Berkman, 1979; Irwin, 1980; Stastny and Tyrnauer, 1982).

These uprisings and the prison writings of famous inmates like George Jackson helped awaken the political consciousness of black, Latino and even white prisoners. Prisoners set up their own elaborate alternative education systems. Many black and Latino prisoners began to regard their imprisonment as expressions of racial, ethnic and economic oppression. The trials and tribulations of notable prisoners and defendants like Eldridge Cleaver, George Jackson and Angela Davis became national and international sensations. Jackson's death under disputed circumstances in August 1971 during an alleged escape attempt further galvanised prisoners across the country and spurred the infamous uprising and bloody crackdown at New York's Attica Prison in September 1971.

Even in the aftermath of the Attica bloodshed, public sympathy for prisoners was considerable. The Attica uprising prompted an outpouring of public and scholarly interest in how to make prisons more humane and in how to reduce the prison population (Gottschalk, 2006: 341, n. 124). Public opinion seemed to be on the side of people in prison, not the prison authorities. A number of national advisory commissions at the time called for a moratorium on prison construction. Soon after, however, the public responded by recoiling from prisoners and the left.

Victims all

The US prisoners' rights movement helped drive a cleavage between victims of crime and offenders that penal conservatives were well poised to exploit. As Etheridge Knight said in his preface to a 1970 collection of writings by black prisoners: '[T]he whole experience of the black man in America can be summed up in one word: prison' (Knight, 1970: 5). Victimhood was a central theme of *The Autobiography of Malcolm X* (Malcolm X, 1997) and other prison writings by prominent black activities that became bestsellers.

This helps explain why the notion of victimhood became such a politically charged issue in the USA. In other countries, a movement for victims could develop without first needing to wrest control of the idea of being a victim back from prisoners – many of whom were black – and their advocates. Certain prisoners and former prisoners in the USA became towering public figures unlike anywhere else. They became heroes – or outlaws, depending on your point of view – who staked an important part of their identity on a claim of victimhood based on their prison experience and their marginal status in US society. This greatly reduced the manoeuvrability of the state to engineer a quiet accommodation with the emerging victims of crime movement (as happened in Britain) that would not pit crime victims against offenders.

In the case of the USA, the initial response to the unprecedented prison unrest of the late 1960s and early 1970s was a combination of reform and repression. Over time, reform yielded to repression. Other Western countries experienced revolutionary upsurges in the 1960s and 1970s, but they ran their course without resulting in a wholesale lockdown on prison activism and without reasserting such a divide between offenders and the rest of society, especially victims of crime.

CAPITAL PUNISHMENT AND THE CARCERAL STATE

In the 1970s, the death penalty catapulted to the centre of debates over crime and punishment in the USA and remained stubbornly lodged there, deforming US penal policies and disfiguring US society in ways not seen in other Western countries. By the 1990s, leading candidates for elective office in the USA rarely opposed the death penalty. Politicians regularly boasted about their willingness and indeed eagerness to carry out executions. Capital punishment was critical to reframing the politics of punishment. It fostered the consolidation of the conservative victims' movement that stressed victims' rights and which marginalised fundamental questions about limits to the state's power to punish.

Opportunistic politicians and public officials exploiting the death penalty for electoral or ideological reasons were not the only reason why capital punishment reshaped the broader politics of penal policy. A whole host of legal decisions and legal strategies related to capital punishment fortified the carceral state in subtle but profound ways. They fostered a public debate around the death penalty that reinforced wider punitive tendencies that were then surfacing in the USA and helped them take root.

The battle over capital punishment, initially confined to the courts, helped to enshrine in the USA the view that popular sentiments and passions are paramount in the formulation of penal policy. Furthermore, the judicial decisions and legal arguments surrounding capital punishment over the last four decades or so helped transform the death penalty into 'the ultimate form of public victim recognition', something which had never been seen before in US history.[5]

The 1972 case *Furman* v. *Georgia*[6] was a critical moment not just for capital punishment but also for the construction of the carceral state. From an immediate legal and legislative perspective, the most noteworthy aspects of *Furman* were how it vacated more than 600 death sentences and spurred a mad dash by dozens of state legislatures to rewrite their capital punishment statutes to address the objections the US Supreme Court had raised. From a political point of view, the ruling is significant in how the fiercest opponents and proponents of capital punishment reframed the issue in strikingly similar terms.

The four dissenting justices in *Furman* took direct aim at the central argument of the Legal Defence Fund (LDF) of the National Association for the Advancement of Colored People (NAACP), the lead counsel in the case. The dissenters disputed the LDF's claim that the death penalty 'is a cruel and unusual punishment because it affronts the basic standards of decency of contemporary society' and is at odds with public opinion (Brief for Petitioner in *Aikens* v. *California*,[7] cited in J. Greenberg, 1977).

The dissenting justices denied that the American public had repudiated the death penalty. The LDF and other abolitionists contended that it had. In doing so, both opponents and proponents ended up

---

[5] Simon (1997), 'Violence, vengeance and risk: capital punishment in the near-liberal state', unpublished manuscript, cited in Sarat, 2001: 19.
[6] *Furman* v. *Georgia*, 408 U.S. 238 (1972).   [7] *Aikens* v. *California*, 406 U.S. 813 (1972).

legitimising popular sentiment as an important factor in the making of penal policy. The battle then began to hinge on how to measure, shape and interpret public sentiment on capital punishment and other penal policies.

This dramatic reframing of the capital punishment issue had wider political repercussions. It essentially identified public sentiment as the main political terrain on which capital punishment would be contested and on which the carceral state would be constructed and legitimised over the coming decades. Furthermore, by failing to close the door once and for all on the death penalty by declaring it unconstitutional under all circumstances, the Supreme Court ensured that the courts would remain the main forum to battle about capital punishment.

The political and legislative response to *Furman* was fast and furious. Nearly three dozen states quickly enacted new death penalty statutes, and leading elected officials and politicians began to stake out stridently pro-death positions. The *Furman* decision galvanised such a powerful political backlash not merely because the Supreme Court had ruled that the death penalty (as then practiced) was unconstitutional, nor because the abolitionists were ill-prepared to battle a backlash they did not see coming. President Richard Nixon, former governor of Georgia Lester Maddox and other hardliners seized this moment to make an issue of capital punishment. They were so successful because abolitionists in the USA ended up having to tread a slippery slope of public opinion that their counterparts elsewhere did not have to contend with.

Elected officials in Canada and Western Europe abolished capital punishment in spite of public opinion, not because of public opinion (Gottschalk, 2006: 227–30). In the US case, abolitionists had to prove in the courts that public sentiment had turned decisively against capital punishment – a very tall order. As state legislatures briskly passed dozens of new death penalty statutes, as the number of defendants receiving the death penalty increased to record levels and as public opinion polls showed that support for capital punishment was the highest in two decades, it was hard to make a convincing case that the public had rejected the death penalty (Garland, 2010).

Gregg, deterrence and public opinion

US opponents of the death penalty also were handicapped because another weapon that had proved to be so powerful in defeating capital punishment elsewhere – the hollowness of the deterrence argument – was neutralised. In the USA, private, non-governmental studies demonstrating that the death penalty had no significant deterrent value had to compete with a cacophony of other arguments about the death penalty and public sentiment. And for the first time in many decades, the anti-death penalty movement had to contend with growing elite and organised public support in favour of capital punishment.

Capital punishment in the USA has been stubbornly impervious to rational or scientific arguments that have been its undoing elsewhere. Canada and Britain made considerable investments in publicly financed research on capital punishment in the 1950s and 1960s (Gowers, 1956; J. B. Christoph, 1962; D. Chandler, 1976; Bedau, 1977). This research demonstrated that the death penalty does not deter homicide. Canada and Britain were more at liberty to focus single-mindedly on the deterrence issue and make that a central feature of the national debate because they did not have to contend with claims about how the death penalty was imposed in a racially discriminatory manner. Furthermore, concerns about crime were minimal when the deterrence issue became prominent in Canada and Europe in the 1950s. So the deterrence question took centre stage in a more dispassionate context.

In the case of the USA, capital punishment burst forth as a national concern in the 1970s at just the moment when the number of homicides was escalating in America. Thus it became easy for supporters of the death penalty to blame the de facto moratorium on executions from the mid 1960s to mid 1970s for the rising homicide rate, which was a source of growing public angst. This undermined one of the most powerful arguments against capital punishment – and, by extension, the carceral state – that is, that harsher penalties do not significantly deter people from committing crimes.

The 1976 Gregg v. Georgia decision,[8] which essentially reinstated capital punishment, reaffirmed the centrality of public opinion in the making of penal policy. It also drew public attention to the deterrence issue at an inauspicious movement – when escalating homicide rates coincided with the nation's de facto moratorium on executions. Sophisticated statistical studies proving the absence of any significant deterrent effect had great difficulty competing with these compelling facts on the ground and, as a result, were less effective in restraining penal populism. As in a number of capital punishment cases before and since, the justices demonstrated in Gregg that they paid close attention to public opinion polls, to the dismay of Justice Thurgood Marshall. In

---

[8] Gregg v. Georgia, 428 U.S. 153 (1976).

his dissent in *Gregg*, Marshall argued that the proper yardstick should be 'the opinions of an *informed* citizenry' (cited in *Gregg* v. *Georgia* in J. Greenberg, 1977: 628, emphasis in original).

Offenders and victims after Gregg

The *Gregg* decision did not immediately prompt the expected bloodbath. Executions resumed with a trickle, not a gush. A series of legal decisions soon after *Gregg*, most notably *Woodson* v. *North Carolina* in 1976[9] and *Lockett* v. *Ohio* in 1978,[10] accorded defendants in capital cases expansive rights to present mitigating evidence. This gave defence attorneys wide leeway to portray capital defendants as sympathetic, tragic figures. But it also provided an opening for penal conservatives to claim that the legal process marginalised the grief and grievances of victims' families.

From about 1983 onward, the Supreme Court began a hasty retreat from involvement in many of the procedural details of the administration of the death penalty, and the number of executions rapidly escalated. In the mid 1980s, some Supreme Court justices and other prominent public officials started drawing public attention to the growing backlog of people on death row and the big increase in the average time from sentencing to execution. This fuelled public concern that the courts were bending over backwards for capital defendants while denying victims and their families justice. It reinforced the unfounded idea that imposition of the death penalty would bring about 'closure' and thus provide some significant psychological comfort to victims' families.

In response, prosecutors and other state officials pushed to permit the introduction of victim-impact evidence in capital sentencing hearings. In *Booth* v. *Maryland*[11] and *South Carolina* v. *Gathers*,[12] the Supreme Court ruled that victim-impact evidence was inadmissible. But shortly thereafter the Court reversed itself in *Payne* v. *Tennessee*.[13] As a result, courtrooms in both capital and non-capital cases became dramatic stages to magnify the suffering of all victims, the immorality that taints all offenders and the fundamental antagonism between victims and offenders (Berger, 1992). This was a unique outcome unparalleled in other Western countries.

---

[9] *Woodson* v. *North Carolina*, 428 U.S. 280 (1976). [10] *Lockett* v. *Ohio*, 438 U.S. 586 (1978).
[11] *Booth* v. *Maryland*, 482 U.S. 496 (1987).
[12] *South Carolina* v. *Gathers*, 490 U.S. 805 (1989). [13] *Payne* v. *Tennessee*, 501 U.S. 808 (1991).

All of this helped to solidify a view of capital punishment and other penal sanctions as primarily the result of a contest between victims and offenders in which the state's power to punish was an incidental issue. So were claims about how the death penalty (and the legal process more broadly) discriminated against the poor and people of color. In such an atmosphere, it is not so surprising that the courts and legislators dismissed sophisticated research demonstrating the racially discriminatory manner in which the death penalty is imposed and the absence of any significant deterrence effect.[14]

In short, some of the legal arguments to which the abolitionists appealed were ambiguous and could be infused with different meanings. Conservatives appropriated the claim about the importance of public sentiment in formulating penal policy. They also recognised that the death penalty had enormous potential to frame and redirect how the public felt about broader social and political changes over the last three or four decades.

The regulation of capital punishment in the courts had powerful spillover effects. It helped legitimise the conservative, zero-sum view of victims and offenders. It contributed to an erosion of the separation between state and society in the making of penal policy, allowing blunt measures of public passions, such as opinion polls, to be accorded a central role. This facilitated the prison boom by deflecting attention from the central question of what the limits are, if any, to the state's power to punish and kill. The death penalty that refused to die had another major impact on the carceral state: it helped to make the imposition of life sentences – once a very rare sanction – a widespread practice (Gottschalk, 2012a: 259–65).

GHOSTS OF THE PAST

By the 1990s, the political consensus in favour of 'get-tough' penal policies had become a formidable and defining feature of contemporary American politics, even as the extraordinary extent of the carceral state remained largely invisible and unexamined. The tenacity of this consensus should not lead us to assume that leading politicians and their allies single-handedly propelled the prison boom. Just because political elites desire a certain type of social control (i.e. massive imprisonment of

---

[14] The most notable example is the Supreme Court's decision in McCleskey v. Kemp, 481 U.S. 279 (1987).

African Americans in the wake of the rebellions of the 1960s and the deteriorating economy of the 1970s) or seek to fortify their electoral base by exploiting law-and-order concerns does not mean they automatically get what they want. A variety of political and other factors can stymie or facilitate their goals.

Women's groups, prisoners' rights organisations and the anti-death-penalty movement did not instigate the law-and-order crusade, but they helped propel it once elites declared war on crime and criminals. These movements are not to blame for the rise of the carceral state and the consolidation of a powerful, retributive victims' rights movement. They were *highly* constrained by historical and institutional factors and some strokes of bad luck and bad timing. In some cases, they may have had a real choice to pursue another path. But in many instances, factors beyond their control sharply constricted their options. The immediate political and strategic choices of these movements had many long-term negative consequences, some of which could not have been predicted at the time.

Major shifts in public policy often have unintended negative consequences, and penal policy is no exception. Those seeking today to forge a wider political movement to dislodge the carceral state and not merely nibble around its edges would do well to remember that the road to a more just penal system is littered with bursts of penal optimism that ended up yielding another right turn in penal policy. More than half a century of political agitation finally brought about bans on the convict-leasing system throughout much of the South by the 1920s. But the state-run chain gangs and penal farms that replaced the brutal and corrupt practice of leasing out convicts to the highest bidder, who often worked them to death's door to turn a profit, became enduring symbols of 'southern backwardness, brutality, and racism' (Lichtenstein, 1996: 16). As Robert Perkinson (2010: 151) wryly observes: 'Strange as it seems, the chain gang, in which thousands of prisoners, most of them black, were loaded onto cattle trucks and carted around the state to pound rocks and shovel dirt, was celebrated as a humanitarian advance.'

Moments of apparent left-right convergence on penal policy are fraught with possibility and peril. It was mistakenly assumed four decades ago that shared disillusionment on the right and the left with indeterminate sentences and prison rehabilitation programmes would shrink the prisoner population. Instead, it exploded. Growing disillusionment on the left and right with rehabilitation and judicial discretion in the 1970s provided a huge political opening for conservatives to move penal policy in a more punitive direction for a variety of reasons. The spike in crime rates helped. So did the factors discussed above.

The growing opposition to mass incarceration over the past decade or so at the national level has gravitated toward two different poles. One identifies racial disparities, racial discrimination and institutional racism as the front lines in the challenge to the carceral state. Michelle Alexander's (2010) formidable and provocative characterisation of mass incarceration as 'the new Jim Crow' exemplifies this view. The other pole seeks to find a winning bipartisan path out of mass incarceration by downplaying its stark racial causes and racial consequences. The emphasis instead is on how the economic burden of the vast penal system is increasingly untenable (see McBride, Chapter 11). As Attorney General Eric Holder told the American Bar Association in 2009, the country's extraordinary incarceration rate is 'unsustainable economically' (Pallasch, 2009).

Publications and institutions spanning the political spectrum from the libertarian *Reason* magazine and the Cato Institute to the left-leaning *Nation* and *American Prospect* have embraced framing the problem of the carceral state as primarily a dollar-and-cents issue that begs for a bipartisan solution. They contend that the USA can do more to promote public safety and save money by reducing its reliance on prisons and by ending expensive, misguided criminal justice adventures like the 'war on drugs'. A group of brand name conservatives, including Newt Gingrich, Grover Norquist, Edwin Meese III and William J. Bennett, have joined 'Right on Crime', a national initiative sparked by the Texas Public Policy Foundation, one of the nation's leading state-based conservative think tanks.[15] The NAACP, the country's foremost civil rights organisation, prominently featured its alliance with the 'Right on Crime' coalition when it launched its new campaign against mass incarceration in spring 2011.

These developments have fuelled optimism across the political spectrum that an unprecedented window of opportunity has opened to shrink the carceral state. However, it is unlikely that the crushing economic burden will single-handedly unhinge the carceral state, even in the wake of the wrenching economic upheavals and distress brought on by the 2008 financial collapse and the Great Recession (Gottschalk,

---

[15] This initiative aims to better align the conservative justice agenda on criminal justice reform with traditional conservative concerns about 'limited government, transparency, individual liberty, personal responsibility, and free enterprise' (Right on Crime, n.d.).

2011; in press). The race to incarcerate began in the 1970s at a time when states faced dire financial straits. It persisted over the next four decades despite wide fluctuations in the crime rate, public opinion and the economy. The 2001 recession raised expectations that the prison boom would end as severe budget deficits forced states to close prisons and lay off guards. At the time, fiscally conservative Republicans, previously known for being penal hardliners, championed some of the sentencing and drug-law reforms. But the penal reforms enacted in the wake of that recession did not make a dent in the US incarceration rate, which continued to march upward. Since the onset of the Great Recession, the total number of people in US jails and prisons has largely stabilised, but no major contraction appears in sight.[16]

As argued above, the construction of the carceral state was the result of a complex set of historical, institutional and political developments. No single factor explains its rise and no single factor will bring about its demise. Mounting fiscal pressures will not be enough on their own to spur communities, states and the federal government to make deep and lasting cuts in their prison and jail populations. Leading politicians did not single-handedly create the carceral state. A change of heart by major political and public figures, however welcome, will not be enough to reverse the prison boom. It will take a much broader social and political movement held together by something more than just bottom-line concerns about how prisons are draining state budgets (see Oparah, Chapter 14).

Framing the problem of mass imprisonment as largely an economic issue (i.e., we just cannot afford it anymore) may yield some short-term benefits. But focusing so heavily on the economic burden of the penal system may come at the cost of drawing attention away from how the vast penal system is beginning to fundamentally alter how key social and political institutions operate and to pervert what it means to be a citizen in the USA. The economic argument also slights the compelling civil and human rights arguments that the carceral state raises as it removes wide swaths of the black, Latino and poor populations and members of other disadvantaged groups from their neighbourhoods, leaving devastated families and communities in its wake and raising troubling

---

[16] The number of inmates continued to grow in about half of the states while declining slightly in the other half. Meanwhile, the federal prison population continued to grow at a brisk pace, as did the number of immigrants detained by the federal government (Pew Center on the States, 2010).

THE POLITICS OF THE CARCERAL STATE

questions about the fairness and legitimacy of US political institutions and the broader social order.

The hyper-incarceration of certain groups – most notably African Americans – has been a defining feature of US penal policy. However, a successful movement to challenge the carceral state will have to stake its claim on more than just race-based claims that mass incarceration is 'the new Jim Crow'. The 'new Jim Crow' frame has made some important contributions to our understanding of mass incarceration and has prised open some vital political space to challenge the carceral state. But it has some shortcomings. It has contributed to public misperceptions about the relationship between the war on drugs and the carceral state. Even if we could end the war on drugs tomorrow, without other major changes in US laws and penal policies and practices, the USA would continue to be the world's warden, and a stint in prison or jail would continue to be a rite of passage for many African Americans. Viewing mass incarceration primarily through a racial lens also slights the qualitative dimension of the penal crisis. That is, the USA is exceptional not only because it locks up so many people but also because of the exceptionally brutal and dehumanising conditions in many of its jails and prisons for people of all races and ethnicities.

Viewing the carceral state primarily through a racial lens has come at the cost of a careful excavation of the underlying political, economic and social factors that spark and sustain such punitive policies not only for certain black populations but also for certain white and Latino populations and members of other demographic groups. The racial disparities frame obscures important racial, ethnic, gender and socio-economic shifts recently in who is being incarcerated. Bluntly stated, the USA would still have an incarceration crisis even if black people were sent to prison and jails at 'only' the rate at which white people are currently locked up. This is partly because class is becoming an increasingly important factor in determining who serves time and who does not (see Wacquant, Chapter 4).

Analysts and activists who emphasise the racial dimension of mass incarceration are not blind to the significance of class and other economic factors in building the carceral state. But they often do not insert their racial disparities framework into a wider and more nuanced understanding of shifts in US polity, society and economy that profoundly affect the prospects for rolling back the carceral state. For those few critics of the carceral state who do emphasise economic factors, all too often a denunciation of the awesome power of the prison-industrial complex substitutes for careful analysis of the specific, complex and shifting political and economic factors that sustain the carceral state and that deeply complicate the politics of penal reform. The intense focus on racial disparities obscures not only the significance of socio-economic factors in determining who is punished and for what, but also how wider shifts in the political economy are posing impediments to forging a successful political movement to undo the carceral state. Key features of that context include deep structural changes in the job market, growing income and other inequalities, the escalating political assault on the public sector and organised labour and the economic decline of wide swaths of urban and rural America. As discussed else-where in other chapters, the most significant factor may be the deep penetration of neoliberalism into nearly all aspects of US public policy and politics, which is rapidly eroding democratic institutions.

PART V

ABOLITIONIST ALTERNATIVES

13

SCHOOLING THE CARCERAL STATE: CHALLENGING THE SCHOOL-TO-PRISON PIPELINE

Erica Meiners

On 18 April 2012, following a tantrum in school, 6-year-old Salecia Johnson was handcuffed and taken from her kindergarten class at Creekside Elementary School in Milledgeville, Georgia, to jail by a police officer (A. I. Jefferson, 2012). While Salecia's treatment incited national dialogue, mainly outrage, what happened to Salecia is not unique. In Baltimore, in 2012, three 9-year-olds and an 8-year-old were arrested in school after a fight (Hellgren, 2012). In Queens, in February 2009, 12-year-old Alexa Gonzales was handcuffed and arrested for writing on her desk with a lime green magic marker (R. Monahan, 2010). In November 2009, at the Perspectives Charter Schools in Calumet, twenty-five students were arrested and charged with misdemeanour reckless conduct after a food fight (Bartosik, 2009).

Across the USA, many young people in urban schools have their first interaction with policing and arrest in a public high school. Students who are queer[1] and/or gender-non-conforming, African American, Latino, First Nations and/or with disabilities are grotesquely over-represented not only in arrests that happen in public schools but also in police stops and school-based disciplinary proceedings and in juvenile (in)justice systems. The most current reports document that approximately 93,000 youths, disproportionately youths of color (Petteruti et al., 2009: 1), are held in juvenile justice institutions every day:

---

[1] Queer functions as a proxy term to encompass not just gay, lesbian, bisexual and transgendered but all non-heteronormative and gender-non-conforming identifications.

261

Today, children of color represent 34 percent of the nation's total youth population but constitute 62 percent of youth committed to public facilities after disposition. African American youth represent 16 percent of the total youth population nationwide but constitute 28 percent of all youth arrests and 58 percent of all youth admitted to adult prisons.

(Hewitt et al., 2010: 133)[2]

According to a 2010 research project that followed 15,170 youths over seven years and tracked questions about their sexual orientation, sexual practices and interactions with police and school disciplinary practices, non-heterosexual youth are 40 per cent more likely to be arrested and 30 to 50 per cent more likely to be stopped by the police. Lesbian and bisexual girls were twice as likely to be stopped by police, twice as many times as heterosexual girls. Ironically, this research also documented that lesbian, gay, bisexual, transgendered and queer (LGBTQ) participants engaged in less violent behaviour than their straight counterparts (Himmelstein and Bruckner, 2011).

A range of canonical sociological literature emphasises the role that the institution of schooling plays to reproduce socioeconomic classes and repressive economic and political ideologies (Willis, 1977; Bourdieu, 1998). Building from this scholarship, research identifies that the USA has always tracked particular populations, specifically people of color, toward low-wage work, under- or unemployment or the work available after full white-male employment (Bowles and Gintis, 1976; Anderson, 1988). What is 'new' are the shifting and expanding tentacles of the carceral state. Over the last ten years, across the USA, the concept and the framework of the 'school-to-prison pipe-line' has become a galvanising image and metaphor that continues to mobilise communities to examine the tightening relationships between schools and jails. *School to prison, cradle to tomb, schoolhouse to jailhouse* – while these frameworks have become increasingly popular and have placed the question of the criminalisation of youth onto a national stage, this concept often obscures the need for a wider and deeper analysis capable of supporting sustainable, dynamic and stronger move-ments to end our nation's commitment to penal incarceration.[3]

Many, as Angela Y. Davis (2003) writes, are also raising the question 'are prisons obsolete?' and working to promote the vision and practice of

---

[2] See also Krisberg (2007).

[3] In previous work I have suggested that the use of the 'nexus' might be more accurate, as relationships between schools and jails are less a pipeline and more a nexus or a web of intertwined punitive threads (Meiners, 2007).

prison abolition. In cases where harm against individuals has been committed, prisons merely displace that violence to another location rather than solving the underlying problems that caused the violence in the first place (see Cooper and Sim, Chapter 10; Oparah, Chapter 14). Furthermore, despite popular representations of prisons as repositories for violent individuals, the population of prisons and jails has exploded in direct correlation to the reduction or elimination of social assistance programmes and the increased criminalisation of the options that poor people possess to cope with untenable situations.

With an abolitionist lens, this chapter explores the relationships between schools and the carceral state. First, the chapter sketches the wider contexts of the carceral state and places public education within this framework. Second, the chapter reviews related research and outlines facets of the school-to-prison pipeline. Third, this chapter offers three ongoing challenges within this field of work that is, by definition, theoretically explicit in its advocacy for justice, and closes with a return to an abolitionist framework and pushes scholars and organisers to ask 'why prison?'

CARCERAL LANDSCAPES

The USA has the dubious distinction of locking up more people than any other nation. With 5 per cent of the world's total population but 25 per cent of its overall officially recorded prison population, the number of people incapacitated in the USA has dramatically increased since the 1970s, not because of an increase in violence or crime but because of policies including the 'Three Strikes' legislation, mandatory minimum sentencing and the war on drugs (Mauer, 1999; A. Y. Davis, 2003; R. Gilmore, 2007; Pew Center on the States Public Safety Performance Project, 2008; Alexander, 2010). The 2 million plus people locked up and warehoused in prisons and jails across the USA are poor, mentally ill, under- or uneducated, non-heterosexual and/or gender-non-conforming non-citizens and/or non-white.

Activists, organisers and academics have popularised the term 'prison-industrial complex' to refer to the creation of prisons and detention centres as a perceived growth economy in an era of deindustrialisation and as 'a set of symbiotic relationships among correctional communities, transnational corporations, media conglomerates, guards' unions and legislative and court agendas' (A. Y. Davis, 2003: 107). In conceptualising the prison-industrial complex, I include not only prisons and jails but also all of the tentacles of the dominant punishment regime that expand criminalisation and incarceration, including immigration enforcement and detention, policing, punishment in schools, corporate investments in perpetuating punishment and divestment from social services, housing, education and all the things that would make us feel truly safe. Hence I also use the term 'carceral state' to highlight the multiple and intersecting state agencies and institutions (including not-for-profits that effectively do the regulatory work of the state) that have punishing functions and effectively police poor communities: child and family services, welfare/workfare agencies, public education, immigration, health and human services and more (Roberts, 1997; Wacquant 2009b; Gustafson, 2011; Beckett and Murakawa, 2012). The term carceral state also points to how the logic of punishment shapes other governmental and institutional practices, even those perceived not to be linked to prisons and policing.

While the term prison-industrial complex typically refers to connections between prisons and punishment, the economy and the political sphere, as the opening examples demonstrate, education must be included in any analysis of the carceral state. With the increased use of surveillance and incarceration and punishment technologies (e.g. metal detectors, surveillance cameras, school uniforms, armed security guards and on-site school police detachments), urban schools *look* and *act* a lot like detention centres.

These linkages are not new. There is a strong body of interdisciplinary research demonstrating how and why US public schools are punishing sites within larger economic and political structures (Anyon, 1980; Oakes, 1985; Saltman and Gabbard, 2003; Anyon, 2005; Robbins 2008; Apple, 2010; Lipman, 2011; Kumashiro, 2012). Numerous ethnographic studies continue to document the hetero-gendered and racialised production of disposable youth (Ferguson, 2000; López, 2003; Winn, 2010). All of this research is inextricably linked to historical analysis that outlines the foundational and white supremacist inequities of public education in the USA (Anderson, 1988; Watkins, 2001).

Research in multiple fields also identifies that the growth of an incarceration nation clearly impacts public education, funnelling the limited pool of tax dollars from social service programmes to the carceral state. Decreases in education correlate with higher rates of penal incarceration, most dramatically for African American males (Petit and Western, 2004). Economists suggest that just one more year of high school would significantly reduce penal incarceration (and crime) rates, and raising the male high school graduation rate by 1 per cent would result in the nation saving, by one economist's analysis, $1.4 billion per year (Lochner and Moretti, 2004). Numerous studies also demonstrate that education, in particular higher education while locked up, reduces recidivism (Taylor, 1992; Fine et al., 2001; Steurer et al., 2001), yet Pell Grants were removed in 1994 for people incarcerated. Between 1984 and 2000, across all states and the District of Columbia, state spending on prisons increased six times as much as spending on higher education (Justice Policy Institute, 2002). The Illinois Consortium on Drug Policies has calculated that, in 2002, if post-secondary programmes were offered to incarcerated men and women, then Illinois could have saved 'between $11.8 and $47.3 million' from the reduced recidivism rates (Kane-Willis et al., 2006: 4). As budgets for corrections expand and funding for higher education contracts, visions about the future of select youth are clear.

THE SCHOOL-TO-PRISON PIPELINE

From this landscape a body of research and organising has emerged that focuses on the particular nexus of relationships referred to as the 'school-to-prison pipeline' (Duncan, 2000; Browne, 2003; Meiners, 2007; Simmons, 2009; Advancement Project, 2010; Winn, 2010). The majority of research and intervention efforts centre on practices inside schools that move young people between prisons and schools. The conception of the term school-to-prison pipeline aims to highlight a complex network of relations that naturalise the movement of youth of color from our schools and communities into under- or unemployment and permanent detention. As previously noted, and this merits re-emphasising, the targeted under- or uneducation of particular populations is nothing new, and the USA has always tracked poor, non-white, non-able-bodied, non-citizens and/or queers toward under- or uneducation, non-living-wage work, participation in a permanent war economy and/or permanent detention. White supremacy has always been central to our nation's public education system and to our carceral state. Educational scholar and activist Garrett Albert Duncan (2000: 36) writes, 'Far from being novel, today's prison industrial system is a variation on past educational and legal measures aimed at subjugating people of color in the U.S.' While the educational outcomes are not new, the expansion of our prison nation in the USA over the last three decades has strengthened policy, practice and ideological linkages between schools and prisons.

Below, I briefly highlight several areas of focus that have emerged in related organising and/or scholarship as predictors of future incarceration. Racial 'disproportionality' is threaded through all of these interlocking categories. For example African American, Latino and First Nations students are over-represented in select 'soft' disability categories and are subsequently targeted for suspension and expulsion. These same students are often pushed into alternative schools – because they have been suspended or expelled – or have been caught up in schools that are hyper-policed.

Discipline

Research consistently demonstrates that disciplinary sanctions in schools disproportionately target youth of color. As summarised in a 2010 article in the *Educational Researcher* surveying available national research on disciplinary sanctions (Gregory et al., 2010), schools actively target youth of color: males of all racial and ethnic groups are more likely than females to receive disciplinary sanctions. In 2004, only 1 per cent of Asian Pacific Islander females were suspended, compared with 11 per cent of Asian Pacific Islander males. Expulsion data from that same year showed that white females were half as likely to be expelled as white males (p < .001), and, similarly, black females were half as likely to be expelled as black males (p < .05). Black males are especially at risk for receiving discipline sanctions, with one study showing that black males were sixteen times as likely as white females to be suspended (Gregory et al., 2010: 60). These gendered and racialised practices of removing students from an educational setting, the most dramatic educational sanction available, start before preschool.

In a 2005 survey of 40 states' pre-kindergarten programmes, boys were expelled at a rate over 4.5 times that of girls. African Americans attending state-funded pre-kindergarten were approximately twice as likely to be expelled as Latino and Caucasian children and over five times as likely to be expelled as Asian-American children (Gilliam, 2005: 3). Head Start programmes and public schools had the lowest rates of expulsions for this age group, with faith-based organisations at the top. The rates of preschool expulsion in all states but three in the forty-state survey exceeds the rate of expulsion in K-12 classrooms (Gilliam, 2005).

Important to note is that all the available data on suspensions indicates that suspensions do not improve academic achievement or students' behaviour, and suspensions are not for acts of violence. In one state-wide study, 'only 5% of all out-of-school suspensions were issued for disciplinary incidents that are typically considered serious or dangerous, such as possession of weapons or drugs. The remaining 95% of suspensions fell into two categories: disruptive behavior and other' (Losen and Skiba, 2010: 9).

One example, the City of Chicago, is representative of most urban school districts. Data from the Department of Education's Office for Civil Rights documents that while African American students represented 45 per cent of the Chicago Public Schools' enrolment in 2009–2010, 76 per cent of students receiving at least one out-of-school suspension that year were black (Civil Rights Data Collection, 2012). Excessively punitive disciplinary measures that disproportionately target the most marginalised in school contexts made national headlines in 2011, highlighting the educational cost to young people when they are pushed out of school (Losen and Skiba, 2010; Schwarz, 2011; Himmelstein and Bruckner, 2011; St. George, 2012).

Special education

In addition to racial disproportionality in school suspension and expulsions, research highlights how students of color are over-represented in 'soft' disability categories (Losen and Orfield, 2002; McNally, 2003; Smith and Erevelles, 2004; Harry and Klingner, 2006), warranting two formal investigations (1982 and 2002) by the National Academy of Sciences. Classification as special education masks segregation, and pathologising 'students of color as disabled allows their continued segregation under a seemingly natural and justifiable label' (Reid and Knight, 2006: 19). Students labelled with these disabilities receive differential access to high-quality education, are not tracked toward college, experience higher rates of suspension and expulsion and are disproportionately represented in juvenile justice prisons (Burrell and Warboys, 2000; Losen and Orfield, 2002; McNally, 2003; Harry and Klingner, 2006).

Not unlike the subjectivity of school-based disciplinary actions, where *disrespect* or *acting out* move children into the category of a disciplinary problem, a number of subjective factors are responsible for placing largely male youth of color in these soft disability categories. In *Why Are There So Many Minority Students in Special Education*, Harry and Klingner (2006) document how soft disability categories are reliant on assessment practices that are much more subjective, including mental

retardation, emotional disturbance and learning disability. These disabilities are differentially interpreted across states, and researchers have
found that diagnostic criteria are not applied uniformly within districts
and schools.

The use of each of these categories also shifts across time, a further
indication of 'a sign of the instability and ambiguity of the categories
themselves' (Harry and Klingner, 2006: 4). A number of factors are
responsible for placing youth in the category of special education:

> When a child's referral actually got to 'the table,' it was clear that neither
> 'rationality' nor 'science' were in control. Rather, we noted six 'soft
> places' that either informed, influenced, and at times distorted the out-
> comes of conferences on eligibility and placement: school personnel's
> impressions of the family, a focus on intrinsic deficit rather than class-
> room ecology, teachers' informal diagnoses, dilemmas of disability defi-
> nitions and criteria, psychologists philosophical positions, and pressure
> from high stakes testing to place a student in special education.
>
> (Harry and Klingner, 2006: 103)[4]

An entire special issue of *Educational Researcher* (2006) examined racial
(and gendered) disproportionality in special education and aimed to
invite readers to think about how these flexible practices of classification
educationally disqualify certain communities and function as forms of
racialised and gendered social control. It is central to link these practices
of classification and their concurrent political and economic impacts to
wider bodies of scholarship. Prominent sociologists such as Stanley
Cohen (1985) and Dorothy Smith (1990) have produced germinal
works that intimately track how communities produce punishing
norms and manage dissent through not just prisons and punishment
but other related punitive structures.

Compulsory heteronormativity and gender conformity
Sexuality and gender are central to the movement of youth, in particular
youth of color, toward penal incarceration. Sexual and gender violence
towards girls increases the likelihood that girls will drop out/be pushed
out of school, and researchers have linked interpersonal sexual violence
as a 'powerful indicator' of future incarceration for young girls (Simkins
et al., 2004; Winn, 2010). Sexually righteous young women, including
pregnant and parenting teens, are offered no protection for their sexual

[4] See also Losen and Orfield (2002).

lives in school and are punished if they exceed the state's impoverished expectations (Fine and McClelland, 2006). Not surprisingly, research identifies that gay, bisexual and lesbian youth are more likely to be punished by courts and schools, even though they are less likely than straight peers to engage in serious crimes, and 'consensual same-sex acts more often trigger punishments than equivalent opposite sex behaviors' (Himmelstein and Bruckner, 2011: 50).[5] Scholarship and organising on the school-to-prison nexus must account for the myriad ways in which schools actively discriminate and concurrently push out lesbian, gay, bisexual, transgendered and gender-non-conforming youth and how sexual violence targeted at girls and women participates in augmenting the school-to-prison nexus.

As a short sidebar, these intersections are key when thinking through strategies to respond to injustices in schools and communities. For example, as anti-bullying legislation and policies have recently gained measures of success, specifically those that recognise the decades-long failure to provide even a measure of 'safety' for LGBTQ and gender-non-conforming youth in schools, all too often these policies heavily sanction perpetrators. The turn to a criminalisation of perpetrators of this 'anti-gay' violence in schools results in more school sanctions, more punishment, potentially more push-out in an educational context where school disciplinary actions disproportionately harm youth of color. Our 'remedies' have collateral damages. Intervention in the movement of youth of color from schools to prisons requires that organisations and scholars engage in inter- and intra-movement analysis.

Criminalisation of schools and youth

Perhaps the most highly visible manifestation of the school-to-prison nexus is the criminalisation of youth 'misconduct' in schools. Most urban public schools have on-site police detachments that conduct drug tests and searches at schools, and the naturalisation of this police presence creates a seamless and interlocking relationship between the school and the juvenile justice systems. In Chicago public schools in 2010 there were 5,574 school-based arrests of juveniles under 18 years old on school property. Unsurprisingly, black youth accounted for 74 per cent of school-based juvenile arrests in 2010; Latino youth

---

[5] This research by Himmelstein and Bruckner follows a decade of work by advocacy organisations including the Gay, Lesbian and Straight Educators Network that clearly outlines how LGBTQ and gender-non-conforming youth are also disproportionately targeted for suspension and expulsion and also denied the right to an education (e.g., see Kosciw and Diaz, 2009).

represented 22.5 per cent of arrests (Kaba and Edwards, 2012). The New York Police Department released data in 2012 acknowledging that in the last three months of 2011, five students were arrested in New York schools every day and these students were, again, disproportionately black and Latino. Again, the majority of these students were arrested for 'disorderly conduct' (New York Civil Liberties Union, 2012). Asserting and affirmatively challenging police conduct in schools is particularly salient when research demonstrates that one of the most popular reasons students are referred to juvenile courts is, again, subjective: 'disorderly conduct' (Florida, 2007–2008) and 'disrupting schools' (South Carolina, 2007–2008) (Hewitt et al., 2010: 112). It is challenging to secure students' rights, in particular the right to due process within schools and to privacy in a context where courts are relatively reluctant to seriously infringe upon the power of schools. For example, the 1985 decision in *New Jersey* v. *T.L.O.*[6] stated that while the Fourth Amendment does apply to students, because schools have 'special needs', 'school administrators need only reasonable suspicion, rather than probable cause, to search students' (Hewitt et al., 2010: 115).

Bodies that count as children are also highly policed, and schools are public spaces that are under continuous surveillance. Often this criminalisation occurs under the guise of safety or protection. For example, almost every state has adopted 'drug-free zones' around schools, but as a 2006 Justice Policy Institute Report identified, these zones overwhelmingly blanket neighbourhoods in urban areas where predominantly people of color reside, including '76 percent of Newark, and over half of Camden and Jersey City' (Greene et al., 2006: 26). These zones – ostensibly created in the name of safety – result in the targeting of communities of color by police, yet they fail to keep drugs away from schools. Along these same lines, the mobility and public space restrictions attached to sex offender registries, the most potent and current component of our expanding prison-industrial complex, centre around public places where children congregate: schools and parks. But with the Bureau of Justice Statistics acknowledging that over 70 per cent of all reported sexual assaults against children are committed in a residence, usually the victim's, this emphasis on policing public spaces is misplaced (Bureau of Justice, 2000).

[6] *New Jersey* v. *T.L.O.* [1985] Certiorari to the Supreme Court of New Jersey No. 83–712, Judgement of 15 January 1985.

MOVEMENT-BUILDING/MOVEMENT ASSESSMENT

Networks and organisation have also emerged to concentrate research and resources around the school-to-prison pipeline, to convene high-profile meetings and to translate research into more accessible materials for mainstream audiences. Some of these organisations include the Advancement Project, the American Civil Liberties Union, the Charles Hamilton Houston Institute for Race and Justice, the Civil Rights Project/Proyecto Derechos Civiles, Dignity in Schools and the Southern Poverty Law Centre. Advocacy organisations that work on juvenile and educational justice issues in many states have developed initiatives – for example, the Juvenile Justice Project of Louisiana's Schools First! project centring the school-to-prison pipeline as an organisational focus.[7]

Grassroots and youth-centred community groups across the USA have placed interrupting the schoolhouse-to-jailhouse track on their advocacy agenda. Youth-led projects including Chicago's Blocks Together, teacher-facilitated journals such as *Rethinking Schools* and national grassroots conferences such as Education for Liberation have all provided leadership, analysis and movement-building around challenging discriminatory educational policies at the local and state level that track youth to prisons. Notably, one component of the 'schools not jails' movement was also a staunchly youth-led movement with a fierce critique of the 'status quo of schooling' (including non-relevant curriculum and a sharp analysis of the unequal forms of schooling available to urban youth), yet some of this analysis gets lost in more mainstream scholarship on the relationships between education and penal incarceration, which simply posits schooling as the antidote to carceral expansion, without linking the two structures (Acey, 2000).

While the work of these organisations and scholars is compelling and has raised the visibility of the racialisation (generally weakly identified as a problem of 'disproportionality') of school discipline policies and practices and the increased presence of police in public schools, I raise three challenges for this field of organising and research based from my local

---

[7] Advancement Project (www.advancementproject.org, www.stopschoolstojails.org/), the American Civil Liberties Union (www.aclu.org/racial-justice/school-prison-pipeline), the Charles Hamilton Houston Institute for Race and Justice (www.charleshamiltonhouston.org), the Civil Rights Project/Proyecto Derechos Civiles (www.civilrightsproject.ucla.edu), Dignity in Schools (www.dignityinschools.org), the Southern Poverty Law Center (www.splcenter.org/what-we-do/children-at-risk) and the Juvenile Justice Project of Louisiana's Schools First! project (http://jjpl.org/programs/schools-first).

and national work, reading and engagement. These tensions are ones I struggle with myself and they are offered in the service of building stronger collective movements and paradigms for justice work. More importantly, I offer these as central concepts to track for those committed to ending our nation's investments in a carceral state: (i) how do we negotiate work that often centres youth or juveniles as 'exceptional' within the larger mess of the justice system?; (ii) how do we negotiate shifting state structures capable of appropriating our justice work?; and (iii) why is it important to also focus labour on how to change and build practices and paradigms of public safety that are not reliant on punishment, isolation and stigma? For each, I offer a short theorised summary, with brief examples where possible, of what these questions resemble in practice.

Trouble with the child

Research and organising within the framework of the school-to-prison pipeline struggles with the tensions involved in working with and challenging *a portion* of a system and a structure that is flawed. The strategy of focusing work around the school-to-prison pipeline becomes particularly troubling as this labour and focus is reliant on prioritising a category, 'youth', that is also constructed and flexible. Scholarship and advocacy in this field often starts with a shared assumption that youth are different than adults. This *a priori* case for a kind of exceptionalism creates problems for both wider justice movements and for work with youth as well.[8]

Contemporary age requirements – to drink alcohol, to vote, to serve in the military, to have sex – are mobile and often incoherent and/or contradictory when mapped onto one another. Those 15 years of age, for example, may be held culpable for crimes as adults, yet that same age cohort is protected by laws that stipulate that a 15-year-old is not legally competent to consent to heterosexual acts (except in some states where a girl of said age may marry a man with parental consent) (Schaffner, 2002). New developmental categories, meanwhile, continue to emerge. For young black men, going to prison has become akin to entering a new 'life stage', similar to joining the military or getting married (Petit and Western, 2004). At the same time, for college-educated, relatively affluent young people, 'emerging adulthood' is being posited as a phase

---

[8] See also Nancy Fraser's related analysis for a discussion of the challenges of movements that focus political organising goals on recognition rather than redistribution (Fraser, 1997).

when the secure markers of their class – and often racial and gendered status, including marriage, employment and home ownership – have yet to be achieved (P. Cohen, 2010). So while black men (and increasingly black women) are moved directly from childhood to adulthood and effectively denied adolescence, more affluent, better educated young people are granted a new status and attendant benefits, such as extended access to their parents' health insurance (Arnett, 2000).

The suppleness of *childhood* is not arbitrary. Ruth Gilmore (2007: 28) defines racism as 'the state-sanctioned or extralegal production and exploitation of group-differentiated vulnerability to premature death'. The *child* produces – and simultaneously masks traces of that production – forms of group-differentiated vulnerability. For example, the nineteenth-century construction of childhood innocence explicitly excluded non-white children. White children were innocent and sentient and therefore fully human, while black children were excluded from innocence and access to sentience and deemed not fully human (Bernstein, 2011). Contemporary eligibility for participation in any of the categories of child, youth or adult and their accompanying legal, political and social conditions are never produced in isolation from race, sexuality, gender, ability, geography, socioeconomics and more. Not everyone benefits from an affiliation with childhood, and some bodies are simply excluded from inhabiting the categories of childhood or youth, including 12-year-old boys who are charged as adults and 9-year-old girls who are held as juveniles in detention centres. When the unit of analysis for research or organising is 'the child', the presumption is that this category is neutral, but I argue the category *child* masks the transactions of who has access to innocence, sentience and full humanity.

Shifting state

As prison reform organisations lobby for 'alternatives' to incarceration (particularly for populations afforded 'exceptionality' status, like pregnant women and juveniles), it is important to trace how these alternatives are created, developed and implemented and to track the relationships of these alternatives to the carceral state. The construction of alternatives to incarceration also offers us the opportunity to engage with the changing conceptions of the state and the corresponding ways identities are sutured, often through affect, to these new state practices/formations.

By alternatives to incarceration and punishment, I refer to a range of programmes like the 'culture of calm' in Chicago public schools

(Huston, 2010) and, more widely, the limited moves in some school systems to include forms of restorative justice and the extension in many states to include boot camps and military programmes into their menu of public educational options. I also include the growing number of programmes that are often court-mandated for 'at-risk' youth: anger management (men) and self-esteem (women). Academics and those invested in prison reform (or educational reform) are often called to support these alternatives and we often evaluate, grant-write and endorse these options because these are 'alternatives' to prison or detention for young people.

Yet these alternatives, often provided by community-based, non-profit entities that wield considerable power, participate in forming a neoliberal state capable of 'government from a distance' (N. Rose, 1999; see also Cooper and Sim, Chapter 10 of this volume). It is not immediately clear whether these programmes extend or soften the carceral state. The relationships between these programmes and the state are nuanced, forming networks of power that remind us that the decentralisation key to neoliberal policies does not mean that the state withdraws – rather, the state's relationships and abilities to negotiate power, to 'govern' from a distance, shift and potentially expand. A key concern is whether young people are made more vulnerable by supporting and implementing, for example, the proliferation of anger management programmes in lieu of in-school detentions.

Questions remain as we move into this terrain: 'how do these programmes facilitate or advance our collective goals of liberation?' and 'how do these programmes function as part of the carceral state?' When 'community' programmes such as Alcoholics Anonymous become court-mandated and/or state-organised, potentially radical, democratic and healing practices are transformed. When schools start to offer restorative justice practices and these practices are tied to juvenile justice systems, there must be assessments about what is won and what is lost with these moves. These should not be investigations that limit us but rather challenge and question our work.

Building safer communities and schools

Parents want security guards and surveillance cameras in schools because they perceive schools as unsafe spaces. Teachers want detention and a school discipline officer because they don't know what to do with students in their classrooms who harm themselves or their peers.

People often ask for more police on the streets and tougher laws because they want to feel safe.

The prevailing contemporary carceral logic recycles the false notion that safety can be achieved through essentially more of the same: more guards, fences, surveillance, suspensions, punishment etc. Yet building more youth detention centres and prisons, funnelling more youth into suspensions or expulsions and placing more police and cameras in schools will not make schools safer, or our communities stronger. Scholars that are invested in work that interrupts and transforms the school-to-prison nexus must build other futures and participate in rethinking safety.

Building safer schools requires not only challenging mass incarceration/ hyper-incarceration policies but also grappling directly with questions and feelings of safety and, in particular, how a gendered and often racialised fear – for example, of sexual assault of white women and children – is publicly deployed to augment the prison system (see Gottschalk, Chapter 12). Our classrooms are not immune from these stereotypes and fears. Our schools receive and can reproduce powerful mythologies: violent teenaged super predators, 'bad' neighbourhoods, crack babies, 'bad and lazy' parents and disordered and dangerous youth.

Shifting from a punishment and detention-based approach to a definition of safety that incorporates relationships and community inside and outside our schools requires engagement with the lived experience of being and feeling safe (see Oparah, Chapter 14). This is complicated work. We need research and organising that explores what schools and communities are doing to create safe and strong environments without relying on more detention rooms, truancy officers, surveillance cameras and school security guards.[9]

Unpacking carceral logic from feelings and experiences of being unsafe or fearful can demonstrate how punishment logic masks the real question: 'how do we build stronger and safer communities?' As many, from Audre Lorde (1984) to Feel Tank Chicago (2008: 3) have pointed out, politics and political engagement is a 'world of orchestrated feeling'. Addressing questions of fear and safety in a landscape where sexual and other forms of harm are endemic is difficult because building responses to these forms of state and interpersonal violence necessitates multifaceted

---

[9] Across the globe, formal and ad hoc groups are working on this challenge, include the Story Telling and Organizing Project/Creative Interventions and the Audre Lorde Project/Safe OUTside the System.

labours. We must consider how our responses mobilise disgust, defensiveness and pity and to subsequently use this thinking to shape our organising efforts. In schools, these practices are no different, and we need allies willing to focus research and other labours on the fledgling restorative and transformative justice practices that are happening in schools: peace circles, peer juries, motivational interviewing and many other forms of relationships and community building. Ending the school-to-prison pipeline requires building other sustainable frameworks for public safety and engaging the question of why prisons have been naturalised as responses to harm in our communities.

ORGANISING ABOLITION FUTURES

Victor Rios (2011) in his ethnographic research in Oakland, California, with forty young Latino and black men over a three-year period, the overwhelming majority of whom had their first encounter with police in or near a public school, offers scholars and organisers concrete insights into how increasingly integrated carceral systems – prison, police, school and more – punish young men. While studying sociology in graduate school, Rios chafed at the frameworks provided to understand poverty, as these failed to highlight a key factor he had learned: the carceral state is not broken; it is doing precisely what it was designed to do.

> The state had not abandoned the poor; it had reorganized itself, placing priority on its punitive institutions, such as the police, and embedding crime control discourses and practices into welfare institutions, such as schools.
>
> (Rios, 2011: xiii)

For Rios, the pathways taken by young men he works with are neither surprising nor arbitrary.

While mainstream media may feature stories of outrage at the arrest or detention of young people, including those I have cited in this article (Salecia Johnson and Alexa Gonzales), as Rios states, the experiences of these youth are not surprising. Rios reminds us that the carceral state is a designed and manufactured set of interlocking systems and the response is not to tweak or adjust this system. We do not need better trained police in schools, or improved juvenile justice prisons. We must rebuild schools and communities that do not require these structures: abolition.

While an abolition epistemology also pushes for an end to the school-to-prison pipeline through the elimination of punitive school disciplinary policies, we must also work to open up other avenues and question how our communities and practices have naturalised punishment and isolation (see Scott, Chapter 15). Prisons, Angela Y. Davis (2005: 96–7) states, have 'thrived over the last century precisely because of the absence of those resources and the persistence of some of the deep structures of slavery. They cannot be eliminated unless new institutions and resources are made available to those communities that provide, in large part, the human beings that make up the prison population.'[10] To build stronger and safer communities and schools, we must *transform* our conceptions of what makes us secure and what makes our lives and communities just. If we are invested in moving away from our punishing democracy, our schools-to-prisons pipeline, our incarceration nation, it is not enough to take down prisons: *we must name how our democratic institutions continue to shut out millions from the 'best of' pathways and then remake these institutions.* This has never been more vital.

Horrified at the 'downstate' trips to adult prison offered to Chicago's 15-year-old youth of color? Then let us reshape our institutions to ensure that other pathways, including college and/or flourishing wage employment, are not just imaginable but available and expected.

[10] Also see Salah-El (2001).

277

14

WHY NO PRISONS?

Julia C. Oparah

Since the late 1990s, a vibrant anti-prison movement has emerged in the USA in response to the hyper-incarceration[1] of predominantly racialised minorities from distressed urban communities. This movement has popularised the term 'prison-industrial complex' to describe a symbiotic relationship between politicians, corporations, media and correctional institutions that generates political and economic profit from penal expansion. Movement actors – described as the 'new abolitionists' – identify connections between the incomplete abolition of slavery and the rise of the prison-industrial complex and push for a radical rethinking of how society responds to harm. This chapter argues that any examination of the role of the prison must consider the insurgent knowledge produced by these anti-prison activists. It then examines five arguments for the end of prisons put forward by the new abolitionists and explores how activists have mobilised around them as the basis for political praxis. The chapter closes with a discussion of moratorium, decarceration and community accountability as steps toward an abolition that is lived now rather than in some future utopia.

---

[1] The abolitionist scholars and activists discussed in this paper generally use the term 'mass incarceration' to describe the exponential increase in prison and jail populations since the 1970s and to capture the immense impact penal expansion has had on marginalised communities of color. Loïc Wacquant (2010a) argues that 'hyper-incarceration' more accurately describes the intensive targeting of low-income African-American neighbourhoods as well as the relative insulation from surveillance experienced by residents of middle- and upper-class communities, regardless of race. While Wacquant's analysis erases the targeting of Latinos, Native Americans, immigrants and women of color, his thesis – when expanded to include these groups – usefully brings attention to the selective impact of the US carceral regime and thus helps to explain continued popular and bipartisan support for tough-on-crime politics.

In early 2012, Corrections Corporation of America (CCA) wrote a letter to forty-eight states in which it offered to assist them in managing 'challenging correctional budgets' by purchasing publicly owned prisons (Kirkham, 2012). In return for the injection of much-needed resources into the budgets of cash-strapped states, the state would sign a management contract of at least twenty years with CCA guaranteeing a minimum 90 per cent occupancy rate. Barely veiled behind the rationale of enhanced efficiencies and mutually beneficial public-private partnerships was a Faustian bargain that would have locked states overburdened with the financial consequences of uncontrolled prison expansion into continuing a failed social experiment with hyper-incarceration. CCA's move was designed to buy long-term insulation against the risks associated with decarcerative strategies, such as sentencing and parole reforms, which are increasingly appealing during an economic downturn. But this attempt to capitalise on state budget crises was not to succeed. The letter was leaked to a major progressive investigate news site (Kirkham, 2012) and the story was quickly picked up by bloggers and activists (Navarro, 2012). CCA became the target of a campaign by a coalition of non-profits and religious organisations, which urged states to reject the offer (American Civil Liberties Union, 2012). Tolling a death knoll to the ambitious plan, Louisiana, the second state targeted by the corporation, voted against a plan to sell off three prisons, after the state treasurer memorably compared the plan to 'a junkie selling the television set and radio to generate money for his next fix' (Kirkham, 2012: 3).

There are important lessons to be learned from CCA's offer and from their very public, but certainly temporary, humiliation. First, this incident unveils a symbiotic relationship between state correctional machinery and corporate profit-making that drives prison growth and undermines efforts to shift dependency on incarceration as a panacea for social ills. Making visible the *business* of imprisonment should encourage us to interrogate the assumption in much prison studies literature: that the only significant players involved in penal policy are state actors (see Cooper and Sim, this Chapter 10). This assumption leads to policy initiatives by advocacy organisations as well as liberal academics that erroneously assume a causal relationship between governmental decision-making and evidence-based claims by non-governmental actors. In this chapter, I examine alternative strategies developed by activists in the USA who believe that providing state actors with 'better knowledge' is not enough; instead they promote a model of change based on pressure exerted on both private and public actors within the context of popular movement-building.

This brings us to the second lesson. What is notable about CCA's debacle is the swift, well-coordinated and effective nature of the response from opponents of the plan. While the USA is the site of immense and interlocking pro-carceral forces, these political and economic forces do not wield uncontested power. Rather, the emergence of a transnational prison-industrial complex and the associated prison- and jail-building boom has spurred the development of a vibrant abolitionist movement. This is no armchair abolitionism; rather, the new abolitionists are deeply engaged in movement-building with the communities most affected by hyper-incarceration (see Meiners, Chapter 13). In so doing, they have been highly effective in disseminating counter-hegemonic ideas about racial and economic politics of punishment. These new understandings popularised by the anti-prison movement have spread to newspapers, websites, non-profit organisations and classrooms, building an educated citizenry who are becoming equipped to call out and successfully confront endless penal expansion.

FORGING A MOVEMENT

The new abolitionist movement in the USA exploded into public awareness in September of 1998, when over 3,000 activists, scholars, students, artists, prisoners, former prisoners and their families came together at a conference and strategy session at the University of California, Berkeley (Critical Resistance, 2000).[2] Entitled *Critical Resistance: Beyond the Prison Industrial Complex*, the event was more than an academic conference. Instead, passionate first-hand testimonies by former prisoners and their family members, visual arts, popular theatre, puppetry and spoken word were interwoven with critical analyses of the political economy of prisons. As an unexpected number of attendees poured into the event, it was clear that a new abolitionist politic was being generated, one that was at once urgent, deeply personal and politically radical. In the following months Critical Resistance became the foundation for a new social movement, establishing chapters and affiliates across the country, building popular understanding of the

[2] The author was a member of the conference planning committee.

prison-industrial complex and disseminating a model of grassroots organising that could adapt to local conditions.[3]

In 2008, Critical Resistance 10 (CR10) brought together a new generation of young activists alongside some of the original organisers to 'assess the successes and challenges of the movement to abolish the prison-industrial complex during the past ten years, to examine how the prison-industrial complex has adapted to the challenges our work has posed and what we must do to gain ground over the next 10 years' (Critical Resistance, 2008: 2). CR10's theme – *Dismantle. Change. Build.* – indicated the maturation of the movement. From a focus on critiquing the prison-industrial complex and confronting prison expansion in its early years, Critical Resistance and other movement actors had shifted toward a focus on building alternatives to the prison-industrial complex. These included both broad-based social transformation such as providing 'food, shelter, meaningful work and freedom' for all as a means to create genuine security, as well as 'alternative systems of accountability' that address harms in ways that foster social stability and sustainability (ibid.: 2).

From its inception, Critical Resistance reached far beyond the small prison abolitionist and reform community. Organising for the first conference had deliberately targeted numerous sectors – from the American Indian Movement and Puerto Rican nationalists to homeless advocates and sex-worker rights activists. This coalitional politics built on the understanding that a mass movement powerful enough to make meaningful change to the penal goliath must involve more than those directly touched by penal incarceration. At the same time, organisers recognised the importance of creating space for the leadership of those who have survived prison and can combine political analysis with the ability to speak bitterness about the reality of life inside. Organisers therefore developed a two-prong approach, relying heavily on the moral authority of (formerly) imprisoned intellectuals and leaders such as Angela Y. Davis, Ramona and Pam Africa, Leonard Peltier, Dylcia Pagan and Frank 'Big Black' Smith, while also promoting the principle that the prison is not only toxic for those captured within it, but that its negative social, economic and environmental impacts leach out into the lives of all those who live in a society characterised by hyper-incarceration.

---

[3] Subsequent regional conferences took place in New York in 2001 and the Tremé district of New Orleans in 2003.

The new abolitionist movement, like all 'new' social movements, is both a marker of a new set of strategies, actors and understandings and a continuation of older currents of organising. Critical Resistance's critique of the multiple functions of the prison – as machinery for state repression of marginalised and resurgent communities; as warehouse for indigent and racialised communities; as factory for the US war machine and corporate capital; and as site for the manufacture and maintenance of systemic racial, sexual violence – was informed by radical imprisoned intellectuals who emerged from the movements of the 1960s and 1970s. These activists suffered brutal state repression and lengthy sentences as punishment for their opposition to state violence at home and imperialist interventions abroad, and also witnessed the exploding prison system from the inside, experiences that shaped their abolitionist politics.[4] Thus Critical Resistance can actually be seen as both a resurgence and a new iteration of the anti-imperialist, anti-capitalist, black and Chicano liberation, Puerto Rican and indigenous sovereignty movements. This is not to suggest a stagnant exhumation of past battles; rather, Critical Resistance's anti-racist, anti-capitalist critique was informed by insights from the feminist and lesbian, gay, bisexual, transgender and queer (LGBTQ) movements, as well as the youth activism of the hip-hop generation, thus forging a more nuanced, inter-generational and multi-issue politic.

WHY ABOLITION?

While we can identify intellectual and political influences shaping anti-prison activism in the USA, the movement does not have a manifesto or dogma to which movement actors are expected to adhere. Rather, a fluid and mutable leadership, a multiplicity of analytic perspectives, local responsiveness and autonomy and radical democratic and non-hierarchical decision-making structures characterise the new abolitionist movement. Despite this multiplicity and complexity, we can identify five key arguments by movement actors that together comprise a radical democratic, anti-racist critique and rationale for the abolition of prisons. First, prisons are rooted in and perpetuate a brutal racial history traceable to the Plantation South and thus like slavery, must be abolished, not

---

[4] In particular, Critical Resistance's analysis of the political economy of prisons was shaped by anti-imperialist political prisoner Linda Evans, co-author of a pamphlet distributed at Critical Resistance (Evans and Goldberg, 1998), and Angela Y. Davis, who hosted planning meetings.

reformed. Second, prisons do not make us safe; rather, they construct a dangerous racialised 'other' in order to govern through a politics of fear. Third, a symbiotic relationship between prisons, corporations and the military promotes private profit at the expense of public goods like education, healthcare and community infrastructure. Fourth, prisons squelch dissent, impoverish the radical imagination and undermine democracy. And fifth, prisons and the criminal punishment system more broadly are primary sites for the reproduction of violence against women as well as those who do not conform to normative expectations of sexual conduct or gender expression.

Unfinished liberation

One of the most effective strategies used by Critical Resistance to win support for the abolition rather than reform of prisons is to point to a continuity between slavery and contemporary incarceration. Imprisoned African Americans have a long tradition of using the narrative of slavery to describe their experiences (K. Gilmore, 2000). Kemba Smith, who received a 24.5-year mandatory minimum sentence for 'conspiracy' in a drug-related incident is a vocal opponent to the war on drugs. In a letter written while in prison, she invoked a powerful history of racialised repression and resistance:

> With the entering of the New Year, I want to give you the gift of vision, to see this system of modern-day slavery for what it is. The government gets paid $25,000 a year by you (taxpayers) to house me (us). The more of us that they incarcerate, the more money they get from you to build prisons.
>
> (K. Smith, 2005: 106)

Kemba also drew on the trope of severed mother-child bonds, an emotionally charged image that was used by female slavery abolitionists to win support from northern white women:

> On December 12, 1994, still imprisoned, I gave birth to my son. Thirteen days after his birth, I spent Christmas staring at jail cell bars, partially understanding what our ancestors were forced to endure when torn apart from their babies in the Motherland.
>
> (K. Smith, 2005: 105)

The massive racial disparities in the US criminal punishment system (African Americans are incarcerated at nearly six times the rate of the white population), as well as the imagery of large numbers of black prisoners controlled and forced to work or to relinquish their children by white guards, provides a ready foundation for the slavery-prison analogy (Mauer and King, 2007: 3).[5] Anti-prison scholars have provided historical contextualisation for, and explored the usefulness of, this analogy while also noting the differences between the two modes of regulation. Their discussion focuses on the historical origins of hyper-incarceration at the end of the Civil War and the unfinished liberation marked by the Thirteenth Amendment of the US Constitution; the historical connections between convict-leasing, the Black Codes, the racialisation of crime and contemporary prison labour (A. Y. Davis, 2003: 22–39); and the linkages between the social death of slavery and the abrogation of civil rights signified by contemporary imprisonment (Rodriguez, 2006: 223–55).

Labelling the Thirteenth Amendment an 'enslaving anti-enslavement document' (K. Gilmore, 2000: xxi), activist scholars draw attention to the exemption clause of the Amendment, which outlawed slavery and involuntary servitude 'except as a punishment for crime whereof the party shall have been duly convicted' (A. Y. Davis, 2003: 28). Since slavery was not abolished (only regulated and limited), prison abolitionists argue that they are picking up where slavery abolitionists left off. With involuntary labour allowed under the supervision of the criminal punishment system, convict leasing became an important way to regulate black labour in the postwar South. Former slave states passed Black Codes that prohibited African Americans from a range of activities permissible for the white population, such as insulting gestures, breach of job contracts, possession of firearms and vagrancy (A. Y. Davis, 2003: 28–9). The Black Codes provided ample fodder for the burgeoning penal system and transformed the racial composition of southern prison populations. Subsequent penal regimes in the USA, including contemporary patterns of hyper-incarceration, would continue the racial logics of the post-emancipation era, from the racialisation of crime and punishment to the normalisation of racially targeted laws. This exploration of the roots of modern patterns of imprisonment in slavery has proven to be an effective tool.[6] Maya, an activist working for the freedom of political exile, and former Black

---

[5] Of course, this imagery erases the presence of Latinos who are incarcerated at double the rate of the white population (Mauer and King, 2007: 3), and Native Americans whose disproportionate incarceration is often rendered invisible in official statistics (ibid.: 2).

[6] But see also Luana Ross (1998) and Stormy Ogden (2005) for an alternative genealogy rooted in forced indigenous labour in the Southwest missions, tribal relocations and the Indian boarding schools.

Panther Assata Shakur exemplifies the effectiveness of this argument in winning people over to the abolitionist cause:

> The first time I found out about the Thirteenth Amendment was in Assata's book, and a lot of people didn't know that the Thirteenth Amendment had a 'but' clause. So that means people are still legally enslaved in this country... If you are against enslavement, how are you for prison?
>
> (Sudbury, 2011: 300)

The slavery-prison analogy is also an efficacious strategy for countering the common allegation that prison abolition is unrealistic or utopian. As Angela Y. Davis (2003) points out:

> Slavery, lynching and segregation are certainly compelling examples of social institutions that, like the prison, were once considered to be as everlasting as the sun. Yet, in the case of all three examples, we can point to movements that assumed the radical stance of announcing the obsolescence of these institutions.
>
> (A.Y. Davis, 2003: 25)

By invoking a powerful history of significant and unimagined social transformations engendered by popular resistance, and by positioning themselves as the inheritors of the abolitionist movements of the nineteenth century, the new abolitionists claim moral currency, reignite consciousness about the radical possibilities offered by abolition and generate a sense of agency against apparently overwhelming odds.

But what do we do with the rapists? Toward real security

In one of its popular pamphlets, Critical Resistance addresses the question: 'What about the rapists, child molesters and murderers. Aren't there some people who really need to be locked up?' (Critical Resistance, n.d.). This question, commonly directed at abolitionists, reflects a concern for safety that is informed by lived experiences of harm, as well as an embedded assumption that prisons do in fact keep 'us' safe. Safety is an issue which is particularly pertinent for people from communities most impacted by hyper-incarceration because they have less access to cars, alarmed properties, well lit streets, respectful policing and economic choices (to leave a violent relationship, for example) which may lead to some measure of safety in the context of societies plagued by poverty, inequality, untreated addiction and violence. Decoupling safety from policing and prisons has therefore been a critical step toward building a broad-based popular movement to dismantle the prison-industrial complex.

In addressing this concern, activists have used a number of strategies. First, they have educated the public about the people who fill our prisons and jails. Popular media representations of prisons and the criminal punishment system in the USA tend to focus on sensationalised cases that promote an image of the prison as a warehouse for dangerous racialised men who have committed violent crimes. These images, as well as the combative court system, create and reify a rigid dichotomy between victim and perpetrator, 'us' and 'them', that encourages the majority to disidentify from and dehumanise people in prison. One way prison activists have combated this tendency is to break down the social isolation generated by the prison. Prisoners suffer from a simultaneous invisibility and hyper-visibility that erases their lived experiences and replaces them with graphic dramatised narratives; creating opportunities for people outside of prison to hear the voices of people in prison, through phone-ins at conferences, reading letters from people inside and foregrounding the testimonies of those who have been inside is a key strategy in challenging their social death and dehumanisation.

Art and poetry are also powerful tools that abolitionists have used to enable people in prison to make important human connections with potential allies on the outside. Silent auctions at events by Critical Resistance and other anti-prison organisations allow people in prison to showcase their art while also raising funds for the movement, demonstrating the agency and resourcefulness of people inside. Prison art exhibits such as *Interrupted Life: Incarcerated Mothers in the U.S.* also challenge controlling images of 'the criminal', 'the inmate' and the 'unfit mother' by creating space for women in prison to express maternal grief and aspirations for themselves and their children. In common with other forms of movement-oriented art, prison art provides the artist an opportunity to communicate, inspire and mobilise. However, prison art is unique in that the conditions of its production are structured by coercive relations of ruling and the constant threat of sanctions for forms of expression that transgress those relations. Prison art is therefore a translated, negotiated and mediated expressive form, which nevertheless allows the artist to reclaim the self and exert agency in the world outside.

A second approach deployed by abolitionists has been to create a dialogue about the question 'what makes us feel safe?' In their abolitionist toolkit, Critical Resistance shares an exercise in which participants are invited to make two lists. In the first, they list things that make them feel safe; in the second, things that make them feel unsafe. This exercise begins to interrogate the common sense idea that policing and prisons help to safeguard public safety. Instead, Critical Resistance continues:

> Police, prisons, and the wider effect of the prison-industrial complex create major barriers to other kinds of safety we need to live. With most financial resources going to policing and controlling people... there is less of an opportunity for people most affected by crime and poverty to get resources to deal with those concerns where they live... people of color, poor people, queer people, and others are often made unsafe by the incursions of police – whether they suffer physical abuse, constant harassment, or removal from their communities.
>
> (Critical Resistance, n.d: 30)

The popular education curricula developed by Critical Resistance, the Prison Moratorium Project and other anti-prison organisations emphasise building on participants' lived experiences. Rather than relying on abstract theoretical analysis to build a case for abolition, they encourage participants to share their own experiences of surveillance, policing and imprisonment and to use that as a basis for critical interrogations of the concept of safety. By demonstrating through the participants' experiences that the criminal punishment system provides (limited) safety for some, while exacerbating insecurity and harm for many, these organisations develop a collective analysis of the links between race, class, gender, sexuality, state regulation and punishment. They then provide an alternative vision of 'human security', based on the provision of basic needs for food, clothing, shelter, education, health care; a sustainable relationship with the environment that provides clean water and air; and respect for human dignity, equality and cultural identities as well as protection from avoidable harm. In this sense, genuine security cannot be bought with bigger and better locks, alarm systems, prisons or armies but implies:

> support for community gardens, farmer's markets, credit unions, and small-scale worker-owned businesses and markets. It implies local control over transnational corporations and the reduction of poor countries' debt. It means living more simply; recycling materials; mending clothes, shoes and appliances; bartering for some of the things we need.
>
> (Okazawa-Rey and Kirk, 2000: 121)

By redefining and broadening our understanding of security, anti-prison organisers successfully channel the desire for safety – a common barrier to imagining a world without prisons – into support for an abolitionist vision.

Who profits? The business of imprisonment

The development and articulation of the concept of the 'prison-industrial complex' is a key third component to the abolitionist critique. The concept is derived from the 'military-industrial complex', a term coined by Dwight Eisenhower to describe the 'conjunction of an immense military establishment and a large arms industry' (Eisenhower, 1961: 1035–40). The term 'prison-industrial complex' was first used by Mike Davis (1995: 260) to describe a multibillion-dollar prison-building boom in California that, he argued, 'rivals agribusiness as the dominant force in the life of rural California and competes with land developers as the chief seducer of legislators in Sacramento'. Elaborated on by California-based scholars and prison intellectuals associated with Critical Resistance (Ruth Wilson Gilmore, Linda Evans, Angela Y. Davis and myself), the concept helped to explain why that state had continued a hugely expensive prison-building binge throughout the 1990s, even as crime rates were falling and unemployment rates were relatively low (A. Y. Davis, 2003; Sudbury, 2004).

The prison-industrial complex incorporates two related processes. The first is the transformation of prisoners into profits. This occurs in both public- and privately run prisons. When a new prison, jail or detention centre is built to create beds for the perpetually swelling ranks of people sentenced to time behind bars, profits are generated for construction companies, architects and the suppliers of high tech surveillance equipment and other materials. New prisons also create profits for the companies that underwrite the costs of construction, turning prisons into a commodity on the stock market and investors into jailers. Prison labour also generates profits for companies that pay less than minimum wage to workers who receive no benefits, paid leave or maternity pay, as well as saving money for states that use prison labour to clean highways or dig graves. Finally a plethora of secondary economic interests repackage hyper-incarceration for sale via crime-themed television, movies, news shows, clothes and music videos.

Anti-prison activists have used highly visible and often entertaining ways to bring attention to the business of imprisonment. Giant puppets and papier maché figures featuring dollar bills, conservative political leaders and prison bars are common at demonstrations opposing the construction of new prisons or the passage of pro-incarceration bills. Poster and mural art has also been a useful vehicle for disseminating information about the connection between prisons, profit and cuts to public services. For example, Critical Resistance's poster series rewrote the 'It's the Cheese' advertising campaign with eye-catching data: 'California, No. 41 in education spending, No. 1 in prison spending.' Similarly, Christine Wong's mural, created for an event opposing a juvenile crime bill that would have channelled more young people into adult courts, features a woman of color[7] in a prison cell sewing undergarments which are worn by a white model in a Victoria's Secret poster, pointing to the commodification and racialisation of punishment.[8] Posters, murals and puppetry alongside popular education workshops and publications have proven effective in popularising the concept of the prison-industrial complex. In this way, the movement has successfully shifted popular conversations about crime and punishment to include an understanding of the commodification of prisoners' bodies.

The second process that drives the prison-industrial complex is the cementing of prisons, jails and detention centres into local economies. 'Industrialised punishment' has become a key economic development strategy for rural towns devastated by the economic restructuring brought about by globalisation. In the context of farm bankruptcies and factory closures caused by the rise of corporate agribusiness and the influx of foreign produce, politicians and business elites in rural towns have promoted the policy of prison construction as economic development, touting prisons as a recession-proof and non-polluting industry (Dhondt, 2002). The jobs and construction contracts promised by new public or private prisons and detention centres are touted as a panacea for economic stagnation and population loss, leading small towns to compete in a bid to offer the most attractive package of tax breaks, cheap land and other incentives (R. Gilmore, 2007). With the prison population in the USA increasing 500 per cent in thirty years, hyper-incarceration became *the* fastest expanding industry in rural areas during the late 1980s and 1990s.

In order to challenge the prisonisation of rural economies, abolitionists more familiar with organising in highly policed urban communities have moved to small rural towns and farming communities. In their fight against Delano II, a 5,160-bed prison ultimately constructed in

---

[7] The term 'women of color' was developed in the 1980s by African American, Chicana/Latina, Native American, Asian American, Pacific Islander and diasporic women in the USA as a basis for coalition politics and, like the term 'black' when used as an umbrella term in the UK, connotes an oppositional collective identity.

[8] An excerpt from the mural can be seen on the cover of *Global Lockdown* (Sudbury, 2005c).

California's central valley for example, Critical Resistance and the
California Prison Moratorium Project (CPMP) built coalitions with local
youth, immigrant workers, the United Farm Workers and environmental
justice organisations by uniting around the 'three Ps: police, pollution and
prisons' (Braz and Gilmore, 2006: 96). While urban communities of color
tend to focus on the negative social and economic impacts of removing
large numbers of community members to remote prisons, rural inhabitants
are more concerned with how a new prison would impact farmland, ground
water, traffic and air quality, local protected species, housing prices,
schools and jobs. By combining grassroots actions with a legal case against
the cumulative environmental impacts of prison construction, Critical
Resistance and CPMP were successful in significantly delaying the new
prison and creating a model for cooperation between rural/urban and anti-
prison/environmental justice communities.

Eisenhower's critique of the relationship between the state and the
arms industry was rooted in the 'unwarranted influence' waged by the
business sector over government policy. Similarly, the corporate prison
lobby and other economic interests exercise significant influence over
criminal punishment policies. This influence occurs in three main ways:
campaign donations, lobbying and funding and participation in the
American Legislative Exchange Council, a New Right foundation that
provides templates of pro-incarceration bills to legislators (Sarabi and
Bender, 2000). Prison corporations use campaign donations as part of a
strategy to create a pro-privatisation environment, to maximise the size
of the corrections market and to minimise the 'risk' posed by decarcerative measures.[9] In addition, lobbyists working on behalf of the prison
industry influence lawmakers through the provision of corporate largesse
such as travel, lavish dinners and (sometimes illegal) gifts.[10] Such tactics
have had two main achievements: (i) to promote privatisation in states
previously ambivalent or opposed; and (ii) to generate tough-on-crime
legislation leading to larger prison populations.[11] By making visible the

---

[9] For example, private prison-industry donations of nearly 1 million dollars to Florida campaigns
in 2010 were rewarded with a plan to privatise prisons in a third of the cash-strapped state, and to
quadruple the number of private prisons (National Institute on Money in State Politics, 2012).

[10] For example, Correctional Services Corporation (CSC) was forced to pay a $300,000 fine after
an investigation by the New York State Lobbying Commission found that they had failed to
report their lobbying expenditures and had given gifts beyond the legal limit to legislators. CSC
also provided staff free of charge, including drivers, public relations aides, security guards and
workers for political campaigns, and was suspected of inviting legislators to participate in a sex
ring (Correction Corporation of America, 2003).

[11] For example, the Institute on Money in State Politics identified clear evidence of legislators
introducing or voting favourably on pro-industry bills that would benefit the private prison

power of corporations to influence penal policy, abolitionists demonstrate that prisons benefit economic and political elites rather than those they purport to protect. Using shaming as a tool to discredit politicians who have been seduced by corporate interests, activists end the impunity and invisibility surrounding these transactions. They also seek to make corporations – from Victoria's Secret to Bank of America – accountable for their relationships with the prison-industrial complex.

The end of democracy? Prisons and dissent

The fourth argument for the abolition of prisons developed by movement activists is that prisons undermine democracy by silencing dissent and abrogating the rights of low-income and racialised citizens to participate in the political process (see Barker, Chapter 7). The focus on prisons as the primary vehicle for state censorship of radical and insurgent perspectives is informed by the involvement of political prisoners, prisoners of war and their allies. The ruthless and sometimes illegal activities of the FBI's Counter Intelligence Program (COINTELPRO) under the leadership of J. Edgar Hoover in the 1960s and early 1970s led to the premature deaths, incarceration and exile of hundreds of revolutionaries and independentistas. These radicals, like Leonard Peltier, Assata Shakur and Mumia Abu Jamal, have inspired organisers to establish organisations dedicated to their vindication and freedom.[12] In addition, former political prisoners and prisoners of war who have been released as a result of clemencies, parole hearings or successful appeals continue to oppose state repression and raise awareness about those who remain behind bars through their writings, speeches and organising work (Bukhari, 2010; Rosenberg, 2011).[13]

Abolitionists are not unified in their definition of political prisoners or their analysis of the role of political prisoner campaigns in anti-prison work (James, 2003: bxi). For some, the focus on radical individuals creates a narrow politics in which the public is encouraged to support

companies that had donated to their campaigns in Mississippi, Georgia, Florida, Oklahoma and North Carolina during the 2000 election cycle (E. Bender 2002: 4). For a discussion of the influence of US prison corporations on UK corrections policy, see Sudbury (2000: 135–7).

[12] Organizations include: Millions for Mumia (www.millions4mumia.org), Black August (http://mxgm.org/blackaugust/blackaugust-history), Hands Off Assata (www.assatashakur.org), The Leonard Peltier Defense Offense Committee (www.whoisleonardpeltier.info), The Jericho Movement (www.thejerichomovement.com) (all accessed 29 July 2012) and Sparks Fly (Shakur et al., 1998).

[13] Of course, this use of state power to isolate and silence radicalism did not end with the termination of COINTELPRO in 1971; rather, state and federal governments continue to surveil, prosecute and imprison anti-prison activists, as well as radicals from the anti-globalisation, anti-war, environmental justice and student movements.

the release of those wrongfully imprisoned for their political affiliations and actions, while overlooking the unjust laws and economic motives that lead to the incarceration of millions of 'common' (non-political) prisoners. For others, making visible the violent use of state power to neutralise and isolate movement leaders is not incompatible with a radical critique of notions of innocence and guilt or a vision of liberation for all those captured and exploited by the prison-industrial complex (Buck, 2000: 25–8). Adding further complexity, Dylan Rodriquez's call for a transgressive engagement with the radical prison practice produced by 'imprisoned radical intellectuals' includes 'politically unrecognized captives [who] compose the vast majority of those who have become activists and political intellectuals *while imprisoned*' (Rodriquez, 2006: 5, emphasis in original).[14]

Radical imprisoned intellectuals trace their lineage back to traditions of marronage, communities of free Africans and indigenous peoples who created and lived an alternative political vision, whose existence made the abolition of slavery a present possibility rather than a utopian future (Sudbury, 2011). Non-imprisoned abolitionists such as Joy James, Dylan Rodriquez and Angela Y. Davis have played a key role in disseminating the knowledge produced by this group with progressive communities on the outside. This has been achieved through publications of writings and poetry by and in collaboration with imprisoned radicals, and through letters, audio and video recordings from inside prison and from exile in Cuba. These engagements expand the radical imagination, reminding younger activists of earlier revolutionary visions of global solidarity and political and economic systems run by and for the people. In a context in which politicians and pundits receive media airtime to argue that health care for all is a first foothold in a communist takeover, the need for radical ideas from beyond the narrow spectrum of US party politics is never more urgently needed.

Since the 2000 election of George W. Bush, abolitionists have turned their attention to the impact of hyper-incarceration on the ability of communities of color to vote for politicians who represent their interests. Slavery abolitionists viewed the vote as the only way to guarantee the limited freedoms and citizenship rights granted by the Thirteenth and Fourteenth Amendments and worked vigorously to

---

[14] This definition does not include white supremacists and right-wing extremists who are incarcerated for violent acts against the state like the 1995 Oklahoma City bombing, who as Joy James argues, are reactionaries rather than radicals, seeking to restore old systems of supremacy and waging war against a state that they view as overly progressive and supportive of minority interests (James, 2003: xi).

win the franchise for black men (and in some cases black women). During the short era of Radical Reconstruction, when federal militias protected black-male voting rights, legislatures in the South changed dramatically, with the new multiracial senates passing legislation that provided free public education, more equitable taxation and laws against racial discrimination (Foner, 2002). This radical experiment with multiracial and multiclass democracy was rapidly curtailed once federal reconstruction ended, and the short-lived era of black electoral participation was terminated legally through poll taxes and grandfather clauses, and extra-legally through the lynch mob and burning cross.

Drawing on this history, and its legacy of resistance, organisations like the NuLeadership Policy Group and All of Us Or None organise to promote the leadership of former prisoners and to end post-incarceration discrimination against people with felony convictions. An important part of this work has been to campaign against the disenfranchisement of predominantly African American men as a result of laws that prohibit people on probation, parole or, in some instances those who have completed their sentence from voting.[15] As Michelle Alexander (2010) argues, felony disenfranchisement has led to a new form of Jim Crow segregation. Revealing that more African American men were disenfranchised in 2004 than in 1870 when the Fifteenth Amendment passed, Alexander (2010) points to a growing undercaste who are permanently relegated to second-class citizenship and legally discriminated against in housing, employment, access to education and public benefits. In their work for voting rights for all, All of Us Or None (n.d.), a 'national organising initiative of prisoners, former prisoners and felons', emphasises the impact of felony disenfranchisement on the political freedoms of African Americans, and therefore on election outcomes. Since the 1970s, as rates of (penal) incarceration have increased exponentially for low-income communities of color, political parties have been progressively able to ignore the political visions and preferences of these communities because of the large proportion who are denied the vote. Dorsey Nunn, a formerly incarcerated abolitionist, Critical Resistance member and founding member of the organisation, articulates this formula:

> The voting rights of incarcerated and formerly incarcerated people and people with past convictions have been violated over the course of

[15] As of 2010, 5 million citizens were ineligible to vote, including 1 in every 8 black men (Porter, 2010).

decades, at a minimum through benign neglect, and at worst deliberate disenfranchisement of hundreds of thousands of people. The lessons coming out of Florida in 2000 were not only a question of hanging chads, but the open suppression of Black votes through the manipulation of felony conviction status.

(All of Us Or None, n.d.; see also Nunn, 2012)

The mass disenfranchisement of black men and to a lesser degree women and other men of color contributes further to the narrowing of political possibilities begun in the 1970s with the targeting and removal of radicals from these communities. By illustrating the intersections between hyper-incarceration and the racial politics of voting, new abolitionists suggest a very different vision of Obama's America than the mythical post-racial society imagined by some commentators. Rather, they demonstrate that the racialised exclusion cemented through white supremacy and racial terrorism in the nineteenth century continues to shape the political landscape.

Rethinking gender violence

The final argument for abolition is that prisons reproduce gender violence, while perpetuating the myth that retributive state violence protects women and queers. The relationship between prison abolitionists and anti-violence activists has often been fraught due in part to the accusation by the latter that abolitionists do not provide adequate strategies for keeping survivors of sexual assault, domestic violence and hate crimes safe from further harm. New abolitionists have addressed this tension by challenging dominant understandings of gender violence, identifying forms of violence such as homophobic and transphobic harassment by police officers, prison rape, strip searches and shackling of pregnant women, which are perpetrated rather than prevented by the criminal punishment system. They have thus convinced large numbers of anti-violence organisers that more policing and prisons is not a solution to gender violence. In the late 1960s and early 1970s when the women's liberation and 'gay' liberation movements first made visible various forms of gender violence, from incest, rape and domestic violence to 'gay bashing', their struggles largely took the form of grassroots expressions of collective power and self-help such as Take Back the Night and Pride marches, community patrols, protests against police harassment and the establishment of shelters and hotlines. These activities were located outside of the state and frequently confronted state violence.

By the 1980s and 1990s, however, feminist agendas had begun to penetrate the corridors of power, with 'women's issues' – such as domestic violence, sexual assault and child abuse – appearing in public policy discussions, and police and courts instructed to aggressively pursue perpetrators of violence against women with the same vigour that they brought to other criminal cases (Dempsey, 2009; see also Gottschalk, Chapter 12 of this volume). For anti-violence activists, this appeared to represent an important achievement. Many anti-violence activists embraced new initiatives that promoted law-and-order solutions to gender violence, including mandatory arrest laws, more funding for law enforcement – often attached to the establishment of police domestic violence units – and longer sentences for those convicted of battering and sexual assault. In so doing, they provided legitimacy for the exponential growth in police, court and prison/jail budgets and thus unwittingly supported the transfer of public resources from community-based services – many of which offered alternatives for women and LGBTQ people escaping violence and the attendant homelessness, poverty, trauma and addiction – to the criminal punishment system (A. Smith, 2005: 139). The passage of the Violence Against Women Act in 1994 reinforced the symbiotic relationship between the anti-violence movement and the criminal justice system by providing state resources for domestic violence shelters and sexual assault centres (see Gottschalk, Chapter 12). This funding required groups to apply for charitable 501c3 status, to formalise a hierarchical structure and to work closely in partnership with the police and courts. As a result, the political challenge of feminist anti-violence work was absorbed by the state, and tough-on-crime sentencing and prison expansion reified as the only imaginable solution (Richie, 2012). The state had successfully positioned itself as protector and defender of survivors, prosecutor and rehabilitator of perpetrators and provider and partner of feminist and LGBTQ organisations.

Women of color within the anti-prison movement have played a critical role in generating a critique of the state's capacity to protect women and queers from gender violence. Our close relationships to both the anti-violence and anti-prison movements have provided a unique legitimacy to our arguments. In 2000, a group of 'women of color' activists from a cross-section of movements convened a conference and strategy session in Santa Cruz, California entitled *The Colour of Violence* (A. Smith, 2001). Attended by 2,000 women, the conference shifted understandings of violence against women and exploded the mainstream movement's narrow focus on domestic violence and sexual assault by highlighting the many forms of violence experienced by women of color. Speakers demonstrated the need to address state and intimate violence simultaneously and moved toward articulating a new approach to confronting violence against women, queers and communities of color.

The powerful energy generated by the conference was harnessed in the creation of a national organisation of radical women of color called INCITE! Women of Color Against Violence.[16] INCITE! has been instrumental in building a feminist-of-color abolitionist politic and in encouraging mainstream anti-violence activists and organisations to become accountable for the consequences of their relationships with the criminal-punishment industry (INCITE! Women of Color Against Violence, 2006). The Critical Resistance-INCITE! statement, a collaboration between Critical Resistance and INCITE!, which provides a blueprint for activist work that simultaneously works to dismantle oppressive systems of law enforcement and incarceration and to end all forms of gender violence, has been an important activist tool (Critical Resistance and INCITE! 2003). INCITE! has also carried out participatory action research into the violence experienced by women and transgender people of color at the hands of law enforcement agencies (INCITE! Women of Color Against Violence, n.d.). By making visible the violence routinely carried out by local and state police, immigration enforcement (such as Immigration and Customs Enforcement, Border Patrol and Customs, Drug Enforcement Agents), the FBI, private security agents and military forces, INCITE! interrupts the symbiotic relationship between the anti-violence movement and the 'state as protector' in order to unveil and confront the reality of the 'state as perpetrator' in the lives of many women of color (see Meiners, Chapter 13).

The argument that the criminal punishment system is a primary organiser of multiple forms of gender violence has been made most powerfully by survivors of state violence, including incarcerated women and transgender activists (Stanley and Smith, 2011; Richie, 2012). Organisations working alongside women and transgender people in prison have been particularly effective in providing a conduit for the

---

[16] 'INCITE! is a national activist organization of radical feminists of color advancing a movement to end violence against women of color and our communities through direct action, critical dialogue, and grassroots organizing' (www.incite-national.org (accessed 14 July 2012).

voices of people in prison so that they can shape conversations about the nature of and solutions to violence. For example, California Coalition for Women Prisoners' newsletter *The Fire Inside*, written mostly by people in women's prisons and distributed to communities in and outside prison, provides a platform where people in women's prisons can share their experiences of injustice and resilience. Trans/forming Justice, a coalition of organisations working alongside transgender people in prison, uses YouTube, video diaries and testimonials to enable transgender survivors of imprisonment to articulate and disseminate an analysis of the connections between transphobic violence and discrimination, social exclusion, policing and imprisonment.

The strategic importance of efforts to provide an opportunity for gender-oppressed people in prison to speak for themselves is illustrated in Justice Now's campaign against the California Department of Corrections and Rehabilitation's $294 million 'gender responsive prison expansion' plan (C. Chandler, 2010). The Gender Responsive Strategies Commission – an advisory committee to the California Department of Corrections and Rehabilitation comprising correctional officials, city and state officials and criminologists specialising in women's imprisonment – proposed the plan. Identifying 4,500 non-violent, 'low-risk' women who could be released from state prison, the Commission proposed that 4,500 additional prison beds should be created in new female rehabilitative community correctional centres. Californians United for a Responsible Budget (CURB), an abolitionist-led coalition of organisations seeking to stem spending on policing and prisons, opposed the proposal, arguing that: the 4,500 people identified as low risk should be discharged and provided with six months' housing costs; that funds from the proposed prison construction should instead be directed to social services and education; and that one women's prison should then be closed (CURB, 2007: 300). However, it was Justice Now's strategic mobilisation of 3,000 people in women's prisons, and their dramatic unfurling of a 33-foot banner containing 2,500 signatures, that removed the proposal's progressive mantle and revealed it as 'a fraud' – that, far from creating alternatives to prison, would 'have the effect of massively expanding our already mammoth prison system' (CURB, 2007: 6). From their vantage point inside prison, women and transgender people have successfully demonstrated that prisons are fundamentally violent, punitive environments and that efforts to create a women-centred, community-based prison regime ultimately serve expansionist agendas, draining the resources that could be used to support women in their efforts to escape violence, recreate family ties and rebuild their lives.

STOP!/SHRINK/BUILD: STEPS TO ABOLITION

As we launched a new abolitionist movement in the late 1990s, we faced almost overwhelming odds. In the context of a culture that normalises incarceration as a solution to a plethora of social ills, we sought to dismantle an almost universal, uncritical acceptance of the necessity of the prison. Over a decade later, anti-prison activists have made significant gains, particularly in low-income communities of color and among students and other young people. We have popularised the concept of the prison-industrial complex so that the notion that prisons produce benefits for elites at the expense of racialised and marginalised communities is now commonplace. We have educated young people about the connections between slavery and imprisonment, building support for a renewed abolitionist movement to complete the unfinished business of the Thirteenth Amendment. And we have mobilised an educated citizenry to oppose unfettered prison expansion, forcing pro-expansion forces to utilise new, subtler strategies such as gender-responsiveness to win support for their agenda.

Abolition begins with a transformation of consciousness, a shift in the popular imagination, so that large numbers of people begin to ask themselves what a world with no prisons would look like. But arguments against prisons are not enough in themselves; we also need practical strategies that can contend with the powerful political and economic forces that shape penal policy. Activists working to 'shrink the system into non-existence' have identified three steps to abolition, building on the strategies developed by abolitionists since the nineteenth century (B. Aptheker, 1971; Mathiesen, 1974; Knopp, 1976; H. Aptheker, 1989; R. Morris 1998; West and Morris, 2000). The first step, moratorium, seeks to end prison expansion. Despite the awareness by many state and federal legislators that the snowballing costs of imprisonment are holding hostage public spending on social goods from education to social services, senior correctional officials continue to collaborate with politicians and corporate interests to push for more prison construction. There is a close relationship between prison-expansion and prison-reform activism, since campaigns and lawsuits against inhumane conditions or inadequate health care and programming can easily be co-opted as a justification for more construction. In contrast, when abolitionists work in solidarity with people in prison on survival issues such as access to health care and the violence caused by overcrowding, we take the stance that the state cannot build its way out of the problems inherent in penal regimes. From that starting point, moratorium efforts include campaigns by local residents to prevent the construction of a specific prison, as well as legislative activism against initiatives that would provide funds for additional construction.

The second step is decarceration: shrinking the prison population. People in US prisons face dangerous levels of overcrowding, which will be exacerbated if moratorium efforts are successful. For moratoria to be sustainable, they must be followed swiftly by decarceration initiatives. Decarceration campaigns tend to focus on a subsector of the prison population that the public does not see as threatening, such as people sentenced for non-violent drug offences, women or the elderly. For example, CURB's proposal to dramatically reduce California's prison population includes geriatric parole for elderly prisoners serving long sentences, compassionate release and medical parole for prisoners with serious and life-threatening illnesses, expanded alternative custody options for women and improved re-entry supports for parolees. While starting with these non-threatening subgroups does not promote the overall dismantling of prisons (and can even reify a false dichotomy between those who do and do not 'belong' in prison), it does provide an opportunity to begin a conversation about who is actually in prison, how much it costs to keep them there and what else could be done with those funds to support those individuals and their communities (see McBride, Chapter 11). Decarceration campaigns can also promote an abolitionist message. For example, Free Battered Women, an organisation that works for the release of women imprisoned for assaulting their abusers, also draws attention to the large number of women in prison who are survivors of intimate violence. They thereby challenge the myth of the state as paternalistic protector and call for alternatives to relying on the criminal punishment system to address intimate violence, as part of a broader vision of a world without prisons 'where all people have access to the material, educational, emotional, and spiritual resources necessary to be safe and thrive in our communities'.[17]

The third step toward abolition is building what Critical Resistance has termed 'abolition now'. Recognising that people will not support dismantling prisons if they feel reliant on them and cannot envision

---

[17] www.freebatteredwomen.org/aboutus.html (accessed 18 July 2012).

alternatives, anti-prison activists have turned their attention to creating alternative ways to build security and address harm. These projects include Harm Free Zones, in which urban communities targeted by both over-policing and street violence take back control by creating new forms of community accountability:

> Community accountability refers to the ability and desire of community members to adopt a harm-free way of thinking. This includes developing the mechanisms to prevent harm, to intervene directly when harm occurs, to repair harm amongst community members, and to transform individual and collective relationships... Autonomous communities deal with intra-social/intra-communal/inter-personal harm as communities and without the intervention of representatives of the state. Their way of dealing with social harm does not mimic but disrupts the manner in which the state deals with us and our communities.[18]

They also include community accountability strategies adopted by feminists of color, youth and other social-justice oriented communities. These practices hold people who commit harm accountable for their actions, keep survivors of violence as safe as possible and bring about change in the community relations and power dynamics that supported the harmful act. A key aspect of these 'community accountability' practices is a commitment to recognise the humanity of everyone involved in order to break the cycle of racialised and gender violation in communities of color. Innovative strategies developed by community organisations and collectives demonstrate that it is possible to empower communities to dismantle the flawed belief that we can 'fix' violence with more violence, and to release our attachment to retributive justice (Sista II Sista, 2006; Communities Against Rape and Abuse (CARA), 2006; Kelly, 2012; Kim, 2012). By envisioning and creating community accountability strategies, these new abolitionists are building a world without prisons, not in some distant utopia but in our everyday lives and within the limitations of the communities we inhabit. By 'living abolition', they enable us to decouple our imaginations from the prison-industrial complex so that we can redistribute the massive resources currently dedicated to surveillance, punishment and control and begin to build real safety, based on social justice, radical democracy and collective healing.

[18] Southern Coalition for Social Justice (2012: 1).

15

UNEQUALLED IN PAIN

David Scott

Penological studies have time and time again emphasised that imprison-ment has much in common with other sites of state detention and that the emergence some two centuries ago of the modern prison is intimately tied to a broader 'confinement project' (S. Cohen, 1985; Mathiesen, 1990). Many of the inherent harms of imprisonment are shared by different sites of confinement, and the boundaries between forms of incarceration have always been blurred and permeable: prisons hold recalcitrant mental health patients and foreign nationals; high-security hospitals and asylums hold the 'criminally insane'; and immigration detention centres hold foreign national ex-prisoners and may be *experi-enced* like prisons. Influential arguments have also been made concern-ing the overlaps and convergences between the modern prison and other 'institutions', such as the monastery, nunnery, reformatory, workhouse, plantation, slavery, asylum, hospital, factory, school, army barracks, boot camp, concentration camp, immigration detention centre, Jim Crow regime and black ghetto (Rothman, 1971; Foucault, 1977; Melossi and Pavarini, 1981; S. Cohen, 1985; Dobash et al., 1986; Scott, 1996/2011; Wacquant, 2001; Scull, 2006; Bosworth, 2008; Alexander, 2011; A. Y. Davis, 2012; Ugelvik, 2012). Yet whilst identification of symbiotic intersections remains important, the danger is that prison can become conceptually indistinguishable from other forms of confinement. We must be careful not to 'obfuscate or ignore' (Scull, 2006: 201) the ideological and institutional differences between the separate sites of incarceration, for each have their own unique *raison d'être*. Prisons are designed to deliberately create human suffering, hurt and injury.

Saturated in time consciousness in an environment bereft of love, dignity and respect, the prison is a profoundly painful institution (Scott and Codd, 2010). Other sites of state detention (and other social institutions) may at times be experienced as equally or even more painful than prison, but pain infliction is not their primary intention. The task of the prison is to classify, discipline and *punish* (Foucault, 1977; S. Cohen, 1985). Pain and the allocation of blame are the very reasons why prison exists (Christie, 1981).

Bernard Harcourt (2011: 222–4) has talked persuasively about the increasing dominance of a penal logic shaping contemporary forms of confinement. Drawing upon data on the institutionalisation of mental health patients in the USA in the 1930s through to the 1970s, he highlights that from 1938 to 1963, mental health institutions consistently had a patient rate of over 600 per 100,000 of the general population and that the total incarceration rate stood at more than 800 per 100,000. There was a rapid decline in the incarceration rate from 1964 to 1974 to around 400 per 100,000, but since this time whereas the number of confined mental health patients has continued to fall, the prison population in the USA has escalated at an astonishing rate. This move from the asylum to the prison as the primary form of incarceration indicates an ideological shift in responding to social problems that privileges the penal over welfare interventions (Hudson, 1993), a development that appears to have been reproduced in many other countries across the globe. So why has penal incarceration expanded so rapidly and what can we do right now to halt and reverse penal colonisation? This chapter considers these two questions. It begins by locating global hyper-incarceration within the context of mounting economic inequalities and the social inequalities of class, 'race', gender and sexuality, which signal disparities in power and status. Consideration is then given to a number of factors driving the intensification of penal logic, focusing upon the legal jurisdiction of England and Wales as an illustrative example. The chapter comes to a close with a discussion of 'what is to be done' through promotion of radical social policy interventions from an abolitionist real utopia perspective.

ECONOMIC AND SOCIAL INEQUALITIES

Whilst there is considerable evidence to suggest that genuine equality leads to empathetic identification, understanding, solidarity, collective responsibility and a concern for the wellbeing of others, economic and social inequalities appear to have the opposite effect (Greenberg, 1999). Inequalities weaken social bonds, generate false hierarchies, spawn intolerance, create anxieties and suspicion and promote moral judgments based on individual responsibility that subsequently lead to resentment and hostility to those classified as 'other'. Unequal societies are highly conducive to the attribution of blame and the deliberate infliction of pain (Christie, 1981, 2000; Lappi-Seppala, 2012) and it has long been established that penal severity and income inequality are intimately connected (Wilkins and Pease, 1987; Wilkins, 1991; Pease, 1994). Though economic and social inequalities walk hand in hand with capitalist political economy, it is widely acknowledged that capitalist economies are diverse rather than monolithic (Hall and Soskice, 2001; Cavadino and Dignan, 2006; Lacey, 2008). The two main current varieties of capitalism are 'coordinated market economies' and 'liberal market economies'. Coordinated market economies exist in societies which promote social democracy, egalitarianism, generous welfare provision and so-called 'consensus' political cultures (Green, 2008). Liberal market economies (often referred to as neoliberal) exist in – and perpetuate – extremely unequal, socially divided 'free-market' societies that have relatively low welfare provision, low levels of trust, highly competitive media and majoritarian political cultures (Lacey, 2011).[1] Whilst the penal policies of any given nation are determined through a complex interaction between its historical, socioeconomic, cultural and political characteristics (Webster and Doob, 2007), data from international prison rates indicate that penal excess is much more prevalent in grossly unequal neoliberal/liberal market economies (Cavadino and Dignan, 2006; J. Pratt, 2008a, 2008b; Lacey, 2008, 2011).

Today, 1 per cent of the 7 billion people on planet earth own 40 per cent of all assets, with the richest 10 per cent owning a staggering 85 per cent of global wealth (Irvin, 2008). If we consider economic inequality in just two Anglophone liberal market economies (the USA and the UK), we find that the richest 10 per cent of Americans own 70 per cent of the nation's wealth whilst the top 1 per cent in the UK own almost a quarter (24 per cent) of its wealth. At its extremes, income inequality

---

[1] A number of authors in this volume have referred to this current form of capitalism as neoliberalism. I have used the term 'liberal market economy' rather than 'neoliberalism' simply because the former more strongly emphasises the varieties in capitalism. This being noted, I broadly concur with the expansive definitions of neoliberalism outlined by Emma Bell and Loïc Wacquant (both in this volume).

becomes so severe that for those at the bottom of the social structure such disparity can only be described as 'poverty'. The poorest 50 per cent in the UK have possession of just 6 per cent of marketable wealth and one in four live below the average national income (Grover, 2008). Three broad policy options are available to governments regarding the problem of poverty: (i) the management of poverty through welfare; (ii) the discipline and control of the poor through punishment (and welfare); and (iii) the abolition of poverty through radical social policies. Needless to say, policies in advanced capitalist societies have oscillated between those promoting welfare and punishment, and for critical thinkers such as Rusche and Kirchheimer (1939/2003), Beckett and Western (2001) and Loïc Wacquant (2009b), welfare and punishment have historically intersected in a complementary fashion.

The strategy adopted to deal with the problem of poverty has an impact not only on the lived experiences of the poor but also upon the nature and extent of the penal apparatus of the capitalist state. There is a growing body of evidence that prisoner population rates have a close relationship to the proportion of gross domestic product (GDP) a nation spends on welfare (Beckett and Western, 2001; Cavadino and Dignan, 2006; Lacey, 2008). In an important examination of welfare-spending and rates of penal incarceration in nineteen member countries of the Organisation for Economic Co-operation and Development (OECD), Downes and Hansen (2006) found that the seven OECD countries in the sample with the highest levels of imprisonment had below average welfare-spending, whereas the eight countries with the lowest number of prisoners all had above average welfare-spending. It should not go unnoted, however, that even those nations with coordinated market economies spending high proportions of their GDP on welfare continue to operate within the logic of capitalism and consequently remain trapped within its inherent contradictions and subsequent manifestations of class conflict. Further, in such nations, attempts have been made only to manage poverty, not to abolish it. Recourse to imprisonment continues and the pains of penal incarceration, even in countries with relatively low prison populations, remain intense and sometimes even deadly (Mathiesen, 2012; Pratt and Erickson, 2012).

In the last four decades, liberal market economies, such as the USA and UK, have witnessed the gradual dismantling of welfare provision and reductions in welfare spending. In periods of economic contraction, labourers are increasingly required to take responsibility for providing their own welfare and social needs. The free, rational, empowered and self-governing subject is conceived as morally responsible for the good or bad choices they make, and thus for minimising or maximising potential risks. When bad things happen, blame falls squarely on the 'flawed consumer', and if they have not appropriately prepared for financial troubles, poverty will quickly ensue (Wacquant, 2009b). In this time of the 'great recession' (see McBride, Chapter 11), rather than provide welfare assistance, the capitalist state focuses instead upon discipline and punishment (Foucault, 1977; Mathiesen, 1990). It is this drift towards a greater intensification in the control of the poor that has spawned global hyper-incarceration and the substantial penal colonisation of remaining welfare provisions and other sites of state detention. Such a 'penalisation of the social sphere' (Mary and Nagels, 2012: 87) has promoted policies that aim to provide security *from* the poor rather than security *for* the poor (Hudson, 2012).

It is essential that the rather old-fashioned and often-maligned notion of class is not ignored or obscured. Undoubtedly prisons overwhelmingly house people from impoverished backgrounds and, as Alessandro De Giorgi (2006: 131) has argued, the control of the poor 'is a *leitmotiv* in the history of the institution itself'. The historical evidence to support this assertion is overwhelming (Rusche and Kirchheimer, 1939/2003; S. Cohen, 1985; Garland, 1985) and it remains a truism for contemporary times (De Giorgi, 2011). Bruce Western (2006: 73–8), for example, has used the indexes of education, employment and wages to shine a light upon the class inequalities of prisoners in the USA, demonstrating that those with little schooling, and especially 'high school drop outs', have a very strong likelihood of being imprisoned. Yet class analysis alone is not enough to adequately contextualise global hyper-incarceration and contemporary forms of penal colonisation, for of equal import are the social inequalities concerning 'race', gender and sexuality.

In many countries around the world the prison casts a huge shadow over the daily lives of indigenous and black or minority ethnic (BME) populations (see Scott, Chapter 1). For the influential commentator Angela Y. Davis (2012), imprisonment is structured by racism and must be conceptualised as a direct descendent of slavery. In a similar vein, Michelle Alexander (2011) has powerfully argued that the USA today is witnessing the rise of a new black caste system that draws direct parallels with the 'Jim Crow' regime. Whereas blatant racism and racist stereo-typing are no longer seen as permissible, the US criminal process is now used 'to label people of color "criminals" and then engage in all the [stigmatising] practices we supposedly left behind' (Alexander, 2011: 8). The end results are the same: the racist subjugation of indigenous and BME communities forced to endure impoverished living conditions and live like second-class citizens. But it is not just in the USA where penal policies and laws echo and reproduce racist ideologies. Penal systems in Europe reflect the growing scope of 'state racism' (Gordon, 1983; Sivanandan, 2001) and presents us with not only a contemporary reflection of racist constructs of 'national identity' but also a terrible reminder of the legacies of colonialism and slavery. Migrant and BME communities have poor living conditions and precarious employment opportunities. They are marginalised and pushed to the edges of social life. Migrant and BME populations are vulnerable to the insecure labour market, and 'irregular migrants' may be totally excluded from social welfare support altogether. It should come perhaps as no surprise that such populations are grossly over-represented in prison populations in Europe and that this is 'to a degree comparable, nay in most places superior, to the "racial disproportionality" afflicting blacks in the United States' (Wacquant, 2006: 86).

Global hyper-incarceration is also profoundly gendered. The prison is deployed as a means to regulate men and women who transcend the boundaries of conservative masculinity and emphasised femininity. Hegemonic masculinity – the ideological construct underpinning conservative masculinity – is steeped in ideologies of power and violence (Sim, 1994), but paradoxically it is those men who follow this ideology to its logical conclusion – through public acts of violence – who are the fodder of the penal sanction. The prison is a physical manifestation of violence, perpetuating institutionalised sexual abuse such as intimate strip searches, and the women contained within have largely not only broken the law but also transgressed rules of feminine behaviour and/or heterosexuality (Poulantzas, 1978; Scott and Codd, 2010). Women prisoners are often 'survivors' of racialised and sexualised violence and the collateral consequences of the racialised feminisation of poverty. Indeed, interpersonal sexual violence is now recognised as a major indicator of future imprisonment (Sudbury, 2005a). Further, a substantial body of literature also identifies how lesbian, gay, bisexual, transgendered and queer (LGBTQ) and the gender-nonconforming are much more likely to be subjected to police surveillance, arrest and punishment by the courts, even though they are less likely than heterosexuals to engage in highly problematic and illegal conducts (see Meiners, Chapter 13).

In capitalist, neocolonial, patriarchal and heteronormative societies, penal incarceration is shaped through the complex intersections of class, 'race', gender and sexuality and must be analysed as such (Sudbury, 2005a; Barton et al., 2006; A. Y. Davis, 2012). It also is important, however, to recognise that prisons are embedded within the distinct policies and practices of a given legal jurisdiction and its historical, political and policy dynamics (Melossi, 2011). What is required is an understanding of the wider global and structural inequalities discussed above alongside a sensitive and nuanced approach to the specific development of imprisonment within any given country (Tonry, 2007). The discussion below examines recent penal politics and policies in England and Wales to illustrate the growth of penal colonisation in a neoliberal/ liberal market economy disfigured by gendered, racialised and other social inequalities.

TOUGH TALK, SUITABLE ENEMIES AND THE PUNITIVE TRAP

Since the mid 1990s, the prison population in England and Wales has risen to unprecedented levels. In December 1992, the prison population stood at 40,600. At the time of writing (September 2012), this figure had surpassed 86,000. Though data from official crime rates and the British Crime Survey indicate that for much of the last twenty years 'crime' has been in decline, there is no political will to reverse the current expansionist penal trajectory. The message from the Minister of Justice for England and Wales, Chris Grayling, is clear and unequivocal:

> Prison is not meant to be a place that people enjoy being in. I don't want to see prisoners in this country sitting in cells watching the Sunday afternoon [live football] match on Sky Sports. . . Am I planning to reduce the number of prison places? No I'm not. I do not want to set a target to reduce the prison population.
>
> (*Guardian*, 2012)

The ideological message is unambiguous: prisons are to be places of pain and blame and high prison rates are politically acceptable. The harsh stance of the current Minister of Justice and that largely of his predecessors over the last two decades reflects a consolidation, intensification and further entrenchment of what Hall et al. (1978) described some thirty-five years ago as the 'law-and-order society'. Following Stuart Hall, it can be seen that penal excess in England and Wales is the direct

307

result of a deliberate and consciously chosen political strategy aiming to manipulate anxieties to gain electoral advantage (Downes, 2001)./ Whilst this strategy has its roots in the 1970s, it is only since the mid 1990s that politicians from both of the two main political parties have competed to demonstrate who can be 'toughest on crime' (Newburn, 2007). For more than twenty years, penal policy in England and Wales has been shaped by political spin, knee-jerk reactions to unique high-profile problematic incidents and attempts to avoid being labelled as 'soft on crime' (Garland, 2001c; Green, 2008). Presentation is everything.[The national media in England and Wales is highly competitive, the 'news of the day' being determined by certain identifiable newsworthy criteria rather than objective coverage (Chibnall, 1977).] 'Crime news' must be immediate and dramatic, and highly contentious individual troublesome acts are much more likely to grab the headlines and provide a sensation than the less dramatic official data on recorded 'crime', especially if the rate is in decline. In such a context, a heinous 'crime' may be reconstructed, repackaged or replayed in such a way that it has a hugely disproportionate impact upon policy formation and the subsequent application of the criminal law (Green, 2008). In such a manner, the repetitive media coverage of CCTV footage from one single terrible event – the murder of 2-year-old James Bulger by two 10-year-old boys in 1992 – alongside subsequent public disquiet and claims by moral entrepreneurs of an impending social crisis proved decisive in persuading the Labour Party, then in opposition, to compete with the Conservative Party on who could deliver the harshest and most punitive penal policy (Downes, 2007; Newburn, 2007; Green, 2007; Tonry, 2007).

England and Wales is governed through a majoritarian democracy, and the national media perform a key role in the battle for the hearts and minds of the populace (Lijphart, 1999). In the cut-throat and adversarial zero-sum mentality of majoritarian democracies, false dualisms, polarisation, a politics of simplicity, superficial slogans and sound bites generally win the day as politicians compete to grab the headlines. Rather than discussing constructive solutions to pressing social issues, politicians become preoccupied merely with 'scoring points' and discrediting their political opponents (Tonry, 2007; Green, 2008; Lacy, 2011; Lappi-Seppala, 2012; Verfaillie, 2012). Rational arguments and talk of penal reduction fall by the wayside as *populist*, rather than popular (see Bell, Chapter 3) and punitive sound bites like 'tough on crime, tough on the causes of crime', 'prison works', 'making punishment work' or 'tough but intelligent' dominate political debate. Nicola Lacey (2008: 242) has described the current state of affairs as the *prisoners' dilemma*: neither the Labour Party nor the Conservative Party – nor indeed the Liberal Democratic Party – can abandon this costly and counter-productive electoral strategy in case they lose floating voters to the opposition. In other words, politicians have created a 'punitive trap'.

⸹ The political utility of punitive policies must be understood within its referential context and the wider meanings and emotions that 'crime' talk engenders, most notably that 'crime' is a metaphor for social insta-bility, chaos and the breakdown of *English*[2] – albeit profoundly class-distorted – society. By advocating the repression and control of 'crime', politicians leave opponents with little room for manoeuvre: if they challenge such interventions they may appear not only weak but as actively promoting social disorder, turmoil and immorality. More than any other issue, 'the liberal voice is most constrained, conventional definitions are hardest to resist [and] alternative definitions are hardest to come by' when 'crime' talk is engendered (Hall et al., 1978: 90). Even without the authoritarianism of the current political climate, it is hard to denounce a social harm, injury or hurt successfully labelled as 'crime' whilst at the same time question the appropriateness of penalisation and rising prison populations. For Hall et al. (1978: 150):

> Crime is summoned. . . as the evil which is the reverse of the normality of Englishness, and an evil which if left unchecked can rot away the stable order of normality. The reaction to crime, then, is deep rooted, both materially and ideologically. This combination is an extremely powerful one, and, for the dominant classes, an extremely fruitful one. Crime allows all 'good men and true' to stand up and be counted – at least metaphorically – in the defence of normality, stability and 'our way of life'. It allows the construction of a false unity out of the very different social conditions in which this 'way of life' is lived, and under which crime is experienced.

Although the deliberate exploitation of 'crime' by politicians is rela-tively recent, the traditional ideologies of 'crime' have a long history and are deeply embedded within English common sense. The problem is: now that 'crime' has been politicised and the punitive pendulum has

---

[2] Although the discussion is about England and Wales, I use the term 'English' as this chapter develops. This reflects the historical and cultural dominance of England and also is the term used in *Policing the Crisis* (Hall et al., 1978).

gotten into full swing, it seems extremely hard to stop. Yet if we are to understand what activated the punitive trap, we must also explore how the control of the 'crimes of the poor' plays a significant role in the political and ideological management of the contradictions of liberal market economies and its collateral consequences (Hall et al., 1978; Hudson, 1993; Sim, 2009).

The acute economic and structural crises of advanced capitalist societies and neoliberal/liberal market economies in particular are reconstructed in terms of a crisis of individual self-discipline, the collapse of moral order and the undermining of the rule of law (Hall et al., 1978). Orchestrated from above, calls for discipline and moral regulation from below dovetail with a shift towards greater coercive authority and reliance upon the penal apparatus of the capitalist state (Hall et al., 1978; Mathiesen, 1990; Sim, 2009). These insights have perhaps been given their most sophisticated recent application in the writings of Jonathon Simon (2007) and especially in his notion 'governing through crime'. Recognising that there has been an authoritarian drift in social and penal policies, Simon (2007) argues that governments target 'crime' as a means of reassuring an anxious general public, even though many insecurities are created by the social and political fall-out of an increasingly divided and unequal society. As Joe Sim (2009) contends, penal policy becomes one way of managing existing structural fault lines and re-legitimising the capitalist state.

Bernard Harcourt (2011) has powerfully argued that government interventions in liberal market economies are shaped by an ideological myth – a belief in the natural order. According to the myth of natural order, the workings of the capitalist market are beyond both the penal sphere and governmental competence. Consequently, the central role of government is the control and punishment of those 'crimes' that occur outside of the capitalist market place. Yet 'our free markets are far from free' (Harcourt, 2011: 18). The capitalist market, in fact, is highly regulated and has been for centuries. Assumptions about the myth of natural order, however, result in both the naturalisation of unequal wealth distribution and the belief that penal incarceration, rather than social welfare, is the most appropriate and effective form of government action.[3] Consequently, when governments in liberal market economies do withdraw from actively managing the economy, penalisation provides one clear and unambiguous way in which politicians can make

[3] This can also open the door for penal privatisation (see Bell, Chapter 3).

their mark. As Andrew Gamble (1988) maintained some time ago, by punishing the marginalised and relatively weak (working class) 'criminal' and other 'enemies within', governments appear strong and legitimate, for a prison sentence sends reassuring signals that the government is prepared to safeguard the interests of, and provide security for, the general populace. This not only demonstrates strength but can also become an invaluable mechanism through which politicians in liberal market economies can mystify and direct attention away from the growing gap between the rich and the poor and the radical retrenchment and penal reorientation of social welfare provision (Mathiesen, 1974, 1990). All that is required is the identification and subsequent suppression of an appropriate scapegoat. This 'suitable enemy' (Christie, 1986; Wacquant, 2009b) is often referred to as the 'Folk Devil' (S. Cohen, 1972), a person or identifiable group:

> on to whom all our most intense feelings about things going wrong, and all our fears about what might undermine our fragile securities are projected... [The Folk Devil] is a sort of alter ego of virtue... He [sic] is the reverse image, the alternative to all we know: *the negation*... When things threaten to disintegrate, the Folk Devil becomes not only the bearer of all our social anxieties, but we turn against him [sic] the full wrath of our indignation.
>
> (Hall et al., 1978: 161, emphasis in original)

The Folk Devil and other such 'shadowy categories of persons' – the criminal, the ill-disciplined, the irresponsible, the lazy, the unrespectable poor, welfare scroungers, single parents, the unemployed and the feral members of the so-called 'underclass' – present a direct threat to the natural existence of the English way of life (Hall et al., 1978; Scraton and Chadwick, 1991; see also Cooper and Sim, Chapter 10 of this volume). The call of the respectable and law-abiding is for those in positions of authority to provide even greater discipline and control of those not adhering to English characteristics, thus providing legitimacy to mechanisms of marginalisation, penalisation and social exclusion (Hall et al., 1978). The immoral, unrespectable and feckless poor – the subproletariat – are held morally responsible for both their dire poverty and the criminality that arises from such conditions. Undoubtedly the material and ideological legacies of colonialism from the seventeenth to the twentieth century have badly disfigured constructions of the English imagination and lay ideologies of Englishness. 'Non-white' and 'non-English' people are conceived as inferior beings, and lawlessness and 'crime' are portrayed as actions undertaken by the non-English 'other'. Ideologies of nationhood and citizenship are therefore deeply entrenched within everyday practices and institutional cultures of 'crime' control (Hall et al., 1978). In recent times the false dichotomy of the law-abiding respectable English 'us' and the criminal and unrespectable non-English 'them' has become even more deeply entrenched. New and old enemies are touted as threats to the English way of life – foreigners, migrants, asylum seekers, refugees, enemy combatants and 'terror suspects' (see Kaufman and Bosworth, Chapter 9). For Barbara Hudson (2006), these Folk Devils are subsequently categorised as 'non-persons', ensuring that 'aliens' become defined as dangerous 'monsters' in need of containment. To combat these threats to Englishness and the citizens of the English nation, the government must 'declare war' on the non-English Folk Devil, utilising penal incarceration as its primary weapon to contain a (foreign) enemy propelled to our doorsteps through the turbulence of transnational capitalism (Feeley and Simon, 1994; Sparks, 2006; Melossi, 2011; A. Y. Davis, 2012).

It has long been established that prisons perform a key role in protecting moral and social boundaries (Box, 1983). In the globalised labour market, migrant workers, refugees and asylum seekers transcend boundaries of nation and have become some of the main bearers of contemporary insecurities and anxieties (Bosworth, 2010a; see also De Giorgi, Chapter 2 and Bell, Chapter 3 of this volume). Though not perhaps as straightforward as sometimes made out, both immigration laws and the scope and application of the criminal sanction have become more punitively orientated and more closely interconnected (Dow, 2004). The end result of such 'crimmigration' is that the non-English[4] may be regarded as inherently criminal and thus requiring harsh penal control (Stumpf, 2012; see also Kaufman and Bosworth, Chapter 9 of this volume). Indeed, for Loïc Wacquant (2006) the migrant and the criminal have become virtually synonymous. In current times when the non-English Folk Devil is not only at the gate but roaming freely through our streets, the prison is called upon to perform a central role in constructing boundaries to protect our nation and the maintenance of our territorial borders against the hordes of foreigners poised to swamp the country (Hall et al., 1978; Bosworth, 2010a).

[4] The signifier non-English in many but not all cases could be replaced with 'non-British'.

The war against the non-English Folk Devil reasserts the sovereignty of the capitalist state and demonstrates its power and legitimacy, for it provides security for the English nation's borders alongside controlling the threat posed to law-abiding English citizens from its enemies (Bosworth, 2010a). The intensification and amplification of penalisation is order of the day, whichever of the various sites of state detention the enemies of the 'good people of England' are housed within. Immigration detention centres become in effect immigration prisons as those holding the power to punish tighten their grip (Dow, 2004). The ideology is clear: penalisation shows strength; penalisation is the legitimate role of government; and penalisation works in the interests of the English nation.

WHAT IS TO BE DONE?

The prison is unequalled in pain. Uniquely designed and operationalised through deliberate pain infliction, it performs a key function in the maintenance of blatantly unequal societies through the control of poor, marginalised and disproportionately BME male lawbreakers. Above, I have attempted to diagnose and critique this power to punish in liberal market economies, specifically the legal jurisdiction of England and Wales. But diagnosis and critique is not enough. It is also essential that consideration is given to feasible, policy-relevant and progressive interventions that can challenge gross economic and social inequalities and mitigate the humanitarian crises confronting contemporary penal practices, without abandoning the broader obligation to promote radically alternative responses to troublesome human conduct and the logic of capitalist accumulation. This necessitates recognition and engagement with the problems and possibilities of our historical moment alongside a disruption of the ideological limitations placed upon what are considered appropriate and feasible means of social and penal transformation. Such engagement must be rooted in a 'normative framework' – what I have described elsewhere as the 'abolitionist compass' (Scott, in press (c)) – that can assist our navigation away from deeply entrenched social inequalities and the problems associated with the criminal process.

Alternatives to liberal market capitalism and the penal apparatus of the capitalist state should be informed by the principles of human rights, social justice and democratic accountability. Principles of human rights precipitate the recognition of a fellow human being's innate dignity and

313

the symbolic and cultural respect of other people's shared humanity and provide a basis for critiquing dehumanisation through valorising basic human characteristics that must be promoted and protected at all costs. Principles of social justice problematise the current application of the criminal label (which overwhelmingly punishes the poor) and actively promotes interventions that aim to meet human need alongside aiming to foster values of care, love, kindness, forgiveness and solidarity. Principles of democratic accountability highlight the importance of adhering to democratic values which require unhindered participation, processes of shared decision-making and validity for the voices of all concerned in the creation of social norms, whilst at the same time emphasising the importance of legal guarantees and safeguards. To 'remain in the game', alternatives must also be able to 'compete' with advanced capitalism and the criminal process by drawing upon interventions grounded in historically immanent potentialities and simultaneously possess an emancipatory logic that 'contradicts' current institutions and practices of repression by undermining capitalist and punitive rationales. Interventions dealing with troublesome human conducts should be non-punitive and in practice it must be demonstrated that they actually do replace a penal sentence of the criminal courts.

It should be made clear at this point that it is not my intention to explore each possible alternative in depth or to outline all of their strengths and weakness. Rather, my hope is that through highlighting a number of feasible, realisable and immanent interventions I illustrate *existing potentialities for progressive radical change* and demonstrate that with sufficient political will, economic and social inequalities and penal colonisation can be dramatically reduced. In other words, my purpose is not to be comprehensive but to simply show that immediate change is possible. It should also be recognised that the historical experience of any country or region is unique and that both penal culture and penal change are embedded within given geographic, historical, socioeconomic and political contexts (Melossi, 2011). Each nation has its own specific risk and protective factors, and what works best in terms of penal reductionism is likely to vary on a country-by-country basis (Tonry, 2007). This being said, the problems of global hyper-incarceration and the penal colonisation of social welfare and state detention must be located within wider structural contexts. Effective challenges to penal excess must first address the economic and social inequalities which plague advanced capitalist societies, meaning that radical social policies calling for the redistribution of wealth must be promoted on a global scale.

An 'abolitionist real utopia' requires the realisation of at least nine interlinked strategic objectives. These nine objectives will now be discussed in turn.

1. Acknowledgement that social inequalities and penal responses are intimately tied

It is now more than 100 years since the Dutch pioneer of critical criminology, Willem Adrian Bonger (1905/1916), identified in *Criminalité et Conditions Economiques*[5] that the problems associated with inequalities and 'crime' – and subsequently those of punishment – are intimately connected. Political recognition and action are long overdue. Economic and social inequalities breed anxieties, insecurities and the need for scapegoats (Hall et al., 1978) and provide fertile ground for the rapid growth of penalisation (Hudson, 1993). Both inequality and the deliberate infliction of pain destroy human health and wellbeing. In the long term, rampant social inequalities and penalisation are likely to make society less caring, weaken social bonds and create more problematic incidents (Christie, 2000; Scott, 2009). In our time of increasing social polarisation, prisons maintain the status quo by disciplining and controlling certain segments of the working class (Mathiesen, 1990; Christie, 2000). It is time for politicians all around the globe to stand up and tell the truth about the collateral consequences of advanced capitalism and the absolute failure of the confinement project. There needs to be moves towards the stigmatising of high prison rates and expanding prison populations and every effort made to limit the reach of the punitive rationale. One pragmatic way forward that could help facilitate penal de-escalation is for politicians, their spin doctors and the mainstream media to place much greater emphasis on informing the general public about the social harms created by economic and social inequalities. Political strength could then be demonstrated by challenging the dreadful injustices of poverty on both a national and global level rather than blaming and then punishing the poor.

2. Escape from the punitive trap

The analysis above has indicated how central political culture and the media are in the rise of global hyper-incarceration (Green, 2008). We urgently need to find ways in which politicians can escape a punitive trap of their own making. To do so, it is essential that in

[5] This title is the original French Title. The book was published in English in 1916 under the title *Criminality and Economic Conditions*.

neoliberal/liberal market economies politicians and the media down-play 'crime' and place high-profile single issue 'crimes' into appropriate context. This indicates the necessity of a de-politicisation of 'crime' and, especially in majoritarian democracies, a move towards a 'crime' and punishment armistice between the main political parties. Although the obligation for initiating this will inevitably fall upon the party in power, moral and political pressure, through concerted lobbying, needs to be directed to all mainstream political parties. Politicians need to recognise that it is possible to orchestrate a de-escalation of penalisation if they have the appropriate political will. Governments need to be asked to reflect seriously about the mantra 'the less punishment, the better'. The general public's view is polycentric and contradictory, and the more information people are given about an individual case, the greater their understanding and leniency (Lappi-Seppala, 2007). A well-funded pub-lic media campaign on the facts about 'crime' and punishment would help in such endeavours. Alongside this, however, the power of the national media itself also needs to be weakened. In the first instance, this requires steps towards a de-monopolisation of the ownership of the media; the de-nationalisation of media so that journalists make local issues and serving local audiences their main priority; and that inves-tigative and serious journalism in the public interest are the rationale behind news selection, rather than the drive for profits through news-worthiness criteria (Chibnall, 1977; S. Cohen, 2001; Green, 2008).

3. Generate knowledge from below and fostering moral responsibility

Much greater emphasis must also be placed on fostering informed public opinion beyond the restrictive remit of mainstream media. Superficial consumption of penal knowledge results in a failure to understand the painful realities of imprisonment and undermines democratic engage-ment with, and critically scrutiny of, pain delivery (see Michelle Brown, Chapter 6). Providing a platform for the voices of prisoners to be heard, whether through public presentations, video or audio recordings or written testimonies, may be one way to achieve this. Showcasing pris-oner art and poetry may also provide a more sophisticated insight into prison life, as may independent prison documentaries.[6] This 'knowledge

---

[6] See, for example, independent documentaries like *Punishment: A Failed Social Experiment* (direc-ted by Dale Hallatt, released in January 2012) or *Visions of Abolition: From Critical Resistance to a New Way of Life* (directed by Watkins and Naqi, released in March 2011).

from below' may initiate new in-depth understandings, meanings and empathy alongside providing concrete links between theory and practice. It is also more likely than the pre-packaged news of the national media to produce what Stanley Cohen (2001: 290–6) calls 'acknowledgement'. Acknowledgement occurs when someone has knowledge of human suffering, recognises the full reality of the pain and harm this information imparts and identifies the personal implications of possessing such knowledge, leading ultimately to some form of action that attempts to mitigate or end the injuries inflicted upon their fellow humans. In short, it means knowing the truth about the devastation created by advanced capitalism and penal incarceration and doing something about them through interventions rooted in the principles of human rights and social justice.

4. Creation of an alternative public space
To effectively turn the tide on penal excess and growing social polarisation requires morally responsible discussion of human needs and rational responses to problematic human conduct. It also requires adherence to the principles of democratic accountability. De-democratisation facilitates distance between the perceived law-abiding 'us' and the perceived lawless 'them' (Christie, 1981, 2000, 2004). The breakdown in democratic participation in penal politics has eroded social bonds and made the punishment of 'enemies within' appear more palatable (see Barker, Chapter 7). Increased social distance has also made it easier to withdraw welfare support and allow the development of the privatisation of (social) security. Genuine democracy requires unhindered participation, processes of shared decision-making and validity for the voices of all concerned in the creation of social norm. To facilitate such a vision of democracy, Thomas Mathiesen (2001: 33) has talked about the creation of an 'alternative public space' where 'argumentation and principled thinking represents the dominant values'. This alternative public space would require significant time and investment so that it could compete with the mainstream media and allow genuine democratic debate on the key issues of the day, but if successful, would be a significant step forward in providing a genuinely legitimate form of governance.

5. Humanising aliens and monsters
Relatively equal societies do not need symbolic punitive acts to shore up fragile social solidarities as they are likely to have a greater sense of a

317

shared moral responsibility for social problems (Durkheim, 1893/1984; Christie, 1981, 2000; Lappi-Seppala, 2012). In such circumstances we do not need to search for suitable enemies but rather to search for suitable *friends*. Greater economic equality on a global scale reduces global migration and increases levels of social justice in countries with weak economies and a low GDP. Rather than conceive the 'non-national stranger' as a potential threat, competitor in the labour market or service user for relatively scarce welfare services, the encounter with the stranger could be considered an opportunity to learn new insights, share experiences and develop new understandings. This 'humanising of aliens' requires us to acknowledge that the arrival of 'strangers' may sometimes benefit all and that 'others', 'enemies' and 'aliens' have the ability to feel pain and suffering in prison and elsewhere. This would also include highlighting the discrepancies between the criminalisation and punishment of 'crimes' of the powerful and the powerless; the problem of conflating 'good' and 'evil' with good and bad people through the construction of a negative, dehumanised one-dimensional caricature of the offender situated solely in the nature of her/his 'crime'; and ultimately point to the universality of criminal activity and in the end the similarities between those inside and outside the prison walls. In short, we must stress we are all united by a common or shared humanity and must learn to live with the inherent ambivalence of human society. Humanisation requires a reassertion of non-punitive values that emphasises the best of humanity – fraternity, friendship, solidarity, trust, love, compassion, hospitality, kindness and forgiveness – and recognition of a fellow human being's innate dignity, whatever their biographies or backgrounds (S. Cohen, 2001; Christie, 2004).

6. Radical reduction of economic and social inequalities

The ideological myth of the 'natural order' that economic regulation is beyond the legitimate scope of government needs to be exposed and undermined (Harcourt, 2011). Legitimacy can, and should, be derived from interventions which aim to provide a more equitable distribution of the social product and where humans, whatever their backgrounds, are treated fairly and given the opportunity to flourish. Social policy interventions need to strive towards 'abolition democracy' which demands that our present social order is radically transformed in accordance with the principles of social justice (A. Y. Davis, 2005: 72; 2012). Beckett and Herbert (2010) have championed a 'harm reduction model' that places social harms at the centre of analysis and recognises that whilst it may be impossible to totally eradicate certain problems, appropriate help and support can transform lived experiences. In this model, focus is placed on job creation, full medical care and appropriate forms of welfare. There could also be a concerted attempt to challenge inequalities in public services. This would include the further enhancement of existing commitments to provide free transport, health care and education. More could also be done to improve housing and accommodation, including the introduction of rent guarantees. These interventions could dramatically reduce the harm, suffering and dehumanisation associated with wealth and income disparities whilst at the same time contradict the logic of capitalist accumulation. For Beckett and Herbert (2010: 158), there requires recognition that:

> [e]xtreme inequality adversely impacts us all, that poverty stems from structural dynamics that extend well beyond the lone denizen of the street, that security means something more than protection for middle-class whites from the discomforts or urban life, that justice includes the proposition that everyone enjoy a minimal quality of life, and that tolerance of diversity is integral to democracy.

A number of other social policy interventions could also instantaneously reduce economic inequalities. A very small percentage of the people who live in England and Wales (and indeed most countries in the world) own the vast majority of material wealth. Challenging the legitimacy of such wealth inequalities through progressive taxation would entail significant increases in the tax rate for the richest 100,000 people in England and Wales but would dramatically reduce inequalities and provide funding for essential public services. Another straightforward historically immanent policy that could greatly diminish wealth disparities would be to introduce higher inheritance taxes, or, more radically, follow the suggestion of Emile Durkheim and abolish inheritance altogether. There could be the introduction of a maximum wage to ensure that the accumulation of wealth in future generations is more tightly restrained and creates clear boundaries between the top and bottom of the pay structure. The most desirable policies, however, are those that can *abolish* poverty, such as a universal basic income (Wacquant, 2009b; Scott, in press (c)). A universal basic income would both end poverty and provide a direct challenge to the very logic of capitalist accumulation. Whilst its introduction would likely be strongly objected to by capitalists, if successfully implemented its implications would be immense. People could choose to work, or not, and whilst the balance of power would still favour the capitalist, labourers would have considerably more choice than at present.

7. Radical reduction of prison populations

Critical criminologists have long held that we must work both with and against the capitalist state to challenge and exploit its contradictory nature in the interests of human freedom (Poulantzas, 1978; Sim et al., 1987; Sim 2009). One feasible strategy that engages with the capitalist state is the 'attrition model' (Knopp, 1976; Mathiesen, 1986; see also Oparah, Chapter 14 of this volume). Directed at the mechanics of the criminal process, this model can be utilised right now.[7] It entails the following:

1. *Decriminalisation, diversion and minimal legal intervention*: keeping people out of prison through interventions like raising the minimum age of criminal responsibility; police warnings; diverting certain vulnerable people from criminal proceedings; and removing legal prohibitions on certain 'victimless crimes'.
2. *Negative reforms*: enhancing existing practices that protect the shared humanity of those subjected to penalisation through greater legal safeguards and legal rights; strict adherence to due process; and challenging authoritarian occupational cultures.
3. *Permanent international moratorium on prison building*: international, national and local campaigns, political lobbying and legal cases which challenge the moral, economic and political viability of building more prisons.
4. *Decarceration*: deploying pragmatic ways of getting those currently incarcerated out of prison as quickly as possible, such as early release; probation; shorter sentences; home monitoring; amnesties; part-time incarceration; and the introduction of waiting lists.

8. Promotion of radical alternatives

Without rational alternatives, the penal apparatus of the capitalist state may still appear permanent and inevitable (de Haan, 1990). The word 'alternative' should be used cautiously here to mean practices which are not derived from criminal processes but with recognition that in

---

[7] In California, the prison population is currently falling by around 2,000 every month. From July 2011 to July 2012, the California prison rate declined by 16.5 per cent (see McBride, Chapter 11).

everyday life people use many strategies to handle conflicts. People generally try to deal with problems as pragmatically and effectively as possible, and only on relatively rare occasions do they turn to the police and the criminal process. Alternatives are then those interventions which contrast with the practices of state punishment and question the logic of penalisation. To prevent 'net widening' (S. Cohen, 1985), such interventions must avoid co-option by the capitalist state, which today includes devolved and decentralised agencies and networks (Corcoran, 2011; Davies, 2011; Moore and Scott, 2012; see also Cooper and Sim, Chapter 10 of this volume). Alternatives must therefore always be *in place of* rather than merely *additions to* existing criminal processes, and there are a number of non-punitive interventions which could be advocated.

1. *Turn the system on its head.* The current focus of the penal system is on punishing the offender, whereas the victim is largely ignored. One radical alternative would be to turn the system on its head – rather than inflict pain and suffering, the aim of interventions would be to provide assistance, help and support for the person who has been harmed (Mathiesen and Hjemdal, 2011). This would ultimately mean providing massive investment in support for victims and redirecting criminal-justice-system budgets to public social services to help rebuild lives for all. Such 'justice reinvestment' could be used to support women's refuges; shelters for homeless people, drug takers and other troubled people; or drying-out centres.

2. *Reject the penal law.* Abolitionist initiatives have often focused on the civil law and the concept of tort where compensation rather than penalty is the objective of proceedings (Scott, in press (c)). Alternative means of handling conflicts have also been suggested that engage more constructively with the community rather than the capitalist state. Through peace circles, peer juries and motivational interviewing, for example, community members can become involved in delivering safety and building new social bonds (see Meiners, Chapter 13; Oparah, Chapter 14). New relationships can be developed that build solidarity and trust rather than deploying the penal law which undermines it.

3. *Provide help and support.* The shift away from punishment can be augmented by a drive towards help and support for all people in society. For children and young adults in trouble, greater leisure

facilities could be made available such as youth clubs; adventure playgrounds; and educational programmes in music and art. Adult lawbreakers could be helped with community-based employment and job-skills training.

4. *Intentional and therapeutic communities.* The vast majority of people who break the criminal law are not dangerous and should not be considered as such. There are some people who may, however, benefit from a change of context and environment. One idea would be to develop 'intentional communities' where wrongdoers – and perhaps their families if they so wished – could be relocated to small villages in sparsely populated areas, such as in the northern parts of Scotland. Here they could learn new skills, develop more pro-social attitudes and look to rebuild their lives. Such an intentional community for lawbreakers could also become a form of 'sanctuary' where serious offenders could be placed in quarantine to allow for time to cool off; establish grounds for negotiations; and attempt to deliver what might be considered acceptable solutions. Additionally, the idea of developing an 'intentional' or new community could also be available for less serious harms. As a place where people live and share problems together, it could become an option for people with family difficulties. Residential family projects, where each family has a 'family worker', could follow a similar model. Some people embroiled within the penal law would undoubtedly benefit from therapeutic interventions, and those people who have mental health problems, substance usage problems or require other forms of medical interventions could be offered effective voluntary noncustodial treatments and options to participate in alternative 'non-punitive' therapeutic communities.

9. Building grass roots activism and abolitionist praxis

The mobilisation of grass roots activists and abolitionist social movements is necessary for any sustained radical transformation of current penal and social realities. In England and Wales, the radical penal lobby over the last forty years has included a diverse range of organisations, including Radical Alternatives to Prison (RAP), Women in Prison, INQUEST and No More Prison. The publications and radical lobbying of INQUEST on deaths in custody and the campaigns by members of Women in Prison on the experiences of incarcerated women and girls in the UK have delivered clear and principled critiques of penal incarceration and helped facilitate progressive humanitarian change. Such important interventions noted, however, that in recent times the connections between abolitionist thought and political practice have been weak in England and Wales. RAP, which operated from 1970 until the mid-1980s, was unique in that it aimed to challenge both economic inequalities and penal colonisation. Its key aim was to present a 'fundamental critique of the existing economic and political order and the manner in which we chose to define and correct deviant behaviour' (Ryan, 1978: 2). RAP both visualised and supported radical alternatives to handling social and individual problems, especially in its early days, and advocated concrete 'negative reforms' of penal incarceration grounded on the principles of human rights, especially in its later days. The research, campaigns and activism of RAP members provided an essential challenge to the capitalist state's exclusive role in defining 'penal truth' and provided a vehicle for collective mobilisation. Although in the last three decades abolitionist social movements in England and Wales have faltered,[8] lessons can be learned from the past and contemporary abolitionist social movements like Critical Resistance in the USA (see Oparah, Chapter 14). Critical Resistance grounds its opposition to penal incarceration in coalition politics promoting anti-violence, anti-imperialism, anti-capitalism and black and women's liberation. Their activism and community interventions offer testimony of how global hyper-incarceration is not justified in their name. Abolitionist social movements can help foster a politics of inclusion based on shared humanity and can highlight the abnormality of prison and the dehumanising context of poverty and social inequalities. Most significantly of all, abolitionist praxis is essential in the creation of an alternative power base that can be utilised to challenge the role, function and legitimacy of the penal apparatus of the capitalist state and the unequal society it upholds.

An 'abolitionist real utopia' requires immediate direct policy interventions alongside the fostering of community-based social movements that can join forces in struggles for freedom and recognition of human dignity for all. Anti-prison activists and theorists must continue to aspire to live in, and fight for, a *world without prisons* alongside advocating non-punitive interventions rooted in immanent possibilities that can start to

---

[8] No More Prison was established in 2006 in London but has had only a very marginal impact, and in the last three years has been little more than an internet forum. On 13 September 2012, however, a new Reclaim Justice Network was formed in London, England that could develop in an abolitionist direction.

323

roll back the penal colonisation of the life world. In the long term, of course, the best way to protect and guarantee the safety and security of citizens is to ensure that there is a socially just, democratic and accountable distribution of the social product. Though this seems some way off, the time to act is *now*.

BIBLIOGRAPHY

Aas, K. F., (2011), '"Crimmigrant" bodies and the bona fide traveller: surveillance, citizenship and global governance', *Theoretical Criminology*, 15, pp. 331–46.

Acey, C., (2000), 'This is an illogical statement: dangerous trends in anti-prison activism', *Social Justice Journal*, 27(3), pp. 206–11.

Adams, D., (1988), 'Fundamental considerations: the deep meaning of Native American schooling, 1880–1900', *Harvard Educational Review*, 58(1), pp. 1–28.

Adlam, J. and Scanlon, C., (2005), 'Personality disorder and homelessness: membership and "unhoused minds", in forensic settings', *Group Analysis*, 38(3), pp. 452–66.

Advancement Project, (2010), *Test, Punish, and Push Out: How Zero Tolerance and High-Stakes Testing Funnel Youth into the School-to-Prison Pipeline*, Washington, DC: Advancement Project.

Agamben, G., (1995), 'We refugees', *Symposium*, 49, pp. 114–19, trans. by Michael Rocke.

(2005), *State of Exception*, The University of Chicago Press.

Aglietta, M., (1979), *A Theory of Capitalist Regulation*, London: New Left Books.

Ahmed, S., (2001), 'The organization of hate', *Law and Critique*, 12, pp. 345–65.

Alexander, M., (2010), *The New Jim Crow: Mass Incarceration in the Age of Colorblindness*, New York: The New Press.

(2011), 'The New Jim Crow', *Ohio State Journal of Criminal Law*, 9(1), pp. 7–26.

Aliverti, A. (2012). 'Exploring the function of criminal law in the policing of foreigners: the decision to prosecute immigration-related offences', *Social & Legal Studies*, 21(4), pp. 511–27.

All of Us Or None, (n.d.), *Voting Rights for All*, available at: www.allofusor-none.org/newsite/campaigns/voting-rights-for-all (accessed 13 March 2013).

Allen, R., Levenson, J. and Garside, R., (2003), *A Bitter Pill to Swallow: The Sentencing of Foreign National Drug Couriers*. London: Rethinking Crime and Punishment.

Althusser, L., (1971), *Lenin and Philosophy and Other Essays*, London: New Left Books.

American Civil Liberties Union, (2012), *Prisoners of Profit: Immigrants and Detention in Georgia*, Atlanta, GA: American Civil Liberties Union Foundation of Georgia.

Amin, A., (ed.), (1995), *Post-Fordism: A Reader*, Oxford: Blackwell.

Anderson J., (1988), *The Education of Blacks in the South, 1860–1935*, Chapel Hill, NC: University of North Carolina Press.

Andreas, P. and Nadelmann, E., (2006), *Policing the Globe: Criminalization and Crime Control in International Relations*, New York: Oxford University Press.

Angel-Ajani, A., (2003), 'A question of dangerous races?', *Punishment and Society* 5(4), pp. 433–48.

(2005), 'Domestic enemies and carceral circles: African American women and criminalization in Italy', in Sudbury, J. (ed.), *Global Lockdown*, London/New York, NY: Routledge, pp. 3–17.

Anyon, J., (1980), 'Social class and the hidden curriculum of work', *Journal of Education*, 162, pp. 67–92.

(2005), *Radical Possibilities*, New York, NY: Routledge.

Apple, M., (2010), *Global Crises, Social Justice, and Education*, New York, NY: Routledge.

Aptheker, B., (1971), 'The social functions of the prisons in the U.S.', in Davis, A. Y., (ed.), *If They Come in the Morning*, Rochelle, NY: Third Press, pp. 39–48.

Aptheker, H., (1989), *Abolitionism: A Revolutionary Movement*, Boston, MA: Twayne Publishers.

(1951), *The Origins of Totalitarianism*, New York, NY: Schocken Books.

Arendt, H., (1973), *The Origins of Totalitarianism*, (rev. edn), New York, NY: Harcourt Brace Jovanovich.

Armstrong, S. and McAra, L., (2006), 'Audiences, borders, architecture: the contours of control', in Armstrong, S. and McAra, L. (eds.), *Perspectives on Punishment*, Oxford University Press, pp. 1–30.

Arnett, J., (2000), 'Emerging adulthood: a theory of development from the late teens through the twenties', *American Psychologist*, 55(5), pp. 469–80.

Ashworth, A. and Zedner, L., (2010), 'Preventive orders: a problem of under-criminalization?', in Duff, R. A., Farmer, L., Marshal, S. E., Renzo, M. and Tadros, V. (eds.), *The Boundaries of the Criminal Law*, Oxford University Press, pp. 59–87.

(2011), 'Just prevention: preventive rationales and the limits of the criminal law', in Duff, R. A. and Green, S. (eds.), *Philosophical Foundations of Criminal Law*, Oxford: Oxford University Press, pp. 279–303.

Association of Chief Executives of Voluntary Organisations (ACEVO), (2011), *Cuts to the Third Sector: What Can We Learn from Transition Funds Applications*, London: ACEVO.

Augustine, H., (1996), 'J C Prichard's concept of moral insanity: a medical theory of the corruption of human nature', *Medical History*, 40, pp. 311–43.

Australian Bureau of Statistics, (2012), *Corrective Services, Australia, March 2012*, Canberra: Australian Bureau of Statistics.

Australian Human Rights Commission, (2002), *Report of an Inquiry into a Complaint by Six Asylum Seekers Concerning their Transfer from Immigration Detention Centres to State Prisons and their Detention in those Prisons*, HREOC Report No. 21, available at: www.humanrights.gov.au/legal/humanrightsreports/hrc_report_21.html (accessed 1 January 2013).

Bacon, C., (2005), 'The evolution of immigration detention in the UK: the involvement of private prison companies', RSC Working Paper No. 27, pp. 1–36.

Baldry, E., (2001), *Homelessness and the Criminal Justice System*, Summit Paper on Homelessness, Parliament of New South Wales, Australia, available at: http://parliament.nsw.gov.au (accessed 1 January 2013).

Ball, S., (2003), *Class Strategies and the Education Market: The Middle Classes and Social Advantage*, Abingdon: Routledge Falmer.

Bandes, S., (1999), *The Passions of Law*, New York University Press.

Banks, J., (2011), 'Foreign national prisoners in the UK: explanations and implications', *Howard Journal of Criminal Justice*, 50(2), pp. 184–98.

Barabas, J., (2004), 'How deliberation affects public opinion', *American Political Science Review*, 98(4), pp. 687–701.

Barker, V., (2009), *The Politics of Imprisonment: How the Democratic Process Shapes the Way America Punishes Offenders*, New York, NY: Oxford University Press.

Barton, A. and Cooper, V., (2012), 'Hostels and community justice for women: the "semi-penal" paradox', in Malloch, M. and McIvor, G., (eds.), *Women, Punishment and Social Justice: Human Rights and Penal Practices*, London: Routledge, pp. 136–51.

Barton, A., Corteen, K., Scott, D. and Whyte, D., (2006), 'Developing a criminological imagination', in Barton, A., Corteen, K., Scott, D. and Whyte, D., (eds.), *Expanding the Criminological Imagination*, Cullompton: Willan/Routledge, pp. 1–25.

Bartosik, M., (2009), 'Kids arrested for food fight. students kept at police station for hours, parents say', *NBC Chicago*, 10 November, available at: www.nbcchicago.com/news/local/Kids-Arrested-for-Food-Fight-69575092.html (accessed 1 January 2013).

Bauman, Z., (2000), *Modernity and the Holocaust*, Ithaca, NY: Cornell University Press.

BBC, (2006), 'UK seeks human rights law review', *BBC News Online*, 20 May, available at: http://news.bbc.co.uk/1/hi/uk_politics/5000238.stm (accessed 1 January 2013).

Beaumont, G. de and de Tocqueville, A., (1979), *On the Penitentiary System in the United States and Its Application in France*, Carbondale, IL: Southern Illinois University Press.

Beck, U., (1992), *Risk Society: Towards a New Modernity*, London/Thousand Oaks, CA: Sage.

Becker, G., (1968), 'Crime and punishment: an economic approach', *Journal of Political Economy*, 76(2), pp. 169–217.

Beckett, K., (1997a), *Making Crime Pay: Law and Order in Contemporary American Politics*, New York, NY: Oxford University Press.

(1997b), 'Political preoccupation with crime leads, not follows, public opinion', in Tonry, M. (ed.), (2001), *Penal Reform in Overcrowded Times*, Oxford University Press, pp. 40–5.

Beckett, K. and Herbert, S., (2010), *Banished: The New Social Control in Urban America*, Oxford University Press.

Beckett, K. and Murakawa, N., (2012), 'Mapping the shadow carceral state: towards an institutionally capacious approach to punishment', *Theoretical Criminology*, 16, pp. 221–44.

Beckett, K. and Western, B., (2001), 'Governing social marginality: welfare, incarceration, and the transformation of state policy', in Garland, D., (ed.), *Mass Imprisonment*, London: Sage, pp. 35–50.

Bedau, H. A., (1977), *The Courts, the Constitution, and Capital Punishment*, Lexington Books.

Bell, E., (2011), *Criminal Justice and Neoliberalism*, Basingstoke and New York: Palgrave Macmillan.

Bender, E., (2002), *A Contributing Influence: The Private-Prison Industry and Political Giving in the South*, available at www.followthemoney.org/press/ZZ/20020430.pdf (accessed 15 July 2012).

Bender, J., (1987), *Imagining the Penitentiary: Fiction and the Architecture of Mind in Eighteenth Century England*, The University of Chicago Press.

Bentham, J., (1995), *The Panopticon Writings*, London/New York: Verso.

Berger, V., (1992), 'Payne and suffering – a personal reflection and a victim-centered critique', *Florida State University Law Review*, 20, pp. 21–65.

Berkman, R., (1979), *Opening the Gates: The Rise of the Prisoners' Movement*, Lexington Books.

Berlant, L., (2011), *Cruel Optimism*, Durham: Duke University Press.

Berman, G., (2012), *Prison Population Statistics*, London: House of Commons, available at www.parliament.uk/Templates/BriefingPapers/Pages/BPPdf Download.aspx?bp-id=SN04334 (accessed 22 May 2012).

Bernstein, R., (2011), *Racial Innocence: Performing American Childhood from Slavery to Civil Rights*, New York University Press.

Beveridge, W., (1942), *Social Insurance and Allied Services*, London: HMSO.

Bhui, H., (2004), *Going the Distance: Developing Effective Policy and Practice with Foreign National Prisoners*. London: Prison Reform Trust.

(2007), 'Alien experience: foreign national prisoners after the deportation crisis', *Probation Journal*, 54(4): pp. 368–82.

Biehl, J., Good, B. and Kleinman, A., (eds.), (2007), 'Introduction: rethinking subjectivity', in *Subjectivity: Ethnographic Investigations*, Berkeley, CA: University of California Press, pp. 1–22.

Birkbeck, C., (2011), 'Imprisonment and internment: comparing penal institutions north and south', *Punishment and Society*, 13, pp. 307–32.

Blackstone, W., (1766/1979), *Commentaries on the Laws of England: Book the First*, reprinted, The University of Chicago Press.

Blair, T., (1996), *New Britain: My Vision of a Young Country*, London: Fourth Estate.

Blair, T., (2004a), Speech made on launching the government's new five-year crime strategy, 19 June.

(2004b), Speech on antisocial behaviour, 28 October.

Blumstein, A. and Wallman, J., (eds.), (2000), *The Crime Drop in America*, New York, NY: Oxford University Press.

Boltanski, L., (1987), *The Making of a Class: Cadres in French Society*, Cambridge University Press.

(2011), *On Critique: A Sociology of Emancipation*, Cambridge, MA: Polity.

Bonelli, L., (2008), *La France a peur. Une histoire sociale de l'insécurité*, Paris: La De´couverte.

Bonger, W. A., (1905/1916), *Criminality and Economic Conditions*, New York, NY: Little, Brown and Company.

Borrill, J. and Taylor, D. A., (2009). 'Suicides by foreign national prisoners in England and Wales 2007: mental and cultural issues', *Forensic Psychiatry and Psychology*, 20(6): pp. 886–905.

Bosworth, M., (2007), 'Immigration detention', in Lee, M. (ed.), *Human Trafficking*. Collumpton: Willan Publishing, pp. 159–77.

(2008), 'Immigration detention', *Criminal Justice Matters*, 71, pp. 24–5.

(2010a), *Explaining U.S. Imprisonment*, London: Sage.

(2010b), 'Introduction: reinventing penal parsimony', *Theoretical Criminology*, 14, pp. 251–6.

(2011a), 'Deporting foreign national prisoners in England and Wales', *Citizenship Studies*, 15(5), pp. 583–95.

(2011b), 'Human rights and immigration detention', in Dembour, M.-B. and Kelly, T. (eds.), *Are Human Rights for Migrants? Critical Reflections on the Status of Irregular Migrants in Europe and the United States*. Abingdon: Routledge, pp. 165–83.

(2012), 'Subjectivity and identity in detention: punishment and society in a global age', *Theoretical Criminology*, 16, pp. 123–40.

(in press (a)), 'Can immigration detention be legitimate?', in Aas, K. and Bosworth, M. (eds.), *Migration and Punishment: Citizenship, Crime Control, and Social Exclusion*, Oxford University Press.

(in press (b)), *Inside Immigration Detention: Foreigners in a Carceral Age*.

Bosworth, M. and Guild, M., (2008), 'Governing through migration control: security and citizenship in Britain', *The British Journal of Criminology*, 48 (6), pp. 703–19.

Bosworth, M. and Kellezi, B., (2012), *Quality of Life in Detention: Results from the MQLD Questionnaire Data Collected in IRC Yarl's Wood, IRC Tinsley House and IRC Brook House, August 2010 – June 2011*. Oxford: Centre for Criminology.

(in press), 'The quality of life in detention'. *Prison Service Journal*.

Bosworth, M. and Kaufman, E., (2011), 'Foreigners in a carceral age: immigration and imprisonment in the U.S.', *Stanford Law and Policy Review*, 22, pp. 101–27.

Bourdieu, P., (1984), *Distinction: A Social Critique of the Judgement of Taste*, London: Routledge.

(1994), 'Rethinking the state: on the genesis and structure of the bureaucratic field', *Sociological Theory*, 12(1), pp. 1–19.

(1998), *State Nobility: Elite Schools in the Field of Power*, Cambridge, MA: Polity.

(1999), 'The abdication of the state', in Bourdieu, P. et al., *The Weight of the World: Social Suffering in Contemporary Society*, Cambridge, MA: Polity, pp. 181–8.

(2005), *The Social Structures of the Economy*, Cambridge, MA: Polity.

(2012), *Sur l'État*, Paris: Editions Seuil/Raisons d'agir.

Bourdieu, P. et al., (1999), *The Weight of the World: Social Suffering in Contemporary Society*, Cambridge, MA: Polity.

Bowles, H. and Gintis, H., (1976), *Schooling in Capitalist America: Educational Reform and the Contradictions of Economic Life*, New York, NY: Basic Books.

Box, S., (1983), *Power, Crime and Mystification*, London: Routledge.

Box, S. and Hale, C., (1985), 'Unemployment, imprisonment, and prison overcrowding', *Contemporary Crises*, 9, pp. 209–28.

Braithwaite, J. and Pettit, P., (1990), *Not Just Deserts*, Oxford: Clarendon Press.

Brannan, B., (2011), 'Brown's prison plan has a hitch: county jails are overcrowded too', *Sacramento Bee*, 18 January, available at: http://inlandpolitics.com/blog/2011/01/18/sacbee-browns-prison-plan-has-a-hitch-county-jails-are-overcrowded-too (accessed 1 January 2013).

Braz, R. and Gilmore. C., (2006), 'Joining forces: prisons and environmental justice in recent California organizing', *Radical History Review*, 96, pp. 95–111.

Brenner, N. and Theodore, N., (eds.), (2002), *Spaces of Neoliberalism: Urban Restructuring in North America and Western Europe*, New York, NY: Wiley/ Blackwell.

Brodeur, J. P., (2007), 'Comparative penology in perspective', in Tonry, M., (ed.), *Crime, Punishment and Politics in Comparative Perspective*, London: The University of Chicago Press, pp. 49–91.

Brown, E., (2006), 'The dog that did not bark: punitive social views and the "professional middle classes"', *Punishment and Society*, 8(3), pp. 287–312.

Brown, Michelle, (2005), '"Setting the conditions" for Abu Ghraib: the prison nation abroad', *American Quarterly*, 57, pp. 973–97.

(2009), *The Culture of Punishment: Prison, Society, and Spectacle*, New York University Press.

(2011a), 'Prevention and the security state: observations on an emerging jurisprudence of risk', *Champ pénal/Penal field, nouvelle revue internationale de criminologie*, available at: http://champpenal.revues.org/8016 (accessed 1 January 2013).

(2011b), 'Preventive detention and the control of sex crime: receding visions of justice in Australian case law', *Alternative Law Journal*, 36, pp. 10–15.

(2012), 'Empathy and punishment', *Punishment and Society*, 14, pp. 1–19.

Browne, J. A., (2003), *Derailed: The School to Jailhouse Track*, Washington, DC: The Advancement Project.

Buck, M., (2000), 'Prisons, social control and political prisoners', *Social Justice*, 27(3), pp. 25–8.

Bukhari, S., (2010), *The War Before: The True Life Story of Becoming a Black Panther, Keeping the Faith, Fighting for Those Left Behind*, New York, NY: Feminist Press.

Bumiller, K., (2008), *In an Abusive State*, Durham, NC: Duke University Press.

Bureau of Justice Statistics, (2000), *Sexual Assault of Young Children as Reported to Law Enforcement: Victim, Incident, and Offender Characteristics in 2000*, Bureau of Justice Statistics, available at: www.ojp.usdoj.gov/bjs/pub/pdf/saycrle.pdf (accessed 1 January 13).

(2011), *Prisoners in 2010*, Washington, DC: Department of Justice.

Burrell, S. and Warboys, L., (2000), 'Special education and the juvenile justice system', *Juvenile Justice Bulletin*, available at: www.ncjrs.gov/html/ojjdp/2000_6_5/contents.html (accessed 1 January 2013).

Butler, J., (2004), *Precarious Life: The Powers of Mourning and Violence*, London/New York: Verso.

(2005), *Giving an Account of Oneself*, New York, NY: Fordham University Press.

(2009), *Frames of War: When is Life Grievable?*, London/New York, NY: Verso.

Cabinet Office, (2010), 'Spending review 2010 – Ministry of Justice', available at: http://nds.coi.gov.uk/content/detail.aspx?NewsAreaId=2&ReleaseID=416082&SubjectId=2 (accessed 22 May 2012).

Cain, M., (2009), *Globality, Crime and Criminology*, London: Sage.

Calavita, K., (2005), *Immigrants at the Margins: Law, Race, and Exclusion in Southern Europe*, Cambridge University Press.

Californians United for a Responsible Budget (CURB), (2007), *Reducing the Number of People in California Women's Prisons: How 'Gender-Responsive*

Prisons' Harm Women, Children, and their Families, available at http://curb-prisonspending.org/wp-content/uploads/2010/05/curb_report_v5_all_hi_res.pdf (accessed 15 July 2012).

Cameron, D., (2006), 'Thugs – beyond redemption?', speech to the Centre for Social Justice, 10 July.

(2011a), Press conference on sentencing reform, London, 21 June.

(2011b), Speech on the fight-back after the riots, Witney, 15 August.

Campbell, M. C., (2012), 'Ornery alligators and soap on a rope: Texas prosecutors and punishment reform in the Lone Star State', *Theoretical Criminology*, 16, pp. 289–312.

Campbell, J. and Pedersen, O. (eds.), (2001), *The Rise of Neoliberalism and Institutional Analysis*, Princeton University Press.

Carlen, P., (1993), '"Underclass", crime and imprisonment: the continuing need for agendas of utopianism, abolitionism and socialism', in *Criminology and Criminal Justice*, Fourth Willem Bonger Lecture, University of Amsterdam, 14 May.

(1996), *Jigsaw: A Political Criminology of Youth Homelessness*, Buckingham: Open University.

(2002), 'Carceral clawback: the case of women's imprisonment in Canada', *Punishment and Society*, 4(1), pp. 115–21.

(2003), 'A strategy for women offenders? Lock them up, programme them... and then send them out homeless', *Criminal Justice Matters*, 53(1), pp. 34–5.

(2008), 'Imaginary penalities and risk-crazed governance', in Carlen, P., (ed.), *Imaginary Penalities*, Cullompton: Willan, pp. 1–25.

(2012), 'Against rehabilitation, for reparative justice', Twenty Second Lecture in Honour of Eve Saville, London, 6 November.

Carlen, P. and Worrall, A., (2004), *Analysing Women's Imprisonment*, Cullompton: Willan.

Casey, L., (2006), Speech on socially-excluded families, 20 March.

Cavadino, M. and Dignan, J., (2006), *Penal Systems*, London: Sage.

Cesaroni, C. and Doob, A., (2003), 'The decline in support for penal welfarism: evidence of support among the elite for punitive segregation', *British Journal of Criminology*, 43(2), pp. 434–41.

Chambers, P., (2011), 'Society has been defended: following the shifting shape of state through Australia's Christmas Island', *International Political Sociology*, 5, pp. 18–34.

Chambliss, W. J., (1999), *Power, Politics, and Crime*, Boulder, CO: Westview Press.

Chandler, C., (2010), 'The gender-responsive prison expansion movement', in Solinger, R., Johnson, P., Raimon, M. and Reynolds, T. (eds.), *Interrupted Life: Experiences of Incarcerated Women in the United States*, Berkeley, CA: University of California Press, pp. 332–7.

Chandler, D., (1976), *Capital Punishment in Canada: A Sociological Study of Repressive Law*, Toronto: McClelland and Stewart.

Chermack, S., Bailey F. Y. and Brown M. (eds.), (2003), *Media Representations of September 11*, Westport, CT: Praeger Publishers.

Chibnall, S., (1977), *Law and Order News*, Oxford: Martin Robertson.

Chih Lin, A., (1998), 'The troubled success of crime policy', in Weir, M. (ed.), *The Social Divide: Political Parties and the Future of Activist Government*, Washington, DC: Brookings Institution/Russell Sage Foundation, pp. 312–57.

Childres, R. D., (1975), 'Compensation for criminally inflicted personal injury,' in Hudson, J. and Galaway, B. (eds.), *Considering the Victim: Readings in Restitution and Victim Compensation*. Springfield, IL: Charles C. Thomas, pp. 363–92.

Christie, N., (1977), 'Conflicts as property', *British Journal of Criminology*, 17(1), pp. 1–15.

(1981), *Limits to Pain*, Oxford: Martin Robertson.

(1986), 'Suitable enemies', in Bianchi, H. and Swaaningen, R. van, (eds.), *Abolitionism*, Amsterdam: Free University Press, pp. 42–54.

(1993), *Crime Control as Industry*, New York, NY: Routledge.

(2000), *Crime Control as Industry*, (3rd edn), London: Routledge.

(2004), *A Suitable Amount of Crime*, London: Routledge.

(2007), *Limits to Pain: The Role of Punishment in Penal Policy*. Eugene, OR: Wipfand Stock.

Christoph, G., (2010), 'Le néolibéralisme: un essai de définition', in Espiet-Kilty, R., *Libéralisme(s)?*, Clermont Ferrand: Presses Universitaires Blaise Pascal.

Christoph, J. B., (1962), *Capital Punishment and British Politics: The British Movement to Abolish the Death Penalty, 1945–57*, The University of Chicago Press.

Civil Rights Data Collection, (2012), *Civil Rights Data Collection*, Office of Civil Rights, available at: www2.ed.gov/about/offices/list/ocr/data.html (accessed 1 January 2013).

Clandestina, (2009), 'Greek government's "six-point plan" for the war against immigrants in the Aegean', 23 June, available at http://clandestinenglish.wordpress.com/2009/06/23/greek-governments-six-point-plan-for-the-war-against-immigrants-in-the-aegean (accessed 8 June 2012).

Clarke, K., (2010), 'The government's vision for criminal justice reform', speech delivered to the Centre for Crime and Justice Studies, 30 June.

(2011), 'Prison with a purpose', speech to the Conservative Party Conference, October 4.

Clarke, J. and Newman, J., (2006), *The Managerial State*, (2nd edn), London/Thousand Oaks, CA: Sage.

Clear, T., (2008), *Imprisoning Communities: How Mass Incarceration Makes Disadvantaged Neighborhoods Worse*, New York, NY: Oxford University Press.

Cohen, P., (2010), 'Long road to adulthood is growing even longer', *New York Times*, 11 June, available at: www.nytimes.com/2010/06/13/us/13generations.html (accessed 1 January 2013).

Cohen, S., (1972), *Folk Devils and Moral Panics*, London: Routledge.

(1980), 'Preface', in Dronfield, L., (1980), *Outside Chance*, London: RAP, pp. 2–6.

(1985), *Visions of Social Control*, Cambridge, MA: Polity.

(2001), *States of Denial*, Cambridge, MA: Polity.

Coker, D., (2001), 'Crime control and feminist law reform in domestic violence law: a critical review', *Buffalo Criminal Law Review*, 4(2), pp. 801–60.

Coleman, R., Sim, J., Tombs, S. and Whyte, D., (2009), 'Introduction: state, power, crime', in Coleman, R., Sim, J., Tombs, S. and Whyte, D., (eds.), *State, Power, Crime*, London: Sage, pp. 1–19.

Comaroff, J. and Comaroff, J. L. (eds.), (2001), *Millennial Capitalism and the Culture of Neoliberalism*, Durham, NC/London: Duke University Press.

Communities Against Rape and Abuse, (CARA), (2006), 'Taking risks: implementing grassroots community accountability strategies', in INCITE! Women of Color Against Violence (eds.), *Color of Violence: The Incite! Anthology*, Boston, MA: South End Press.

Constitutional Court of Germany, (2011), 'Provisions on preventive detention unconstitutional', Press Release No 31/2011 of 4 May, available at: www.bundesverfassungsgericht.de/en/press/bvg11-031en.html (accessed 6 June 2012).

Corcoran, M., (2011), 'Dilemmas of institutionalisation in the penal voluntary sector', *Critical Social Policy*, 31(1), pp. 30–52.

Corporate Watch, (2012), *Revealed: The Punishing Reality of the Coalition's Welfare Reforms*, London: Corporate Watch.

Correction Corporation of America, (2003), 'CSC announces conclusion of investigation by the new state temporary Commission on Lobbying', Press Release, 26 February.

Council of Europe, (2005), *Twenty Guidelines on Forced Return*, adopted by the Committee of Ministers on 4 May at the 925th meeting of the Ministers' Deputies.

(2007), *Secret Detentions and Illegal Transfers of Detainees Involving Council of Europe Member States: Second Report*, Doc. 11302 rev., 11 June.

(2008), *Memorandum by Thomas Hammarberg, Council of Europe Commissioner for Human Rights, following his visit to France from 21 to 23 May 2008*, commDH(2008)34, Strasbourg, 20 November.

(2012), *SPACE I Annual Penal statistics of the Council of Europe: Survey 2010*, Strasbourg: Council of Europe.

Critical Resistance, (2000), 'The history of Critical Resistance', *Social Justice* 27(3), pp. 6–9.

(2008), *CR10: Strategy and Struggle to Abolish the Prison Industrial Complex Program Book*, Oakland, CA: Critical Resistance.

(n.d.), *The Abolitionist Toolkit*, available at http://criticalresistance.org/resources/the-abolitionist-toolkit (accessed 14 July 2012).

Critical Resistance and INCITE!, (2003), 'Critical Resistance–INCITE! statement on gender violence and the prison-industrial complex', *Social Justice*, 30(3) pp. 141–51.

Crompton, R., (2008), *Class and Stratification*, Cambridge, MA: Polity.

Crouch, C., (2011), *The Strange Non-Death of Neoliberalism*, Cambridge and Malden, MA: Polity.

Cruikshank, B., (1999), *The Will to Empower: Democratic Citizens and Other Subjects*, London: Cornell University Press.

Cummins, E., (1994), *The Rise and Fall of California's Radical Prison Movement*, Stanford University Press.

Cunneen, C., Baldry, E., Brown, D., Brown, M., Schwartz, M. and Steel, A., (2013), *Penal Culture and Hyperincarceration: The Revival of the Prison*, Aldershot: Ashgate.

Daily Mail, (2006). 'Home Office blunders left foreign rapists in UK', *Mail Online*, 26 April, available at: www.dailymail.co.uk/news/article-384183/Home-Office-blunders-left-foreign-rapists-UK.html (accessed 1 January 2013).

Dardot, P. and Laval, C., (2009), *La nouvelle raison du monde: Essai sur la société néolibérale*, Paris: Éditions de la Découverte.

Das, V., (2007), *Life and World: Violence and the Descent into the Ordinary*, Berkeley, CA: University of California Press.

Davies, J., (2011), *Challenging Governance Theory: From Networks to Hegemony*, Bristol: Policy Press.

Davis, A. Y., (2003), *Are Prisons Obsolete?*, New York, NY: Seven Stories Press.

(2005), *Abolition Democracy*, New York, NY: Seven Stories Press.

(2012), *The Meaning of Freedom and Other Difficult Dialogues*, San Francisco, CA: City Light Books.

Davis, M., (1995), 'Hell factories in the field: a prison-industrial complex', *The Nation*, 20 February, pp. 229–34.

Dayan, C., (2005), 'Legal terrors', *Representations*, 92(1), pp. 42–80.

(2011), *The Law is a White Dog: How Legal Rituals Make and Unmake Persons*, Princeton University Press.

De Genova, N. and Peutz, N. (eds.), (2010), *The Deportation Regime: Sovereignty, Space, and the Freedom of Movement*, Durham: Duke University Press.

De Giorgi, A., (2006), *Re-thinking the Political Economy of Punishment: Perspectives on Post-Fordism and Penal Politics*, Aldershot: Ashgate.

(2010), 'Immigration control, post-Fordism, and less eligibility: a materialist critique of the criminalization of immigration across Europe', in *Punishment and Society*, 12(2), pp. 147–67.

(2011), 'Post-Fordism and penal change: the new penology as a post-disciplinary social control strategy', in Melossi, D., Sozzo, M. and Sparks, R. (eds.), *Travels of the Criminal Question*, Oxford: Hart Publishing, pp. 113–46.

(2012), 'Punishment and political economy', in Simon. J. and Sparks, R. (eds.), *Handbook of Punishment and Society*, London: Sage, pp. 40–59.

de Haan, W., (1990), *The Politics of Redress*, London: Unwin Hyman.

DeClerk, P., (2006), 'The necessary suffering of the homeless', in Scholar, R., (ed.), *Divided Cities*, Oxford University Press.

Dempsey, M. M., (2009), *Prosecuting Domestic Violence: A Philosophical Analysis*, New York, NY: Oxford University Press.

Detention Watch, (2009), 'European Court to rule on preventive detention in Germany', 17 December, available at: www.dw.de/dw/article/0,,5018994,00.html (accessed 6 June 2012).

(2012), 'The influence of the private prison industry on immigration detention', available at: www.detentionwatchnetwork.org/privateprisons (accessed 6 June 2012).

Dhondt, G., (2002), *Big Prisons and Small Towns*, Amherst, MA: Center for Popular Economics.

Dobash, R. E. and Dobash, R. P., (1992), *Women, Violence and Social Change*, London/New York, NY: Routledge.

Dobash, R. P., Dobash, R. E and Gutteridge, S., (1986), *The Imprisonment of Women*, Oxford: Blackwell.

Dolovich, S., (2011), 'Exclusion and control in the carceral state', *The Berkeley Journal of Criminal Law*, 16(2), pp. 259–339.

(2012), 'Creating the permanent prisoner', in Ogletree, C. Jr. and Sarat, A. (eds.), *Life Without Parole: America's New Death Penalty*, New York University Press.

Doron, M. G., (2000), 'The dead zone and the architecture of transgression', *City, Analysis of Urban Trends, Culture, Theory, Policy, Action*, 4(2), pp. 247–63.

Dow, M., (2004), *American Gulag – Inside U.S. Immigration Prisons*, London: University of California Press.

Downes, D., (2001), 'The macho penal economy: mass incarceration in the United States – a European perspective', in Garland, D. (ed.), *Mass Imprisonment*, London: Sage, pp. 51–69.

(2007), 'Visions of penal control in the Netherlands', in Tonry, M. (ed.), *Crime, Punishment and Politics in Comparative Perspective*, London: The University of Chicago Press, pp. 93–125.

(2012), 'Political economy, welfare and punishment in comparative perspective', in Snacken, S. and Dumortier, E., *Resisting Punitiveness in Europe?*, London: Routledge, pp. 23–34.

Downes, D. and Hansen, K., (2006), 'Welfare and punishment in comparative perspective', in Armstrong, S. and McAra, L., (eds.), *Perspectives on Punishment*, Oxford University Press, pp. 133–54.

Duff, R. A., (2003), *Punishment, Communication, and Community*, New York: Oxford University Press.

(2010), 'A criminal law for citizens', *Theoretical Criminology*, 14(3), pp. 293–309.

Dullum, J. and Ugelvik, T., (2012), 'Exceptional prisons, exceptional societies', in Ugelvik, T. and Dullum, J. (eds.), *Penal Exceptionalism?*, London: Routledge, pp. 1–10.

Duménil, G. and Lévy, D., (2004), *Capital Resurgent: Roots of the Neoliberal Revolution*, Cambridge: Harvard University Press.

Dumm, T., (1987), *Democracy and Punishment: Disciplinary Origins of the United States*, Madison, WI: University of Wisconsin Press.

Duncan, G. A., (2000), 'Urban pedagogies and the celling of adolescents of color', *Social Justice: A Journal of Crime Conflict and World Order*, 27, pp. 29–42.

Durkheim, E., (1893/1933), *The Division of Labour in Society*, New York, NY: The Free Press.

(1933/1984), *The Division of Labor in Society*, transl. by W. D. Halls, New York, NY: Macmillan.

Edkins, J. and Pin-Fat, V., (2005), 'Through the wire: relations of power and relations of violence,' *Millennium: Journal of International Studies*, 34, pp. 1–26.

Egelko, B., (2012), 'Bid to end death penalty headed to the ballot', *The San Francisco Chronicle*, 2 March.

Ehrenreich, B., (2001), *Nickel and Dimed: On (not) Getting by in America*, New York, NY: Holt.

Ehrenreich, B. and Hochschild, A. R., (2002), *Global Woman: Nannies, Maids, and Sex Workers in the New Economy*, New York, NY: Holt.

Eigen, J., (1999), 'Lesion of the will: medical resolve and criminal responsibility in Victorian insanity trials', *Law and Society Review*, 33, pp. 425–59.

Eisenhower, D., (1961), 'Military-industrial complex speech', Public Papers of the Presidents, Dwight D. Eisenhower, pp. 1035–40, available at: www.h-net.org/~hst306/documents/indust.html (accessed 30 April 2012).

Elias, R., (1983), *Victims of the System*, New Brunswick, NJ: Transaction Books.

Estreich, L., (2011), 'Samuel Delany's lumpen worlds and the problem of representing marginality', in Bourke, A., Dafnos, T. and Kip, M. (eds.), *Lumpencity: Discourses of Marginality, Marginalising Discourses*, Ottawa: Red Quill Books.

European Commission, (2005), *Placement and Treatment of Mentally Ill Offenders: Legislation and Practice in EU Member States*, Mannheim, Germany: Central Institute of Mental Health.

Evans, L. and Goldberg, E., (1998), *The Prison Industrial Complex and the Global Economy*, Berkeley, CA: Kersplebedeb.

Feel Tank Chicago, (2008), Retrieved from Manifesto. www.feeltankchicago. net/

Feeley, M. and Rubin, E., (1999), *Judicial Policy Making and the Modern State: How the Courts Reformed America's Prisons*, Cambridge University Press.

Feeley, M. and Simon, J., (1994), 'Actuarial justice: the emerging new criminal law', in Nelken, D. (ed.), *The Futures of Criminology*, London: Sage, pp. 173–201.

Ferguson, A. A., (2000), *Bad Boys: Public Schools in the Making of Black Masculinity*, Ann Arbor, MI: University of Michigan Press.

Ferree, M. M., (1987), 'Equality and autonomy: feminist politics in the United States and West Germany', in Katzenstein, M. F. and Mueller, C. M. (eds.), *The Women's Movements of the United States and Western Europe*, Philadelphia, PA: Temple University Press, pp. 172–95.

Ferrell, J., Hayward, K. and Young, J., (2008), *Cultural Criminology: An Invitation*, Los Angeles, CA: Sage.

Festa, L., (2006), *Sentimental Figures of Empire in Eighteenth-century Britain and France*, Baltimore, MD: Johns Hopkins University Press.

Fine, M. and McClelland, S., (2006), 'Sexuality education and desire: still missing after all these years', *Harvard Educational Review*, 76(3), pp. 297–338.

Fine, M., Boudin, K., Bowen, I., Clark, J., Hylton, D., Martinez, M. 'Missy', Roberts, R., Smart, P., Torre, M. and Upegu, D., (2001), *Changing Minds: The Impact of College in Prison*, available at: www.changingminds.ws (accessed 1 January 2013).

Fink, B., (1995), *The Lacanian Subject: Between Language and Jouissance*, Princeton University Press.

Fitzgerald, M. and Sim, J., (1982), *British Prisons*, (2nd edn), Oxford: Blackwell.

Fligstein, N., (2001), *The Architecture of Markets: An Economic Sociology of Twenty-First-Century Capitalist Societies*, Princeton University Press.

Flynn, M., (2011), *Immigration Detention and Proportionality*, Global Detention Project Working Paper No. 4, Geneva: The Graduate Institute.

Foley, M. and Lennon, J., (2000), *Dark Tourism: The Attraction of Death and Disaster*, New York, NY: Continuum.

Foner, E., (2002), *Radical Reconstruction: America's Unfinished Revolution, 1863–1877*, New York, NY: Harper Perennial.

Foucault, M., (1967), *Madness and Civilisation*, London: Routledge.
    (1976), *Mikrophysik der Macht*, Berlin: Merve Verlag.

(1977), *Discipline and Punish*, London, Harmondsworth: Penguin/Peregrine.

Frase, R. S., (2001), 'Comparative perspectives in sentencing research', in Tonry, M. and Frase, R. S., (eds.), *Sentencing and Sanctions in Western Countries*, Oxford University Press, pp. 259–92.

Fraser, N., (1997), *Justice Interruptus: Critical Reflections on the 'Postsocialist' Condition*, New York, NY: Routledge.

Freiberg, A. and Carson, W. G., (2010), 'The limits of evidence-based policy: evidence, emotion and criminal justice', *Australian Journal of Public Administration*, 69, pp. 152–64.

Friere, P., (1992), *Pedagogy of Hope: Reliving Pedagogy of the Oppressed*, New Nork, NY: Continuum.

Frow, J., (1995), *Cultural Studies and Cultural Value*, Oxford: Clarendon Press.

Furillo, A., (2010), 'California prepares to release thousands more prisoners', *Sacramento Bee*, 15 February, available at: http://lapd.com/news/headlines/ california_prepares_to_release_thousands_more_prisoners (accessed 1 January 2013).

G4S, (2011), *Working Prisons, Working People*, available at: www.g4s.uk.com/ EN-GB/What%20we%20do/Services/Care%20and%20justice%20serv-ices/Custodial%20Services/Working%20Prisons (accessed 22 May 2012).

Gamble, A., (1988), *The Free Market and the Strong State*, London: Macmillan.

Gammeltoft-Hansen, T., (2011), *Access to Asylum: International Refugee Law and the Globalisation of Migration Control*, Cambridge University Press.

Gans, H. J., (1995), *The War against the Poor*, New York, NY: Basic Books.

Garland, D., (1985), *Punishment and Welfare*, Aldershot: Gower.

(1990), *Punishment and Modern Society: A Study in Social Theory*, The University of Chicago Press.

(1995), 'Penal modernism and postmodernism', in Bloomberg, T. and Cohen, S. (eds.), *Punishment and Social Control*, New York, NY: Aldine De Gruyter, pp. 181–209.

(1996), 'The limits of the sovereign state: strategies of crime control in contemporary society', *British Journal of Criminology*, 36(4), pp. 445–67.

(2000), 'The culture of high crime societies: some preconditions of recent "law and order" policies', *British Journal of Criminology*, 40(3), pp. 347–75.

(2001a), 'Epilogue: the new iron cage', in Garland, D., (ed.), *Mass Imprisonment: Causes and Consequences*, London: Sage, pp. 179–81.

(ed.) (2001b), *Mass Imprisonment: Causes and Consequences*, London: Sage

(2001c), *The Culture of Control: Crime and Social Order in Contemporary Society*, Oxford University Press.

(2001d), 'The meaning of mass imprisonment', in Garland, D., (ed.), *Mass Imprisonment*, London: Sage, pp. 1–3.

(2005a), 'Capital punishment and American culture', *Punishment and Society*, 7, pp. 347–76.

(2005b), 'Penal excess and surplus meaning: public torture lynchings in twentieth-century America', *Law and Society Review*, 39, pp. 793–834.

(2006), 'Concepts of culture in the sociology of punishment', *Theoretical Criminology*, 10, pp. 419–47.

(2010), *Peculiar Institution*, Oxford University Press.

(2012), 'Punishment and social solidarity', in Simon, J. and Sparks, R. (eds.), *The SAGE Handbook of Punishment and Society*, London: Sage, pp. 23–39.

Gartner, R., Doob, A. and Zimring, F., (2011), 'The past as prologue? Decarceration in California then and now', *Criminology and Public Policy*, 10(2), pp. 291–325.

Gelsthorpe, L., Sharpe, G. and Roberts, J., (2007), *Provision for Women Offenders in the Community*, London: Fawcett Society.

Geoghegan, R., Boyd, E. and Gibbs, B., (2011), *Inside Job: Creating a Market for Real Work in Prison*, London: Policy Exchange.

Gibney, M. (2008), 'Asylum and the expansion of deportation in the United Kingdom', *Government and Opposition*, 43(2), pp. 146–67.

Giddens, A., (1998), 'Risk society: the context of British politics', in Franklin, J., (ed.), *The Politics of Risk Society*, Cambridge and Malden, MA: Polity/IPPR, pp. 23–34.

Gill, N., (2009), 'Governmental mobility: the power effects of the movement of detained asylum seekers around Britain's detention estate', *Political Geography*, 28(3): 186–96.

Gilliam, W., (2005), *Prekindergarteners Left Behind: Expulsion Rates in State Prekindergarten Programs*, FCD Brief Series No. 3, May, available at: www.fcd-us.org/PDFs/ExpulsionFinalProof.pdf (accessed 1 January 2013).

Gilmore, K., (2000), 'Slavery and prisons – understanding the connections', *Social Justice*, 27(3), pp. 195–205.

Gilmore, R., (2007), *The Golden Gulag*, Berkeley, CA: University of California Press.

Gilmore, J., Moore, J. M. and Scott, D. (eds.), (2013), *Critique and Dissent*, Ottawa: Red Quill.

Gilroy, P., (1987), *There Ain't No Black in the Union Jack*, London: Routledge.

Glaze, L. E., (2011), *Correctional Population in the United States, 2010*, Washington, DC: Department of Justice.

Global Detention Project (2011), *United Kingdom Detention Profile*, available at: www.globaldetentionproject.org/countries/europe/united-kingdom/introduction.html (accessed 1 January 2013).

Golash, D., (2005), *The Case against Punishment*, London: New York University Press.

Gómez-Jara Díez, C., (2008), 'Enemy combatants versus enemy criminal law: an introduction to the European debate regarding enemy criminal law and its relevance to the Anglo-American discussion on the legal status of unlawful enemy combatants', *New Criminal Law Review*, 11, pp. 529–62.

Gooman, N., (1978), *Ways of Worldmaking*, Indianapolis, IN: Hackett.

Gordon, P., (1983), *White Law*, London: Pluto Press.

Gornick, J., Burt, M. R. and Pittman, K. J., (1985), 'Structure and activities of rape crisis centers in the early 1980s', *Crime and Delinquency*, 31(2), pp. 247–68.

Gottschalk, M., (2000), *The Shadow Welfare State: Labor, Business, and the Politics of Health Care in the United States*, Ithaca, NY: Cornell University Press.

(2006), *The Prison and the Gallows: The Politics of Mass Incarceration in America*, Cambridge/New York, NY: Cambridge University Press.

(2010), 'Cells blocks and red ink: mass incarceration, the great recession and penal reform', *Daedalus*, 139(3), pp. 62–73.

(2011), 'The Great Recession and the Great Confinement: the economic crisis ad the future of penal reform', in Rosenfeld, R., Quinet, K. and Garcia, C., (eds.), *Contemporary Issues in Criminological Theory and Research: The Role of Social Institutions*, Belmont, CA: Wadsworth/ Cengage, pp. 343–70.

(2012a), 'No way out? Life sentences and the politics of penal reform', in Ogletree, C. J. Jr. and Sarat, A., (eds.), *Life Without Parole: America's New Death Penalty?*, New York University Press, pp. 227–81.

(2012b), 'The carceral state and the politics of punishment', in Simon, J. and Sparks, R. (eds.), *The SAGE Handbook of Punishment and Society*, London: Sage, pp. 205–41.

(in press), *Caught: Race, Neoliberalism, and the Future of the Carceral State and American Politics*.

Governor's Budget Summary, (2012), 'Corrections and Rehabilitation, 2011–2012', State of California Budget Office, available at: http://2011-12. archives.ebudget.ca.gov/pdf/BudgetSummary/CorrectionsandRehabilitation. pdf (accessed 27 November 2012).

Gowers, E., (1956), *A Life For a Life? The Problem of Capital Punishment*, London: Chatto and Windus.

Grandquillot, D., (2009), *RSA Revenu de solidarite´ active*, Paris: Gualino Editeur.

Green, D., (2006), 'Public opinion versus public judgment about crime: correction the "comedy of errors"', *British Journal of Criminology*, 46, pp. 131–54.

(2007), 'Comparing penal cultures: child on child homicide in England and Norway', in Tonry, M. (ed.), *Crime, Punishment and Politics in Comparative Perspective*, London: The University of Chicago Press, pp. 591–643.

(2008), *When Children Kill Children*, Oxford: Clarendon Press.

Greenberg, D., (1977), 'The dynamics of oscillatory punishment processes', *Journal of Criminal Law and Criminology*, 68, pp. 643–51.

341

(1980), 'Penal sanctions in Poland: a test of alternative models', *Social Problems*, 28(2), pp. 194–204.

(1999), 'Punishment, division of labour and social solidarity', in Adler, F. and Laufer, W. S. (eds.), *The Criminology of Criminal Law*, Piscataway, NJ: Transaction Publishers, pp. 283–362.

Greenberg, J., (1977), *Cases and Materials on Judicial Process and Social Change: Constitutional Litigation*, St. Paul, MN: West Publishing Co.

Greene, J. and Mauer, M., (2010), *Downscaling Prisons: Lessons from Four States*, available at: www.sentencingproject.org (accessed 29 October, 2012).

Greene, J., Pranis, K. and Ziedenberg, J., (2006), *Disparity by Design: How Drug-Free Zone Laws Impact Racial Disparity – And Fail to Protect Youth*, Washington, DC: Justice Policy Institute, available at: www.justicepolicy.org/reports/SchoolZonesReport306.pdf (accessed 1 January 2013).

Gregory, A., Skiba, R. and Noguera, P., (2010), 'The achievement gap and the discipline gap: two sides of the same coin?', *Educational Researcher*, 39(1), pp. 59–68.

Grewcock, M., (2009), *Border Crimes: Australia's War on Illicit Migrants*, Sydney: Institute of Criminology Press.

Grover, C., (2008), *Crime and Inequality*, Cullompton: Willan.

(2011), 'Social protest in 2011: material and cultural aspects of economic inequalities', *Sociological Research Online*, 16(4), pp. 1–8, available at: www.socresonline.org.uk/16/4/18.html>10.5153/sro.2538 (accessed 8 December 2011).

Guardian, (2012), 'Chris Grayling takes hard line on prison', 20 September, available at: www.guardian.co.uk/politics/2012/sep/20/chris-grayling-take-hardline-prison (accessed 1 January 2013).

Gustafson, K., (2011), *Cheating Welfare: Public Assistance and the Criminalization of Poverty*, New York University Press.

Gutman, A. and Thompson, D., (2004), *Why Deliberative Democracy*, Princeton University Press.

Habermas, J., (1981), *The Theory of Communicative Action*, Boston, MA: Beacon Press.

Hakim, D. and Confessore, N., (2011), 'Speech suggests pro-business approach by Cuomo', *New York Times*, 5 January, available at: www.nytimes.com/2011/01/06/nyregion/06cuomo.html?pagewanted=all (accessed 1 January 2013).

Hakim, D. and Kaplan, T., (2011), 'As republicans resist closing prisons, Cuomo is said to scale back plans', *New York Times*, 28 January, available at: www.nytimes.com/2011/01/29/nyregion/29prisons.html (accessed 1 January 2013).

Hall, S., (1988), *The Hard Road to Renewal*, London: Verso.

(2011), 'The neoliberal revolution', *Soundings*, 48, pp. 9–27.

Hall, P. A. and Soskice, D., (2001), *Varieties of Capitalism*, Oxford Univeristy Press.

Hall, S. and Scraton, P., (1981), 'Law, class and control', in Fitzgerald, M., McLennan, G. and Pawson, J., (compilers), *Crime and Society*, London: Routledge, pp. 385–416.

Hall, S., Critcher, C., Jefferson, T., Clark, J. and Roberts, B., (1978), *Policing the Crisis*, London: Macmillan.

Hallatt, D. (director), (2012), *Punishment: A Failed Social Experiment*, New Future Media.

Hallett, M., (2008), 'Militarism and colonialism in the global punishment economy', in Muraskin, R. and Roberts, A. R., *Visions for Change: Crime and Justice in the 21st Century*, (5th edn), New York, NY: Prentice Hall.

Hamm, T., (2001), *Rebel and a Cause: Caryl Chessman and the Politics of the Death Penalty in Postwar California, 1948–1974*. Berkeley, CA: University of California Press.

Handler, J. F. and Hasenfeld, Y., (1991), *The Moral Construction of Poverty: Welfare Reform in America*, London: Sage.

Haney, L., (2004), 'Introduction: gender, welfare and states of punishment', *Social Politics*, 11(3), pp. 333–62.

(2010), *Offending Women: Power, Punishment, and the Regulation of Desire*, Berkeley, CA: University of California Press.

Hannah-Moffat, K., (2002), 'Creating choices: reflecting on choices', in Carlen, P. (ed.), *Women and Punishment: The Struggle for Justice*, Cullompton: Willan, pp. 199–219.

Hannah-Moffat, K. and Lynch, M., (2012), 'Special issue: theorizing punishment's boundaries', *Theoretical Criminology*, 16, pp. 119–21.

Harcourt, B., (2006), 'From the asylum to the prison: rethinking the incarceration revolution', *Texas Law Review*, 84, pp. 1752–86.

(2011), *The Illusion of Free Markets*, London: Harvard University Press.

Hardt, M. and Negri, A., (2000), *Empire*. Cambridge, MA: Harvard University Press.

Hare, R., (1991), *The Hare Psychopathy Checklist – Revised*, Toronto: Multi-Health Systems.

Harper, E. and Symonds, S., (2009), 'Borders, Citizenship and Immigration Act 2009: Ministerial Statements', prepared for The Immigration Law Practitioners' Association, London: ILPA.

Harris, N., (1997), *The New Untouchables: Immigration and the New World Worker*, Harmondsworth: Penguin.

Harry, B. and Klingner, J. K., (2006), *Why Are There So Many Minority Students in Special Education?: Understanding Race and Disability in Schools*, New York, NY: Teachers College Press.

Harvey, D., (2007), *A Brief History of Neoliberalism*, (2nd edn), Oxford University Press.

Hasenfeld, Y., (1972), 'People processing organizations: an exchange approach', *American Sociological Review*, 37(3), pp. 256–63.

Hellgren, M., (2012). 'Baltimore police handcuff, arrest 4 children under age 10 at their school', *CBS Baltimore*, 30 March, available at: http://baltimore. cbslocal.com/2012/03/30/baltimore-police-handcuff-arrest-4-children-under-age-10-at-their-school (accessed 1 January 2013).

Henderson, L. N., (1985), 'The wrongs of victim's rights', *Stanford Law Review*, 37(4), pp. 937–1021.

Henrichson, C. and Delaney, R., (2012), *The Price of Prisons: What Incarceration Costs Taxpayers*, New York, NY: Vera Institute of Justice.

Herrnstein Smith, B., (1988), *Contingencies of Value: Alternative Perspectives for Critical Theory*, Cambridge, MA: Harvard University Press.

Hewitt, D., Kim, C. and Losen, D., (2010), *The School to Prison Pipeline: Structuring Legal Reform*, New York University Press.

Hillyard, P., (1995), *Suspect Community*, London: Pluto Press.

Himmelstein, K. and Bruckner, H., (2011), 'Criminal-justice and school sanctions against non-heterosexual youth: a national longitudinal study', *Pediatrics*, 127(1), pp. 48–57.

HM Chief Inspector of Prisons, (2012a), *Report on an Unannounced Full Follow-up Inspection of HMP Liverpool 8–16 December 2011*, London: Her Majesty's Inspectorate of Prisons.

(2012b), *Report on an Unannounced Full Follow-up Inspection of HMP Styal 5–15 July 2011*, London: Her Majesty's Inspectorate of Prisons.

HM Inspectorate of Prisons, (2005), *Recalled Prisoners. A Short Review of Recalled Adult Male Determinate-Sentenced Prisoners*, London: Her Majesty's Inspectorate of Prisons, available at: www.abs.gov.au/ausstats/abs@.nsf/Latestproducts/4512.0Main%20Features2March%202012? opendocumentandtabname=Summaryandprodno=4512.0andissue=March%202012andnum=andview= (accessed 1 January 2013).

HM Prison Service, (2006), *Prison Service Order 4630: Immigration and Foreign Nationals in Prison*, London: MoJ.

(2007), *Prison Service Instruction 21/2007: Immigration and Foreign Nationals in Prison (Amended Version)*, London: MoJ.

(2008), *Prison Service Order 4630: Immigration and Foreign Nationals in Prison*, London: MoJ.

Home Office, (1960), *Prisons and Borstals: Statement of Policy and Practice in the Administration of Prisons and Borstal Institutions in England and Wales*, London: HMSO.

(2012), *Immigration Statistics October – December 2011*, London: Home Office.

Hörnqvist, M., (2010), *Risk, Power and the State: After Foucault*, Abingdon: Routledge.

Howard, M., (1993), Speech to the Conservative Party Conference, citation transcribed from a recording compiled by Peter Hill and BBC News, Great Political Speeches (audio cassette).

Hudson, B. A., (1993), Penal Policy and Social Justice, London: Macmillan.

(2003), Justice in the Risk Society, London: Sage.

(2006), 'Punishing monsters and judging aliens: justice at the borders of community', Australian and New Zealand Journal of Criminology, 39(2), pp. 232–47.

(2012), 'Who needs justice? Who needs security?', in Hudson, B. and Ugelvik, S. (eds.), Justice and Security in the Twenty-first Century, London: Routledge, pp. 6–23.

Hudson, R. and Williams, A. M., (2000), Divided Britain, (2nd edn), Paris: Mallard Éditions.

Hulsman, L., (1986), 'Critical criminology and the concept of crime', Contemporary Crises, 10, pp. 63–80.

Huston, W., (2010), 'CPS creates "calm" environment for students, Chicago Defender, 28 January, available at: www.chicagodefender.com/article-7032-cps-creates-lscalmrs.html (accessed 1 January 2013).

Huxley, A., (1936), Eyeless in Gaza, London: Chatto and Windus.

Ignatieff, M., (1978), A Just Measure of Pain, Harmondsworth: Penguin.

INCITE! Women of Color Against Violence, (2006), Color of Violence: The Incite! Anthology, Boston, MA: South End Press.

(n.d.), Law Enforcement Violence Against Women of Color and Trans People of Color: A Critical Intersection of Gender Violence and State Violence, available at: www.incite-national.org/media/docs/3696_TOOLKIT-FINAL.pdf (accessed 14 July 2012).

Institute of Penitentiaries, (2012), The Spanish Prison System, Madrid: Institute of Penitentiaries.

International Centre for Prison Studies, (2012), World Prison Brief, available at: www.prisonstudies.org/info/worldbrief (accessed 10 July 2012; 26 November 2012).

Irvin, G., (2008), Super Rich, Cambridge, MA: Polity.

Irwin, J., (1980), Prisons in Turmoil, Boston, MA: Little, Brown.

Jacobs, J. B., (1979), 'Race relations and the prisoner subculture', in Morris, N. and Tonry, M. (eds.), Crime and Punishment: An Annual Review of Research, vol. 1, The University of Chicago Press, pp. 1–27.

(1980), 'The prisoners' rights movement and its impacts, 1960–80', in Morris, N. and Tonry, M. (eds.), Crime and Justice: A Review of Research, vol. 2, The University of Chicago Press, pp. 429–70.

James, J. (ed.), (2003), Imprisoned Intellectuals: America's Political Prisoners Write on Life, Liberation and Rebellion, Lanham, MD/Boulder, CO/New York, NY: Rowman and Littlefield.

James, A. and Raine, J., (1998), *The New Politics of Criminal Justice*, London: Longman.

Jankovic, I., (1977), 'Labour market and imprisonment', *Crime and Social Justice*, 8, pp. 17–31.

Janus, E., (2010), 'The preventive state: when is prevention of harm harmful', in Nash, M. and Williams, A., (eds.), *Handbook of Public Protection*, Cullompton: Willan, pp. 316–36.

Janus, E., Alexander, S. and Graf, L., (2012), *M. v. Germany: The European Court of Human Rights Takes a Critical Look at Preventive Detention*, Legal Studies Research Paper Series, Paper No. 2012–03, William Mitchell College of Law.

Jefferson, A. I., (2012), 'Salecia Johnson's parents want answers', *The Root*, 20 April, available at: www.theroot.com/views/salecia-johnsons-parents-still-want-answers (accessed 1 January 2013).

Jefferson, A. M., (2012),'Comparisons at work: exporting exceptional norms', in Ugelvik, T. and Dullum, J., (eds.), *Penal Exceptionalism?*, London: Routledge, pp. 100–17.

Jessop, B., (1990a), 'Regulation theories in retrospect and prospect', *Economy and Society*, 19(2), pp. 153–216.

(1990b), *State Theory*, Cambridge, MA: Polity.

(2002), *The Future of The Capitalist State*, Cambridge, MA: Polity.

(2008), *State Power*, Cambridge, MA: Polity.

Jessop, R., (1994), 'Post-Fordism and the state', in Amin, A. (ed.), *Post-Fordism: A Reader*, Oxford: Basil Blackwell, pp. 251–79.

Johnson, N., (1990), *Restructuring the Welfare State: A Decade of Change 1980–1990*, Hemel Hempsted: Harvester Wheatsheaf.

Johnstone, G., (2000), 'Penal policy making: elitist, populist or participatory', *Punishment and Society*, 2(2), pp. 161–80.

Jones, C. and Novak, T., (1999), *Poverty, Welfare and the Disciplinary State*, London/New York: Routledge.

Jones, T. and Newburn, T., (2006), *Policy Transfer and Criminal Justice*, Chichester: Open University Press.

Joseph Rowntree Foundation (JFR), (2001), *Recruiting and Employing Offenders: The Impact of the Police Act*, London: JRF.

(2012), *Serving Deprived Communities in a Recession*, York: JRF.

Justice Policy Institute, (2002), *Cellblocks or Classrooms? The Funding of Higher Education and Corrections and its Impact on African American Men*, available at: www.justicepolicy.org/images/upload/0209_REP_CellblocksClassrooms_BBAC.pdf (accessed 1 January 2013).

Kaba, M. and Edwards, F., (2012), *Policing Chicago Public Schools: A Gateway to the School-to-Prison Pipeline*, available at: http://policeincps.com.

Kane-Willis, K., Janichek, J. and Clark, D., (2006), *Intersecting Voices: Impacts of Illinois' Drug Policies*, The Institute for Metropolitan Affairs: The Illinois

Consortium on Drug Policies, available at: www.roosevelt.edu/ima/pdfs/ intersectingVoices.pdf (accessed 1 January 2013).

Karstedt, S., (2002), 'Emotions and criminal justice', *Theoretical Criminology*, 6, pp. 299–317.

Karstedt, S. and Farrall, S., (2007), *Law-Abiding Majority? The Everyday Crimes of the Middle Classes*, London: Centre for Crime and Justice Studies.

Karstedt, S., Loader, I. and Strang, H., (2011), *Emotions, Crime and Justice*, Portland, OR: Hart Publishing.

Katz, M. B. and Stern, M. J., (2006), *One Nation Divisible: What America Was and What It Is Becoming*, New York, NY: Russell Sage Foundation.

Kaufman, E., (2012a), 'Finding foreigners: race and the politics of memory in British prisons', *Population, Space and Place*, 18(6), pp. 701–14.

(2012b), *Foreign Bodies: The Prison's Place in a Global World*, Doctoral Dissertation, University of Oxford.

(in press). 'Hubs and spokes: the transformation of the British prison', in Aas, K. and Bosworth, M. (eds.), *Migration and Punishment: Citizenship, Crime Control, and Social Exclusion*, Oxford University Press.

Kelly, E. L., (2012), 'Philly stands up: inside the politics and poetics of transformative justice and community accountability in sexual assault situations', *Social Justice*, 37(4), pp. 44–58.

Kendal, K., (2002), 'Time to think again about cognitive behavioural programmes', in Carlen, P. (ed.), *Women and Punishment*, Cullompton: Willan, pp. 182–98.

Kim, M., (2012), 'Moving beyond critique: creative interventions and reconstructions of community accountability', *Social Justice*, 37(4), pp. 14–36.

King, D. S., (1998), 'A strong or weak state? Race and the US federal government in the 1920s', *Ethnic and Racial Studies*, 21(1), pp. 21–47.

(1995), *Separate and Unequal: Black Americans and the U.S. Federal Government*, Oxford: Clarendon Press.

Kirkham, C., (2012), 'Private prison corporation offers cash in exchange for state prisons', *Huffington Post*, 14 February, available at: www.huffingtonpost.com/ 2012/02/14/private-prisons-buying-state-prisons_n_1272143.html (accessed 11 March 2013).

Knight, E. (ed.), (1970), *Black Voices from Prison*, New York, NY: Pathfinder Press.

Knopp, F. H., (1976), *Instead of Prisons: A Handbook for Abolitionists*, Prison Research Education Action Project, Brooklyn, NY: Faculty Press.

Koch, M., (2006), *Roads to Post-Fordism: Labour Markets and Social Structures in Europe*, Aldershot: Ashgate.

Kocka, J., (1981), 'Class formation, interest articulation, and public policy: the origins of the German white-collar class in the late nineteenth and early twentieth centuries', in Berger, S. (ed.), *Organizing Interests in Western Europe*, Cambridge University Press, pp. 63–82.

(2004), 'The middle classes in Europe', in Kaelble, H. (ed.), *The European Way: European Societies in the 19th and 20th Centuries*, Oxford: Berghahn.

Kohn, M. and McBride, K., (2011), *Political Theories of Decolonization: Postcolonialism and the Problem of Foundations*, Oxford University Press.

Kosciw, J. G. and Diaz, E. D., (2009), *Shared Differences: The Experience of Lesbian, Gay, Bisexual and Transgendered Students of Color in Our Nation's Schools*, New York, NY: GLSEN.

Krasmann, S., (2007), 'The enemy on the border: critique of a programme in favour of a preventive state', *Punishment and Society*, 9, pp. 301–18.

Krisberg, B., (2007), *And Justice for Some: Differential Treatment of Youth of Color in the Justice System*, National Center on Crime and Delinquency, available at: www.nccd-crc.org/nccd/pubs/2007jan_justice_for_some.pdf (accessed 1 January 2013).

Kumashiro, K., (2012), *Bad Teacher!*, New York, NY: Teachers College Press.

KVS, (2000), *Kriminella gängbildningar: en pilotundersökning om gängbildningar vid landets anstalter*, Norrköping: Kriminalvårdsstyrelsen.

(2002), *Intagna som kräver extra resurser avseende säkerhet och omhändertagande*, Norrköping: Kriminalvårdsstyrelsen.

KVV, (2000), *Reasoning and Rehabilitation (reviderad upplaga). Utdrag ur Handbok för undervisning i Cognitive Skills*, Norrköping: Kriminalvårdsverket/T3 Associates Training and Consulting Inc.

LA Times, (2009), 'Schwarzenegger's prison reform burden', *Los Angeles Times*, 17 September, available at: http://articles.latimes.com/2009/sep/17/opinion/ed-prisons17 (accessed 1 January 2013).

Lacan, J., (1992), *The Seminar of Jacques Lacan. Book VII, The Ethics of Psychoanalysis: 1959–1960*, London: Routledge.

(1999), *The Seminar of Jacques Lacan. Book XX, On Femine Sexuality, the Limits of Love and Knowledge: Encore 1972–1973*, New York/London: W. W. Norton.

Lacey, N., (2008), *The Prisoner's Dilemma*, Cambridge University Press.

(2011), 'Why globalisation doesn't spell convergence: models of institutional variation and the comparative political economy of punishment', in Crawford, A. (ed.), *International and Comparative Criminal Justice and Urban Governance*, Cambridge University Press, pp. 214–50.

Lamont, M., (2000), *The Dignity of Working Men: Morality and the Boundaries of Race, Class, and Immigration*, New York, NY: Russell Sage Foundation.

Lappi-Seppala, T., (2007), 'Penal policy in Scandinavia', in Tonry, M. (ed.), *Crime, Punishment and Politics in Comparative Perspective*, London: The University of Chicago Press, pp. 217–95.

(2012), 'Explaining national differences in the use of imprisonment', in Snacken, S. and Dumortier, E., *Resisting Punitiveness in Europe?*, London: Routledge, pp. 35–72.

Lawler, S., (2005), 'Disgusted subjects: the making of middle-class identities', *Sociological Review*, 53(3), pp. 429–46.

Leerkes, A. and Broeders, D., (2010), 'A case of mixed motives? Formal and information functions of administrative immigration detention', *British Journal of Criminology*, 50, pp. 830–50.

Levy, J. D. (ed.), (2006), *The State after Statism: New State Activities in the Age of Liberalizatio*, Cambridge, MA: Harvard University Press.

Leys, C., (2003), *Market-Driven Politics: Neoliberal Democracy and the Public Interest*, (2nd edn), London/New York, NY: Verso.

Lichtenstein, A., (1996), *Twice the Work of Free Labor: The Political Economy of Convict Labor in the New South*, London: Verso.

Lijphart, A., (1999), *Patterns of Democracy: Government Forms and Performance in Thirty-six Countries*, Yale University Press.

Lilly, R. and Knepper, P., (1993), 'The corrections-commercial complex', *Crime and Delinquency*, 42(1), pp. 150–66.

Lipman, P., (2011), *The New Political Economy of Urban Education: Neoliberalism, Race, and the Right to the City*, New York, NY: Routledge/ Falmer.

Liverpool City Council, (2009), *The Indices of Multiple Deprivation 2007*, Liverpool City Council.

(2012), *Liverpool Homelessness Review 2011*, Liverpool City Council.

Liverpool City Region, (2012), *Child Poverty and Life Chances Strategy 2011–2014, Liverpool*, Liverpool City Region.

Loader, I. and Sparks, R., (2012), 'Beyond lamentation: towards a democratic egalitarian politics of crime and justice', in Newburn, T. and Peay, J. (eds.), *Policing: Politics, Culture and Control*, Oxford: Hart Publishing, pp. 11–41.

Lochner, L. and Moretti, E., (2004), 'The effect of education on crime: evidence from prison inmates, arrests, and self-reports', *American Economic Review*, 94(1), pp. 155–89.

Lockwood, D., (1995), 'Marking out the middle class(es)', in Butler, T. and Savage, M. (eds.), *Social Change and the Middle Classes*, University College London Press.

Loh, W. D., (1981), 'Q: what has reform of rape legislation wrought? A: truth in criminal labeling', *Journal of Social Issues*, 37(4), pp. 28–51.

López, N., (2003), *Hopeful Girls, Troubled Boys: Race and Gender Disparity in Urban Education*, New York, NY: Routledge.

Lorde, A., (1984), *Sister Outsider: Essays and Speeches*, New York, NY: The Crossing Press.

Losen, D. J. and Orfield, G. (eds.), (2002), *Racial Inequality in Special Education*, Cambridge, MA: Harvard Education Press.

Losen, D. J. and Skiba, R., (2010), *Suspended Education: Urban Middle Schools in Crisis*, Southern Poverty Law Center, available at: www.splcenter.org/sites/default/files/downloads/publication/Suspeded_Education.pdf (accessed 1 January 2013).

Lynch, M., (2009), *Sunbelt Justice: Arizona and the Transformation of American Punishment*, Palo Alto, CA: Stanford University Press.

Lynch, J. P. and Simon, R., (2003), *Immigration the World Over: Statutes, Policies, and Practices*, Lanham, MD: Rowman and Littlefield.

Madriz, E. I., (1997), 'Images of criminals and victims: a study on women's fear and social control', *Gender and Society*, 11(3), pp. 342–56.

Maguire, M. and Pointing, J., (1988), 'Introduction: the rediscovery of the crime victim', in Maguire, M. and Pointing, J. (eds.), *Victims of Crime: A New Deal?*, Milton Keynes: Open University Press.

Makaremi, C., (2009), *On Technologies of Control of Foreigners, Border Control in Europe*, available at: www.libertysecurity.org (accessed 1 January 2013).

Malcolm X, (1997), *The Autobiography of Malcolm X*, Harmondsworth: Penguin.

Manza, J. and Uggen, C., (2006), *Locked Out: Felon Disenfranchisement and American Democracy*, New York, NY: Oxford University Press.

Marazzi, C., (2011), *Capital and Affects: The Politics of the Language Economy*. New York, NY: Semiotext(e).

Marshall, I. H. (ed.), (1997), *Minorities, Migrants, and Crime*. London: Sage.

Martinez, R. and Valenzuela, A. (eds.), (2006), *Immigration and Crime. Race, Ethnicity, and Violence*, New York University Press.

Marvasti, B. A., (2003), *Being Homeless: Textual and Narrative Constructions*, Lanham, MD: Lexington Books.

Marx, K., (1859/1961), 'Preface to *A Contribution to the Critique of Political Economy*', in Bottomore, T. B. and Rubel, M. (eds.), *Karl Marx: Selected Writings in Sociology and Social Philosophy*, Harmondsworth: Penguin, pp. 67–9.

(1867/1976), *Capital*, vol. 1, Harmondsworth: Penguin.

(1963), *The Eighteenth Brumaire of Louis Bonaparte*, New York, NY: International Publishers.

Mary, P. and Nagels, J., (2012), 'Penalisation and social policies', in Snacken, S. and Dumortier, E., *Resisting Punitiveness in Europe?*, London: Routledge, pp. 86–103.

Mathiesen, T., (1974), *The Politics of Abolition*, London: Martin Robertson.

(1980), *Law, Society and Political Action*, London: Academic Press.

(1986), 'The politics of abolition', in *Contemporary Crises*, 10, pp. 81–94.

(1990), *Prison on Trial*, London: Sage.

(2000), *Prison on Trial*, (2nd edn), Winchester: Waterside Press.

(2001), 'Television, public space and prison population', in Garland, D. (ed.), *Mass Imprisonment*, London: Sage, pp. 28–34.

(2004), *Silently Silenced: Essays on the Creation of Acquiescence in Modern Society*, Winchester: Waterside Press.

(2006), *Prison on Trial*, (3rd edn), Winchester: Waterside Press.

(2011), 'Fra "nothing works" til "what works?" – hvor stor er forskjellen?' ('From "nothing works" to "what works" – how great is the difference?'), in Mathiesen, T., *Kritisk sosiologi – en invitasjon (Critical Sociology – An Invitation)*, Novus Publishers, pp. 239–55.

(2012), 'Scandinavian exceptionalism in penal matters: reality or wishful thinking?', in Ugelvik, T. and Dullum, J. (eds.), *Penal Exceptionalism?*, London: Routledge, pp. 13–37.

(in press), *Towards a Surveillant State: The Rise of Surveillance Systems in Europe*, Winchester, Waterside Press.

Mathiesen, T. and Hjemdal, O. K., (2011), 'A new look at victim and offender – an abolitionist approach', in Bosworth, M. and Hoyle, C. (eds.), *What is Criminology?*, Oxford University Press, pp. 223–34.

Matthews, N. A., (1994), *Confronting Rape: The Feminist Anti-Rape Movement and the State*, New York, NY/London: Routledge.

Mauer. M., (1999), *Race to Incarcerate*, New York, NY: New Press.

(2002), 'Mass imprisonment and the disappearing voters', in Mauer, M. and Chesney-Lynd, M. (eds.), *Invisible Punishment: The Collateral Consequences of Mass Imprisonment*, New York, NY: The New Press, pp. 50–8.

(2006), *Race to Incarcerate*, (2nd edn), New York, NY: The New Press.

Mauer, M. and Chesney-Lynd, M. (eds.), (2002), *Invisible Punishment: The Collateral Consequences of Mass Imprisonment*, New York, NY: The New Press.

Mauer, M. and King, R., (2007), *Uneven Justice: State Rates of Incarceration by Race and Ethnicity*, Washington, DC: The Sentencing Project, available at: www.sentencingproject.org/doc/publications/rd_stateratesofincbyra-ceandethnicity.pdf (accessed 14 July 2012).

Maurin, L. and Savidan, P., (2008), *L'Etat des ine´galite´s en France. Donne´es et analyses*, Paris: Belin.

Mawby, R. I. and Gill, M. L., (1987), *Crime Victims: Needs, Services and the Voluntary Sector*, London: Tavistock.

May, T., (2002), Speech to the Conservative Party Conference, 7 October.

McBride, K., (2005), *Collective Dreams: Political Imagination and Community*, University Park, PA: Penn State University Press.

(2007), *Punishment and Political Order*, Ann Arbor, MI: University of Michigan Press.

McConville, S., (1981), *A History of English Prison Administration. Volume I: 1750–1877*, London: Routledge and Kegan Paul.

McDermott, T. E. III., (1975), 'California rape evidence reform: an analysis of Senate Bill 1678', *Hastings Law Journal*, 26, pp. 1551–73.

McDonald, F. (ed.), (2009), *Immigration, Crime and Justice*, Bingley: Emerald Publishing.

McNally, J., (2003), 'Black over-representation in special education not confined to segregation states', *Rethinking Schools Online*, 17(3).

McSherry, B. and Keyzer, P., (2009), *Sex Offenders and Preventive Detention: Politics, Policy and Practice*. Annandale, NSW: The Federation Press.

Mehta, A., (2008), 'Fit for purpose: OASys assessments and parole decisions, a practitioner's view', *Probation Journal*, 55(2), pp. 189–94.

Meiners, E., (2007), *Right to be Hostile: Schools, Prisons and the Making of Public Enemies*, New York, NY: Routledge.

Mele, C. and Miller, T., (2005), *Civil Penalties, Social Consequences*, New York, NY: Routledge.

Melossi, D., (1993), 'Gazette of morality and social whip: punishment, hegemony, and the case of the U.S., 1970–1992', *Social and Legal Studies*, 2, pp. 259–79.

(2003), 'In a peaceful life: migration and the crime of modernity in Europe/ Italy', *Punishment and Society*, 5(4), pp. 371–97.

(2008), *Controlling Crime, Controlling Society*, Cambridge, MA: Polity.

(2011), 'Neo-liberalism's elective affinities: penality, political economy and international relations', in Melossi, D., Sozzo, M. and Sparks, R. (eds.), *Travels of the Criminal Question*, Oxford: Hart Publishing, pp. 45–64.

Melossi, D. and Pavarini, M., (1981), *The Prison and The Factory*, London: Macmillan.

Meranze, M., (1996), *Laboratories of Virtue: Punishment, Revolution, and Authority in Philadelphia, 1760–1835*, Chapel Hill, NC: University of North Carolina Press.

Merkel, G., (2011), 'Case note – retrospective preventive detention in Germany: a comment on the ECHR decision Haidn v. Germany of 13 January 2011', *German Law Journal*, 12, pp. 968–77.

MigrEurope, (2010), *European Borders: Controls, Detention and Deportations*, Paris: MigrEurope.

Miller, L., (2008), *The Perils of Federalism: Race, Poverty and the Politics of Crime Control*, New York, NY: Oxford University Press.

Ministry of Justice (MoJ), (2007a), Letter from Maria Eagle, MP, to Mr. John Shine, Chair of the Independent Monitoring Board, 20 September.

(2007b), 'Not Locked Up but Subject to Rules': An Inquiry into Managing Offenders in Approved Premises (Hostels), following the Panorama Programme Broadcast on 8 November 2006, London: MoJ.

(2007c), *Story of the Prison Population: 1995–2007*, London: MoJ.

(2009), *Story of the Prison Population 1995–2009 England and Wales*, available at: www.justice.gov.uk/publications/docs/story-prison-population.pdf (accessed 20 May 2010).

(2010), *Breaking the Cycle*, London: HMSO, available at: www.justice.gov.uk/downloads/consultations/breaking-the-cycle.pdf (accessed 22 May 2012).

(2011), *Prison Population Projections 2011–2017*, London: MoJ.

(2012a), *Prison Population Projections 2011–2017 England and Wales*, available at: www.justice.gov.uk/downloads/statistics/mojstats/prison-pop-projections-2011-17.pdf (accessed 22 May 2012).

(2012b), *What are Approved Premises?*, London: MoJ.

Ministry of Justice (MoJ) and UK Border Agency (UKBA), (2009), *Service Level Agreement to Support the Effective and Speedy Removal of Foreign National Prisoners*, available at: http://www.irr.org.uk/pdf2/FNP_SLA.pdf (accessed 1 January 2013).

Minow, M., (1998), 'Between vengeance and forgiveness: feminist responses to violent injustice', *New England Law Review*, 32(4), pp. 367–81.

Mladek, K., (2004), 'The psychic life of punishment (Kant, Nietzsche, Freud)', *Punishment, Politics, and Culture*, 30, pp. 211–45.

Monahan, R., (2010), 'Queens girl Alexa Gonzalez hauled out of school in handcuffs after getting caught doodling on desk', *Daily News*, 5 February, available at: http://articles.nydailynews.com/2010-02-05/local/27055388_1_desk-doodling-handcuffs (accessed 1 January 2013).

Monahan, T., (2010), *Surveillance in the Time of Insecurity*, New Brunswick, NJ: Rutgers University Press.

Moore, J. and Scott, D., (2012), 'It's not just about the profits: privatisation, social enterprise and the "John Lewis" prison', *Criminal Justice Matters*, 87(1), pp. 42–3.

Morris, L., (1994), *Dangerous Class: The Underclass and Social Citizenship*, New York, NY: Routledge.

Morris, R., (1998), *Penal Abolition, the Practical Choice: A Practical Manual on Penal Abolition*, Toronto: Canadian Scholars' Press.

Mountz, A., (2010), *Seeking Asylum: Human Smuggling and Bureaucracy at the Border*, Minneapolis, MN: University of Minnesota Press.

Murray, C., (1990), *The Emerging British Underclass*, Choice in Welfare Series No. 2, London: Institute of Economic Affairs.

(1997), *Does Prison Work?* London: Institute of Economic Affairs.

Musterd, S., Murie, A. and Kesteloot, C., (2006), *Neighbourhoods of Poverty: Urban Social Exclusion and Integration in Comparison*, London: Palgrave Macmillan.

Naipaul, V. S., (1964), *An Area of Darkness*, London: The Reprint Society.

National Commission on Law Observance and Enforcement, (1931), *Report on Crime and the Foreign Born*, Washington, DC: US Government Printing Office.

National Inquiry into Children in Immigration Detention, (2004), *Report*, Canberra: Australian Human Rights Commission.

National Institute on Money in State Politics, (2012), 'Private prison money flows to Florida's political campaigns', available at: www.followthemoney. org/Newsroom/index.phtml?r=471 (accessed 19 April 2012).

Navarro, M. W., (2012), 'Why we shouldn't sell our prisons to for-profit corporations', 14 February, available at: http://friendsofjustice. wordpress.com/2012/02/14/why-we-shouldnt-sell-our-prisons-to-for-profit-corporations (accessed 11 March 2013).

Neumann, C. B., (2012), 'Imprisoning the soul', in Ugelvik, T. and Dullum, J., (eds.), *Penal Exceptionalism?* London: Routledge, pp. 139–55.

New York Civil Liberties Union, (2012), *New NYPD Data Shows Racial Disparities in NYC School Arrests*, available at: www.nyclu.org/news/new-nypd-data-shows-racial-disparities-nyc-school-arrests (accessed 1 January 2013).

New York Daily News, (2011), 'Private immigration jails make big bucks locking up the poor', 9 October, available at: http://articles.nydailynews.com/2011-10-09/local/30281437_1_immigrant-rights-immigrant-detainees-immigration#ixzz1aIsiWnWc (accessed 5 June 2012).

New York Times, (2010), 'Editorial: Justice Kennedy on prisons', 15 February, available at: www.nytimes.com/2010/02/16/opinion/16tue3.html?_r=0 (accessed 1 January 2013).

(2011), 'Companies use immigration crackdown to turn a profit', 28 September, available at: www.nytimes.com/2011/09/29/world/asia/getting-tough-on-immigrants-to-turn-a-profit.html?_r=3andpagewanted=all (accessed 5 June 2012).

Newburn, T., (2007), '"Tough on crime": penal policy in England and Wales', in Tonry, M., (ed.), *Crime, Punishment and Politics in Comparative Perspective*, London: The University of Chicago Press, pp. 425–70.

Nietzsche, F., (1986), *Human, All Too Human*, Cambridge University Press.

(1989), *On the Genealogy of Morals*, New York, NY: Random House.

(2011), *Zur Genealogie der Moral*, Hamburg: Tradition.

Novak, T., (1984), *Poverty and Inequality*, London: Pluto Press.

Nunn, D., (2012), *By the Way President Obama, We Have to Fix This Too: Voting is a Right, not a Privilege*, available at: www.prisonerswithchildren.org/2013/01/blog-post-4 (accessed 11 March 2013).

Nyers, P., (2009), *Securitizations of Citizenship*, New York, NY: Routledge.

Oakes, J., (1985), *Keeping Track: How Schools Structure Inequality*, Birmingham, NY: Vail-Ballou Press.

Ogden, S., (2005), 'The prison-industrial complex in indigenous California', in Sudbury, J. (ed.), *Global Lockdown: Race, Gender and the Prison-Industrial Complex*, London/New York, NY: Routledge, pp. 57–66.

Ogletree, C. Jr. and Sarat, A. (eds.), (2012), *Life Without Parole: America's New Death Penalty*, New York University Press.

Okazawa-Rey, M. and Kirk, G., (2000), 'Maximum security', *Social Justice*, 27(3), pp. 120–32.

O'Neill, W. L., (1969), *Everyone was Brave: The Rise and Fall of Feminism in America*, Chicago, IL: Quadrangle.

Packer, H., (1968), *The Limits of the Criminal Sanction*, Palo Alto, CA: Stanford University Press.

Padfield, N., (2012), 'Recalling conditionally released prisoners in England and Wales', *European Journal of Probation*, 4(1), pp. 34–45.

Padfield, N. and Maruna, S., (2006), 'The revolving door at the prison gate: exploring the dramatic increase in recalls to prison', *Criminology and Criminal Justice*, 6(3), pp. 329–52.

Page, J., (2011), *The Toughest Beat: Politics, Punishment and the Prison Officers Union in California*, New York, NY: Oxford University Press.

Palidda, S., (ed.), (2009), *Criminalisation and Victimisation of Migrants in Europe*, Genoa: CRIMPREV.

(2011), *The Racial Criminalization of Migrants in the 21st Century*, Aldershot: Ashgate.

Pallas, J. and Barber, R., (1972), 'From riot to revolution', *Issues in Criminology*, 7(2), pp. 1–19.

Pallasch, A., (2009), 'Prisons not the answer to crime problems: Attorney General', *Chicago Sun-Times*, 3 August.

Pandya, A., (2012), 'Ken Clarke's criminal justice policy is failing and increasing crime nationally', *Daily Mail*, 11 January, available at: www.dailymail.co.uk/debate/article-2085087/Ken-Clarkes-criminal-justice-policy-failing-increasing-crime-nationally.html (accessed 1 January 2013).

Pashukanis, E. B., (1924/1978), *General Theory of Law and Marxism: A General Theory*, London: Ink Links.

Pease, K., (1994), 'Cross national imprisonment rates: limitations of method and possible conclusions', *British Journal of Criminology*, 34, pp. 116–30.

Perkinson, R., (2010), *Texas Tough: The Rise of America's Prison Empire*, New York, NY: Metropolitan.

Petersilia, J., (2003), *When Prisoners Come Home: Parole and Prisoner Reentry*, New York, NY: Oxford University Press.

Petit, B. and Western, B., (2004), 'Mass imprisonment and the life course: race and class inequality in US incarceration', *American Sociological Review*, 69(2), pp. 151–69.

Petteruti, A., Walsh, N. and Velázquez, T., (2009), *The Costs of Confinement: Why Good Juvenile Justice Policies Make Good Fiscal Sense*, Washington, DC: Justice Policy Institute, available at: www.justicepolicy.org/images/upload/09_05_REP_CostsOfConfinement_JJ_PS.pdf (accessed 1 January 2013).

Pew Center for Research on the States, Public Safety Performance Project, (2012), *Time Served: The High Cost, Low Return of Longer Prison Terms*, Washington DC: The Pew Charitable Trust.

Pew Center on the States, (2010), *Prison Count 2010*, March, Washington, DC: Pew Center on the States.

Pew Center on the States Public Safety Performance Project, (2008), *One in 100: Behind Bars in America 2008*, available at: www.pewcenteronthestates.org/uploadedFiles/One%20in%20100.pdf.

Piven, F. F., (2010), 'A response to Wacquant', *Theoretical Criminology*, 14, pp. 111–16.

Piven, F. F. and Cloward, R. A., (1971/1993), *Regulating the Poor: The Functions of Public Welfare*, New York, NY: Vintage.

Player, E., (2007), 'Remanding women in custody', *Modern Law Review*, 70(3), pp. 402–26.

Political Cleanup, (2012), *The Corporate Political Nexus: No Change!*, 7 February, available at: http://political-cleanup.org/?p=2199 (accessed 22 May 2012).

Porter, N., (2010), *Expanding the Vote: Felony Disenfranchisement Reform 1997–2010*, Washington DC: The Sentencing Project, available at: www.sentencingproje536org/doc/publications/publications/vr_ExpandingtheVoteFinalAddendum.pdf (accessed 14 July 2012).

Poulantzas, N., (1975), *Classes in Contemporary Capitalism*, London: New Left Books.

——— (1978), *State, Power, Socialism*, London: Verso.

Pratt, A., (2006), *Securing Borders: Detention and Deportation in Canada*, Vancouver: University of British Columbia Press.

Pratt, J., (1998), 'Toward the decivilising of punishment?', *Social and Legal Studies*, 7(4), pp. 487–515.

——— (2000), 'Civilization and punishment', *Australian and New Zealand Journal of Criminology*, 33, pp. 183–201.

——— (2002), *Punishment and Civilization: Penal Tolerance and Intolerance in Modern Society*, London: Sage.

——— (2007), *Punitive Populism*, London: Routledge.

——— (2008a), 'Scandinavian exceptionalism in an era of penal excess. Part I: the nature and origins of Scandinavian exceptionalism', *British Journal of Criminology*, 48(2), pp. 119–37.

——— (2008b), 'Scandinavian exceptionalism in an era of penal excess. Part II: does Scandinavian exceptionalism have a future?', *British Journal of Criminology*, 48(3), pp. 275–92.

——— (2011), 'Penal excess and penal exceptionalism: welfare and imprisonment in Anglophone and Scandinavian societies', in Crawford, A. (ed.), *International and Comparative Criminal Justice and Urban Governance*, Cambridge University Press, pp. 251–75.

Pratt, J. and Eriksson, A., (2012), 'In defence of Scandinavian exceptionalism', in Ugelvik, T. and Dullum, J. (eds.), *Penal Exceptionalism?*, London: Routledge, pp. 235–60.

Prichard, J. C., (1835), *A Treatise on Insanity and Other Disorders Affecting the Mind*, London: Sherwood, Gilbert, and Piper.

Prison Labour, (2012), www.prisonlabour.org.uk/documents.htm (accessed 22 May 2012).

Prison Officers' Association, (2011), *Briefing Paper: The Private Finance Initiative and the Hidden Costs of Prison Privatisation*, available at: www.poauk.org.uk/index.php?prisons-are-not-for-profit-1 (accessed 2 May 2012).

Prison Reform Trust, (2012), *Bromley Briefings Prison Factfile: June 2012*, available at: www.prisonreformtrust.org.uk/Portals/0/Documents/FactfileJune2012.pdf (accessed 26 November 2012).

Putnam, R., (1993), *Making Democracy Work: Civic Traditions in Modern Italy*, Princeton University Press.

(2000), *Bowling Alone: The Collapse and Revival of American Community*, New York, NY: Simon and Schuster.

Quadagno, J., (1995), *The Color of Welfare*, New York, NY: Oxford University Press.

Quinn T. and Meiners, E., (2009), *Flaunt It! Queers Organizing for Public Education and Justice*, New York, NY: Peter Lang.

Rabinow, P., (1984), 'Introduction', in Rabinow, P. (ed.), *The Foucault Reader*, Harmondsworth: Penguin, pp. 3–30.

Rafter, N., (2006), *Shots in the Mirror: Crime Films and Society*, (2nd edn), New York, NY: Oxford University Press.

Rafter, N., and Brown, M., (2011), *Criminology Goes to the Movies: Crime Theory and Popular Culture*, New York University Press.

Ranulf, S., (1938), *Moral Indignation and Middle Class Psychology*, Copenhagen: Levin and Munksgaard.

Reid, K. and Knight, M., (2006), 'Disability for justification of exclusion of minorities: a critical history grounded in disability studies', *Educational Researcher*, 35(6), pp. 18–24.

Reiner, R., (2007), *Law and Order: An Honest Citizen's Guide to Crime and Control*, Cambridge, MA: Polity.

Rhodes, L. A., (2004), *Total Confinement: Madness and Reason in the Maximum Security Prison*, Berkeley, CA: University of California Press.

Richie, B., (2012), *Arrested Justice: Black Women, Violence and America's Prison Nation*, New York University Press.

Riddell, W., (1923), 'The slave in Upper Canada', *Journal of the American Institute of Criminal Law and Criminology*, 14, pp. 249–78.

Right on Crime, (2012), *A Statement of Principles*, available at: www.right-oncrime.com/the-conservative-case-for-reform/statement-of-principles (accessed 27 November 2012).

(n.d.), 'Statement of principles', available at: www.rightoncrime.com/the-conservative-case-for-reform/statement-of-principles (accessed 31 October 2011).

Rios, V., (2011), *Punished: Policing the Lives of Black and Latino Boys*, New York University Press.

Robbins, C., (2008), *Expelling Hope: The Assault on Youth and the Militarization of Schooling*, New York, NY: State University of New York Press.

Roberts, D., (1997), *Killing the Black Body: Race, Reproduction, and the Meaning of Liberty*. New York, NY: Vintage Books.

Roberts, J. V. and Hough, M., (2005), *Understanding Public Attitudes to Criminal Justice*, Buckingham: Open University Press.

Rock, P., (1990), *Helping Victims of Crime: The Home Office and the Rise of Victim Support in England and Wales*, Oxford: Clarendon Press.

Rodriguez, D., (2006), *Forced Passages: Imprisoned Radical Intellectuals and the U.S. Prison Regime*, Minneapolis, MN: University of Minnesota Press.

Rojek, C., (1993), *Ways of Escape: Modern Transformations in Leisure and Travel*, London: Palgrave Macmillan.

Rose, G., (2000), *Visual Methodologies*, Thousand Oaks, CA: Sage.

(2007), *Visual Methodologies*, (2nd edn), Thousand Oaks, CA: Sage.

Rose, N., (1999), *Powers of Freedom: Reframing Political Thought*, New York, NY: Cambridge University Press.

Rosenberg, S., (2011), *An American Radical: A Political Prisoner in My Own Country*, New York, NY: Citadel.

Ross, L., (1998), *Inventing the Savage: The Social Construction of Native American Criminality*, Austin, TX: University of Texas Press.

Rothman, D., (1971), *Discovery of the Asylum: Social Order and Disorder in the New Republic*, New York, NY: Little, Brown.

Ruggiero, V., (2000), *Crime and Markets: Essays in Anti-Criminology*, Oxford University Press.

Ruggiero, V., Ryan, M., and Sim, J. (eds.), (1996), *Western European Penal Systems*, London: Sage.

Rusche, G., (1930/1980), 'Prison revolts or social policy: lessons from America', *Social Justice*, 13, pp. 41–4.

(1933/1978), 'Labor market and penal sanction: thoughts on the sociology of punishment', *Social Justice*, 10, pp. 2–8.

Rusche, G. and Kirchheimer, O., (1939/2003), *Punishment and Social Structure*, London: Transaction Publishers.

Ryan, M., (1978), *The Acceptable Pressure Group: Inequality in the Penal Lobby – A Case Study of the Howard League and RAP*, Farnborough: Saxon House.

Salah-El, T. A., (2001), 'A call for the abolition of prisons', reprinted in James, J. (ed.), (2005), *The New Abolitionists: (Neo)Slave Narratives and*

Contemporary Prison Writings, Albany, NY: State University of New York Press, pp. 69–74.

Saltman, K. and Gabbard, D. (eds.), (2003), *Education as Enforcement: The Militarization and Corporatization of Schools*, New York, NY: Routledge/Falmer.

Sampson, R. J., (2008), 'Rethinking crime and immigration', *Contexts*, 7(1), pp. 28–33.

Sampson, R. J. and Loeffler, C., (2010), 'Punishment's place: the local concentration of mass incarceration', *Daedalus*, Summer, pp. 20–31.

Sander, T. H. and Putnam, R. D., (2010), 'Still bowling alone? The post-9/11 split', *Journal of Democracy*, 21(1), pp. 9–16.

Sarabi, B. and Bender, E., (2000), *Prison Payoff: The Role of Politics and Private Prisons in the Incarceration Boom*, Portland, OR: Western Prison Project.

Sarat, A., (2000), 'Imagining the law of the father: loss, dread, and mourning in *The Sweet Hereafter*', *Law and Society Review*, 34, pp. 3–46.

(2001), *When the State Kills: Capital Punishment and the American Condition*, Princeton University Press.

Sarat, A. and Kearns, T., (1993), 'A journey through forgetting: toward a jurisprudence of violence', in Sarat, A. and Kearns, T. (eds.), *The Fate of Law*, Ann Arbor, MI: University of Michigan Press.

Savage, M., (2000), *Class Analysis and Social Transformation*, Buckingham: Open University Press.

Savage, M., Barlow, J., Dickens, P. and Fielding, T., (1992), *Property, Bureaucracy and Culture: Middle-Class Formation in Contemporary Britain*, London: Routledge.

Savelsberg, J., (1994), 'Knowledge, domination and criminal punishment', *American Journal of Sociology*, 99(4), pp. 911–43.

Sayer, A., (2001), 'For a critical cultural political economy', *Antipode*, 33(4), pp. 687–708.

Schaffner, L., (2002), 'An age of reason: paradoxes in the US legal constructions of adulthood', *International Journal of Children's Rights*, 10, pp. 201–32.

Schlosser, E., (1998), 'The prison-industrial complex', *Atlantic Monthly*, December, available at www.theatlantic.com/magazine/archive/1998/12/the-prison-industrial-complex/304669 (accessed 1 January 2013).

Schmitt, F. E. and Martin, P. Y., (1999), 'Unobtrusive mobilization by an institutionalized rape crisis center: "all we do comes from victims"', *Gender and Society*, 13(3), pp. 364–84.

Schoenfeld, H., (2009), 'The politics of prison growth: from chain gangs to work release centers and supermax prisons, Florida, 1955–2000', Ph.D dissertation, Northwestern University.

(2010), 'Mass incarceration and the paradox of prison conditions litigation', *Law & Society Review*, 44, pp. 731–68.

Schor, J., (1992), *The Overworked American*, New York, NY: Basic Books.

Schwarz, A., (2011), 'School discipline study raises fresh questions', *New York Times*, 11 April, available at: www.nytimes.com/2011/07/19/education/19discipline.html?_r=0 (accessed 1 January 2013).

Scott, D., (1996/2011), *Heavenly Confinement?*, London: Lambert Academic Press.

(2008), *Penology*, London/Thousand Oaks, CA: Sage.

(2009), 'Punishment', in Hucklesby, A. and Wahidin, A. (eds.), *Criminal Justice*, Oxford University Press, pp. 83–102.

(in press (a)), *The Caretakers of Punishment*, London: Palgrave Macmillan.

(in press (b)), 'The politics of prisoner legal rights', *Howard Journal of Criminal Justice*.

(in press (c)), 'Visualising an abolitionist real utopia: principles, policy and praxis', in Malloch, M. and Munro, W. (eds.), *Crime, Critique and Utopia*, London: Palgrave Macmillan.

Scott, D. and Codd, H., (2010), *Controversial Issues in Prisons*, Buckingham: Open University Press.

Scraton, P. and Chadwick, K., (1991), 'Challenging new orthodoxies: the theoretical and political priorities of critical criminology', in Stenson, K. and Cowell, D. (eds.), *The Politics of Crime Control*, London: Sage, pp. 161–87.

Scraton, P., Sim, J. and Skidmore, P., (1991), *Prisons under Protest*, Milton Keynes: Open University Press.

Scull, A., (1993), *The Most Solitary of Afflictions*, London: Yale University Press.

(2006), 'Power, social control and psychiatry: some critical reflections', in Armstrong, S. and McAra, L. (eds.), *Perspectives on Punishment*, Oxford University Press, pp. 197–216.

Seaton, A. V., (1999), 'War and thanatourism: Waterloo 1815–1914', *Annals of Tourism Research*, 26, pp. 130–58.

Sellin, T., (1938), *Culture Conflict and Crime*, New York, NY: Social Science Research Council.

Senate Joint Select Committee on Australia's Immigration Detention Network, (2012), *Final Report*, Canberra: Commonwealth of Australia.

Sennett, R., (1998), *The Corrosion of Character. The Personal Consequences of Work in the New Capitalism*, New York, NY: Norton.

Seymour, M. and Costello, L., (2005), *A Study of the Number, Profile and Progression Routes of Homeless Persons before the Court and in Custody*, report commissioned by the Department of Justice, Equality and Law Reform, Dublin: PWS.

Shakur, A., Buck, M. and Whitehorn, L., (1998), *Sparks Fly: Women Political Prisoners and Prisoners of War*, Oakland, CA: Regent Press.

Sharff-Smith, P., (2012), 'A critical look at Scandinavian exceptionalism', in Ugelvik, T. and Dullum, J. (eds.), *Penal Exceptionalism?*, London: Routledge, pp. 38–57.

Sharpley, R. and Stone, P., (2009), *The Darker Side of Travel: The Theory and Practice of Dark Tourism*, Bristol: Channel View Publications.

Shipler, D. K., (2004), *The Working Poor: Invisible in America*, New York, NY: Vintage.

Sieh, E. W., (1989), 'Less eligibility: the upper limits of penal policy', *Criminal Justice Policy Review*, 3(2), pp. 159–83.

Silverman, S. and Hajela, R., (2012), *Briefing: Immigration Detention in the UK*, Oxford, Migration Observatory, available at: http://migrobs.vm.bytemark.co.uk/sites/files/migobs/Immigration%20Detention%20Briefing%20v2_0.pdf (accessed 5 June 2012).

Sim. J., (1990), *Medical Power in Prison*, Milton Keynes: Open University Press.
    (1994), 'Tougher than the rest', in Newburn, T. and Stanko, E. (eds.), *Just Boys Doing Business*, London: Routledge, pp. 100–17.
    (2004), 'Thinking about imprisonment', in Muncie, J. and Wilson, D. (eds.), *Student Handbook of Criminal Justice and Criminology*, London: Cavendish, pp. 249–64.
    (2005), 'At the centre of the new professional gaze: women, medicine and confinement', in Chan, W., Chunn, D. and Menzies, R. (eds.), *Women, Madness and the Law*, London: Glasshouse, pp. 211–26.
    (2009), *Punishment and Prisons: Power and the Carceral State*, London: Sage.

Sim, J., Scraton, P. and Gordon, P., (1987), 'Crime, the state and critical analysis', in Scraton, P. (ed.), *Law, Order and the Authoritarian State*, Milton Keynes: Open University Press, pp. 1–70.

Simkins, S., Hirsh, A., Horvat, E. and Moss, M., (2004), 'The school to prison pipeline for girls: the role of physical and sexual abuse', *Children's Legal Rights Journal*, 24(4), pp. 56–72.

Simmons, L., (2009), 'End of the line: tracing racial inequality from school to prison', *Race/Ethnicity: Multidisciplinary Global Perspectives*, 2(2), pp. 215–41.

Simon, J., (1987), 'The emergence of a risk society: insurance, law and the state', *Socialist Review*, 95, pp. 61–89.
    (1998), 'Refugees in a carceral age: the rebirth of immigration prisons in the United States', *Public Culture*, 10(3), pp. 577–607.
    (2001), 'Fear and loathing in late modernity reflections on the cultural sources of mass imprisonment in the United States', in Garland, D. (ed.), *Mass Imprisonment: Social Causes and Consequences*, Thousand Oaks, CA: Sage, pp. 15–27.
    (2007), *Governing Through Crime*, New York, NY/London: Oxford University Press.

(2010), 'Beyond the panopticon: mass imprisonment and the humanities', *Law, Culture and the Humanities*, 6, pp. 327–40.

Sista II Sista, (2006), 'Sistas makin' moves: collective leadership for personal transformation and social justice', in INCITE! Women of Color Against Violence (eds.), *Color of Violence: The Incite! Anthology*, Boston, MA: South End Press.

Sivanandan, A., (2001), 'Poverty is the new black', *Race and Class*, 43(2), pp. 1–6.

Skeggs, B., (2004), *Class, Self, Culture*, London: Routledge.

Skiba, R. J. and Knesting, K., (2002), 'Zero tolerance, zero evidence: an analysis of school disciplinary practice', in Skiba, R. J. and Noam, G. G. (eds.), *New Directions for Youth Development. 92: Zero Tolerance: Can Suspension and Expulsion Keep Schools Safe?*, San Francisco, CA: Jossey-Bass.

Skiba, R. J., Michael, R. S., Nardo, A. C. and Peterson, R. L., (2002), 'The color of discipline: sources of racial and gender disproportionality in school punishment', *The Urban Review*, 34(2), pp. 317–42.

Skocpol, T., (2002), *Diminished Democracy: From Membership to Management in American Civic Life*, Norman, OK: University of Oklahoma Press.

Skolnick, J. H., (1969), *The Politics of Protest*, New York, NY: Ballantine Books.

Smith, A., (2001), 'The color of violence: violence against women of color', *Meridians: Feminism, Race, Transnationalism*, 1(2), pp. 65–72.

(2005), *Conquest: Sexual Violence and American Indian Genocide*, Boston, MA: South End Press.

Smith, C., (2009), *The Prison and the American Imagination*, New Haven, CT: Yale University Press.

Smith, D., (1990), *Texts, Facts, and Femininity: Exploring the Relations of Ruling*, London: Routledge Press.

Smith, K., (2005), 'Modern day slavery: inside the prison-industrial complex', in Sudbury, J. (ed.), *Global Lockdown: Race, Gender and the Prison-Industrial Complex*, London/New York, NY: Routledge, pp. 105–8.

Smith, P., (2008), *Punishment and Culture*, The University of Chicago Press.

Smith, R. M. and Erevelles, N., (2004), 'Toward an enabling education: the difference that disability makes', *Educational Researcher*, 23(8), pp. 31–6.

Smith, S. R. and Freinkel, S., (1988), *Adjusting the Balance: Federal Policy and Victim Services*, Westport, CT: Greenwood.

Snacken, S. and Dumortier, E., (2012), 'Resisting punitiveness in Europe?', in Snacken, S. and Dumortier, E., *Resisting Punitiveness in Europe?*, London: Routledge, pp. 1–20.

Social Exclusion Unit, (2002), *Reducing Re-offending by Ex-prisoners: Summary of the Social Exclusion Report*, London: HMSO.

Sontag, D., (2002), 'Fierce entanglements', *New York Times Magazine*, 17 November, available at: www.nytimes.com/2002/11/17/magazine/fierce-entanglements.html?pagewanted=all&src=pm (accessed 1 January 2013).

Southern Coalition for Social Justice, (2012), *Harm Free Zone Project General Framework*, available at: http://current.workingdirectory.net/projects/iw-working/downloads/hfz/framework.pdf (accessed 18 July 2012).

Sparks, R., (2006), 'Ordinary anxieties and states of emergency: statecraft and spectatorship in the new politics of insecurity', in Armstrong, S. and McAra, L. (eds.), *Perspectives on Punishment*, Oxford University Press, pp. 31–48.

Sparks, R. F., (1982), *Research on Victims of Crime: Accomplishments, Issues and New Directions*, Rockville, MD: National Institute of Mental Health, Center for Studies of Crime and Delinquency.

St. George, D., (2012), 'Federal data show racial gaps in school arrests', *Washington Post*, 5 March, available at: www.washingtonpost.com/national/federal-data-show-racial-gaps-in-school-arrests/2012/03/01/gIQApbjvtR_story.html (accessed 1 January 2013).

Standing, G., (2011), *The Precariat: The New Dangerous Class*, New York, NY: Bloomsbury Academic.

Stanley, E. A. and Smith, N. (eds.), (2011), *Captive Genders: Trans Embodiment and Prison-Industrial Complex*, Oakland, CA: AK Press.

Stanton, S., (2010), 'California inmate release plan begins', *Sacramento Bee*, 25 January, available at: http://lapd.com/news/headlines/california_inmate_release_plan_begins (accessed 1 January 2013).

Stastny, C. and Tyrnauer, G., (1982), *Who Rules the Joint? The Changing Political Culture of Maximum-Security Prisons in America*, Lexington, MA: D.C. Heath.

Steurer, S., Tracy, A. and Smith, L., (2001), *Three State Recidivism Study*, Lanham, MD: Correctional Education Association.

Stinson, P., (2004), 'Restoring justice: how congress can amend the one-strike laws in federally-subsidized housing to ensure due process, avoid inequity, and combat crime', *Georgetown Journal on Poverty Law and Policy*, 11, pp. 435–94.

Strange, C. and Kempa, M., (2003), 'Shades of dark tourism: Alcatraz and Robben Island', *Annals of Tourism Research*, 30, pp. 386–405.

Streeck, W. and Thelen, K. (eds.), (2005), *Beyond Continuity: Institutional Change in Advanced Political Economies*, Oxford University Press.

Streeten, P., (1981), *First Things First: Meeting Basic Human Need in the Developing Countries*, New York, NY: Oxford University Press.

Stumpf, J., (2007), *The Crimmigration Crisis: Immigrations, Crime and Sovereign Power*, Paper No. 2007-2, Lewis and Clark Law School Legal Research Paper Series.

(2011), 'Doing time: crimmigration law and the perils of haste', *UCLA Law Review*, 58, pp. 1705–48.

(2012), 'The justice of crimmigration law and the security of home', in Hudson, B. and Ugelvik, S. (eds.), *Justice and Security in the Twenty-First Century*, London: Routledge, pp. 43–63.

Sturken, M., (2007), *Tourists of History: Memory, Kitsch, and Consumerism from Oklahoma City to Ground Zero*, Durham, NC: Duke University Press.

Sudbury, J., (1998), *Other Kinds of Dreams: Black Women's Organisations and the Politics of Transformation*, London: Routledge.

(2000), 'Transatlantic visions: resisting the globalization of mass incarceration', *Social Justice*, 27(3), pp. 133–49.

(2004), 'A world without prisons: resisting militarism, globalized punishment and empire', *Social Justice*, 31(1–2), pp. 9–30.

(2005a), 'Feminist critiques, transnational landscapes, abolitionist visions', in Sudbury, J. (ed.), *Global Lockdown*, London/New York, NY: Routledge, pp. xi–xxviii.

(2005b), '"Mules", "Yardies" and other folk devils: mapping cross border imprisonment in Britain', in Sudbury, J. (ed.), *Global Lockdown*, London/New York, NY: Routledge, pp. 167–83.

(ed.), (2005c), *Global Lockdown: Race, Gender, and the Prison-Industrial Complex*, London/New York, NY: Routledge.

(2011), 'Maroon abolitionists: black gendered-oppressed activists in the anti-prisons movement in the U.S. and Canada', in Stanley, E. A. and Smith, N. (eds.), *Captive Genders: Trans Embodiment and the Prison Industrial Complex*, Oakland, CA: AK Press, pp. 293–321.

Sudbury, J. and Okazawa-Rey, M. (eds.), (2009), *Activist Scholarship: Antiracism, Feminism and Social Change*, Boulder, CO: Paradigm.

Supreme Court of the United States, (2010), *Citizens United vs. Federal Election Commission*, available at: www.supremecourt.gov/opinions/09pdf/08-205.pdf (accessed 18 July 2012).

Svallfors, S., (2006), *The Moral Economy of Class: Class and Attitudes in Comparative Perspective*, Palo Alto, CA: Stanford University Press.

Taslitz, A., (2012), 'The criminal republic: democratic breakdown as a cause of mass incarceration', *Ohio State Journal of Criminal Law*, 9(1), pp. 133–93.

Taylor, J., (1992), 'Post-secondary correctional education: an evaluation of effectiveness and efficiency', *Journal of Correctional Education*, 43(3), pp. 132–41.

Thatcher, M., (1987), Interview for *Woman's Own*, 23 September, available at: www.margaretthatcher.org (accessed 21 May 2010).

The Sentencing Project, (2012), *Trends in U.S. Corrections*, available at: www.sentencingproject.org (accessed 1 January 2013).

Tilly, C., (1997), 'Parliamentarization of popular contention in Great Britain, 1758–1834', *Theory and Society*, 26(April), pp. 245–73.

Tocqueville, de A. and Beaumont, de G., (1833/1970), *The Penitentiary System in the United States and Its Application in France*, New York, NY: Augustus Kelly.

Tombs, S. and Whyte, D., (2010), 'A deadly consensus: worker safety and regulatory degradation under New Labour', *British Journal of Criminology*, 50(1), pp. 46–55.

Tonry, M. (ed.), (1997), *Ethnicity, Crime, and Immigration: Comparative and Cross-National Perspectives*, The University of Chicago Press.

(2001), 'Punishment policies and patterns in Western countries', in Tonry, M. and Frase, R. S. (eds.), *Sentencing and Sanctions in Western Countries*, Oxford University Press, pp. 3–28.

(2004), *Thinking about Crime: Sense and Sensibility in American Penal Culture*, New York, NY: Oxford University Press.

(2007), 'Determinants of penal policies', in Tonry, M. (ed.), *Crime, Punishment and Politics in Comparative Perspective*, London: The University of Chicago Press, pp. 1–48.

Toynbee, P., (2012), 'Cameron's big cut "idea" will only backfire on the Tories', *Guardian*, 26 June, p. 28.

Travis, A. and Williams, Z., (2012), 'Revealed: government plans for police privatisation', *Guardian*, 2 March, available at: www.guardian.co.uk/uk/2012/mar/02/police-privatisation-security-firms-crime (accessed 1 January 2013).

Trenka, J. J., Oparah. J. C and Yung Shin, S. (eds.), (2006), *Outsiders Within: Writing on Transracial Adoption*, Cambridge, MA: South End Press.

Turkle, S., (2011), *Alone Together: Why We Expect More from Technology and Less from Each Other*, New York, NY: Basic Books.

Turnbull, R., (1796), *A Visit to a Philadelphia Prison*, Philadelphia, PA: Budd and Bertram Press.

Tzanelli, R., O'Brien, M. and Yar, M., (2005), '"Con me if you can": exploring crime in the American cinematic imagination', *Theoretical Criminology*, 9, pp. 97–117.

Ugelvik, T., (2012), 'Imprisoned on the border: subjects and objects of the state in two Norwegian prisons', in Hudson, B. and Ugelvik, S. (eds.), *Justice and Security in the Twenty-First Century*, London: Routledge, pp. 64–82.

Uggen, C., Manza, J. and Thompson, M., (2006), 'Citizenship, democracy and the civic reintegration of criminal offenders', *ANNALS of the American Academy of Political and Social Science*, 605, pp. 281–310.

United Nations, (1988), *Body of Principles for the Protection of All Persons under Any Form of Detention or Imprisonment*, A/RES/43/173, 76th plenary meeting, 9 December 1988.

(2005), *Report of the Working Group on Arbitrary Detention*, E/CN.4/2006/7, Commission on Human Rights, 62nd session, 12 December 2005.

United Nations High Commissioner for Refugees, (1999), *Revised Guidelines on Applicable Criteria and Standards Relating to the Detention of Asylum-Seekers*, Geneva: Office of the United Nations High Commissioner for Refugees.

(2010), *Joint Study on Global Practices in Relation to Secret Detention in the Context of Countering Terrorism*, A/HRC/13/42, 19 February 2010.

United States Census Bureau, (2012), *Elections: Voting-Age Population and Voter Participation*, available at: www.census.gov/compendia/statab/cats/elections/ voting-age_population_and_voter_participation.html (accessed 29 October 2012).

Useem, B. and Kimball, P., (1989), *States of Siege: U.S. Prison Riots, 1971–1986*, New York, NY: Oxford University Press.

Valverde, M., (2012), 'Analysing punishment: scope and scale', *Theoretical Criminology*, 16, pp. 245–53.

Van Kalmthout, A. M., Hofstee-van der Meulen, F. B. A. M. and Dünkel, F. (eds.), (2007), *Foreigners in European Prisoners*. Nijmegen: Wolf Legal Publishers.

Verfaillie, K., (2012), 'Punitive needs, society and public opinion: an explorative study of ambivalent attitudes to punishment and criminal justice', in Snacken, S. and Dumortier, E., *Resisting Punitiveness in Europe?*, London: Routledge, pp. 225–46.

Vine, J., (2012), *Thematic Inspection of How the UK Border Agency Manages Foreign National Prisoners: February – May 2011*, London: Independent Chief Inspector of the UK Border Agency.

Wacquant, L., (1991), 'Making class: the middle class(es) in social theory and social structure', in McNall, S., Levine, R. and Fantasia, R. (eds.), *Bringing Class Back In: Contemporary and Historical Perspectives*, Boulder, CO: Westview Press, pp. 39–64.

(2001), 'Deadly symbiosis: when ghetto and prison meet and mesh', in Garland, D. (ed.), (2001), *Mass Imprisonment*, London: Sage, pp. 82–120.

(ed.), (2005), *The Mystery of Ministry: Pierre Bourdieu and Democratic Politics*, Cambridge, MA: Polity.

(2006), 'Penalisation, depoliticisation, racialisation: on the over-incarceration of immigrants in the European Union', in Armstrong, S. and McAra, L. (eds.), *Perspectives on Punishment*, Oxford University Press, pp. 83–100.

(2008a), 'Ordering insecurity: social polarization and the punitive upsurge', *Radical Philosophy Review*, 11(1), pp. 9–27.

(2008b), *Urban Outcasts: A Comparative Sociology of Advanced Marginalit*, Cambridge, MA: Polity.

(2009a), *Prisons of Poverty*, Minneapolis, MN: University of Minnesota Press.

(2009b), *Punishing the Poor: The Neoliberal Government of Social Insecurity*, Durham: Duke University Press.

(2010a), 'Class, race and hyper-incarceration in revanchist America', *Daedalus*, 139(3), pp. 70–80.

(2010b), 'The wedding of workfare and prisonfare revisited', *Social Justice*, 38(1–2), pp. 203–21.

(2013), *Deadly Symbiosis: Race and the Rise of the Penal State*, Cambridge, MA: Polity.

Walker, A., (1997), 'Introduction: the strategy of inequality', in Walker, A. and Walker, C. (eds.), *Britain Divided: The Growth of Social Exclusion in the 1980s and 1990s*, London: Child Poverty Action Group.

Walker, S., (1999), *In Defense of American Liberties: A History of the ACLU*, (2nd edn), Carbondale, IL: Southern Illinois Press.

Walmsley, R., (2012), *World Prison Population List*, (9th edn), Essex: International Centre for Prison Studies.

Wardhaugh, J., (2000), *Subcity: Young People Homelessness and Crime*, Aldershot: Ashgate.

Warrell, H., (2012), 'Incentives to find jobs for ex-prisoners', *Financial Times*, 6 March, available at: http://www.ft.com/cms/s/0/50865658-6771-11e1-b4a1-00144feabdc0.html#axzz2NWvIufTi (accessed 1 January 2013).

Watkins, W., (2001), *The White Architects of Black Education: Ideology and Power in America, 1865–1954*, New York, NY: Teachers College Press.

Watkins, C. and Naqi, P., (2011), *Visions of Abolition: From Critical Resistance to a New Way of Life*, available at: www.visionsofabolition.org (accessed 1 November 2012).

Weber, M., (English edn 1930, German original 1904–5), *The Protestant Ethic and the Spirit of Capitalism*, Unwin University Books.

Webster, C. M. and Doob, A. N., (2007), 'Punitive trends and stable imprisonment rates in Canada', in Tonry, M. (ed.), *Crime, Punishment and Politics in Comparative Perspective*, London: The University of Chicago Press, pp. 297–396.

Weeks, K. M., (1970), 'The New Zealand criminal injuries compensation scheme', *Southern California Law Review*, 43, pp. 107–21.

Weiss, R. and South, N. (eds.), (1998), *Comparing Prison Systems*, London: Routledge.

West, W. G. and Morris, R. (eds.), (2000), *The Case for Penal Abolition*, Toronto: Canadian Scholars' Press.

Western, B., (2006), *Punishment and Inequality in America*, New York, NY: Russell Sage Foundation.

Wheelock, D., Wald, P. and Shchukin, Y., (2012), 'Managing the socially marginalized: attitudes toward welfare, punishment, and race', *Journal of Poverty*, 16(1), pp. 1–26.

Whitehead, T., (2012), 'Ken Clarke to double number of prisoners working full time', *Daily Telegraph*, 3 January, available at: www.telegraph.co.uk/

news/uknews/law-and-order/8984942/Ken-Clarke-to-double-number-of-prisoners-working-full-time.html (accessed 1 January 2013).

Whitman, J. Q., (2003), *Harsh Justice: Criminal Punishment and the Widening Divide between America and Europe*, New York, NY: Oxford University Press.

Who's Lobbying, (2012), http://whoslobbying.com/uk/g4s (accessed 22 May 2012).

Wilkins, L., (1991), *Punishment, Crime and Market Forces*, Aldershot: Dartmouth.

Wilkins, L. and Pease, K., (1987), 'Public demand for punishment', *International Journal of Sociology and Social Policy*, 7(3), pp. 16–29.

Wilkinson, R. and Pickett, K., (2010), *The Spirit Level: Why Equality is Better for Everyone*, London: Penguin.

Willis, P., (1977), *Learning to Labor: How Working Class Kids Get Working Class Jobs*, New York, NY: Columbia University Press.

Wilsher, D. (2011). *Immigration Detention: Law, History, Politics*, Cambridge University Press.

Wilson, D. and Anderson, M., (2011), 'Understanding Obama's discourse on urban poverty', in Bourke, A., Dafnos, T. and Kip, M. (eds.), *Lumpencity: Discourses of Marginality, Marginalising Discourses*, Ottawa: Red Quill Books, pp. 43–74.

Wilson, D. and O'Sullivan, S., (2005), 'Re-theorizing the penal reform functions of the prison film: revelation, humanization, empathy and bench-marking', *Theoretical Criminology*, 9, pp. 471–91.

Wilson, W. J., (1987), *The Truly Disadvantaged: The Inner City, the Underclass, and Public Policy*, The University of Chicago Press.

(1996), *When Work Disappears: The World of the New Urban Poor*, NewYork, NY: Knopf.

Winn, M., (2010), *Girl Time: Literacy, Justice, and the School-to-Prison Pipeline*, New York, NY: Teachers College Press.

Wollebæk, Dag., Enjolras, B., Steen-Johnsen, K. and Ødegård, G. (2011), *Hva gjør terroren med oss som sivilsamfunn?* (*How Does the Terror Affect Us As a Civil Society?*), Senter for forskning på sivilsamfunn og frivillig sector (Center for Research on Civil Society and Voluntary Sector).

Wollebæk, Dag., Enjolras, B., Ødegård, G. and Steen-Johnsen, K. (2012), *Ett år etter 22 juli. Har rosetoget gått?* (*One Year after 22 July. Has the Rose Procession gone?*), Senter for forskning på sivilsamfunn og frivillig sector (Center for Research on Civil Society and Voluntary Sector).

Wright, E. O., (1985), *Classes*, London: Verso.

Young, J., (1999), *The Exclusive Society*, London: Sage.

Young, W. and Brown, M., (1993), 'The use of imprisonment: trends and cross-national comparisons', in Tonry. M. (ed.), *Crime and Justice: An Annual Review of Research*, The University of Chicago Press.

Zedner, L., (1994), 'Victims', in Maguire, M., Morgan, R. and Reiner, R. (eds.), *The Oxford Handbook of Criminology*, Oxford: Clarendon Press, pp. 1207–46.

(2003), 'Too much security?', *International Journal of the Sociology of Law*, 31, pp. 155–84.

(2009), *Security*, London: Taylor and Francis.

Zimring, F. E. and Hawkins, G., (1995), *Incapacitation: Penal Confinement and the Restraint of Crime*, Oxford University Press.

Zimring, F. E., Hawkins, G. and Kamin, S., (2001), *Punishment and Democracy: Three Strikes and You're Out in California*, New York, NY: Oxford University Press.

Žižek, S., (1994), *The Metastases of Enjoyment: Six Essays on Woman and Causality*, London: Verso.

(1997), *The Plague of Fantasies*, London: Verso.

(2006), *The Parallax View*, Cambridge, MA: MIT Press.

INDEX

Lightning Source UK Ltd.
Milton Keynes UK
UKOW07n1838040215

245706UK00006B/29/P